THE CIVIL WAR

A TREASURY OF
ART AND LITERATURE

THE CIVIL WAR

A TREASURY OF
ART AND LITERATURE

Edited by Stephen W. Sears

Hugh Lauter Levin Associates, Inc.

Distributed by Macmillan Publishing Company, New York

Copyright © 1992, Hugh Lauter Levin Associates, Inc.
Design by Philip Grushkin
Typeset by U. S. Lithograph, typographers, New York City
Printed in Hong Kong
ISBN 0-88363-970-x

Samuel W. Crawford. *The Genesis of the Civil War*. First published in 1887, Hartford, Conn.

C. Vann Woodward, ed. *Mary Chesnut's Civil War*. © 1981 by C. Vann Woodward, Sally Bland Metts, Barbara G. Carpenter, Sally Bland Johnson, and Katherine W. Herbert. Reproduced by permission of Yale University Press.

Walt Whitman. "Beat! Beat! Drums!" "Ashes of Soldiers." "O Captain! My Captain!" "When Lilacs Last in the Dooryard Bloom'd." "The Thought of Graves." Reprinted from *Walt Whitman's Civil War*. Walter Lowenfels, ed. © 1960 by Walter Lowenfels. Published by Alfred A. Knopf, Inc.

James Russell Lowell. "The Pickens-and-Stealin's Rebellion." From *Political Essays*, vol. V of *The Works of James Russell Lowell*. Published by Houghton, Mifflin & Co., 1899.

Testimony of Mrs. Mary A. Ward. *Report of the Committee of the Senate upon the Relations between Labor and Capital, and Testimony Taken by the Committee*. Published by the U.S. Government Printing Office, 1885.

Warren Lee Goss. "Going to the Front." From *Battles and Leaders of the Civil War*, vol. I. Robert U. Johnson and Clarence C. Buel, eds. New York: The Century Co., 1888.

Ulysses S. Grant. *Personal Memoirs of U. S. Grant*. New York: Charles L. Webster & Co., 1885.

Frederick Douglass. *Douglass' Monthly*, August 1861, March 1862.

Benjamin P. Thomas. *Abraham Lincoln*. © 1952 by Benjamin P. Thomas. Reprinted by permission of Alfred A. Knopf, Inc.

J. B. Jones. *A Rebel War Clerk's Diary At the Confederate States Capital*, vol. I. Howard Swiggett, ed. New York: Old Hickory Bookshop, 1935.

Howard K. Beale, ed. *Diary of Gideon Welles*, vol. I. Published by W. W. Norton & Company, Inc., 1960.

Allan Nevins. *The War for the Union*, vol. II. © 1960 Allan Nevins; copyright renewed 1988. Reprinted by permission of Charles Scribner's Sons, an imprint of Macmillan Publishing Company.

Richard Taylor. *Destruction and Reconstruction: Personal Experiences of the Late War*. New York: D. Appleton & Co., 1879, 1900.

Shelby Foote. *The Civil War: A Narrative*. © 1958 by Shelby Foote. Reprinted by permission of Random House, Inc.

Don E. Fehrenbacher. *Lincoln in Text and Context: Collected Essays*. © 1987 by the Board of Trustees of the Leland Stanford Junior University. Reprinted with the permission of the publisher, Stanford University Press.

Roy P. Basler, ed. *The Collected Works of Abraham Lincoln*, vols. V, VI. © 1953 by Abraham Lincoln Association. Reprinted with permission of Rutgers University Press.

Bruce Catton. *A Stillness at Appomattox*. © 1953 by Bruce Catton. Used by permission of Doubleday, a division of Bantam Doubleday Dell Publishing Group, Inc.

War Letters, 1862–1865, of John Chipman Gray and John Codman Ropes. Cambridge: Houghton, Mifflin & Co., The Riverside Press, 1927.

Thomas Wentworth Higginson. "Regular and Volunteer Officers." *Atlantic Monthly*, September, 1864.

Mark Twain. "The Private History of a Campaign That Failed." *Century Magazine*, December, 1885.

Thomas W. Hyde. *Following the Greek Cross or, Memories of the Sixth Army Corps*. Cambridge: Houghton, Mifflin & Co., The Riverside Press, 1895.

Michael Shaara. *The Killer Angels*. © 1974 by Michael Shaara. Reprinted by permission of David McKay Co., a division of Random House, Inc.

Stephen Crane. *The Red Badge of Courage*. First published in 1895.

Sam R. Watkins. "Co. Aytch," *Maury Grays, First Tennessee Regiment; or, A Side Show of the Big Show*. First published in 1882.

Robert Penn Warren. *Wilderness: A Tale of the Civil War*. © 1961 by Robert Penn Warren. Published by Random House.

Walt Whitman. "A Glimpse of War's Hell-Scenes." "The Wounded from Chancellorsville." "Released Union Prisoners from the South." Letter of Condolence. Reflections on the Battle of Bull Run. Dispatch to the *New York Times*, February 26, 1863. Journal Entry, February 23, 1865. Reprinted from *Walt Whitman's Civil War*. Walter Lowenfels, ed. © 1960 by Walter Lowenfels. Published by Alfred A. Knopf, Inc.

Alexander Hunter. *Johnny Reb and Billy Yank*. New York: Neale Publishing Company, 1905.

John W. De Forest. "Forced Marches." *Galaxy*, 1868.

J. B. Polley. *A Soldier's Letters to Charming Nellie*. New York: Neale Publishing Company, 1908.

Harold A. Small, ed. *The Road to Richmond: The Civil War Memoirs of Major Abner R. Small*. © 1939 The Regents of the University of California. Reprinted by permission of University of California Press.

Carlton McCarthy. *Detailed Minutiae of Soldier Life in the Army of Northern Virginia, 1861–1865*. Richmond: Carlton McCarthy & Co., 1882.

John D. Billings. *Hardtack and Coffee or The Unwritten Story of Army Life*. Boston: G. M. Smith, 1887.

Sidney Lanier. *Centennial Edition of the Works of Sidney Lanier: Letters of 1857–1868*, vol. VII. Baltimore/London: The Johns Hopkins University Press, 1945, pp. 46–49.

C. G. Chamberlayne, ed. *Ham Chamberlayne-Virginian: Letters and Papers of an Artillery Officer*. Richmond: Press of the Dietz Printing Co., 1932.

Norwood Penrose Hallowell. *Selected Letters and Papers of N. P. Hallowell*. Published by The Richard R. Smith Co., Inc., 1963.

Letters written by William Stillwell, James Keenan, Benjamin Abbott, and N. J. Brooks. From "*Dear Mother: Don't Grieve About Me. If I Get Killed, I'll Only be Dead.*" *Letters from Georgia Soldiers in the Civil War*. Mills Lane, ed. Savannah, Georgia: Beehive Press, 1977.

Nathaniel Hawthorne. "Chiefly About War Matters." *Atlantic Monthly*, July, 1862.

Alfred W. Ellet. "Ellet and His Steam-Rams at Memphis." From *Battles and Leaders of the Civil War*, vol. I. Robert U. Johnson and Clarence C. Buel, eds. New York: The Century Co., 1888.

"The Cruise of the *Alabama* and the *Sumter*, from the Private Journals and Other Papers of Commander R. Semmes, C. S. N., and Other Officers." From *Battles and Leaders of the Civil War*, vol. IV. Robert U. Johnson and Clarence C. Buel, eds. New York: The Century Co., 1888.

James Morris Morgan. *Recollections of a Rebel Reefer*. London: Constable & Co., 1918.

John McIntosh Kell. "Cruise and Combats of the *Alabama*." From *Battles and Leaders of the Civil War*, vol. IV. Robert U. Johnson and Clarence C. Buel, eds. New York: The Century Co., 1888.

John C. Kinney. "Farragut at Mobile Bay." From *Battles and Leaders of the Civil War*, vol. IV. Robert U. Johnson and Clarence C. Buel, eds. New York: The Century Co., 1888.

William B. Cushing. "The Destruction of the *Albemarle*." From *Battles and Leaders of the Civil War*, vol. IV. Robert U. Johnson and Clarence C. Buel, eds. New York: The Century Co., 1888.

Sallie Putnam. *Richmond During The War: Four Years of Personal Observation by a Richmond Lady*. New York: G. W. Carleton, 1867.

George Washington Cable. "New Orleans Before the Capture." From *Battles and Leaders of the Civil War*, vol. II. Robert U. Johnson and Clarence C. Buel, eds. New York: The Century Co., 1888.

Herman Melville. "Malvern Hill." Reprinted from *Selected Poems of Herman Melville*. Henning Cohen, ed. Published by Anchor Books, Doubleday, 1964.

William L. Lusk, ed. *War Letters of William Thompson Lusk*. © 1911 by William Chittenden Lusk. Privately Printed, New York.

Oliver Wendell Holmes. "My Hunt After the Captain." *Atlantic Monthly*, December, 1862.

Heros Von Borcke. *Memoirs of the Confederate War for Independence*, vol. I. London, 1866.

Alexander K. McClure. "The Invasion of Pennsylvania." From *The Rebellion Record by Frank Moore*. Published by Putnam, 1863.

George Augustus Sala. *My Diary in America in the Midst of War*, vol. I. London: Tinsley Brothers, 1865.

Robert Hunt Rhodes, ed. *All for the Union: A History of the 2nd Rhode Island Volunteer Infantry in the War of the Great Rebellion As told by the Diary and Letters of Elisha Hunt Rhodes*. Published by Orion Books/Crown, 1991.

Shelby Foote. *The Civil War: A Narrative*, vol. I. © 1958 by Shelby Foote. Reprinted by permission of Random House, Inc.

Henry Ropes. Letter to father, June 3, 1862. 20th Massachusetts Regiment Collection, Boston Public Library.

Rufus R. Dawes. *Service with the Sixth Wisconsin Volunteers*. Reprinted by the Press of Morningside Bookshop, Dayton, Ohio.

William Faulkner. *Intruder in the Dust*. © 1948 by Random House, Inc. Reprinted by permission of Random House, Inc.

Constance Cary Harrison. "Virginia Scenes in '61." From *Battles and Leaders of the Civil War*, vol. I. "Richmond Scenes in '62." From *Battles and Leaders of the Civil War*, vol. II. Robert W. Johnson and Clarence C. Buel, eds. New York: The Century Co., 1888.

John Esten Cooke. *Outlines from the Outpost*. Richard Harwell, ed. Chicago: The Lakeside Press, R. R. Donnelley & Sons Company, 1961.

Thomas H. Johnson, ed. From *The Letters of Emily Dickinson*. © 1958, 1968 by the President and Fellows of Harvard College. Reprinted by permission of The Belknap Press of Harvard University Press, Cambridge.

Ambrose Bierce. From *The Collected Writings of Ambrose Bierce*. Clifton Fadiman, ed. New York: The Citadel Press, 1946. Published by arrangement with Carol Publishing Group.

S. S. Boggs. *Eighteen Months a Prisoner under the Rebel Flag*. Published in 1887.

Julia Ward Howe. *Reminiscences, 1819–1899*. Boston: Houghton, Mifflin & Co., 1899.

Julia Ward Howe. "Battle Hymn of the Republic." *Atlantic Monthly*, February, 1862.

Lydia Minturn Post, ed. Letter from Robert Gould Shaw in *Soldiers' Letters from Camp, Battle-field and Prison*. New York: Bunce & Huntington, 1865.

George W. Cable, ed. "A Woman's Diary of the Siege of Vicksburg. Under Fire from the Gunboats." *Century Magazine*, VIII, 1885.

Allan Nevins and Milton Halsey Thomas, eds. *The Diary of George Templeton Strong*. © 1952 The Macmillan Company, copyright renewed 1980 by Milton Halsey Thomas. Reprinted with the permission of Macmillan Publishing Company.

Gurdon Grovenor in William E. Connelley, ed. *Quantrill and the Border Wars*. Iowa: Torch Press, 1910.

Bruce Catton. *Glory Road: The Bloody Route from Fredericksburg to Gettysburg*. © 1952 by Bruce Catton. Used by permission of Doubleday, a division of Bantam Doubleday Dell Publishing Group, Inc.

Frank Wilkeson. *Recollections of a Private Soldier in the Army of the Potomac*. New York & London: G. P. Putnam's Sons, The Knickerbocker Press, 1887.

Frederic Bancroft, ed. *Speeches, Correspondence and Political Papers of Carl Schurz*, vol. 1. New York: G. P. Putnam's Sons, 1913.

Tyler Dennett, ed. *Lincoln and the Civil War in the Diaries and Letters of John Hay*. © 1939 by Dodd Mead & Company, Inc., New York.

Nathaniel Paige. "The Attack on Fort Wagner," *New York Tribune*. From *The Rebellion Record*, VII. Frank Moore, ed., 1864.

Stephen D. Ramseur. Letter to his wife, October 10, 1864. Southern Historical Collection, Library of the University of North Carolina at Chapel Hill.

William Tecumseh Sherman. *Memoirs of General William T. Sherman*. New York: D. Appleton, 1875.

Herman Melville. "Marching to the Sea." "The Wilderness." Reprinted from *Collected Poems of Herman Melville*. Howard P. Vincent, ed. Chicago: Hendricks House, 1947.

Entry from Mary S. Mallard's Journal. Letter from Charles C. Jones, Jr. From *The Children of Pride: A New, Abridged Edition*; Selected Letters of the Family of the Rev. Dr. Charles Colcock Jones from the Years 1860-1868, with the Addition of Several Previously Unpublished Letters. Robert Manson Myers, ed. © 1972, 1984 by Robert Manson Myers. Reproduced by permission of Yale University Press.

M. A. DeWolfe Howe, ed. *Home Letters of General Sherman*. New York: Charles Scribner's Sons, 1909.

Gary W. Gallagher, ed. *Fighting for the Confederacy: The Personal Recollections of General Edward Porter Alexander*. © 1989 The University of North Carolina Press. Reprinted by permission of the publisher.

Charles Royster. From *The Destructive War*. © 1991 by Charles Royster. Reprinted by permission of Alfred A. Knopf, Inc.

Abraham Lincoln. "Second Inaugural Address." Reprinted from *Messages and Papers of the Presidents*, VI. James D. Richardson, ed. New York, 1904.

Gilbert E. Govan and James W. Livingood, eds. From *The Haskell Memoirs: The Personal Narrative of a Confederate Officer*. © 1960 by Gilbert E. Govan and James W. Livingood. Published by G. P. Putnam's Sons, New York. Reprinted by permission of Gilbert E. Govan and James W. Livingood.

Ulysses S. Grant. *Personal Memoirs of U. S. Grant*. 1885.

Joshua Lawrence Chamberlain. *The Passing of the Armies, An Account of the Final Campaign of the Army of the Potomac, Based upon Personal Reminiscences of the Fifth Army Corps*. New York: G. P. Putnam's Sons, 1915.

Richard M. Ketchum. "Faces From the Past." © Richard M. Ketchum, 1961. American Heritage Press.

Douglas S. Freeman. *The Last Parade*. Richmond: Whittet & Shepperson, 1932.

Bruce Catton. Excerpt from *The American Heritage Picture History of the Civil War*. © 1960 by American Heritage, a division of Forbes, Inc.

PHOTO CREDITS:

ROBERT E. LEE from *The Civil War: Lee Takes Command*. Photograph by Larry Sherer, © 1984 Time-Life Books, Inc.

THE PROCLAMATION OF EMANCIPATION from *The Civil War: Twenty Million Yankees*. Photograph by Larry Sherer, © 1985 Time-Life Books, Inc.

PRESENTATION OF THE CHARGER "COQUETTE" TO COLONEL MOSBY BY THE MEN OF HIS COMMAND, DECEMBER, 1864 from *The Civil War: Spies, Scouts and Raiders*. Photograph by Larry Sherer, © 1985 Time-Life Books, Inc.

A NEWSPAPER IN THE TRENCHES from *The Civil War: Death in the Trenches*. Photograph by Larry Sherer, © 1986 Time-Life Books, Inc.

THE BATTLE OF CHICKAMUAGA, SEPTEMBER 19, 1863 AND GENERAL HOOKER AT LOOKOUT MOUNTAIN, NOVEMBER 24, 1863 from *The Civil War: The Fight for Chattanooga*. Photograph by Larry Sherer, © 1985 Time-Life Books, Inc.

BURIAL OF LATANÉ from *The Civil War: Lee Takes Command*. Photograph by Larry Sherer, © 1984 Time-Life Books, Inc.

PETERSBURG REFUGEE FAMILY from *The Civil War: Rebels Resurgent*. Photograph by Larry Sherer, © 1985 Time-Life Books, Inc.

FORT SUMTER INTERIOR AT SUNRISE, DEC. 9, 1864 from *The Civil War: The Coastal War*. Photograph by Larry Sherer, © 1984 Time-Life Books, Inc.

CONTENTS

LANDSCAPE OF WAR

DAYS OF BATTLE

TOLL OF BATTLE

AN END TO WAR

THE CIVIL WAR

A TREASURY OF
ART AND LITERATURE

INTRODUCTION

The American Civil War did not produce one singularly great American literary masterpiece. No *War and Peace* sprang from this nineteenth-century cataclysm, perhaps simply because no American Tolstoy emerged to write it. Yet the Civil War did produce a massive outpouring of literature that is notable for its quality, its variety, and its eloquence. The selection from this literature that follows is notable too for its wide range of authorship. There are poets here, literary lights, novelists, historians, and journalists, generals of the armies, soldiers in the ranks, men on ships at sea, women in the home place, and even a president. More than eighty different voices are heard here, and each of them has something to say about what the Civil War was like.

Here, too, is the best work of the numerous artists who painted the Civil War, their paintings and watercolors reproduced in color. There is as well a generous sampling of sketches, drawings, prints, and photographs of the people, places, and incidents of the war that remains the most important single event in our national history.

There is no attempt in these pages to recount the history of the Civil War—there are any number of other books that do that. Rather, the intent is to give, in words and pictures, impressions of that war. These are incidents and scenes experienced by the authors, or imagined by them, and recorded in paint, watercolor, pencil, and on photographic plates by artists of the day. Both text and pictures are therefore arranged by topic rather than restricted by chronology: Soldier Life—Landscape of War—Civilians at War—Days of Battle. Each selection represents a perspective on events that is distinct and indeed unique. The result is a mosaic that reveals patterns in the longest four years in the American experience.

In his day Walt Whitman expressed doubts about the literature of the Civil War. He wrote that "Future years will never know the seething hell and the black infernal background of countless minor scenes and interiors (not the official surface courteousness of the generals, not the few great battles) of the Secession War; and it is best they should not. The real war will never get in the books." In fact (and due in part to Whitman himself) the real war *has* gotten into the books. When it came to the Civil War, the Victorian squeamishness and sentiment of the time gave way often enough to unblinking realism and unselfconscious reporting. Today we know much about 1861–1865's seething hells and black infernal backgrounds that Whitman doubted we would know.

A prime example of this reality is found in the words of Abraham Lincoln. As the critic Edmund Wilson points out, "the tautness and hard distinction" of Lincoln's writing was unique among political figures of the nineteenth century. An important measure of Lincoln's greatness was his literary skill; indeed he is regarded today as one of the country's major literary figures. Lincoln scholar Don E. Fehrenbacher observes here, in "The Words of Lincoln," that the president's addresses and other writings are "contributions to the permanent literary treasure of the nation." Three excerpts from the Lincoln canon are included in these pages, and included as well are views of Lincoln the wartime president as seen from several perspectives.

One of these perspectives is that of Walt Whitman. Of the entire American literary establishment of the day, only Whitman contemplated writing a book about the Civil War—a book, he said in 1863, "full enough of mosaic but all fused in one comprehensive theory." While in the end he never wrote the book, he produced a large body of material for it. The poetry in *Drum-Taps*, which when published in 1865 Whitman regarded as his best work, and his memorable elegies to Lincoln—"O Captain! My Captain!" and "When Lilacs Last in the Dooryard Bloom'd"—were incorporated in later editions of Whitman's masterwork, *Leaves of Grass*.

Whitman's wartime prose is as memorable as his poetry. Much of it grew out of his service as a nurse and hospital aide and confidant of the wounded; he estimated that he made as many as 600 visits to military hospitals during the war years. These half-dozen selections from his prose, sharply drawn, unsparing eye-witness accounts, deal largely with the victims of the conflict. "I comprehended all," Whitman wrote, "whoever came my way, northern or southern, and slighted none."

Herman Melville's war poetry, published in 1866 in *Battle-Pieces and Aspects of the War*, has like Whitman's prose a strong reportorial quality. While Melville's experience of the war was limited to a visit to the Virginia front in 1864 to see a relative serving in the Army of the Potomac, he followed the war's progress anxiously, and poems such as "Malvern Hill" and "The Wilderness" reflect deep thought about those battles. The war, Melville said, is "the great historic tragedy of our time." A latter-day poet, Stephen Vincent Benét, echoes the same sort of intense historical association. Benét's long narrative poem about the Civil War, *John Brown's Body*, from which four excerpts are taken, was published in 1928 and was awarded a Pulitzer prize.

Four other members of the literary generation of Whitman and Melville, represented collectively as "the flowering of New England," also comment here on the war. Emily Dickinson writes a quiet tribute to a young hometown boy who was killed in battle. James Russell Lowell, who edited the *Atlantic Monthly* from 1857 to 1861, analyzes thoughtfully the coming of the war for the magazine's readers. Nathaniel Hawthorne is represented in two excerpts from the article "Chiefly About War Matters" that he wrote for the *Atlantic* in 1862, reporting on his visit to the "seat of war" in Virginia. Oliver Wendell Holmes, the Boston essayist and medical pioneer, offers similarly strong reporting in an account of his battleground search for his son, the future Supreme Court justice, who was gravely wounded at the Battle of Antietam.

Other writers, or future writers, directly experienced the war from the perspective of the armies' ranks. The future poet, Sidney Lanier of Georgia, tells firsthand of camp life in a Confederate regiment. In the Union army, John W. De Forest, "including battles, assaults, skirmishes, & trench duty," saw forty-six days under fire. De Forest, a pioneer of realism with his novel *Miss Ravenel's Conversion from Secession to Loyalty*, records here an incident of war he experienced in the bayou country of the lower Mississippi. Ambrose Bierce, who also fought in the western theater and was described by his commanding officer as "a fearless and trusty man," records in fiction what he saw in the aftermath of the Battle of Chickamauga. Thomas Wentworth Higginson, author and friend of Emily Dickinson, analyzes the characteristics of leadership in a volunteer army, a role he experienced personally as colonel of a regiment of black soldiers.

In 1861, under the impress of patriotic oratory he described as "full of gunpowder and glory," twenty-six-year-old Samuel Clemens signed up with the Marion Rangers in southeastern Missouri and had a taste of the military life. The result of that experience was his story "The Private History of a Campaign That Failed," a memorable account of what it was like in the days when the war was young. After a week of this service, young Sam Clemens left for Nevada Territory and served no more. In Nevada, as a deserter from the Confederate army, he concluded that it would be advisable to take the pseudonym Mark Twain.

Born eight years after the battle was fought that he would depict so brilliantly, Stephen Crane had witnessed no war of any kind when he wrote the odyssey of young Henry Fleming in *The Red Badge of Courage*. While the battle setting is Chancellorsville, Crane's antiheroic novel might be about any great Civil War battle, and Henry Fleming might be any soldier experiencing war for the first time. Following the publication of *The Red Badge of Courage* in 1895, Crane did witness war—the Greco-Turkish War and the Spanish-American War—as a war correspondent for a New York newspaper. When he died in 1900, he was not yet twenty-nine.

Among twentieth-century novels taking the Civil War for their setting, Michael Shaara's *The Killer Angels*, dealing with Gettysburg and the men who fought it, is perhaps the closest in spirit to Stephen Crane's work. Shaara observes that Crane once said that the cold history of a battle was not enough for him; "he wanted to know what it was like to *be* there, what the weather was like, what men's faces looked like. In order to live it he had to write it." He wrote *The Killer Angels*, Shaara said, "for much the same reason." These excerpts from his novel deal with real people—Joshua Chamberlain, Robert E. Lee, and others—confronting the greatest single battle of the war.

Historians are not granted the novelist's luxury of putting thoughts into the heads and words into the mouths of their characters, yet the Civil War offers so broad a canvas for the historian's brush that it has stimulated some of the finest historical literature produced in this country. A half-dozen historians are represented in these pages. Shelby Foote writes of the remarkable Confederate cavalryman Nathan Bedford Forrest, and of the Battle of Shiloh in Tennessee in 1862, which novelist-turned-historian Foote had also taken as the subject of a novel. Allan Nevins offers a perceptive portrait of Robert E. Lee upon that general's taking command of the Army of Northern Virginia in June of 1862. Charles Royster details the terrible days in February 1865 when Sherman's army marched into Columbia, the capital of South Carolina, and then the city was destroyed.

Lincoln biographer Benjamin P. Thomas portrays President Lincoln in the White House, and Richard M. Ketchum follows General Lee home to Richmond from Appomattox. Bruce Catton depicts Lieutenant General U. S. Grant on the occasion of his taking command of all the Union armies in March 1864. Catton also furnishes us with an outstanding example of the historian's art by recreating that day in November 1863 when Mr. Lincoln delivered "a few appropriate remarks" at the dedication of the new military cemetery at Gettysburg, Pennsylvania.

The largest single author category in this selection of the Civil War's literature is made up of the men and women, of high station and low, who were there. In letters and diaries and recollections, writing without pretension or romantic illusion, they testify to what they saw and experienced.

Diarists produced a uniquely personal literature about the war. The brilliantly observant Mary Boykin Chesnut records here the moment she learned when the war began, and at war's end, when President Lincoln was murdered. A clerk in the War Department in Richmond tells of his first meeting with the Confederacy's president, Jefferson Davis. Gideon Welles, head of the Navy Department in Washington, gives his diarist's impression of Union general George B. McClellan. Yankee soldier Elisha Hunt Rhodes describes the war's first battle, and New York lawyer George Templeton Strong records the fearful, deadly rioting in New York City when conscription went into effect. Mr. Lincoln's secretary John Hay records the president's reaction to his re-election in 1864, and a Georgia woman, Mary Mallard, confides to her journal what it was like when Sherman's "bummers" came in 1865.

The American Civil War was the first war in history in which a large percentage of the men in the ranks could read and write. Soldiers wrote letters by the millions to those at home, and waited impatiently for the replies that would soften the monotony of their days. In this sampling of wartime letters, a well-educated Bostonian writes his impressions upon first meeting General Sherman, and a Texan writes to his "Charming Nellie" about his decidedly odd truce with the Yankees. Other men describe their days and their campaigns and their battles, and some of them fell in battle, leaving only their letters to survive them. Some, like Private William Stillwell, told their loved ones at home of their love, and survived the war to demonstrate it.

Countless men and women wrote their recollections of the Civil War and how the war affected them. *Hardtack and Coffee*, *The Blue and the Gray*, *Recollections of a Private*, and books with similar titles were published by the hundreds. Battles on land and sea are recalled here, both by commanders and by private soldiers and sailors. General Grant tells of volunteers in the first weeks of the war, and of taking General Lee's surrender at the end of it. A Richmond woman recalls what it was like in that first heady summer of the war. General Dick Taylor tells of Stonewall Jackson, and Julia Ward Howe tells of writing "The Battle Hymn of the Republic." Private Sam Watkins remembers the fight at Missionary Ridge; Major Rufus Dawes remembers the bloody Cornfield at Antietam; General Porter Alexander remembers the trenches at Petersburg. A signalman hears Farragut damn the torpedoes at Mobile Bay, and George Washington Cable watches the Yankees occupy New Orleans.

Some years after the war, a former Confederate soldier remarked that after so long a time it might be thought impossible "to remember with any degree of accuracy, circumstances that took place then. But these things are indelibly impressed upon my memory. . . ." It is these indelible memories that tell us so much about what it was like living through the Civil War.

If this war produced far more writing by those engaged in it than all previous wars put together, it was also the first war to be lavishly pictured even as it was being fought. Every week of the war, week in and week out, the "pictures in the papers" recorded the events of the conflict as they were seen by what the editor of one of these papers called a "noble army of artists." It was, to be sure, a small army—some twenty-eight professionals called "special artists," along with several hundred amateurs. Their individual work might appear once or twice during the war years. But whatever their number, it was the artists for these papers—*Harper's Weekly, Frank Leslie's Illustrated Weekly,* the *New York Illustrated News*—who brought the war home visually to millions of Americans.

Printing technology of the day did not permit the newspaper artists' drawings to be reproduced directly; instead they had to be converted to woodcut engravings. It was these woodcuts, as well as photographic views (carte de visite, album cards, and stereoptic viewing cards) depicting wartime people and places, that were seen most widely by the Civil War generation. Yet the special artists, and many other artists as well, professional and amateur, also produced thousands of paintings and watercolors of the war.

By far now the most famous of the special artists, and indeed one of the most famous among all American artists, was Winslow Homer. *Harper's Weekly* sent the self-taught, twenty-five-year-old Homer to sketch the scene in Washington in 1861. The next year Homer was with the Army of the Potomac for some two months during the Peninsula campaign, and later in the war he made a second trip (and perhaps a third) to the seat of war in Virginia. He returned from these experiences with his notebook full of sketches of soldiers, camp scenes, and army life that had caught his eye, and in his New York studio he proceeded to explore painting in oils.

With the exception of *A Skirmish in the Wilderness,* a scene from Grant's 1864 campaign, Homer painted not battle scenes but the everyday routines of military life. His men are Northerners but could easily be Southerners. Soldiers amuse themselves in *Pitching Horseshoes* or huddle around a campfire in *A Rainy Day in Camp.* Homer painted men on sick call and undergoing punishment for drunkenness. The tedium of trench warfare is explored in *Inviting a Shot Before Petersburg,* and this final campaign of the war is also dramatized in *Prisoners from the Front.* Homer movingly depicts the final ending of the bloodshed in *The Veteran in a New Field.*

Three other newspaper special artists expanded their wartime views beyond the quick pencil sketches required for the woodcut engravers. Thomas Nast, best known for his savage political cartoons in the postwar years, is represented here by two paintings, one a scene in New York in the first days of the war, the other a scene in Charleston in the war's last days. One of the most prolific of the special artists, Edwin Forbes of *Leslie's,* paints here a quiet camp scene and a depiction of the Federal army on the march after Gettysburg. Frank Vizetelly was one of the most special of the special artists, an Englishman who represented the *London Illustrated News* and who spent most of the Civil War reporting pictorially from the South. Vizetelly's work, most of it in watercolor, offers a distinctive and unusual Confederate perspective on the events he covered.

When the Civil War began, there was but one American artist who had taken military painting as his specialty. James Walker had served in the Mexican War and had painted numerous views of its battles, including one for the U.S. Capitol. Walker's careful rendering of detail and terrain in his Civil War battle scenes is evident in the paintings reproduced here. Edward Lamson Henry was another artist who specialized in rendering his scenes in faultless detail, as will be seen in such paintings as *The Old Westover Mansion* and *City Point, Virginia: Headquarters of General Grant.*

Several of the best known artists of the day found incidents of the war to put on canvas. George Caleb Bingham, painter of the frontier, did his bitter *Order No. 11* as a protest against the Federal army's forcible removal of civilians from their Missouri homes in 1863 for allegedly sheltering Confederate guerrillas. It is Bingham's only Civil War picture. Albert Bierstadt, another painter celebrated for his western subjects, especially his western landscapes, is represented here in a strongly landscaped scene, *Attack on a Picket Post.* Another artist of the time specializing in landscapes was Sanford Robinson Gifford, who combined his painting skills with his membership in the well-known 7th New York militia regiment to produce finely crafted renderings of camp scenes he experienced in his service with the 7th regiment.

Eastman Johnson, noted for his genre or "slice of life" paintings, captures a moment in time in his depiction of fleeing slaves, *A Ride for Liberty.* In quiet contrast is Johnson's *The Letter Home,* in which a woman representing the U.S. Sanitary Commission, a group devoted to the welfare of the troops, writes a letter for a wounded soldier. David Gilmour Blythe, a considerably less finished painter of genre scenes, dealt with such widely divergent subjects as a prisoner-of-war enclosure in Richmond, an army on the march, the Battle of Gettysburg, and a highly symbolic rendering of President Lincoln slaying the dragon of rebellion. A genre painter of more polish, Thomas Waterman Wood, commemorates veterans coming home from the war in *The Return of the Flags.*

Marine painting flourished in the nineteenth century, and the Civil War at sea offered a wide choice of subject matter. Xanthus Russell Smith served in the Union navy and saw extensive service, during which time he did numerous drawings from which he later composed large studio paintings of marine subjects. His canvas reproduced here portrays the 1865 attack by the Federals against Fort Fisher that guarded Wilmington, North Carolina. The war at sea between blockaders and blockade runners attracted several artists, as did the inland river war; *Harper's Weekly* artist Alexander Simplot painted the spectacular naval battle on the Mississippi at Memphis. One of the more unusual paintings of America's Civil War is that by the French master Edouard Manet, who painted the famous naval duel between the *Alabama* and the *Kearsarge* fought off Cherbourg on June 19, 1864.

While there were comparatively few artists portraying the Confederate side of the conflict, one of them, Conrad Wise Chapman, ranks with the best of the Civil War's artists, North or South. Early in the war Chapman served in a Kentucky regiment in the western theater, an experience he drew on for a number of camp scenes. He then transferred to a Virginia regiment posted at Charleston, where he was commissioned by General P. G. T. Beauregard to do a series of paintings of the city's fortifications. As is apparent in this selection, these were superbly designed and executed, described by one authority as "among the most delightful paintings produced during the course of the war."

Of equal artistic merit are the striking watercolors of François Ferdinand d'Orléans, Prince de Joinville. Joinville, of the French royal house of Orléans, served on the staff of Union general McClellan in 1861 and 1862 and recorded numerous incidents and scenes connected with the Army of the Potomac during that period.

Just as there were diarists and letter writers and memoirists in the ranks, there were also soldier artists. The sense of eyewitness factuality in their pictures makes up for any lack of professional polish. As is the case with some of their work illustrated here, sometimes the names of these soldier artists have been lost to history. In other cases, their work offers a unique view of certain events. The sole pictures we have of the Battle of Pea Ridge, for example, fought in Arkansas in March of 1862, are those of a Confederate artilleryman named Hunt P. Wilson; one is reproduced here. Likewise unique are the two paintings by a Union soldier, Samuel J. Reader, that picture Confederate Sterling Price's raid into Kansas in 1864. James Hope of the 2nd Vermont regiment produced the only paintings of the Battle of Antietam, the costliest one day of battle in the nation's history.

Whether amateurs or professionals, whether depicting violent battles or quiet behind-the-front scenes, this "noble army of artists" furnishes us with invaluable perspectives on the Civil War. The editor who spoke of a noble army spoke by extension of all the war's artists when he went on to say in tribute, at war's end, "There never was a war before of which the varying details, the striking and picturesque scenes, the sieges, charges, and battles by land and sea, and all the innumerable romantic incidents of a great struggle have been presented to the eye of the world by the most skillful and devoted artists. . . they were part of all, and their faithful fingers, depicting the scene, have made us a part also."

THE CIVIL WAR

*A TREASURY OF
ART AND LITERATURE*

CALL TO WAR

Samuel Wylie Crawford
FROM THE GENESIS OF THE CIVIL WAR
On South Carolina Leaving the Union

A U.S. Army surgeon stationed at Fort Sumter describes the three crucial days in Charleston—December 18–20, 1860—that initiated the dissolution of the Union.

. . . Crowds of excited people thronged the streets and open squares of the city, and filled the passage and stairways of the hall. Congratulations were exchanged on every side, while earnest dissatisfaction was freely expressed that the passage of the Secession Ordinance had been delayed.

Blue cockades and cockades of palmetto appeared in almost every hat; flags of all descriptions, except the National colors, were everywhere displayed. Upon the gavel that lay upon the Speaker's table, the word "Secession" had been cut in deep black characters. The enthusiasm spread to the more practical walks of trade, and the business streets were gay with bunting and flags, as the tradespeople, many of whom were Northern men, commended themselves to the popular clamor by a display of coarse representations on canvas of the public men, and of the incidents daily presenting themselves, and of the brilliant future in store for them.

The session of the Convention lasted but one hour; there was great unanimity . . . . On the 19th the Convention reassembled at St. Andrews Hall, when the President of the Convention submitted a communication from J. A. Elmore, the Commissioner from Alabama, enclosing a telegram received on the night of the 17th from Governor A. B. Moore, of Alabama.

"Tell the Convention," said he, "to listen to no propositions of compromise or delay"; and Mr. Elmore assures the President of the Convention that the Governor "offers it" in no spirit of dictation, but as the friendly counsel and united voice of the true men of Alabama. . . .

Early on the morning of the 20th knots of men were seen gathered here and there through the main streets and squares of Charleston. The Convention was not to meet until 12 o'clock, but it was understood that the Committee was ready to report the Ordinance of Secession, and that it would certainly pass the Convention that day. The report soon spread. Although this action had been fully anticipated, there was a feverish anxiety to know that the secession of the State was really accomplished, and as the hour of noon approached, crowds of people streamed along the avenues towards St. Andrews Hall and filled the approaches. A stranger passing from the excited throng outside into the hall of the Convention would be struck with the contrast. . . . There was no excitement. There was no visible sign that the Commonwealth of South Carolina was about to take a step more momentous for weal or woe than had yet been known in her history.

Then followed the introduction of a resolution by Mr. R. B. Rhett, that a committee of thirteen be appointed to report an ordinance providing for a convention to form a

GEORGE S. COOK. *Interior of Secession Hall, Charleston. 1861.* Photograph. Library of Congress, Washington, D.C.

Southern Confederacy, as important a step as the secession of the State itself. It was referred to the appropriate committee, when Chancellor Inglis of Chesterfield, the chairman of the committee to report an ordinance proper of secession, arose and called the attention of the President.

An immediate silence pervaded the whole assemblage as every eye turned upon the speaker. Addressing the chair, he said that the committee appointed to prepare a draft of an ordinance proper, to be adopted by the Convention in order to effect the secession of South Carolina from the Federal Union, respectfully report that they have had the matter under consideration, and believe that they would best meet the exigencies of the occasion by expressing in the fewest and simplest words all that was necessary to effect the end proposed, and so to exclude everything which was not a necessary part of the "solemn act of secession." They therefore submitted the following:

"AN ORDINANCE

to dissolve the Union between the state of South Carolina and other States united with her under the compact entitled 'The Constitution of the United States of America.'

"We, the People of the State of South Carolina, in Convention assembled, do declare and ordain, and it is hereby declared and ordained,

"That the Ordinance adopted by us in Convention, on the twenty-third day of May, in the year of our Lord one thousand seven hundred and eighty-eight, whereby the Constitution of the United States of America was ratified, and also, all Acts and parts of Acts of the General Assembly of this State, ratifying amendments to the said Constitution, are hereby repealed; and that the union now existing between South Carolina and other States, under the name of 'The United States of America,' is hereby dissolved."

A proposition that business be suspended for fifteen minutes was not agreed to, and the question was at once put, with the result of a unanimous vote, at 1:30 P.M., of 169 yeas, nays none. An immediate struggle for the floor ensued. Mr. W. Porcher Miles moved that an immediate telegram be sent to the Members of Congress, at Washington, announcing the result of the vote and the Ordinance of Secession. It was then resolved to invite the Governor and both branches of the Legislature to Institute Hall, at seven o'clock in the evening, and that the Convention should move in procession to that hall, and there, in the presence of the constituted authorities of the State and the people, sign the Ordinance of Secession. . . .

The invitations to the Senate and House of Representatives having been accepted, the Convention moved in procession at the hour indicated to Institute Hall, amid the crowds of citizens that thronged the streets, cheering loudly as it passed. The galleries of the hall were crowded with ladies, who waved their handkerchiefs to the Convention as it entered, with marked demonstration. On either side of the President's chair were two large palmetto trees. The Hall was densely crowded. The Ordinance, having been returned engrossed and with the great seal of the State, attached by the Attorney-General, was presented and was signed by every member of the Convention, special favorites being received with loud applause. Two hours were thus occupied. The President then announced that "the Ordinance of Secession has been signed and ratified, and I proclaim the State of South Carolina an independent Commonwealth."

At once the whole audience broke out in a storm of cheers; the ladies again joined in the demonstration; a rush was made for the palmetto trees, which were torn to pieces in the effort to secure mementos of the occasion. . . .

The adjournment of the Convention was characterized by the same dignity that had marked its sessions. Outside, the whole city was wild with excitement as the news spread like wild-fire through its streets. Business was suspended everywhere; the peals of the church bells mingling with salvos of artillery from the citadel. Old men ran shouting down the street. Every one entitled to it, appeared at once in uniform. In less than fifteen minutes after its passage, the principal newspaper of Charleston had placed in the hands of the eager multitude a copy of the Ordinance of Secession. Private residences were illuminated, while military organizations marched in every direction, the music of their bands lost amid the shouts of the people. The whole heart of the people had spoken.

Mary Chesnut

On the Moment in Charleston
When the War Began

Mrs. Chesnut, wife of former South Carolina senator James Chesnut, records in her diary the refusal of Robert Anderson, commander of Fort Sumter in Charleston Harbor, to capitulate, and then the moment on April 12, 1861, when war began.

APRIL 12, 1861. Anderson will not capitulate.

Yesterday was the merriest, maddest dinner we have had yet. Men were more audaciously wise and witty. We had an unspoken foreboding it was to be our last pleasant meeting. Mr. Miles dined with us today. Mrs. Henry King rushed in: "The news, I come for the latest news—all of the men of the King family are on the island"—of which fact she seemed proud.

While she was here, our peace negotiator—or envoy—came in. That is, Mr. Chesnut returned—his interview with Colonel Anderson had been deeply interesting—but was not inclined to be communicative, wanted his dinner. Felt for Anderson. Had telegraphed to President Davis for instructions.

What answer to give Anderson, &c&c. He had gone back to Fort Sumter, with additional instructions.

When they were about to leave the wharf, A. H. Boykin sprang into the boat in great excitement; thought himself ill-used. A likelihood of fighting—and he to be left behind!

I do not pretend to go to sleep. How can I? If Anderson does not accept terms—at four—the orders are—he shall be fired upon.

I count four—St. Michael chimes. I begin to hope. At half-past four, the heavy booming of a cannon.

I sprang out of bed. And on my knees—prostrate—I prayed as I never prayed before.

There was a sound of stir all over the house—pattering of feet in the corridor—all seemed hurrying one way. I put on my double gown and a shawl and went, too. It was to the housetop.

The shells were bursting. In the dark I heard a man say "waste of ammunition."

I knew my husband was rowing about in a boat somewhere in that dark bay. And that the shells were roofing it over—bursting toward the fort. If Anderson was obstinate—he was to order the forts on our side to open fire. Certainly fire had begun. The regular roar of the cannon—there it was. And who could tell what each volley accomplished of death and destruction.

The women were wild, there on the housetop. Prayers from the women and imprecations from the men, and then a shell would light up the scene. Tonight, they say, the forces are to attempt to land. . . .

WILLIAM WAUD. *Confederate Gun, Charleston. Negroes mounting cannon for the assault on Fort Sumter, March, 1861.* Pencil and wash. 9¾ x 14″. Library of Congress, Washington, D.C.

COLORPLATE 1

GEORGE HAYWARD. *Departure of the Seventh Regiment.* 1861. Pencil, watercolor, and gouache. 14½ × 20³⁄₁₆″. Museum of Fine Arts, Boston. M. & M. Karolik Collection. *New York's Seventh Regiment answers President Lincoln's call for troops.*

COLORPLATE 2 *(opposite)*

WILLIAM LUDWELL SHEPPARD. *Equipment, '61.* ca. 1899-1900. Watercolor on paper. 11¼ × 8″. Museum of the Confederacy, Richmond. Eleanor S. Brockenbrough Library. Photo by Katherine Wetzel. *A Virginia officer answers President Davis's call for volunteers.*

COLORPLATE 3

WINSLOW HOMER. *Young Union Soldier; Separate Study of a Soldier Giving Water to a Wounded Companion.* 1861. Oil, gouache, black crayon on canvas. 14⅛ × 6⅞″. Cooper-Hewitt National Museum of Design, Smithsonian Institution / Art Resource, New York. Gift of Charles Savage Homer. Photo by Ken Pelka.

COLORPLATE 4

Artist Unknown. *Fourth Pennsylvania Cavalry.* 1861. Oil on canvas. 36 × 47¾″. Philadelphia Museum of Art. Collection of Edgar William and Bernice Chrysler Garbisch.

Oct 1861

4TH. PA. CAVALRY

COLORPLATE 5

Artist Unknown. *The Army of the Potomac Marching up Pennsylvania Avenue, Washington, D.C. 1861*. 1861. Oil on canvas. 39½ × 50″. West Point Museum, United States Military Academy, West Point, New York.

COLORPLATE 6

THOMAS NAST. *The Departure of the Seventh Regiment to the War, April 19, 1861.* 1869.
Oil on canvas. 66 × 96″. The Seventh Regiment Fund, Inc., New York.

COLORPLATE 7

Artist Unknown. *Off to the Front.* ca. 1861. Oil on canvas. 27¼ × 30″.
West Point Museum, United States Military Academy, West Point, New York.

Charles C. Jones, Jr.

Letter Reflecting a Southerner's View of the North
June 10, 1861

A lawyer in Savannah, Georgia, reflects on the "blinded, fanatical" people of the North who would make war on the Confederate states.

Savannah, *Monday,* June 10th, 1861

My dear Father and Mother,

Ruth has returned after her short visit to Amanda looking pretty well. She suffered one day from an acute attack, but was soon relieved.

I presume you have observed the appointment of Judge Jackson as a brigadier general in the Confederate service. It is a position he has long and most ardently desired, and I doubt not when the hour of combat comes he will do the states no little service.

That hour must soon arrive. Sincerely do I trust and believe that the God of Battles will in that day send the victory where it of right belongs. I cannot bring my mind to entertain even the impression that a God of justice and of truth will permit a blinded, fanatical people, who already have set at naught all rules of equality, of right, and of honor; who flagrantly violate the inalienable right of private liberty by an arrogant suspension of the privilege of habeas corpus, a writ of right than which none can be dearer to the citizen—and that in the face of judicial process issued by the Chief Justice Taney, renowned for his profound legal attainments, respected for his many virtues and high position, and venerable for his many useful labors and constitutional learning; who set at defiance the right of private property by seizing Negroes, the personal chattels of others, without offer of remuneration or consent of the owner; who permit their mercenaries to trifle at will with private virtue; who trample under foot sacred compacts and solemn engagements; who substitute military despotism in the place of constitutional liberty; and who without the fear of either God or man in their eyes recklessly pursue a policy subversive of all that is just and pure and high-minded—to triumph in this unholy war. We have our sins and our shortcomings, and they are many; but without the arrogance of the self-righteous Pharisee we may honestly thank God that we are not as they are. Should they be defeated in this fearful contest, how fearful the retribution! Who can appreciate the terrors of this lifted wave of fanaticism when, broken and dismayed, it recoils in confusion and madness upon itself? Agrarianism in ancient Rome will appear as naught in the contrast.

You will observe that I have issued a proclamation requesting the citizens of Savannah to abstain from their ordinary engagements on Thursday next, the day set apart by the President as a day of fasting and prayer, and with one consent to unite in the due observation of the day. You may also notice an anonymous communication in our city papers signed "Citizen," in which I recommend that the suggestion in reference to the taking up of a collection in all places of public worship on that day for the benefit of our army and of our government should meet with a generous, practical, and patriotic adoption. If this plan be pursued generally on that day throughout these Confederate States, the amount received will be large, and the fund thus realized will prove most acceptable to the present finances of the government. The idea is a good one, and should be everywhere carried into effect. I intend myself conscientiously to observe the day. We should all do so.

We are kept very much in the dark with reference to the true movements of our army

Inauguration of Jefferson Davis as President of the Confederate States of America at Montgomery, Alabama. Feb. 18, 1861. Salt Print. 7⅞ x 5⅞". Library of the Boston Athenaeum, Boston.

in Virginia, and it is proper that this should be so. President Davis' presence inspires great enthusiasm and confidence. He appears to be in every respect the man raised for the emergency. At once soldier and statesman, he everywhere acknowledges our dependence upon and our hope in the guiding influence and the protection of a superintending Providence. I regret to know that his health is feeble. In the event of his death, where would we look for a successor?

The Central Railroad Company have declared a semi-annual dividend payable on and after the 15th inst. of five percent. Very acceptable to all stockholders at the present. I send by this post a copy of Judge Jackson's recent eulogy upon the life and character of the Hon. Charles J. McDonald. We are all well, and unite, my dearest parents, in warmest love to you both. As ever,

Your affectionate son,
Charles C. Jones, Jr.

Walt Whitman
"BEAT! BEAT! DRUMS!"

The poet describes the attitude in the North toward the outbreak of war; from Drum Taps, *Whitman's collection of poetry about the Civil War.*

Beat! beat! drums—blow! bugles! blow!
Through the windows—through doors—burst like a ruthless force,

Into the solemn church, and scatter the congregation,
Into the school where the scholar is studying;
Leave not the bridegroom quiet—no happiness must he have now with his
    bride,
Nor the peaceful farmer any peace, ploughing his field or gathering his grain,
So fierce you whirr and pound you drums—so shrill you bugles blow.

Beat! beat! drums—blow! bugles! blow!
Over the traffic of cities—over the rumble of wheels in the streets;
Are beds prepared for sleepers at night in the houses? no sleepers must sleep
    in those beds,
No bargainers' bargains by day—no brokers or speculators—would they
    continue?
Would the talkers be talking? would the singer attempt to sing?
Would the lawyers rise in the court to state his case before the judge?
Then rattle quicker, heavier drums—you bugles wilder blow.

Beat! beat! drums!—blow! bugles! blow!
Make no parley—stop for no expostulation,
Mind not the timid—mind not the weeper or prayer,
Mind not the old man beseeching the young man,
Let not the child's voice be heard, nor the mother's entreaties,
Make even the trestles to shake the dead where they lie awaiting the hearses,
So strong you thump O terrible drums—so loud you bugles blow.

James Russell Lowell

On a Northerner's View of the South at the Onset of the War

For the readers of the Atlantic Monthly, *the New England critic and poet remarks on the errant sister states of the South.*

The country had come to the conclusion that Mr. Lincoln and his cabinet were mainly employed in packing their trunks to leave Washington, when the "venerable Edward Ruffin of Virginia" fired the first gun at Fort Sumter which brought all the Free States to their feet as one man. That shot is destined to be the most memorable one ever fired on this continent since the Concord fowling-pieces said, "That bridge is ours, and we mean to go across it," eighty-seven Aprils ago. As these began a conflict which gave us independence, so that began another which is to give us nationality. It was certainly a great piece of good-luck for the Government that they had a fort which it was so profitable to lose. The people were weary of a masterly inactivity which seemed to consist mainly in submitting to be kicked. We know very well the difficulties that surrounded the new Administration; we appreciate their reluctance to begin a war the responsibility of which was as great as its consequences seemed doubtful; but we cannot understand how it hoped to evade war, except by concessions vastly more disastrous than war itself.

War has no evil comparable in its effect on national character to that of a craven submission to manifest wrong, the postponement of moral to material interests. There is no prosperity so great as courage. We do not believe that any amount of forbearance would have conciliated the South so long as they thought us pusillanimous. The only way to retain the Border States was by showing that we had the will and the power to do without them. The little Bo-peep policy of:

"Let them alone, and they'll all come home
Wagging their tails behind them"

was certainly tried long enough with conspirators who had shown unmistakably that they desired nothing so much as the continuance of peace, especially when it was all on one side, and who would never have given the Government the great advantage of being attacked in Fort Sumter, had they not supposed they were dealing with men who could not be cuffed into resistance.

The lesson we have to teach them now is that we are thoroughly and terribly in earnest. Mr. Stephens' theories are to be put to a speedier and sterner test than he expected, and we are to prove which is stronger—an oligarchy built *on* men, or a commonwealth built *of* them. Our structure is alive in every part with defensive and recuperative energies; woe to theirs, if that vaunted cornerstone which they believe patient and enduring as marble should begin to writhe with intelligent life.

We have no doubt of the issue. We believe that the strongest battalions are always on the side of God. The Southern army will be fighting for Jefferson Davis, or at most for the liberty of self-misgovernment, while we go forth for the defense of principles which alone make government august and civil society possible. It is the very life of the

E. B. AND E. C. KELLOGG. *The Eagle's Nest.* 1861. Lithograph. New York Public Library, New York. Miriam and Ira D. Wallach Division of Art, Prints, and Photographs. Astor, Lenox and Tilden Foundations.

nation that is at stake. There is no question here of dynasties, races, religions, but simply whether we will consent to include in our Bill of Rights—not merely as of equal validity with our other rights, whether natural or acquired, but by its very nature transcending and abrogating them all—the Right of Anarchy. We must convince men that treason against the ballot-box is as dangerous as treason against a throne, and that, if they play so desperate a game, they must stake their lives on the hazard.

The Government, however slow it may have been to accept the war which Mr. Buchanan's supineness left them, is acting now with all energy and determination. What they have a right to claim is the confidence of the people, and that depends in good measure on the discretion of the press. Only let us have no more weakness under the plausible name of conciliation.

We need not discuss the probabilities of an acknowledgment of the Confederated States by England and France; we have only to say, "Acknowledge them at your peril." But there is no chance of the recognition of the Confederacy by any foreign governments, so long as it is without the confidence of the brokers.

The whole tone of Southern journals, so far as we are able to judge, shows the inherent folly and weakness of the secession movement. Men who feel strong in the justice of their cause, or confident in their powers, do not waste breath in childish boasts of their own superiority and querulous deprecation of their antagonists. They are weak, and they know it.

And not only are they weak in comparison with the Free States, but we believe they are without the moral support of whatever deserves the name of public opinion at home. If not, why does their Congress, as they call it, hold council always with closed doors, like a knot of conspirators? The first tap of the Northern drum dispelled many illusions, and we need no better proof of which ship is sinking than that Mr. Caleb Cushing should have made haste to come over to the old Constitution, with the stars and stripes at her masthead.

We cannot think that the war we are entering on can end without some radical change in the system of African slavery. Whether it be doomed to a sudden extinction, or to a gradual abolition through economical causes, this war will not leave it where it was before. As a power in the state, its reign is already over. The fiery tongues of the batteries in Charleston Harbor accomplished in one day a conversion which the constancy of Garrison and the eloquence of Phillips had failed to bring about in thirty years. And whatever other result this war is destined to produce, it has already won for us a blessing worth everything to us as a nation in emancipating the public opinion of the North.

Mary A. Ward

On the Women of Rome, Georgia, Preparing Soldiers for War

A woman in Rome, Georgia, helps ready the Light Guards for war. Had the men of the South been unwilling to go to war, Mrs. Ward believed "they would have been made to go by the women."

The day that Georgia was declared out of the Union was a day of the wildest excitement in Rome. There was no order or prearrangement about it at all, but the people met each other and shook hands and exchanged congratulations over it and manifested the utmost

*The Richmond Grays
at Harper's Ferry
during the Trial of
John Brown.* 1859.
Ambrotype. Valentine
Museum, Richmond.

enthusiasm. Of course a great many of the older and wiser heads looked on with a great deal of foreboding at these rejoicings and evidences of delight, but the general feeling was one of excitement and joy.

Then we began preparing our soldiers for the war. The ladies were all summoned to public places, to halls and lecture-rooms, and sometimes to churches, and everybody who had sewing-machines was invited to send them; they were never demanded because the mere suggestion was all-sufficient. The sewing-machines were sent to these places and ladies that were known to be experts in cutting out garments were engaged in that part of the work, and every lady in town was turned into a seamstress and worked as hard as anybody could work; and the ladies not only worked themselves but they brought colored seamstresses to those places, and these halls and public places would be just filled with busy women all day long.

But even while we were doing all these things in this enthusiastic manner, of course there was a great deal of the pathetic manifested in connection with this enthusiasm, because we knew that the war meant the separation of our soldiers from their friends and families and the possibility of their not coming back. Still, while we spoke of these things we really did not think that there was going to be actual war. We had an idea that when our soldiers got upon the ground and showed, unmistakably that they were really ready and willing to fight—an idea that then, by some sort of hocus-pocus, we didn't know what, the whole trouble would be declared at an end. Of course we were not fully conscious of that feeling at the time, but that the feeling existed was beyond doubt from the great disappointment that showed itself afterwards when things turned out differently. We got our soldiers ready for the field, and the Governor of Georgia called out the troops and they were ordered out, five companies from Floyd County and three from Rome. They were ordered to Virginia under the command of General Joseph E. Johnston. The young men carried dress suits with them and any quantity of fine linen. . . .

Every soldier, nearly, had a servant with him, and a whole lot of spoons and forks, so as to live comfortably and elegantly in camp, and finally to make a splurge in Washington when they should arrive there, which they expected would be very soon indeed. That is really the way they went off; and their sweethearts gave them embroidered slippers and pin-cushions and needle-books, and all sorts of such little et ceteras, and they finally got off, after having a very eloquent discourse preached to them at the Presbyterian church, by the Presbyterian minister, Rev. John A. Jones. I remember his text very well. It was, "Be strong and quit yourselves like men." I don't know that I have had occasion to think of that sermon for years, but although this occurred more than twenty years ago, I remember it very distinctly at this moment. Then the choir played music of the most mournful character—"Farewell," and "Good Bye," and all that, and there was just one convulsive sob from one end of the church to the other, for the congregation was composed of the mothers and wives and sisters and daughters of the soldiers who were marching away.

The captain of the Light Guards, the most prominent company, a company composed of the *élite* of the town, had been married on the Thursday evening before this night of which I am speaking. He was a young Virginian. His wife came of very patriotic parents, and was a very brave woman herself. She came into the church that day with her husband, and walked up the aisle with him. She had on a brown traveling-dress, and a broad scarf crossed on her dress, and, I think, on it was inscribed, "The Rome Light Guards," and there was a pistol on one side and a dagger on the other. This lady went to the war with her husband, and staid there through the whole struggle, and never came home until the war was over.

Warren Lee Goss
"GOING TO THE FRONT"
On a Massachusetts Recruit Preparing to Go to War

A young Massachusetts man contracts "war fever" and volunteers to fight the secessionists.

Before I reached the point of enlisting, I had read and been "enthused" by General Dix's famous "shoot him on the spot" dispatch; I had attended flag-raisings, and had heard orators declaim of "undying devotion to the Union." One speaker to whom I listened declared that "human life must be cheapened"; but I never learned that he helped on the work experimentally. When men by the hundred walked soberly to the front and signed the enlistment papers, he was not one of them. As I came out of the hall, with conflicting emotions, feeling as though I should have to go finally or forfeit my birthright as an American citizen, one of the orators who stood at the door, glowing with enthusiasm and patriotism, and shaking hands effusively with those who enlisted, said to me:

"Did you enlist?" "No," I said. "Did you?"

"No; they won't take me. I have got a lame leg and a widowed mother to take care of."

I remember another enthusiast who was eager to enlist others. He declared that the family of no man who went to the front should suffer. After the war he was prominent among those who at town-meeting voted to refund the money to such as had expended it to procure substitutes. He has, moreover, been fierce and uncompromising toward the ex-Confederates since the war.

From the first I did not believe the trouble would blow over in "sixty days"; nor did I consider eleven dollars a month, and the promised glory, large pay for the services of an able-bodied young man.

It was the news that the 6th Massachusetts regiment had been mobbed by roughs on their passage through Baltimore which gave me the war fever. And yet when I read Governor John A. Andrew's instructions to have the hero martyrs "preserved in ice and tenderly sent forward," somehow, though I felt the pathos of it, I could not reconcile myself to the ice. Ice in connection with patriotism did not give me agreeable impressions of war, and when I came to think of it, the stoning of the heroic "Sixth" didn't suit me; it detracted from my desire to die a soldier's death.

I lay awake all night thinking the matter over, with the "ice" and "brick-bats" before my mind. However, the fever culminated that night, and I resolved to enlist.

"Cold chills" ran up and down my back as I got out of bed after the sleepless night, and shaved, preparatory to other desperate deeds of valor. I was twenty years of age, and when anything unusual was to be done, like fighting or courting, I shaved.

With a nervous tremor convulsing my system, and my heart thumping like muffled drum-beats, I stood before the door of the recruiting-office, and, before turning the knob to enter, read and re-read the advertisement for recruits posted thereon, until I knew all its peculiarities. The promised chances for "travel and promotion" seemed good, and I thought I might have made a mistake in considering war so serious after all. "Chances for travel!" I must confess now, after four years of soldiering, that the "chances for travel" were no myth; but "promotion" was a little uncertain and slow.

I was in no hurry to open the door. Though determined to enlist, I was half inclined to put it off awhile; I had a fluctuation of desires; I was faint-hearted and brave; I wanted

Officers of the 114th PA at the Poker Table, Petersburg, Virginia. August, 1864. Photograph. Library of Congress, Washington, D.C.

to enlist, and yet—Here I turned the knob, and was relieved. I had been more prompt, with all my hesitation, than the officer in his duty; he wasn't in. Finally he came, and said: "What do you want, my boy?" "I want to enlist," I responded, blushing deeply with upwelling patriotism and bashfulness. Then the surgeon came to strip and examine me. In justice to myself, it must be stated that I signed the rolls without a tremor. It is common to the most of humanity, I believe, that, when confronted with actual danger, men have less fear than in its contemplation. I will, however, make one exception in favor of the first shell I heard uttering its blood-curdling hisses, as though a steam locomotive were traveling the air. With this exception I have found the actual dangers of war always less terrible face to face than on the night before the battle.

My first uniform was a bad fit: my trousers were too long by three or four inches; the flannel shirt was coarse and unpleasant, too large at the neck and too short elsewhere. The forage cap was an ungainly bag with pasteboard top and leather visor; the blouse was the only part which seemed decent; while the overcoat made me feel like a little nubbin of corn in a large preponderance of husk. Nothing except "Virginia mud" ever took down my ideas of military pomp quite so low.

After enlisting I did not seem of so much consequence as I had expected. There was not so much excitement on account of my military appearance as I deemed justly my due. I was taught my facings, and at the time I thought the drill-master needlessly fussy about shouldering, ordering, and presenting arms. At this time men were often drilled in company and regimental evolutions long before they learned the manual of arms, because of the difficulty of obtaining muskets. These we obtained at an early day, but we would willingly have resigned them after carrying them for a few hours. The musket, after an hour's drill, seemed heavier and less ornamental than it had looked to be. The first day I went out to drill, getting tired of doing the same things over and over, I said to the drill-sergeant: "Let's stop this fooling and go over to the grocery." His only reply was addressed to a corporal: "Corporal, take this man out and drill him like h—l"; and the corporal did! I found that suggestions were not so well appreciated in the army as in private life, and that no wisdom was equal to a drill-master's "Right face," "Left wheel," and "Right, oblique, march." It takes a raw recruit some time to learn that he is not to think or suggest, but obey. Some never do learn. I acquired it at last, in humility and mud, but it was tough. Yet I doubt if my patriotism, during my first three weeks' drill, was quite knee-high. Drilling looks easy to a spectator, but it isn't. Old soldiers who read this will remember their green recruithood and smile assent. After a time I had cut down my uniform so that I could see out of it, and had conquered the drill sufficiently to see through it. Then the word came: On to Washington!

Ulysses S. Grant
On Volunteering in Illinois

In his Memoirs, *the former U.S. Army captain and 18th president, Grant, recalls how the men of Galena responded to the call for volunteers to put down the rebellion.*

As soon as the news of the call for volunteers reached Galena, posters were stuck up calling for a meeting of the citizens at the court-house in the evening. Business ceased entirely; all was excitement; for a time there were no party distinctions; all were Union men, determined to avenge the insult to the national flag. In the evening the court-house

J. W. Campbell.
Ulysses S. Grant.
1862. Photograph.
Chicago Historical
Society, Chicago.

was packed. Although a comparative stranger I was called upon to preside; the sole reason, possibly, was that I had been in the army and had seen service. With much embarrassment and some prompting I made out to announce the object of the meeting. Speeches were in order, but it is doubtful whether it would have been safe just then to make other than patriotic ones. There was probably no one in the house, however, who felt like making any other. The two principal speeches were by B. B. Howard, the postmaster and a Breckenridge Democrat at the November election the fall before, and John

A. Rawlins, an elector on the Douglas ticket. E. B. Washburne, with whom I was not acquainted at that time, came in after the meeting had been organized and expressed, I understood afterwards, a little surprise that Galena could not furnish a presiding officer for such an occasion without taking a stranger. He came forward and was introduced, and made a speech appealing to the patriotism of the meeting.

After the speaking was over volunteers were called for to form a company. The quota of Illinois had been fixed at six regiments; and it was supposed that one company would be as much as would be accepted from Galena. The company was raised and the officers and non-commissioned officers elected before the meeting adjourned. I declined the captaincy before the balloting, but announced that I would aid the company in every way I could and would be found in the service in some position if there should be a war. I never went into our leather store after that meeting, to put up a package or do other business.

The ladies of Galena were quite as patriotic as the men. They could not enlist, but they conceived the idea of sending their first company to the field uniformed. They came to me to get a description of the United States uniform for infantry; subscribed and bought the material; procured tailors to cut out the garments, and the ladies made them up. In a few days the company was in uniform and ready to report to the State capital for assignment. The men all turned out the morning after their enlistment, and I took charge, divided them into squads and superintended their drill. When they were ready to go to Springfield I went with them and remained there until they were assigned to a regiment.

There were so many more volunteers than had been called for that the question whom to accept was quite embarrassing to the governor, Richard Yates. The legislature was in session at the time, however, and came to his relief. A law was enacted authorizing the governor to accept the services of ten additional regiments, one from each congressional district, for one month, to be paid by the State, but pledged to go into the service of the United States if there should be a further call during their term. Even with this relief the governor was still very much embarrassed. Before the war was over he was like the President when he was taken with the varioloid: "at last he had something he could give to all who wanted it."

In time the Galena company was mustered into the United States service, forming a part of the 11th Illinois volunteer infantry. . . .

Frederick Douglass

On Slavery as a Cause of the War

Writing in his magazine, Douglass' Monthly, *the black abolitionist reminds his countrymen of "the guilty cause of all our national troubles. . . ."*

———————

We talk of the irrepressible conflict, and practically give the lie to our talk. We wage war against slaveholding rebels, and yet protect and augment the motive which has moved the slaveholders to rebellion. We strike at the effect, and leave the cause unharmed. Fire will not burn it out of us—water cannot wash it out of us, that this war with the slaveholders can never be brought to a desirable termination until slavery, the guilty cause of all our national troubles, has been totally and forever abolished. . . .

We are asked if we would turn the slaves all loose. I answer, Yes. Why not? They

Frederick Douglass.
1856. Ambrotype.
4³⁄₁₆ x 3³⁄₈″. National
Portrait Gallery,
Smithsonian Institution,
Washington, D.C. Gift
of an anonymous donor.

are not wolves nor tigers, but men. They are endowed with reason—can decide upon questions of right and wrong, good and evil, benefits and injuries—and are therefore subjects of government precisely as other men are.

But would you have them stay here? Why should they not? What better is here than there? What class of people can show a better title to the land on which they live—than the colored people of the South? They have watered the soil with their tears and enriched it with their blood, and tilled it with their hard hands during two centuries; they have leveled its forests, raked out the obstructions to the plow and hoe, reclaimed the swamps, and produced whatever has made it a goodly land to dwell in, and it would be a shame and a crime little inferior in enormity to Slavery itself if these natural owners of the Southern and Gulf States should be driven away from their country to make room for others—even if others could be obtained to fill their places.

WAR LEADERS

Benjamin P. Thomas
"PROFILE OF A PRESIDENT"
On Abraham Lincoln

*Lincoln scholar and biographer Benjamin Thomas recounts the daily routine in the
White House when Abraham Lincoln met the people.*

A President's life is wearying and worrisome at best, but in Lincoln's case all the vast
problems of the war were added to the normal tasks of office. [John] Nicolay and [John]
Hay comprised his secretarial staff until William O. Stoddard was brought in to assist
them midway of the war. Edward D. Neill succeeded Stoddard when the latter became
ill, and was in turn succeeded by Charles Philbrick. These young men scrutinized and
questioned visitors, prepared a daily digest of news and military information, read and
sorted the mail, and took care of whatever other details happened to call for attention.
They had rooms at the White House, but walked to Willard's for their meals.

Lincoln started his workday early, for he was a light and fitful sleeper, and sometimes
walked alone across the White House lawn in the gray dawn to summon a newsboy. By
eight o'clock, when breakfast was announced, he had already been at work for an hour
or more. His morning meal consisted of an egg and a cup of coffee; he was so little
concerned about eating that Mrs. Lincoln sometimes invited guests to breakfast to make
sure he would come. After breakfast he put in another hour of work before his door
opened to visitors. . . .

At first Lincoln refused to limit the visiting-hours. "They do not want much," he said
of the throng waiting to see him, "and they get very little. . . . I know how I would feel
in their place." So people began coming before breakfast, and some still remained late
at night. Lincoln realized at last that something must be done to conserve his time, and
agreed to restrict the visiting-period from ten o'clock in the morning till three in the
afternoon. But his other work continued to pile up, and the hours were again shortened,
from ten till one.

Priority was granted to cabinet members, senators, and representatives in that order;
finally, if any time remained, ordinary citizens were admitted. Army officers, many of
whom had made nuisances of themselves with requests for promotion or demands for
redress from supposed injustices, were forbidden to come to Washington without special
permission. . . .

With only Edward Moran, a short, thin, humorous Irishman, who had served since
President Taylor's time, stationed at the front door, and Louis Bargdorf, another White
House veteran, posted in the upstairs corridor, the throng enjoyed access to all the public
rooms and trooped about unhindered. [Ward] Lamon warned Lincoln that eavesdroppers
and traitors lurked among the crowd, and suggested that Allan Pinkerton or some other
shrewd detective be employed to ferret them out. At least everyone should be kept downstairs until his name was called, he thought. But not until November 1864 were four

ALEXANDER GARDNER.
Abraham Lincoln.
February 5, 1865.
Photograph.
Library of Congress,
Washington, D.C.

District of Columbia policemen in plain clothes detailed to the White House. A secretary gave each visitor a final scrutiny, but even so, unworthy persons often managed to intrude upon the President.

Once a visitor had passed the outer barriers and entered Lincoln's office, he encountered no further formality. The President never effused: "I am delighted to see you," unless he meant it; he simply said: "How do you do?" or "What can I do for you?" with a pleasant nod and smile. Lincoln wore no outward signs of greatness. He inspired no awe or embarrassment. He had no pomp, no wish to impress. But along with his awkward angularity he had an innate poise and casual unaffected dignity. Meeting all sorts of people, he shaped his response to their approach. He was lowly to the meek, dignified to the pompous, flippant or stern with the presumptuous, and courteous to everyone, even his foes, when they came to him in good faith. He respected the views of others and listened while they talked, for he knew that in some matters they might see truth more clearly than he, and that men arrive at truth by free discussion. His usual attitude while listening was to cross his long legs and lean forward, hands clasped around his knee, or with one elbow on his knee to support his arm while he stroked his chin.

Samuel R. Suddarth, Quartermaster General of Kentucky, observed after an interview: "His conversational powers are fine—and his custom of interspersing conversation with incidents, anecdotes and witticisms are well calculated to impress his hearers with the kindheartedness of the man. And they are so adroitly and delicately mingled in the thread of his discourse that one hardly notices the digression. His language is good though not select. . . . He is dignified in his manners without austerity." Suddarth was one of very few persons who heard Lincoln use profanity; "He is a damned rascal," the President said of a certain politician, and then added hastily, as though surprised: "God knows I do not know when I have sworn before.". . .

It always gave Lincoln pleasure to be able to grant a request. But the glibbest talkers could not back him down. He seldom gave an outright "No." He was more likely to make the necessity of saying it so obvious that refusal became unnecessary. Or he would turn the conversation with a story or a jest; when petitioners found themselves back in the hall, they wondered how he had got rid of them. Men of the strongest personalities felt Lincoln's quiet dominance. Thurlow Weed went home after a talk with him and wrote: "I do not, when with you, say half I intend, partly because I do not like to 'crank,' and partly because you talk me out of my convictions and apprehensions. So bear with me, please, now, till I free my mind.". . .

With government officials and men of influence so often turned away from Lincoln's office, it is remarkable that so many humble people managed to get in. But if he learned that some anxious old lady or worried wife, or a young soldier in a private's uniform had been waiting patiently from day to day to see him, he would arrange an appointment and if necessary overstay his time to hear his story. His secretaries estimated that he spent at least three quarters of his time in meeting people, despite their efforts to shield him from annoyance. It was as though he tried to make himself the nation's burden-bearer; and when his door swung shut at last, he' was often near exhaustion.

While these daily sessions wore on him physically, they refreshed his mind and spirit. Through them he measured the pulse-beat of the people and learned to key his actions to its changing throb, using caution when it slowed, moving boldly when he felt it quicken. He called them his "public opinion baths," but they were more than that, for they also enabled him to curb the undue harshness of subordinates, and to override bureaucratic arrogance and indifference.

J. B. Jones
On Jefferson Davis, President

A War Department clerk in Richmond meets the president of the Confederate States of America for the first time, and confides his impressions to his diary in 1861.

———————

MAY 17TH—Was introduced to the President to-day. He was overwhelmed with papers, and retained a number in his left hand, probably of more importance than the rest. He received me with urbanity, and while he read the papers I had given him, as I had never seen him before, I endeavored to scrutinize his features, as one would naturally do, for the purpose of forming a vague estimate of the character and capabilities of the man destined to perform the leading part in a revolution which must occupy a large space in the world's history. His stature is tall, nearly six feet; his frame is very slight and seemingly frail; but when he throws back his shoulders he is as straight as an Indian chief. The features of his face are distinctly marked with character; and no one gazing at his profile would doubt for a moment that he beheld more than an ordinary man. His face is handsome, and [on] his thin lip often basks a pleasant smile. There is nothing sinister or repulsive in his manners or appearance; and if there are no special indications of great grasp of intellectual power on his forehead and on his sharply defined nose and chin, neither is there any evidence of weakness, or that he could be easily moved from any settled purpose. I think he has a clear perception of matters demanding his cognizance, and a nice discrimination of details. As a politician he attaches the utmost importance to *consistency*—and here I differ with him. I think that to be consistent as a politician, is to change with the circumstances of the case. When Calhoun and Webster first met in Congress, the first advocated a protective tariff and the last opposed it. This

Jefferson Davis.
Prior to 1860.
Daguerreotype.
Chicago Historical
Society, Chicago.

COLORPLATE 8

Artist Unknown. *Jefferson Davis and His Generals.* From left, P. G. T. Beauregard, Thomas J. "Stonewall" Jackson, President Davis, J. E. B. Stuart, Joseph E. Johnston. West Point Museum, United States Military Academy, West Point, New York.

COLORPLATE 9

Attributed to W. B. Cox. *Robert E. Lee.* 1865. Oil on canvas. 21½ × 17½″.
Virginia Historical Society, Richmond.

COLORPLATE 10

JULIAN SCOTT. *George Brinton McClellan.* No date. Oil on canvas. 40 × 30″. National Portrait Gallery, Smithsonian Institution, Washington, D.C. Bequest of Georgiana L. McClellan, 1953.

COLORPLATE 11

JAMES J. ELDER. *Robert E. Lee.* ca. 1875. Oil on canvas. 49 × 36″.
Washington & Lee University, Lexington, Virginia. Photo by Larry Sherer, copyright © 1984
Time-Life Books, Inc.

COLORPLATE 12

WILLIAM GARL BROWNE. *T. J. "Stonewall" Jackson.* 1869. Oil on canvas. 46 × 35″.
Stonewall Jackson House, Historic Lexington Foundation, Lexington, Virginia.

COLORPLATE 13

E. B. F. JULIO. *The Last Meeting of Lee and Jackson.* 1869. Oil on canvas. 102 × 74".
Courtesy of Robert M. Hicklin Jr., Inc. *The scene is the Battle of Chancellorsville, May 2, 1863. That evening Jackson was mortally wounded.*

COLORPLATE 14

OLE PETER HANSEN BALLING. *Ulysses S. Grant*. 1865. Oil on canvas. 48¼ × 38¼".
National Portrait Gallery, Smithsonian Institution, Washington, D.C.

COLORPLATE 15

CHARLES HOFFBAUER. *Jeb Stuart*. 1913-1920. Mural.
Virginia Historical Society, Richmond.

was told me by Mr. Webster himself, in 1842, when he was Secretary of State; and it was confirmed by Mr. Calhoun in 1844, then Secretary of State himself. Statesmen are the physicians of the public weal; and what doctor hesitates to vary his remedies with the new phases of disease?

When the President had completed the reading of my papers, and during the perusal I observed him make several emphatic nods, he asked me what I wanted. I told him I wanted employment with my pen, perhaps only temporary employment. I thought the correspondence of the Secretary of War would increase in volume, and another assistant besides Major Tyler would be required in his office. He smiled and shook his head, saying that such work would be only temporary indeed; which I construed to mean that even *he* did not then suppose the war to assume colossal proportions.

Gideon Welles
On General George B. McClellan

In his diary, in September 1862, the secretary of the Navy remarks on the Army of the Potomac's first commander, General George B. McClellan. Welles was critical of McClellan's role in the recently fought Second Battle of Bull Run.

SEPTEMBER 3, WEDNESDAY

. . . McClellan is an intelligent engineer but not a commander. To attack or advance with energy and power is not in his reading or studies, nor is it in his nature or disposition to advance. I sometimes fear his heart is not in the cause yet I do not entertain the thought that he is unfaithful. The study of military operations interests and amuses

BRADY STUDIO, WASHINGTON, D.C. *George B. McClellan.* ca. 1861–1862. Photograph. National Archives, Washington, D.C.

him. He likes show, parade and power. Wishes to outgeneral the Rebels, but not to kill and destroy them. In conversation which I had with him in May last at Cumberland on the Pamunkey, he said he desired, of all things, to capture Charleston; he would demolish and annihilate the city. He detested, he said, both South Carolina and Massachusetts, and should rejoice to see both States extinguished. Both were and always had been ultra and mischievous, and he could not tell which he hated most. There were the remarks of the General-in-Chief at the head of our armies then in the field, and as large a proportion of his troops were from Massachusetts as from any State in the Union, while as large a proportion of those opposed, who were fighting the Union, were from South Carolina as from any State. He was leading the men of Massachusetts against the men of South Carolina, yet he, the General, detests them alike.

I cannot relieve my mind from the belief, that to him, in a great degree, and to his example, influence and conduct are to be attributed some portion of our late reverses—more than to any other person on either side. His reluctance to move or have others move, his inactivity, his detention of Franklin, his omission to send forward supplies unless Pope would send a cavalry escort from the battle-field, and the tone of his dispatches, all show a moody state of feeling. The treatment which he and the generals associated with him have received was injudicious, impolitic, wrong perhaps, but is no justification for withholding one tithe of strength in a great emergency, where the lives of their countrymen and the welfare of the country were in danger. The soldiers whom he has commanded are doubtless attached to him. They have been trained to it, and he has kindly cared for them while under him. They have imbibed the prejudices of these officers, and the officers have, I fear, manifested a spirit in some instances more factious than patriotic.

Allan Nevins

FROM THE WAR FOR THE UNION

On Robert E. Lee

On June 1, 1862, Virginia-born Robert E. Lee replaced the wounded Joe Johnston as commander of the Southern army defending Richmond; historian Nevins evaluates the new commander.

While McClellan waited, the enemy resolved to strike, for the Southern army was now headed by a man of lionhearted qualities. If the emergence of Jackson was one of the memorable developments of the war, the replacement of Johnston by Robert E. Lee signalized a quite new phase of the conflict. Since April 23, 1861, by State appointment, Lee had been major-general and commander of the Virginia forces, and since May 10, 1861, he had also held supreme control of all the Confederate forces in Virginia. Primarily concerned with organizing State forces, fortifying Virginia rivers, and (during the winter) improving the defenses of the South Atlantic coast, he had also been Jefferson Davis' military adviser. He kept aloof from the dispute between Davis and Johnston over the latter's rank. By common consent he was easily the ablest man to take Johnston's place, although he had never directed a battle. In the prime of life—fifty-five years old, powerfully built, in superb health—he was glad to exchange his empty if honorable desk eminence for a field command. On June 1 he took charge of the force he named The Army of Northern Virginia, and promptly began planning an offensive.

Lee saw that he could not wait. If McClellan marshaled his hosts and brought his powerful siege guns to bear, Richmond would be lost. Nothing but fierce lunging blows could extricate the Confederacy from its disadvantages of inferior strength. Like Jackson, he was a thinker. Although his symmetry of character was so noble, and his reticence so complete, that many have credited him with greatness of personality rather than intellect, the fact was that he possessed both. In quickness of perception, subtlety of thought, and power of devising complicated operations, he equaled Marlborough or Frederick, as in coolness he surpassed them. He knew that a general must always take chances, that the leader with inferior forces must move swiftly and shrewdly to make his

JULIAN VANNERSON.
Robert E. Lee in Richmond.
1863. Photograph.
Library of Congress,
Washington, D.C.

chances better than even, and that he must realistically equate the power to act with the power to imagine.

If in many ways Lee seemed limited, it was intensity of purpose that limited him. All his thoughts, apart from religion and family, were centered on the profession of arms. He did almost no general reading; he never accumulated a library, never gave a leisure hour to literature, and never once in his letters refers to Shakespeare or Milton, to Dickens or Thackeray. The great scientific advance of the age of Darwin, Huxley, and Spencer made no appeal to him. Even in religion he paid no attention to austere theological thought; the Bible was enough for him. But in strategy and tactics, in engineering, and in what we now call logistics, he made himself proficient by hard study. Nobody in America knew military science so well.

War was in fact a passion with him, and as befitted a son of "Light-Horse Harry" Lee, he delighted in martial problems and exercises. A merciful man, he was sensitively aware of the suffering which war imposes. "You have no idea what a horrible sight a battlefield is," he wrote his family from Mexico. The knightliest of commanders, he set his face sternly, in his invasion of the North, against any retaliation for the devastation and plundering of which many Union forces had been guilty. But his energetic nature, which comprehended a taste for excitement and a delight in seeing intricate mental combinations translated into army evolutions, made conflict a congenial element. Remembering well what his father's unresting activity had accomplished at Stony Point, Paulus Hook, and in the long Southern campaign, he drew a special pleasure from swift movement and battles against odds. When told after the war that such daring decisions as the splitting of his army at Second Manassas had risked the utter ruin of the Confederacy, he replied that this was obvious, "but the disparity of force between the contending forces rendered the risks unavoidable."

Richard Taylor
On "Stonewall" Jackson

Thomas J. "Stonewall" Jackson first gained fame with his Shenandoah Valley campaign in the spring of 1862. Dick Taylor, commanding a Louisiana brigade, meets Stonewall for the first time and tells of it in his Destruction and Reconstruction: Personal Experiences of the Late War.

———————————

After attending to necessary camp details, I sought Jackson, whom I had never met. . . . The mounted officer who had been sent on in advance pointed out a figure perched on the topmost rail of a fence overlooking the road and field, and said it was Jackson. Approaching, I saluted and declared my name and rank, then waited for a response. Before this came I had time to see a pair of cavalry boots covering feet of gigantic size, a mangy cap with visor drawn low, a heavy, dark beard, and weary eyes—eyes I afterward saw filled with intense but never brilliant light. A low, gentle voice inquired the road and distance marched that day.

"Keazletown road, six and twenty miles."

"You seem to have no stragglers."

"Never allow straggling."

"You must teach my people; they straggle badly." A bow in reply. Just then my creoles

RONTZOHN GALLERY, WINCHESTER, VIRGINIA. *Thomas "Stonewall" Jackson.* February, 1862. Photograph. Valentine Museum, Richmond.

started their band and a waltz. After a contemplative suck at a lemon, "Thoughtless fellows for serious work" came forth. I expressed a hope that the work would not be less well done because of the gayety. A return to the lemon gave me the opportunity to retire. Where Jackson got his lemons "no fellow could find out," but he was rarely without one. To have lived twelve miles from that fruit would have disturbed him as much as it did the witty Dean.

Quite late that night General Jackson came to my camp fire, where he stayed some hours. He said we would move at dawn, asked a few questions about the marching of my men, which seemed to have impressed him, and then remained silent. If silence be golden, he was a "bonanza." He sucked lemons, ate hard-tack, and drank water, and praying and fighting appeared to be his idea of the "whole duty of man."

In the gray of the morning, as I was forming my column on the pike, Jackson appeared and gave the route—north—which, from the situation of its camp, put my brigade in advance of the army. After moving a short distance in this direction, the head of the column was turned to the east and took the road over Massanutten gap to Luray. Scarce a word was spoken on the march, as Jackson rode with me. From time to time a courier would gallop up, report, and return toward Luray. An ungraceful horseman, mounted on a sorry chestnut with a shambling gait, his huge feet with outturned toes thrust into his stirrups, and such parts of his countenance as the low visor of his shocking cap failed to conceal wearing a wooden look, our new commander was not prepossessing. . . .

Shelby Foote

FROM THE CIVIL WAR: A NARRATIVE
On Nathan Bedford Forrest

It was April 8, 1862, the day after the Battle of Shiloh in western Tennessee, when General Sherman first encountered the fierce Confederate cavalryman Nathan Bedford Forrest; historian Foote describes the clash.

The place was called the Fallen Timbers, a half-mile-wide boggy swale where a prewar logging project had been abandoned. The road dipped down, then crested a ridge on the far side, where [Sherman] could see enemy horsemen grouped in silhouette against the sky. Not knowing their strength or what might lie beyond the ridge, he shook out a regiment of skirmishers, posted cavalry to back them up and guard their flanks, then

Nathan Bedford Forrest. 1865.
Photograph. Library of Congress,
Washington, D.C.

sent them forward, following with the rest of the brigade in attack formation at an interval of about two hundred yards. The thing was done in strict professional style, according to the book. But the man he was advancing against had never read the book, though he was presently to rewrite it by improvising tactics that would conform to his own notion of what war was all about. "War means fighting," he said. "And fighting means killing." It was Forrest. Breckinridge had assigned him a scratch collection of about 350 Tennessee, Kentucky, Mississippi, and Texas cavalrymen, turning over to him the task of protecting the rear of the retreating column.

As he prepared to defend the ridge, outnumbered five-to-one by the advancing blue brigade, he saw something that caused him to change his mind and his tactics. For as the skirmishers entered the vine-tangled hollow, picking their way around felled trees and stumbling through the brambles, they lost their neat alignment. In fact, they could hardly have been more disorganized if artillery had opened on them there in the swale. Forrest saw his chance. "Charge!" he shouted, and led his horsemen pounding down the slope. Most of the skirmishers had begun to run before he struck them, but those who stood were knocked sprawling by a blast from shotguns and revolvers. Beyond them, the Federal cavalry had panicked, firing their carbines wildly in the air. When they broke too, Forrest kept on after them, still brandishing his saber and crying, "Charge! Charge!" as he plowed into the solid ranks of the brigade drawn up beyond. The trouble was, he was charging by himself; the others, seeing the steady brigade front, had turned back and were already busy gathering up their 43 prisoners. Forrest was one gray uniform, high above a sea of blue. "Kill him! *Kill* the goddam rebel! Knock him off his horse!" It was no easy thing to do; the horse was kicking and plunging and Forrest was hacking and slashing; but one of the soldiers did his best. Reaching far out, he shoved the muzzle of his rifle into the colonel's side and pulled the trigger. The force of the explosion lifted Forrest clear of the saddle, but he regained his seat and sawed the horse around. As he came out of the mass of dark blue uniforms and furious white faces, clearing a path with his saber, he reached down and grabbed one of the soldiers by the collar, swung him onto the crupper of the horse, and galloped back to safety, using the Federal as a shield against the bullets fired after him. Once he was out of range, he flung the hapless fellow off and rode on up the ridge where his men were waiting in open-mouthed amazement. . . .

Don E. Fehrenbacher
"THE WORDS OF LINCOLN"
On Lincoln's Genius

Lincoln's literary skill was a key element in his success as a wartime leader. Lincoln scholar Fehrenbacher analyzes what he terms the president's "genius" in this regard.

Besides their intended meanings and effective meanings within a definite historical context, some of Lincoln's words have acquired *transcendent* meaning as contributions to the permanent literary treasure of the nation. Just why his prose at its best is so splendid, so memorable, has been pondered by all sorts of critics. Edmund Wilson is one of those who emphasize the leanness and muscular strength of Lincoln's style, compared with the more ornate oratorical fashion of the day. Yet, in his more formal pieces especially, Lincoln employed some of the structures and rhetorical devices of eighteenth-century expository writing. In the Gettysburg Address, for example, one scholar finds "two antitheses, five cases of anaphora, eight instances of balanced phrases and clauses, thirteen alliterations." Several critics stress the richness and vigor of Lincoln's imagery, drawn as it was from everyday American experience and culture. Jacques Barzun speaks of his gift of rhythm, "developed to a supreme degree," and of an extraordinary capacity for verbal discipline. "Lincoln," he says, "acquired his power by exacting obedience from words."

Lincoln's literary skill is most readily observable in those instances when he took someone else's prose and molded it to his own use. The first sentence of the House Divided speech, for instance ["If we could first know *where* we are, and *whither* we are tending, we could then better judge *what* to do, and *how* to do it.], was a simpler, crisper version of the rhetorical flourish with which Daniel Webster began his "Second Reply to Hayne." And the familiar opening words of the Gettysburg Address may have been derived from a speech delivered on July 4, 1861, by Galusha A. Grow in assuming office as Speaker of the House of Representatives.

Perhaps the best example, however, is Lincoln's plea for reconciliation in the final paragraph of the First Inaugural—a paragraph drafted originally by his secretary of state, William H. Seward. Let us look first at just the short opening sentence. Seward wrote: "I close." Lincoln changed it to: "I am loth to close." The improvement in cadence is obvious enough, but the addition of three words also makes the sentence throb with connotative meanings and emotive force. It expresses an almost elegiac reluctance to break off discussion of the crisis—a sense of remnant opportunities slipping away, of a cherished world about to be lost. Then Lincoln went on to make the moving appeal that was the first oratorical summit of his presidency: "Though passion may have strained, it must not break our bonds of affection. The mystic chords of memory, stretching from every battlefield, and patriot grave, to every living heart and hearthstone, all over this broad land, will yet swell the chorus of the Union, when again touched, as surely they will be, by the better angels of our nature."

Here was an occasion calling for eloquence; here was an ear keenly tuned to the music of the English language; here were intellectual grasp and moral urgency; here was great emotional power under firm artistic control. Here, in short, was the mastery that we associate with genius.

Abraham Lincoln
Letter to Major General Hooker
January 26, 1863

The president advises the new commander of the Army of the Potomac, "Fighting Joe" Hooker.

Major General Hooker:

Executive Mansion,
Washington, January 26, 1863.

General,

I have placed you at the head of the Army of the Potomac. Of course I have done this upon what appear to me to be sufficient reasons. And yet I think it best for you to know that there are some things in regard to which, I am not quite satisfied with you. I believe you to be a brave and a skilful soldier, which, of course, I like. I also believe you do not mix politics with your profession, in which you are right. You have confidence in yourself, which is a valuable, if not an indispensable quality. You are ambitious, which, within reasonable bounds, does good rather than harm. But I think that during Gen. Burnside's command of the Army, you have taken counsel of your ambition, and thwarted him as much as you could, in which you did a great wrong to the country, and to a most meritorious and honorable brother officer. I have heard, in such way as to believe it, of your recently saying that both the Army and the Government needed a Dictator. Of course it was not *for* this, but in spite of it, that I have given you the command. Only those generals who gain successes, can set up dictators. What I now ask of you is military success, and I will risk the dictatorship. The government will support you to the utmost of it's ability, which is neither more nor less than it has done and will do for all commanders. I much fear that the spirit which you have aided to infuse into the Army, of criticising their Commander, and withholding confidence from him, will now turn upon you. I shall assist you as far as I can, to put it down. Neither you, nor Napoleon, if he were alive again, could get any good out of an army, while such a spirit prevails in it.

And now, beware of rashness. Beware of rashness, but with energy, and sleepless vigilance, go forward, and give us victories.

Yours very truly
A. Lincoln

Bruce Catton
FROM A STILLNESS AT APPOMATTOX
On Grant

The historian appraises Grant, the Union army's general-in-chief, appointed to that post in the spring of 1864. Catton won a Pulitzer Prize in 1953 for A Stillness at Appomattox.

Ulysses S. Grant was a natural—an unmistakable rural Middle Westerner, bearing somehow the air of the little farm and the empty dusty road and the small-town harness shop, plunked down here in an army predominantly officered by polished Easterners. He was slouchy, round-shouldered, a red bristly beard cropped short on his weathered face, with a look about the eyes as of a man who had come way up from very far down; his one visible talent seemingly the ability to ride any horse anywhere under any conditions. These days, mostly, he rode a big bay horse named Cincinnati, and when he went out to look at the troops he set a pace no staff officer could match, slanting easily forward as if he and the horse had been made in one piece, and his following was generally trailed out behind him for a hundred yards, scabbards banging against the sides of lathered horses, the less military officers frantically grabbing hats and saddle leather as they tried to keep up.

Somewhere within the general in chief there hid the proud, shy little West Point graduate who put on the best uniform a brevet second lieutenant of infantry could wear when he went home to Ohio on furlough after graduation, and who got laughed at for a dude by livery-stable toughs, and who forever after preferred to wear the plain uniform of a private soldier, with officer's insignia stitched to the shoulders. He had three stars to put there now—more than any American soldier had worn except George Washington and Winfield Scott—and he had little eccentricities. He breakfasted frequently on a cup of coffee and a cucumber sliced in vinegar, and if he ate meat it had to be cooked black, almost to a crisp: this author of much bloodshed detested the sight of blood, and was made queasy by the sight of red meat. When he prepared for his day's rounds he accepted from his servant two dozen cigars, which were stowed away in various pockets, and he carried a flint and steel lighter with a long wick, modern style, so that he could get a light in a high wind.

He received many letters asking for his autograph, but, he admitted, "I don't get as many as I did when I answered them." He was not without a quiet sense of humor; writing his memoirs, he told about the backwoods schools he went to as a boy, saying that he was taught so many times that "a noun is the name of a thing" that he finally came to believe it. As a man he was talkative but as a general he was closemouthed. When the crack VI Corps was paraded for him and officers asked him if he ever saw anything to equal it (hoping that he might confess that the Army of the Potomac was better drilled than Western troops, which was indeed the case) he remarked only that General So-and-so rode a very fine horse; the general in question, a brigade commander, having recently invested $500 in a fancy new saddle of which he was very proud.

Nobody knew quite what to make of him, and judgments were tentative. One of Meade's staff officers commented that Grant's habitual expression was that of a man who had made up his mind to drive his head through a stone wall, and Uncle John Sedgwick, canniest and most deeply loved of all the army's higher officers, wrote to his sister that he had been "most agreeably disappointed" both with the general's looks and with his obvious common sense. (As it happened, "common sense" was the expression most often used when men tried to say why they liked Sedgwick so much.) Sedgwick was a little bit skeptical. He said that even though Grant impressed him well, it was doubtful whether he could really do much more with the army than his predecessors had done, since "the truth is we are on the wrong road to take Richmond." Having unburdened himself, Sedgwick retired to his tent to resume one of his everlasting games of solitaire, leaving further comment to other ranks.

Other ranks had their own ideas, which did not always approach reverence. A squadron of cavalry went trotting by one day while Grant sat his horse, smoking, and one trooper sniffed the breeze and said that he knew the general was a good man because he smoked such elegant cigars. Two privates in the 5th Wisconsin saw Grant ride past them, and studied him in silence. Presently one asked the inevitable question: "Well, what do you think?" The other took in the watchful eyes and the hard straight mouth under the stubbly beard, and replied: "He looks as if he meant it.". . .

John C. Gray, Jr.
Letter Recording His First Impressions of Sherman December 14, 1864

Major Gray, judge advocate in the Department of the South, meets William Tecumseh Sherman in Savannah after the general's March to the Sea and records his impressions for his Harvard Law School classmate John C. Ropes.

_____

DEAR JOHN,—I have just passed a whole morning in the company of the greatest military genius of the country in the height of his success. If I were to write a dozen pages I could not tell you a tenth part of what he said, for he talked incessantly and more rapidly than any man I ever saw. A despatch boat goes North immediately on our arrival at Hilton Head with the glorious news of Sherman's success, but I will try to scribble a word or two as we go along in this shaky boat. . . .

First about Fort McAllister, the 'all important capture' of which as General S. terms it, secures an excellent base for such supplies as may be needed. The Fort is very strong mounting twenty-one guns, some of which are field pieces, and many months ago beat off three heavy ironclads, inflicting considerable damage; the assault was made by three columns each of three regiments, and twenty-five minutes by the watch, as General Sherman says, after the first order was given the fort was in our possession. The garrison fought desperately, and several refusing to surrender were killed inside of the Fort. Our loss was about eighty, of whom half were killed and wounded by the explosion of torpedoes buried in the ground which were exploded by our men walking over the works after they were captured. General Sherman set the prisoners to work digging them up and informed the commander of the fort that he had it in consideration to shut him up with a number of his men equal to the number of our men who were killed by torpedoes and blow them up by gunpowder.

General Sherman is the most American looking man I ever saw, tall and lank, not very erect, with hair like thatch, which he rubs up with his hands, a rusty beard trimmed

BRADY STUDIO, WASHINGTON, D.C.
William T. Sherman. 1865. Photograph.
National Archives, Washington, D.C.

close, a wrinkled face, sharp, prominent red nose, small, bright eyes, coarse red hands; black felt hat slouched over the eyes (he says when he wears anything else the soldiers cry out, as he rides along, 'Hallo, the old man has got a new hat'), dirty dickey with the points wilted down, black, old-fashioned stock, brown field officer's coat with high collar and no shoulder straps, muddy trowsers and one spur. He carries his hands in his pocket, is very awkward in his gait and motions, talks continually and with immense rapidity, and might sit to *Punch* for the portrait of an ideal Yankee. He was of course in the highest spirits and talked with an openness which was too natural not to be something more than apparent. In striving to recall his talk, I find it impossible to recall his language or indeed what he talked about, indeed it would be easier to say what he did not talk about than what he did. I never passed a more amusing or instructive day, but at his departure I felt it a relief and experienced almost an exhaustion after the excitement of his vigorous presence. . . .

There is a 'whip the creation' and an almost boastful confidence in himself which in an untried man would be very disgusting, but in him is intensely comic. I wish you could see him, he is a man after your own heart. Like Grant he smokes constantly, and producing six cigars from his pocket said they were his daily allowance, but judging at the rate at which he travelled through them while he was on our boat, he must often exceed it. He scouted the idea of his going on ships and said he would rather march to Richmond than go there by water, he said he expected to turn north toward the latter end of December, at the same time the sun did, and that if he went through South Carolina, as he in all probability should, that his march through that state would be one of the most horrible things in the history of the world, that the devil himself could not restrain his men in that state, and I do not think that he (that is Sherman, not the devil) would try to restrain them much; he evidently purposes to make the South feel the horrors of war as much as he legitimately can, and if the men trespass beyond the strict limits of his orders he does not inquire into their cases too curiously. He told with evident delight how on his march he could look forty miles in each direction and see the smoke rolling up as from one great bonfire. . . .

Thomas Wentworth Higginson
"REGULAR AND VOLUNTEER OFFICERS"
On the Art of Leadership

Higginson, in peacetime a Massachusetts clergyman, in wartime an acclaimed combat officer, explains the art of leadership for the Atlantic Monthly, September 1864.

Now that three years have abolished many surmises, and turned many others into established facts, it must be owned that the total value of the professional training has proved far greater, and that of the general preparation far less, than many intelligent observers predicted. The relation between officer and soldier is something so different in kind from anything which civil life has to offer, that it has proved almost impossible to transfer methods or maxims from the one to the other. If a regiment is merely a caucus, and the colonel the chairman,—or merely a fire-company, and the colonel the foreman,—or

The Awkward Squad.

WALTON TABER.
The Awkward Squad.
1886. Pen. 7 x 13".
Century Collection,
New York.

merely a prayer-meeting, and the colonel the moderator,—or merely a bar-room, and the colonel the landlord,—then the failure of the whole thing is a foregone conclusion.

War is not the highest of human pursuits, certainly; but an army comes very near to being the completest of human organizations, and he alone succeeds in it who readily accepts its inevitable laws, and applies them. An army is an aristocracy, on a three-years' lease, supposing that the period of enlistment. No mortal skill can make military power effective on democratic principles. A democratic people can perhaps carry on a war longer and better than any other; because no other can so well comprehend the object, raise the means, or bear the sacrifices. But these sacrifices include the surrender, for the time being, of the essential principle of the government. Personal independence in the soldier, like personal liberty in the civilian, must be waived for the preservation of the nation. With shipwreck staring men in the face, the choice lies between despotism and anarchy, trusting to the common sense of those concerned, when the danger is over, to revert to the old safeguards. It is precisely because democracy is an advanced stage in human society, that war, which belongs to a less advanced stage, is peculiarly inconsistent with its habits. Thus the undemocratic character, so often lamented in West Point and Annapolis, is in reality their strong point. Granted that they are no more appropriate to our stage of society than are revolvers and bowie-knives, that is precisely what makes them all serviceable in time of war. War being exceptional, the institutions which train its officers must be exceptional likewise.

The first essential for military authority lies in the power of command,—a power which it is useless to analyze, for it is felt instinctively, and it is seen in its results. It is hardly too much to say, that, in military service, if one has this power, all else becomes secondary; and it is perfectly safe to say that without it all other gifts are useless. Now for the exercise of power there is no preparation like power, and nowhere is this preparation to be found, in this community, except in regular army-training. Nothing but great personal qualities can give a man by nature what is easily acquired by young men of very average ability who are systematically trained to command.

The criticism habitually made upon our army by foreign observers at the beginning of the war continues still to be made, though in a rather less degree,—that the soldiers are relatively superior to the officers, so that the officers lead, perhaps, but do not command them. The reason is plain. Three years are not long enough to overcome the settled habits of twenty years. The weak point of our volunteer service invariably lies here, that the soldier, in nine cases out of ten, utterly detests being commanded, while the officer, in his turn, equally shrinks from commanding. War, to both, is an episode in life, not a profession, and therefore military subordination, which needs for its efficiency to be fixed and absolute, is, by common consent, reduced to a minimum. The white American soldier, being, doubtless, the most intelligent in the world, is more ready than any other to comply with a reasonable order, but he does it because it is reasonable, not because it is an order. With advancing experience his compliance increases, but it is still because he better and better comprehends the reason. Give him an order that looks utterly unreasonable,— and this is sometimes necessary,—or give him one which looks trifling, under which head all sanitary precautions are yet to apt to rank, and you may, perhaps, find that you still have a free and independent citizen to deal with, not a soldier. *Implicit* obedience must be admitted still to be a rare quality in our army; nor can we wonder at it.

In many cases there is really no more difference between officers and men, in education or in breeding, than if the one class were chosen by lot from the other; all are from the same neighborhood, all will return to the same civil pursuits side by side; every officer knows that in a little while each soldier will again become his client or his customer, his constituent or his rival. Shall he risk offending him for life in order to carry out some hobby of stricter discipline? If this difficulty exist in the case of commissioned officers, it is still more the case with the non-commissioned, those essential intermediate links in the chain of authority. Hence the discipline of our soldiers has been generally that of a town-meeting or of an engine-company, rather than that of an army; and it shows the extraordinary quality of the individual men, that so much has been accomplished with such a formidable defect in the organization. Even granting that there has been a great and constant improvement, the evil is still vast enough. And every young man trained at West Point enters the service with at least this advantage, that he has been brought up to command, and has not that task to learn.

He has this further advantage, that he is brought up with some respect for the army-organization as it is, with its existing rules, methods, and proprieties, and is not, like the newly commissioned civilian, desposed in his secret soul to set aside all its proprieties as mere "pipe-clay," its methods as "old-fogyism," and its rules as "red-tape." How many good volunteer officers will admit, if they speak candidly, that on entering the service they half believed the "Army Regulations" to be a mass of old-time rubbish, which they would gladly reëdit, under contract, with immense improvements, in a month or two,—and that they finally left the service with the conviction that the same book was a mine of wisdom, as yet but half explored!

Certainly, when one thinks for what a handful of an army our present military system was devised, and with what an admirable elasticity it has borne this sudden and stupendous expansion, it must be admitted to have most admirably stood the test. Of course, there has been much amendment and alteration needed, nor is the work done yet; but it has mainly touched the details, not the general principles. The system is wonderfully complete for its own ends, and the more one studies it the less one sneers. Many a form which at first seems to the volunteer officer merely cumbrous and trivial he learns to prize at last as almost essential to good discipline; he seldom attempts a short cut without finding it the longest way, and rarely enters on that heroic measure of cutting red-tape without finding at last that he has entangled his own fingers in the process.

More thorough training tells in another way. It is hard to appreciate, without the actual experience, how much of military life is a matter of mere detail. The maiden at home fancies her lover charging at the head of his company, when in reality he is at that precise moment endeavoring to convince his company-cooks that salt-junk needs five hours' boiling, or is anxiously deciding which pair of worn-out trousers shall be ejected from a drummer-boy's knapsack. Courage is, no doubt, a good quality in a soldier, and luckily not often wanting; but, in the long run, courage depends largely on the haversack. Men are naturally brave, and when the crisis comes, almost all men will fight well, if well commanded. As Sir Philip Sidney said, an army of stags led by a lion is more formidable than an army of lions led by a stag. Courage is cheap; the main duty of an officer is to take good care of his men, so that every one of them shall be ready, at a moment's notice, for any reasonable demand.

A soldier's life usually implies weeks and months of waiting, and then one glorious hour; and if the interval of leisure had been wasted, there is nothing but a wasted heroism at the end, and perhaps not even that. The penalty for misused weeks, the reward for laborious months, may be determined within ten minutes.

Without discipline an army is a mob, and the larger the worse; without rations the men are empty uniforms; without ammunition they might as well have no guns; without shoes they might almost as well have no legs. And it is in the practical appreciation of all these matters that the superiority of the regular officer is apt to be shown. . . .

In those unfortunate early days, when it seemed to most of our Governors to make little difference whom they commissioned, since all were alike untried, and of two evils it was natural to choose that which would produce the more agreeable consequences at the next election-time,—in those days of darkness many very poor officers saw the light. Many of these have since been happily discharged or judiciously shelved. The trouble is, that those who remain are among the senior officers in our volunteer army, in their respective grades. They command posts, brigades, divisions. They preside at court-martials. Beneath the shadow of their notorious incompetency all minor evils may lurk undetected. To crown all, they are, in many cases, sincere and well-meaning men, utterly obtuse as to their own deficiencies, and manifesting (to employ a witticism coeval with themselves) all the Christian virtues except that of resignation.

The present writer has beheld the spectacle of an officer of high rank, previously eminent in civil life, who could only vindicate himself before a court-martial from the ruinous charge of false muster by summoning a staff-officer to prove that it was his custom to sign all military papers without looking at them. He has seen a lieutenant tried for neglect of duty in allowing a soldier under his command, at an important picket-post, to be found by the field-officer of the day with two inches of sand in the bottom of his gun,—and pleading, in mitigation of sentence, that it had never been the practice in his regiment to make any inspection of men detailed for such duty. That such instances of negligence should be tolerated for six months in any regiment of regulars is a thing almost inconceivable, and yet in these cases the regiments and the officers had been nearly three years in service. . . .

The glaring defect of most of our volunteer regiments, from the beginning to this day, has lain in slovenliness and remissness as to every department of military duty, except the actual fighting and dying. When it comes to that ultimate test, our men usually endure it so magnificently that one is tempted to overlook all deficiencies on intermediate points. But they must not be overlooked, because they create a fearful discount on the usefulness of our troops, when tried by the standard of regular armies. I do not now refer to the niceties of dress-parade or the courtesies of salutation: it has long since been tacitly admitted that a white American soldier will not present arms to any number of rows of buttons, if he can by any ingenuity evade it; and to shoulder arms on passing an officer is something to which only Ethiopia or the regular army can attain. Grant, if you please, (though I do not grant,) that these are merely points of foolish punctilio. But there are many things which are more than punctilio, though they may be less than fighting.

The efficiency of a body of troops depends, after all, not so much on its bravery as on the condition of its sick-list. A regiment which does picket-duty faithfully will often avoid the need of duties more terrible. Yet I have ridden by night along a chain of ten sentinels, every one of whom should have taken my life rather than permit me to give the countersign without dismounting, and have been required to dismount by only four, while two did not ask me for the countersign at all, and two others were asleep. I have ridden through a regimental camp whose utterly filthy condition seemed enough to send malaria through a whole military department, and have been asked by the colonel, almost with tears in his eyes, to explain to him why his men were dying at the rate of one a day. The latter was a regiment nearly a year old, and the former one of almost two years' service, and just from the old Army of the Potomac.

The fault was, of course, in the officers. The officer makes the command, as surely as, in educational matters, the teacher makes the school. There is not a regiment in the army so good that it could not be utterly spoiled in three months by a poor commander, nor so poor that it could not be altogether transformed in six by a good one. The difference in material is nothing,—white or black, German or Irish; so potent is military machinery that an officer who knows his business can make good soldiers out of almost anything, give him but a fair chance. The difference between the present Army of the Potomac and any previous one,—the reason why we do not daily hear, as in the early campaigns, of irresistible surprises, overwhelming numbers, and masked batteries,—the reason why the present movements are a tide and not a wave,—is not that the men are veterans, but that the officers are. There is an immense amount of perfectly raw material in General Grant's force, besides the colored regiments, which in that army are all raw, but in which the Copperhead critics have such faith they would gladly select them for dangers fit for Napoleon's Old Guard. But the newest recruit soon grows steady with a steady corporal at his elbow, a well-trained sergeant behind him, and a captain or a colonel whose voice means something to give commands.

INCIDENTS OF WAR

Mark Twain

"THE PRIVATE HISTORY OF A CAMPAIGN THAT FAILED"

Writing in Century *magazine, in December 1885, Twain recounts his brief war effort as a member of the innocent Marion Rangers from his native state of Missouri.*

You have heard from a great many people who did something in the war; is it not fair and right that you listen a little moment to one who started out to do something in it, but didn't. Thousands entered the war, got just a taste of it, and then stepped out again permanently. These, by their very numbers, are respectable, and are therefore entitled to a sort of voice—not a loud one, but a modest one; not a boastful one, but an apologetic one. They ought not to be allowed much space among better people—people who did something. I grant that; but they ought at least to be allowed to state why they didn't do anything, and also to explain the process by which they didn't do anything. Surely this kind of light must have a sort of value.

Out West there was a good deal of confusion in men's minds during the first months of the great trouble—a good deal of unsettledness, of leaning first this way, then that,

COLORPLATE 16

THURE DE THULSTRUP. *Grant at Missionary Ridge.* ca. 1885. Oil on canvas. 15 × 22″.
The Seventh Regiment Fund, Inc., New York.

COLORPLATE 17

Attributed to FRANCIS B. CARPENTER. *Reception at the White House.* ca. 1864. Oil on canvas. 23⅝ × 37⅛″. White House Collection, Washington, D.C. Copyright © White House Historical Association; Photograph by the National Geographic Society. *General Grant is with President Lincoln at right center. Seated at right is General Winfield Scott.*

COLORPLATE 18

OTTO SOMMER. *Union Drover With Cattle for the Army.* 1866. Oil on canvas. 30 × 44″.
Museum of Western Art, Denver. Photo courtesy Maxwell Galleries, San Francisco.

COLORPLATE 19

FRANCIS B. CARPENTER. *The Proclamation of Emancipation.* 1864. Oil on canvas. 108 × 174″.
Collection of the United States Senate, Washington, D.C. Photo by Larry Sherer, copyright
© 1985 Time-Life Books, Inc. *From left, Edwin M. Stanton, Salmon P. Chase, Lincoln,
Gideon Welles, Caleb B. Smith, William B. Seward, Montgomery Blair, Edward Bates.*

76

COLORPLATE 20

JAMES MADISON ALDEN. *Admiral Porter's Gunboats Passing the Red River Dam.* 1864. Watercolor on paper. 15⅜ × 29¼″. Museum of Fine Arts, Boston. M. and M. Karolik Collection. *Building wing dams saved a Federal flotilla from being trapped by low water in Louisiana's Red River, May 1864.*

COLORPLATE 21

PRINCE DE JOINVILLE. *Surprise of the Pickets at Peck's House.* 1861. Watercolor on paper. 6¾ × 9½″. Fondation Saint-Louis, Amboise, France.

COLORPLATE 22

Artist Unknown. *The Fight for the Standard*. 1865. Oil on canvas. 26¾ × 21½″. Wadsworth Atheneum, Hartford. Ella Gallup Sumner and Mary Catlin Sumner Collection. Photo © Wadsworth Atheneum.

COLORPLATE 23

ALBERT BIERSTADT. *Attack on a Picket Post*. 1862. Oil on canvas.
15 × 17¾″. The Century Association, New York.

then the other way. It was hard for us to get our bearings. I call to mind an instance of this. I was piloting on the Mississippi when the news came that South Carolina had gone out of the Union on the 20th of December, 1860. My pilot mate was a New Yorker. He was strong for the Union; so was I. But he would not listen to me with any patience; my loyalty was smirched, to his eye, because my father had owned slaves. I said, in palliation of this dark fact, that I had heard my father say, some years before he died, that slavery was a great wrong, and that he would free the solitary Negro he then owned if he could think it right to give away the property of the family when he was so straitened in means. My mate retorted that a mere impulse was nothing—anybody could pretend to a good impulse; and went on decrying my Unionism and libeling my ancestry. A month later the secession atmosphere had considerably thickened on the Lower Mississippi, and I became a rebel; so did he. We were together in New Orleans the 26th of January, when Louisiana went out of the Union. He did his full share of the rebel shouting, but was bitterly opposed to letting me do mine. He said that I came of bad stock—of a father who had been willing to set slaves free. In the following summer he was piloting a Federal gunboat and shouting for the Union again, and I was in the Confederate army. I held his note for some borrowed money. He was one of the most upright men I ever knew, but he repudiated that note without hesitation because I was a rebel and the son of a man who owned slaves.

In that summer—of 1861—the first wash of the wave of war broke upon the shores of Missouri. Our State was invaded by the Union forces. They took possession of St. Louis, Jefferson Barracks, and some other points. The Governor, Claib Jackson, issued his proclamation calling out fifty thousand militia to repel the invader.

I was visiting in the small town where my boyhood had been spent—Hannibal, Marion County. Several of us got together in a secret place by night and formed ourselves into a military company. One Tom Lyman, a young fellow of a good deal of spirit but of no military experience, was made captain; I was made second lieutenant. We had no first lieutenant; I do not know why; it was long ago. There were fifteen of us. By the advice of an innocent connected with the organization we called ourselves the Marion Rangers. I do not remember that anyone found fault with the name. I did not; I thought it sounded quite well. The young fellow who proposed this title was perhaps a fair sample of the kind of stuff we were made of. He was young, ignorant, good-natured, well-meaning, trivial, full of romance, and given to reading chivalric novels and singing forlorn love-ditties. He had some pathetic little nickel-plated aristocratic instincts, and detested his name, which was Dunlap; detested it, partly because it was nearly as common in that region as Smith, but mainly because it had a [plebeian] sound to his ear. So he tried to ennoble it by writing it in this way: *d'Unlap*. That contented his eye, but left his ear unsatisfied, for people gave the new name the same old pronunciation—emphasis on the front end of it. He then did the bravest thing that can be imagined—a thing to make one shiver when one remembers how the world is given to resenting shams and affectations; he began to write his name so: *d'Un Lap*. And he waited patiently through the long storm of mud that was flung at this work of art, and he had his reward at last; for he lived to see that name accepted, and the emphasis put where he wanted it by people who had known him all his life, and to whom the tribe of Dunlaps had been as familiar as the rain and the sunshine for forty years. So sure of victory at last is the courage that can wait. He said he had found, by consulting some ancient French chronicles, that the name was rightly and originally written d'Un Lap; and said that if it were translated into English it would mean Peterson: *Lap* Latin or Greek, he said, for stone or rock, same as the French *pierre*, that is to say, Peter; *d'*, of or from a stone or a Peter; that is to say, one who is the son of a stone, the son of a Peter—Peterson. Our militia company were not learned, and the explanation confused them; so they called him Peterson Dunlap. He proved useful to us in his way; he named our camps for us and he generally struck a name that was "no slouch," as the boys said. . . .

Well, this herd of cattle started for the war. What could you expect of them? Nothing, I should say. That is what they did. . . .

We occupied an old maple sugar camp, whose half-rotted troughs were still propped against the trees. A long corn-crib served for sleeping quarters for the battalion. On our left, half a mile away, were Mason's farm and house; and he was a friend to the cause. Shortly after noon the farmers began to arrive from several directions, with mules and horses for our use, and these they lent us for as along as the war might last, which they judged would be about three months. The animals were of all sizes, all colors, and all breeds. They were mainly young and frisky, and nobody in the command could stay on them long at a time; for we were town boys, and ignorant of horsemanship. The creature that fell to my share was a very small mule, and yet so quick and active that it could throw me without difficulty; and it did this whenever I got on it. Then it would bray—stretching its neck out, laying its ears back, and spreading its jaws till you could see down to its works. It was a disagreeable animal in every way. If I took it by the bridle and tried to lead if off the grounds, it would sit down and brace back, and no one could budge it. However, I was not entirely destitute of military resources, and I did presently manage to spoil this game; for I had seen many a steamboat aground in my time, and knew a trick or two which even a grounded mule would be obliged to respect. There was a well by the corn-crib; so I substituted thirty fathom of rope for the bridle, and fetched him home with the windlass.

I will anticipate here sufficiently to say that we did learn to ride, after some days' practice, but never well. We could not learn to like our animals; they were not choice ones, and most of them had annoying peculiarities of one kind or another. Steven's horse would carry him, when he was not noticing, under the huge excrescences which form on the trunks of oak trees, and wipe him out of the saddle; in this way Stevens got several bad hurts. Sergeant Bowers's horse was very large and tall, with slim, long legs, and looked like a railroad bridge. His size enabled him to reach all about, and as far as he wanted to, with his head; so he was always biting Bowers's legs. On the march, in the sun, Bowers slept a good deal; and as soon as the horse recognized that he was asleep he would reach around and bite him on the leg. His legs were black and blue with bites. This was the only thing that could ever make him swear, but this always did; whenever his horse bit him he always swore, and of course Stevens, who laughed at everything, laughed at this, and would even get into such convulsions over it as to lose his balance and fall off his horse; and then Bowers, already irritated by the pain of the horse-bite, would resent the laughter with hard language, and there would be a quarrel; so that horse made no end of trouble and bad blood in the command. . . .

In that camp the whole command slept on the corn in the big corn-crib; and there was usually a general row before morning, for the place was full of rats, and they would scramble over the boys' bodies and faces, annoying and irritating everybody; and now and then they would bite someone's toe, and the person who owned the toe would start up and magnify his English and begin to throw corn in the dark. The ears were half as heavy as bricks, and when they struck they hurt. The persons struck would respond, and inside of five minutes every man would be locked in a death-grip with his neighbor. There was a grievous deal of blood shed in the corn-crib, but this was all that was spilled while I was in the war. No, that is not quite true. But for one circumstance it would have been all. I will come to that now.

Our scares were frequent. Every few days rumors would come that the enemy were approaching. In these cases we always fell back on some other camp of ours; we never stayed where we were. But the rumors always turned out to be false; so at least even we began to grow indifferent to them. One night a Negro was sent to our corn-crib with the same old warning: the enemy was hovering in our neighborhood. We all said let him hover. We resolved to stay still and be comfortable. It was a fine warlike resolution, and no doubt we all felt the stir of it in our veins—for a moment. We had been having a very jolly time, that was full of horse-play and school-boy hilarity; but that cooled down now, and presently the fast-waning fire of forced jokes and forced laughs died out altogether, and the company became silent. Silent and nervous. And soon uneasy—worried—apprehensive. We had said we would stay, and we were committed. We could have been persuaded to go, but there was nobody brave enough to suggest it. An almost noise-less movement presently began in the dark by a general but unvoiced impulse. When the movement was completed each man knew that he was not the only person who had crept to the front wall and had his eye at a crack between the logs. No, we were all there; all there with our hearts in our throats, and staring out toward the sugar-troughs where the forest footpath came through. It was late, and there was a deep woodsy stillness everywhere. There was a veiled moonlight, which was only just strong enough to enable us to mark the general shape of objects. Presently a muffled sound caught our ears, and we recognized it as the hoof-beats of a horse or horses. And right away a figure appeared in the forest path; it could have been made of smoke, its mass had so little sharpness of outline. It was a man on horseback, and it seemed to me that there were others behind him. I got hold of a gun in the dark, and pushed it through a crack between the logs, hardly knowing what I was doing, I was so dazed with fright. Somebody said, "Fire!" I pulled the trigger. I seemed to see a hundred flashes and hear a hundred reports; then I saw the man fall down out of the saddle. My first feeling was of surprised gratification; my first impulse was an apprentice-sportsman's impulse to run and pick up his game. Somebody said, hardly audibly, "Good—we've got him!—wait for the rest." But the rest did not come. We waited—listened—still no more came. There was not a sound, not the whisper of a leaf; just perfect stillness; an uncanny kind of stillness, which was all the more uncanny on account of the damp, earthy, late-night smells now rising and pervading it. Then, wondering, we crept stealthily out, and approached the man. When we got to him the moon revealed him distinctly. He was lying on his back, with his arms abroad; his mouth was open and his chest heaving with long gasps, and his white shirt-front was all splashed with blood. The thought shot through me that I was a murderer; that I had killed a man—a man who had never done me any harm. That was the coldest sensation that ever went through my marrow. I was down by him in a moment, helplessly stroking his forehead; and I would have given anything then—my own life freely—to make him again what he had been five minutes before. And all the boys seemed to be feeling in the same way; they hung over him, full of pitying interest, and tried all they could to help him, and said all sorts of regretful things. They had forgotten all about the enemy; they thought only of this one forlorn unit of the foe. Once my imagination per-suaded me that the dying man gave me a reproachful look out of his shadowy eyes, and it seemed to me that I could rather he had stabbed me than done that. He muttered and mumbled like a dreamer in his sleep about his wife and his child; and I thought with a new despair, "This thing that I have done does not end with him; it falls upon *them* too, and they never did me any harm, any more than he."

In a little while the man was dead. He was killed in war; killed in fair and legitimate war; killed in battle, as you may say; and yet he was as sincerely mourned by the opposing force as if he had been their brother. The boys stood there a half-hour sorrowing over him, and recalling the details of the tragedy, and wondering how he might be, and if he were a spy, and saying that if it were to do over again they would not hurt him unless he attacked them first. It soon came out that mine was not the only shot fired; there were five others—a division of the guilt which was a great relief to me, since it in some degree lightened and diminished the burden I was carrying. There were six shots fired at once; but I was not in my right mind at the time, and my heated imagination had magnified my one shot into a volley.

The man was not in uniform, and was not armed. He was a stranger in the country; that was all we ever found out about him. The thought of him got to preying upon me every night; I could not get rid of it. I could not drive it away, the taking of that un-offending life seemed such a wanton thing. And it seemed an epitome of war; that all war must be just that—the killing of strangers against whom you feel no personal ani-mosity; strangers whom, in other circumstances, you would help if you found them in trouble, and who would help you if you needed it. My campaign was spoiled. It seemed to me that I was not rightly equipped for this awful business; that war was intended for men, and I for a child's nurse. I resolved to retire from this avocation of sham soldiership while I could save some remnant of my self-respect. These morbid thoughts clung to me against reason; for at bottom I did not believe I had touched that man. The law of probabilities decreed me guiltless of his blood; for in all my small experience with guns I had never hit anything I had tried to hit, and I knew I had done my best to hit him. Yet there was no solace in the thought. Against a diseased imagination demonstration goes for nothing.

The rest of my war experience was of a piece with what I have already told of it. We kept monotonously falling back upon one camp or another, and eating up the country. I marvel now at the patience of the farmers and their families. They ought to have shot us; on the contrary, they were as hospitably kind and courteous to us as if we had deserved it. In one of these camps we found Ab Grimes, an Upper Mississippi pilot, who afterwards became famous as a dare-devil rebel spy, whose career bristled with desperate adventures. The look and style of his comrades suggested that they had not come into the war to play, and their deeds made good the conjecture later. They were fine horsemen and good revolver shots; but their favorite arm was the lasso. Each had one at his pommel, and could snatch a man out of the saddle with it every time, on a full gallop, at any reasonable distance.

In another camp the chief was a fierce and profane old blacksmith of sixty, and he had furnished his twenty recruits with gigantic home-made bowie-knives, to be swung with two hands, like the *machetes* of the Isthmus. It was a grisly spectacle to see that earnest band practicing their murderous cuts and slashes under the eye of that remorseless old fanatic.

The last camp which we fell back upon was in a hollow near the village of Florida, where I was born — in Monroe County. Here we were warned one day that a Union colonel was sweeping down on us with a whole regiment at his heel. This looked decidedly

A Private of Company F, 4th Michigan Infantry, U.S.A. ca. 1862. Photograph. National Archives, Washington, D.C.

serious. Our boys went apart and consulted; then we went back and told the other companies present that the war was a disappointment to us, and we were going to disband. They were getting ready themselves to fall back on some place or other, and were only waiting for General Tom Harris, who was expected to arrive at any moment; so they tried to persuade us to wait a little while, but the majority of us said no, we were accustomed to falling back, and didn't need any of Tom Harris's help; we could get along perfectly well without him—and save time, too. So about half of our fifteen, including myself, mounted and left on the instant; the others yielded to persuasion and stayed—stayed through the war.

An hour later we met General Harris on the road, with two or three people in his company—his staff, probably, but we could not tell; none of them were in uniform; uniforms had not come into vogue among us yet. Harris ordered us back; but we told him there was a Union colonel coming with a whole regiment in his wake, and it looked as if there was going to be a disturbance; so we had concluded to go home. He raged a little, but it was of no use; our minds were made up. We had done our share; had killed one man, exterminated one army, such as it was; let him go and kill the rest, and that would end the war. I did not see that brisk young general again until last year; then he was wearing white hair and whiskers.

In time I came to know that Union colonel whose coming frightened me out of the war and crippled the Southern cause to that extent—General Grant. I came within a few hours of seeing him when he was as unknown as I was myself; at a time when anybody could have said, "Grant? Ulysses S. Grant? I do not remember hearing the name before." It seems difficult to realize that there was once a time when such a remark could be rationally made; but there *was*, and I was within a few miles of the place and the occasion, too, though proceeding in the other direction.

The thoughtful will not throw this war paper of mine lightly aside as being valueless. It has this value: it is a not unfair picture of what went on in many and many a militia camp in the first months of the rebellion, when the green recruits were without discipline, without the steadying and heartening influence of trained leaders; when all their circumstances were new and strange, and charged with exaggerated terrors, and before the invaluable experience of actual collision in the field has turned them from rabbits into soldiers. If this side of the picture of that early day has not before been put into history, then history has been to that degree incomplete, for it had and has its rightful place there. There was more Bull Run material scattered through the early camps of this country than exhibited itself at Bull Run. And yet it learned its trade presently, and helped to fight the great battles after. I could have become a soldier myself if I had waited. I had got part of it learned; I knew more about retreating than the man that invented retreating.

Thomas W. Hyde

On an Incident at Antietam

The ordeal of the 7th Maine at the Battle of Antietam, September 17, 1862; from the memoir of its major, Following the Greek Cross or, Memories of the Sixth Army Corps.

———————

While we were charging down the valley, Harry Campbell, carrying the colors, was struck in the arm. He held it up to me all bloody, waving the flag. "Take the other hand, Harry,"

said I. When halfway through the orchard, I heard him call out as if in pain behind me, and went back to save the colors if possible. The apple-trees were short and I could not see much, but soon found the pursuing enemy were between me and the regiment, and I read "Manassas" on one of their flags, so I turned about and as quickly as possible gained the corner of the orchard and found the regiment had got through the tall picket fence. While uncertain how to get out, I was surrounded by a dozen or more rebels, but with a cry of "Rally, boys, to save the major," back surged the regiment, the muzzles of their Windsors were pushed between the pickets, and few of my would-be captors got away. Sergeant Hill with his sabre bayonet cut through the rails and I was soon extricated. Our batteries had been for some minutes throwing grape into the orchard, which aided us much, though we were more afraid of the grape than of the enemy. I then formed the regiment on the colors, sixty-five men and three officers, and slowly we marched back toward our place in line. The batteries by Dunker Church opened on us at first, but I guess they thought we had pounding enough, for they stopped after a few shots. But our main line rose up and waved their hats, and when we came in front of our dear comrades, the Vermonters, their cheers made the welkin ring. General Brooks had told their colonels when they begged to follow our charge, "You will never see that regiment again." In my judgment, we only needed the Vermonters behind us to have cut through to the river, and a few more brigades in support would have ended the business, as at that moment Lee's much-enduring army was fought out.

We did not take a large space on the line as we lay down in the falling darkness, and when Channing, Webber, Nickerson, and I got together under one blanket for the night, we were womanish enough to shed tears for our dead and crippled comrades. Fifteen officers and two hundred and twenty-five men in the morning, and this little party at night! We had the consolation of knowing that we had gone farther into the rebel lines than any Union regiment that day, that we had fought three or four times our numbers, and inflicted more damage than we received, but as the French officer at Balaklava said, "It is magnificent, but it is not war." When we knew our efforts were resultant from no plan or design at headquarters, but were from an inspiration of John Barleycorn in our brigade commander alone, I wished I had been old enough, or distinguished enough, to have dared to disobey orders.

Michael Shaara

FROM THE KILLER ANGELS

On Colonel Chamberlain

The novelist's account of new men for Colonel Joshua Lawrence Chamberlain's 20th Maine, on the march toward Gettysburg in 1863.

The Regiment had begun to form. Chamberlain thought: At least it'll be a short speech. He walked slowly toward the prisoners.

Glazier Estabrook was standing guard, leaning patiently on his rifle. He was a thick little man of about forty. Except for Kilrain he was the oldest man in the Regiment, the strongest man Chamberlain had ever seen. He waved happily as Chamberlain came up but went on leaning on the rifle. He pointed at one of the prisoners.

"Hey, Colonel, you know who this is? This here is Dan Burns from Orono. I know his daddy. Daddy's a preacher. You really ought to hear him. Best damn cusser I ever heard. Knows more fine swear words than any man in Maine, I bet. Hee."

Chamberlain smiled. But the Burns boy was looking at him with no expression. Chamberlain said, "You fellas gather round."

He stood in the shade, waited while they closed in silently, watchfully around him. In the background the tents were coming down, the wagons were hitching, but some of the men of the Regiment had come out to watch and listen. Some of the men here were still chewing. But they were quiet, attentive.

Chamberlain waited a moment longer. Now it was quiet in the grove and the clink of the wagons was sharp in the distance. Chamberlain said, "I've been talking with Bucklin. He's told me your problem."

Some of the men grumbled. Chamberlain heard no words clearly. He went on speaking softly so that they would have to quiet to hear him.

"I don't know what I can do about it. I'll do what I can. I'll look into it as soon as possible. But there's nothing I can do today. We're moving out in a few minutes and we'll be marching all day and we may be in a big fight before nightfall. But as soon as I can, I'll do what I can."

They were silent, watching him. Chamberlain began to relax. He had made many speeches and he had a gift for it. He did not know what it was, but when he spoke most men stopped to listen. Fanny said it was something in his voice. He hoped it was there now.

"I've been ordered to take you men with me. I've been told that if you don't come I can shoot you. Well, you know I won't do that. Not Maine men. I won't shoot any man who doesn't want this fight. Maybe someone else will, but I won't. So that's that."

He paused again. There was nothing on their faces to lead him.

"Here's the situation. I've been ordered to take you along, and that's what I'm going to do. Under guard if necessary. But you can have your rifles if you want them. The whole Reb army is up the road a ways waiting for us and this is no time for an argument like this. I tell you this: we sure can use you. We're down below half strength and we need you, no doubt of that. But whether you fight or not is up to you. Whether you come along, well, you're coming."

Tom had come up with Chamberlain's horse. Over the heads of the prisoners Chamberlain could see the Regiment falling into line out in the flaming road. He took a deep breath.

"Well, I don't want to preach to you. You know who we are and what we're doing here. But if you're going to fight alongside us there's a few things I want you to know."

He bowed his head, not looking at eyes. He folded his hands together.

"This Regiment was formed last fall, back in Maine. There were a thousand of us then. There's not three hundred of us now." He glanced up briefly. "But what is left is choice."

He was embarrassed. He spoke very slowly, staring at the ground.

"Some of us volunteered to fight for Union. Some came in mainly because we were bored at home and this looked like it might be fun. Some came because we were ashamed not to. Many of us came . . . because it was the right thing to do. All of us have seen men die. Most of us never saw a black man back home. We think on that, too. But freedom . . . is not just a word."

He looked up in to the sky, over silent faces.

"This is a different kind of army. If you look at history you'll see men fight for pay, or women, or some other kind of loot. They fight for land, or because a king makes them, or just because they like killing. But we're here for something new. I don't . . . this hasn't happened much in the history of the world. We're an army going out to set other men free."

Joshua L. Chamberlain. 1864. Photograph. National Archives, Washington, D.C.

He bent down, scratched the black dirt into his fingers. He was beginning to warm to it; the words were beginning to flow. No one in front of him was moving. He said, "This is free ground. All the way from here to the Pacific Ocean. No man has to bow. No man born to royalty. Here we judge you by what *you* do, not by what your father was. Here you can be *something*. Here's a place to build a home. It isn't the land—there's always more land. It's the idea that we all have value, you and me, we're worth something more than the dirt. I never saw dirt I'd die for, but I'm not asking you to come join us and fight for dirt. What we're all fighting for, in the end, is each other."

Once he started talking he broke right through the embarrassment and there was suddenly no longer a barrier there. The words came out of him in a clear river, and he felt himself silent and suspended in the grove listening to himself speak, carried outside himself and looking back down on the silent faces and himself speaking, and he felt the power in him, the power of his cause. For an instant he could see black castles in the air; he could create centuries of screaming, eons of torture. Then he was back in sunlit Pennsylvania. The bugles were blowing and he was done.

He had nothing else to say. No one moved. He felt the embarrassment return. He was suddenly enormously tired. The faces were staring up at him like white stones. Some heads were down. He said, "Didn't mean to preach. Sorry. But I thought . . . you should know who we are." He had forgotten how tiring it was just to speak. "Well, this is still the army, but you're as free as I can make you. Go ahead and talk for a while. If you want your rifles for this fight you'll have them back and nothing else will be said. If you won't join us you'll come along under guard. When this is over I'll do what I can to see that you get fair treatment. Now we have to move out." He stopped, looked at them. The faces showed nothing. He said slowly, "I think if we lose this fight the war will be over. So if you choose to come with us I'll be personally grateful. Well. We have to move out."

Stephen Crane

FROM THE RED BADGE OF COURAGE
On Approaching Battle for the First Time

In Crane's classic story representing the Battle of Chancellorsville in 1863, the youth and his comrades of the 304th approach battle for the first time.

One morning, however, he found himself in the ranks of his prepared regiment. The men were whispering speculations and recounting the old rumors. In the gloom before the break of the day their uniforms glowed a deep purple hue. From across the river the red eyes were still peering. In the eastern sky there was a yellow patch like a rug laid for the feet of the coming sun; and against it, black and patternlike, loomed the gigantic figure of the colonel on a gigantic horse.

From off in the darkness came the trampling of feet. The youth could occasionally see dark shadows that moved like monsters. The regiments stood at rest for what seemed a long time. The youth grew impatient. It was unendurable the way these affairs were managed. He wondered how long they were to be kept waiting.

As he looked all about him and pondered upon the mystic gloom, he began to believe that at any moment the ominous distance might be aflare, and the rolling crashes of an engagement come to his ears. Staring once at the red eyes across the river, he conceived them to be growing larger, as the orbs of a row of dragons advancing. He turned toward the colonel and saw him lift his gigantic arm and calmly stroke his mustache.

At last he heard from along the road at the foot of the hill the clatter of a horse's galloping hoofs. It must be the coming of orders. He bent forward, scarce breathing. The exciting clickety-click, as it grew louder and louder, seemed to be beating upon his soul. Presently a horseman with jangling equipment drew rein before the colonel of the regiment. The two held a short, sharp-worded conversation. The men in the foremost ranks craned their necks.

As the horseman wheeled his animal and galloped away he turned to shout over his shoulder, "Don't forget that box of cigars!" The colonel mumbled in reply. The youth wondered what a box of cigars had to do with war.

A moment later the regiment went swinging off into the darkness. It was now like one of those moving monsters wending with many feet. The air was heavy, and cold with dew. A mass of wet grass, marched upon, rustled like silk.

There was an occasional flash and glimmer of steel from the backs of all these huge crawling reptiles. From the road came creakings and grumblings as some surly guns were dragged away.

The men stumbled along still muttering speculations. There was a subdued debate. Once a man fell down, and as he reached for his rifle a comrade, unseeing, trod upon his hand. He of the injured fingers swore bitterly and aloud. A low, tittering laugh went among his fellows.

Presently they passed into a roadway and marched forward with easy strides. A dark regiment moved before them, and from behind also came the tinkle of equipments on the bodies of marching men.

The rushing yellow of the developing day went on behind their backs. When the sunrays at last struck full and mellowingly upon the earth, the youth saw that the landscape was streaked with two long, thin, black columns which disappeared on the brow of a hill in front, and rearward vanished in a wood. They were like two serpents crawling from the cavern of the night.

The river was not in view. The tall soldier burst into praises of what he thought to be his powers of perception.

Some of the tall one's companions cried with emphasis that they, too, had evolved the same thing, and they congratulated themselves upon it. But there were others who said that the tall one's plan was not the true one at all. They persisted with other theories. There was a vigorous discussion.

The youth took no part in them. As he walked along in careless line he was engaged with his own eternal debate. He could not hinder himself from dwelling upon it. He was despondent and sullen, and threw shifting glances about him. He looked ahead, often expecting to hear from the advance the rattle of firing.

But the long serpents crawled slowly from hill to hill without bluster of smoke. A dun-colored cloud of dust floated away to the right. The sky overhead was of a fairy blue.

The youth studied the faces of his companions, ever on the watch to detect kindred emotions. He suffered disappointment. Some ardor of the air which was causing the veteran commands to move with glee—almost with song—had infected the new regiment. The men began to speak of victory as of a thing they knew. Also, the tall soldier received his vindication. They were certainly going to come around in behind the enemy. They expressed commiseration for that part of the army which had been left upon the river bank, felicitating themselves upon being a part of a blasting host.

The youth, considering himself as separated from the others, was saddened by the blithe and merry speeches that went from rank to rank. The company wags all made their best endeavors. The regiment tramped to the tune of laughter.

The blatant soldier often convulsed whole files by his biting sarcasms aimed at the tall one.

And it was not long before all the men seemed to forget their mission. Whole brigades grinned in unison, and regiments laughed.

A rather fat soldier attempted to pilfer a horse from a dooryard. He planned to load his knapsack upon it. He was escaping with his prize when a young girl rushed from the house and grabbed the animal's mane. There followed a wrangle. The young girl, with pink cheeks and shining eyes, stood like a dauntless statue.

The observant regiment, standing at rest in the roadway, whooped at once, and entered whole-souled upon the side of the maiden. The men became so engrossed in this affair that they entirely ceased to remember their own large war. They jeered the piratical private, and called attention to various defects in his personal appearance; and they were wildly enthusiastic in support of the young girl.

To her, from some distance, came bold advice, "Hit him with a stick."

There were crows and catcalls showered upon him when he retreated without the horse. The regiment rejoiced at his downfall. Loud and vociferous congratulations were showered upon the maiden, who stood panting and regarding the troops with defiance.

At nightfall the column broke into regimental pieces, and the fragments went into the fields to camp. Tents sprang up like strange plants. Camp fires, like red, peculiar blossoms, dotted the night.

The youth kept from intercourse with his companions as much as circumstances would allow him. In the evening he wandered a few paces into the gloom. From this little distance the many fires, with the black forms of men passing to and fro before the crimson rays, made weird and satanic effects.

He lay down in the grass. The blades pressed tenderly against his cheek. The moon had been lighted and was hung in a treetop. The liquid stillness of the night enveloping him made him feel vast pity for himself. There was a caress in the soft winds; and the whole mood of the darkness, he thought, was one of sympathy for himself in his distress.

He wished, without reserve, that he was at home again making the endless rounds from the house to the barn, from the barn to the house. He remembered he had often cursed the brindle cow and her mates, and had sometimes flung milking stools. But, from his present point of view, there was a halo of happiness about each of their heads, and he would have sacrificed all the brass buttons on the continent to have been enabled to return to them. He told himself that he was not formed for a soldier. And he mused seriously upon the radical differences between himself and those men who were dodging imp-like around the fires.

As he mused thus he heard the rustle of grass, and, upon turning his head, discovered the loud soldier. He called out, "Oh, Wilson!"

The latter approached and looked down. "Why hello, Henry; is it you? What you doing here?"

"Oh, thinking," said the youth.

The other sat down and carefully lighted his pipe. "You're getting blue, my boy. You're looking thundering peeked. What the dickens is wrong with you?"

"Oh, nothing," said the youth.

The loud soldier launched then into the subject of the anticipated fight. "Oh, we've got 'em now!" As he spoke his boyish face was wreathed in a gleeful smile, and his voice had an exultant ring. "We've got 'em now. At last, by the eternal thunders, we'll lick 'em good!"

"If the truth was known," he added more soberly, "*they've* licked *us* about every clip up to now; but this time—this time—we'll lick 'em good!"

"I thought you was objecting to this march a little while ago," said the youth coldly.

"Oh, it wasn't that," explained the other. "I don't mind marching, if there's going to be fighting at the end of it. What I hate is this getting moved here and moved there, with no good coming of it, as far as I can see, excepting sore feet and damned short rations."

"Well, Jim Conklin says we'll get aplenty of fighting this time."

"He's right for once, I guess, though I can't see how it come. This time we're in for a big battle, and we've got the best end of it, certain sure. Gee rod! how we will thump 'em!"

He arose and began to pace to and fro excitedly. The thrill of his enthusiasm made him walk with an elastic step. He was sprightly, vigorous, fiery in his belief in success. He looked into the future with clear, proud eye, and he swore with the air of an old soldier.

The youth watched him for a moment in silence. When he finally spoke his voice was as bitter as dregs. "Oh, you're going to do great things I s'pose!"

The loud soldier blew a thoughtful cloud of smoke from his pipe. "Oh, I don't know," he remarked with dignity; "I don't know. I s'pose I'll do as well as the rest. I'm going to try like thunder." He evidently complimented himself upon the modesty of this statement.

"How do you know you won't run when the time comes?" asked the youth.

"Run?" said the loud one; "run?—of course not!" He laughed.

"Well," continued the youth. "Lots of good-a-'nough men have thought they was going to do great things before the fight, but when the time come they skedaddled."

"Oh, that's all true, I s'pose," replied the other; "but I'm not going to skedaddle. The man that bets on my running will lose his money, that's all." He nodded confidently.

"Oh, shucks!" said the youth. "You ain't the bravest man in the world, are you?"

"No, I ain't," exclaimed the loud soldier indignantly; "and I didn't say I was the bravest man in the world, neither. I said I was going to do my share of fighting—that's what I said. And I am, too. Who are you, anyhow? You talk as if you thought you was Napoleon Bonaparte." He glared at the youth for a moment, and then strode away.

The youth called in a savage voice after his comrade: "Well, you needn't git mad about it!" But the other continued on his way and made no reply.

He felt alone in space when his injured comrade had disappeared. His failure to discover any mite of resemblance in their view points made him more miserable than before. No one seemed to be wrestling with such a terrific personal problem. He was a mental outcast.

He went slowly to his tent and stretched himself on a blanket by the side of the snoring tall soldier. In the darkness he saw visions of a thousand-tongued fear that would babble at his back and cause him to flee, while others were going coolly about their country's business. He admitted that he would not be able to cope with this monster. He felt that every nerve in his body would be an ear to hear the voices, while other men would remain stolid and deaf.

And as he sweated with the pain of these thoughts, he could hear low, serene sentences. "I'll bid five." "Make it six." "Seven." "Seven goes."

He stared at the red, shivering reflection of a fire on the white wall of his tent until, exhausted and ill from the monotony of his suffering, he fell asleep.

When another night came the columns, changed to purple streaks, filed across two pontoon bridges. A glaring fire wine-tinted the waters of the river. Its rays, shining upon the moving masses of troops, brought forth here and there sudden gleams of silver or gold. Upon the other shore a dark and mysterious range of hills was curved against the sky. The insect voices of the night sang solemnly.

After this crossing the youth assured himself that at any moment they might be suddenly and fearfully assaulted from the caves of the lowering woods. He kept his eyes watchfully upon the darkness.

But his regiment went unmolested to a camping place, and its soldiers slept the brave sleep of wearied men. In the morning they were routed out with early energy, and hustled along a narrow road that led deep into the forest.

It was during this rapid march that the regiment lost many of the marks of a new command.

The men had begun to count the miles upon their fingers, and they grew tired. "Sore feet an' damned short rations, that's all," said the loud soldier. There was perspiration and grumblings. After a time they began to shed their knapsacks. Some tossed them unconcernedly down; others hid them carefully, asserting their plans to return for them at some convenient time. Men extricated themselves from thick shirts. Presently few carried anything but their necessary clothing, blankets, haversacks, canteens, and arms and ammunition. "You can now eat and shoot," said the tall soldier to the youth. "That's all you want to do. What you want to do—carry a hotel?"

There was sudden change from the ponderous infantry of theory to the light and speedy infantry of practice. The regiment, relieved of a burden, received a new impetus. But there was much loss of valuable knapsacks, and, on the whole, very good shirts.

But the regiment was not yet veteran like in appearance. Veteran regiments in the army were likely to be very small aggregations of men. Once, when the command had first come to the field, some perambulating veterans, noting the length of their column, had accosted them thus: "Hey, fellers, what brigade is that?" And when the men had replied that they formed a regiment and not a brigade, the older soldiers had laughed, and said, "O Gawd!"

Also, there was too great a similarity in the hats. The hats of a regiment should properly represent the history of headgear for a period of years. And, moreover, there were no letters of faded gold speaking from the colors. They were new and beautiful, and the color-bearer habitually oiled the pole.

Presently the army again sat down to think. The odor of the peaceful pines was in the men's nostrils. The sounds of monotonous axe blows rang through the forest, and the insects, nodding upon their perches, crooned like old women. The youth returned to his theory of a blue demonstration.

One gray dawn, however, he was kicked in the leg by the tall soldier, and then, before he was entirely awake, he found himself running down a wood road in the midst of men who were panting from the first effects of speed. His canteen banged rhythmically upon his thigh, and his haversack bobbed softly. His musket bounded a trifle from his shoulder at each stride and made his cap feel uncertain upon his head.

He could hear the men whisper jerky sentences: "Say—what's all this—about?" "What th' thunder—we—skedaddlin' this way fer?" "Billie—keep off m' feet. Yeh run—like a cow." And the loud soldier's shrill voice could be heard: "What th' devil they in sich a hurry for?"

The youth thought the damp fog of early morning moved from the rush of a great body of troops. From the distance came a sudden spatter of firing.

He was bewildered. As he ran with his comrades he strenuously tried to think, but all he knew was that if he fell down those coming behind would tread upon him. All his faculties seemed to be needed to guide him over and past obstructions. He felt carried along by a mob.

The sun spread disclosing rays, and, one by one, regiments burst into view like armed men just born of the earth. The youth perceived that the time had come. He was about to be measured. For a moment he felt in the face of his great trial like a babe, and the flesh over his heart seemed very thin. He seized time to look about him calculatingly.

But he instantly saw that it would be impossible for him to escape from the regiment. It enclosed him. And there were iron laws of tradition and law on four sides. He was in a moving box.

As he perceived this fact it occurred to him that he had never wished to come to the war. He had not enlisted of his free will. He had been dragged by the merciless government. And now they were taking him out to be slaughtered.

The regiment slid down a bank and wallowed across a little stream. The mournful current moved slowly on, and from the water, shaded black, some white bubble eyes looked at the men.

As they climbed the hill on the farther side artillery began to boom. Here the youth forgot many things as he felt a sudden impulse of curiosity. He scrambled up the bank with a speed that could not be exceeded by a bloodthirsty man.

He expected a battle scene.

There were some little fields girted and squeezed by a forest. Spread over the grass

and in among the tree trunks, he could see knots and waving lines of skirmishers who were running hither and thither and firing at the landscape. A dark battle line lay upon a sun struck clearing that gleamed orange color. A flag fluttered.

Other regiments floundered up the bank. The brigade was formed in line of battle, and after a pause started slowly through the woods in the rear of the receding skirmishers, who were continually melting into the scene to appear again farther on. They were always busy as bees, deeply absorbed in their little combats.

The youth tried to observe everything. He did not use care to avoid trees and branches, and his forgotten feet were constantly knocking against stones or getting entangled in briers. He was aware that these battalions with their commotions were woven red and startling into the gentle fabric of softened greens and browns. It looked to be a wrong place for a battlefield.

The skirmishers in advance fascinated him. Their shots into thickets and at distant and prominent trees spoke to him of tragedies—hidden, mysterious, solemn.

Once the line encountered the body of a dead soldier. He lay upon his back staring at the sky. He was dressed in an awkward suit of yellowish brown. The youth could see that the soles of his shoes had been worn to the thinness of writing paper, and from a great rent in one the dead foot projected piteously. And it was as if fate had betrayed the soldier. In death it exposed to his enemies that poverty which in life he had perhaps concealed from his friends.

The ranks opened covertly to avoid the corpse. The invulnerable dead man forced a way for himself. The youth looked keenly at the ashen face. The wind raised the tawny beard. It moved as if a hand were stroking it. He vaguely desired to walk around and around the body and stare; the impulse of the living to try to read in dead eyes the answer to the Question.

During the march the ardor which the youth had acquired when out of view of the field rapidly faded to nothing. His curiosity was quite easily satisfied. If an intense scene had caught him with its wild swing as he came to the top of the bank, he might have gone roaring on. This advance upon Nature was too calm. He had opportunity to reflect. He had time in which to wonder about himself and to attempt to probe his sensations.

Absurd ideas took hold upon him. He thought that he did not relish the landscape. It threatened him. A coldness swept over his back, and it is true that his trousers felt to him that they were no fit for his legs at all.

A house standing placidly in distant fields had to him an ominous look. The shadows of the woods were formidable. He was certain that in this vista there lurked fierce-eyed hosts. The swift thought came to him that the generals did not know what they were about. It was all a trap. Suddenly those close forests would bristle with rifle barrels. Iron like brigades would appear in the rear. They were all going to be sacrificed. The generals were stupids. The enemy would presently swallow the whole command. He glared about him, expecting to see the stealthy approach of his death.

He thought that he must break from the ranks and harangue his comrades. They must not all be killed like pigs; and he was sure it would come to pass unless they were informed of these dangers. The generals were idiots to send them marching into a regular pen. There was but one pair of eyes in the corps. He would step forth and make a speech. Shrill and passionate words came to his lips.

The line, broken into moving fragments by the ground, went calmly on through fields and woods. The youth looked at the men nearest him, and saw, for the most part, expressions of deep interest, as if they were investigating something that had fascinated them. One or two stepped with over valiant airs as if they were already plunged into war. Others walked as upon thin ice. The greater part of the untested men appeared quiet and absorbed. They were going to look at war, the red animal — war, the blood-swollen god. And they were deeply engrossed in this march.

As he looked the youth gripped his outcry at his throat. He saw that even if the men were tottering with fear they would laugh at his warning. They would jeer him, and, if practicable, pelt him with missiles. Admitting that he might be wrong, a frenzied declamation of the kind would turn him into a worm.

He assumed, then, the demeanor of one who knows that he is doomed alone to unwritten responsibilities. He lagged, with tragic glances at the sky. He was surprised presently by the young lieutenant of his company, who began heartily to beat him with a sword, calling out in a loud and insolent voice: "Come, young man, get up into the ranks there. No skulking'll do here." He mended his pace with suitable haste. And he hated the lieutenant, who had no appreciation of fine minds. He was a mere brute.

After a time the brigade was halted in the cathedral light of a forest. The busy skirmishers were still popping. Through the aisles of the wood could be seen the floating smoke from their rifles. Sometimes it went up in little balls, white and compact.

During this halt many men in the regiment began erecting tiny hills in front of them. They used stones, sticks, earth, and anything they thought might turn a bullet. Some built comparatively large ones, while others seemed content with little ones.

This procedure caused a discussion among the men. Some wished to fight like duellists, believing it to be correct to stand erect and be, from their feet to their foreheads, a mark. They said they scorned the devices of the cautious. But the others scoffed in reply, and pointed to the veterans on the flanks who were digging at the ground like terriers. In a short time there was quite a barricade along the regimental fronts. Directly, however, they were ordered to withdraw from that place.

This astounded the youth. He forgot his stewing over the advance movement. "Well, then, what did they march us out here for?" he demanded of the tall soldier. The latter with calm faith began a heavy explanation, although he had been compelled to leave a little protection of stones and dirt to which he had devoted much care and skill.

When the regiment was aligned in another position each man's regard for his safety caused another line of small entrenchments. They ate their noon meal behind a third one. They were moved from this one also. They were marched from place to place with apparent aimlessness.

The youth had been taught that a man became another being in a battle. He saw his salvation in such a change. Hence this waiting was an ordeal to him. He was in a fever of impatience. He considered that there was denoted a lack of purpose on the part of the generals. He began to complain to the tall soldier. "I can't stand this much longer," he cried. "I don't see what good it does to make us wear out our legs for nothin'." He wished to return to camp, knowing that this affair was a blue demonstration; or else to go into battle and discover that he had been a fool in his doubts, and was, in truth, a man of traditional courage. The strain of present circumstances he felt to be intolerable.

The philosophical tall soldier measured a sandwich of cracker and pork and swallowed it in a nonchalant manner. "Oh, I suppose we must go reconnoitering around the country jest to keep 'em from getting too close, or to develop 'em, or something."

"Huh!" said the loud soldier.

"Well," cried the youth, still fidgeting, "I'd rather do anything 'most than go tramping 'round the country all day doing no good to nobody and jest tiring ourselves out."

"So would I," said the loud soldier. "It ain't right. I tell you if anybody with any sense was a-runnin' this army it——"

"Oh, shut up!" roared the tall private. "You little fool. You little damn' cuss. You ain't had that there coat and them pants on for six months, and yet you talk as if——"

"Well, I wanta do some fighting anyway," interrupted the other. "I didn't come here to walk. I could 'ave walked to home—'round an' 'round the barn, if I jest wanted to walk."

The tall one, red-faced, swallowed another sandwich as if taking poison in despair.

But gradually, as he chewed, his face became again quiet and contented. He could not rage in fierce argument in the presence of such sandwiches. During his meals he always wore an air of blissful contemplation of the food he had swallowed. His spirit seemed then to be communing with the viands.

He accepted new environment and circumstance with great coolness, eating from his haversack at every opportunity. On the march he went along with the stride of a hunter, objecting to neither gait nor distance. And he had not raised his voice when he had been ordered away from three little protective piles of earth and stone, each of which had been an engineering feat worthy of being made sacred to the name of his grandmother.

In the afternoon the regiment went out over the same ground it had taken in the morning. The landscape then ceased to threaten the youth. He had been close to it and become familiar with it.

When, however, they began to pass into a new region, his old fears of stupidity and incompetence reassailed him, but this time he doggedly let them babble. He was occupied with his problem, and in his desperation he concluded that the stupidity did not greatly matter.

Once he thought he had concluded that it would be better to get killed directly and end his troubles. Regarding death thus out of the corner of his eye, he conceived it to be nothing but rest, and he was filled with a momentary astonishment that he should have made an extraordinary commotion over the mere matter of getting killed. He would die; he would go to some place where he would be understood. It was useless to expect appreciation of his profound and fine senses from such men as the lieutenant. He must look to the grave for comprehension.

The skirmish fire increased to a long clattering sound. With it was mingled far-away cheering. A battery spoke.

Directly the youth would see the skirmishers running. They were pursued by the sound of musketry fire. After a time the hot, dangerous flashes of the rifles were visible. Smoke clouds went slowly and insolently across the fields like observant phantoms. The din became crescendo, like the roar of an oncoming train.

A brigade ahead of them and on the right went into action with a rending roar. It was as if it had exploded. And thereafter it lay stretched in the distance behind a long gray wall, that one was obliged to look twice at to make sure that it was smoke.

The youth, forgetting his neat plan of getting killed, gazed spellbound. His eyes grew wide and busy with the action of the scene. His mouth was a little ways open.

Of a sudden he felt a heavy and sad hand laid upon his shoulder. Awakening from his trance of observation he turned and beheld the loud soldier.

"It's my first and last battle, old boy," said the latter, with intense gloom. He was quite pale, and his girlish lip was trembling.

"Eh?" murmured the youth in great astonishment.

COLORPLATE 24

JOHN J. PORTER. *Presentation of the Charger "Coquette" to Colonel Mosby by the Men of His Command, December, 1864.* 1864. Oil on canvas. 14½ × 20¼". Collection of Beverly Mosby Coleman. Photo by Larry Sherer, copyright © 1985 Time-Life Books, Inc. *Confederate partisan leader John Singleton Mosby (left center) is presented with a thoroughbred by his men.*

COLORPLATE 25

JOHN A. ELDER. *The Scout's Return.* No date. Oil on canvas glued to cardboard. 21¾ × 27″.
Virginia Museum of Fine Arts, Richmond. Gift of Mrs. Hugh L. Macneil in memory of Mrs.
Charles E. Bolling. Photo copyright © 1991 Virginia Museum of Fine Arts.

COLORPLATE 26

WINSLOW HOMER. *Defiance: Inviting a Shot Before Petersburg.* 1864. Oil on panel. 12 × 18″.
Detroit Institute of Arts. Gift of Dexter M. Ferry, Jr. Photo copyright © 1991 Detroit Institute of Arts.

COLORPLATE 27

PRINCE DE JOINVILLE. *Sunday Review at Bayley Cross Roads.* 1861.
Watercolor on paper. 6¾ × 9½". Fondation Saint-Louis, Amboise, France.

COLORPLATE 28

PRINCE DE JOINVILLE. *Picnic on the Potomac, Great Falls.* 1861.
Watercolor on paper. 5 × 7". Fondation Saint-Louis, Amboise, France.

COLORPLATE 29

CONRAD WISE CHAPMAN. *Confederate Camp at Corinth.* 1862.
Lithograph. 10⅝ × 15¼″. Valentine Museum, Richmond.

COLORPLATE 30

VOLTAIRE COMBE. *Camp Oliver at New Bern, North Carolina.* 1863. Watercolor on paper.
11¾ × 21½″. Brown University Library, Providence. Anne S. K. Brown Military Collection.

COLORPLATE 31

CONRAD WISE CHAPMAN. *Battery Rutledge, Charleston, Dec. 3, 1864.* 1864. Oil on board.
11½ × 15½″. Museum of the Confederacy, Richmond. Photo by Katherine Wetzel.

COLORPLATE 32

Edwin Forbes. *Mess Boy Asleep*. 1867. Oil on canvas. 14 × 20¼″. Wadsworth Atheneum, Hartford. Ella Gallup Sumner and Mary Catlin Sumner Collection. Photo copyright © Wadsworth Atheneum.

"It's my first and last battle, old boy," continued the loud soldier. "Something tells me——"

"What?"

"I'm a gone coon this first time and—and I w-want you to take these here things—to—my—folks." He ended in a quavering sob of pity for himself. He handed the youth a little packet done up in a yellow envelope.

"Why, what the devil——" began the youth again.

But the other gave him a glance as from the depths of a tomb, and raised his limp hand in a prophetic manner and turned away.

The brigade was halted in the fringe of a grove. The men crouched among the trees and pointed their restless guns out at the fields. They tried to look beyond the smoke.

Out of this haze they could see running men. Some shouted information and gestured as they hurried.

The men of the new regiment watched and listened eagerly, while their tongues ran on in gossip of the battle. They mouthed rumors that had flown like birds out of the unknown. . . .

The din in front swelled to a tremendous chorus. The youth and his fellows were frozen to silence. They could see a flag that tossed in the smoke angrily. Near it were the blurred and agitated forms of troops. There came a turbulent stream of men across the fields. A battery changing positions at a frantic gallop scattered the stragglers right and left.

A shell screaming like a storm banshee went over the huddled heads of the reserves. It landed in the grove, and exploding redly flung the brown earth. There was a little shower of pine needles.

Bullets began to whistle among the branches and nip at the trees. Twigs and leaves came sailing down. It was as if a thousand axes, wee and invisible, were being wielded. Many of the men were constantly dodging and ducking their heads.

The lieutenant of the youth's company was shot in the hand. He began to swear so wondrously, that a nervous laugh went along the regimental line. The officer's profanity sounded conventional. It relieved the tightened senses of the new men. It was as if he had hit his fingers with a tack hammer at home.

He held the wounded member carefully away from his side so that the blood would not drip upon his trousers.

The captain of the company, tucking his sword under his arm, produced a handkerchief and began to bind with it the lieutenant's wound. And they disputed as to how the binding should be done.

The battle flag in the distance jerked about madly. It seemed to be struggling to free itself from an agony. The billowing smoke was filled with horizontal flashes.

Men running swiftly emerged from it. They grew in numbers until it was seen that the whole command was fleeing. The flag suddenly sank down as if dying. Its motion as it fell was a gesture of despair.

Wild yells came from behind the walls of smoke. A sketch in gray and red dissolved into a moblike body of men who galloped like wild horses.

The veteran regiments on the right and left of the 304th immediately began to jeer. With the passionate song of the bullets and the banshee shrieks of shells were mingled loud catcalls and bits of facetious advice concerning places of safety.

But the new regiment was breathless with horror. "Gawd! Saunder's got crushed!" whispered the man at the youth's elbow. They shrank back and crouched as if compelled to await a flood.

The youth shot a swift glance along the blue ranks of the regiment. The profiles were motionless, carven; and afterward he remembered that the color sergeant was standing with his legs apart, as if he expected to be pushed to the ground.

The following throng went whirling around the flank. Here and there were officers carried along in the stream like exasperated chips. They were striking about them with their swords and with their left fists, punching every head they could reach. They cursed like highwaymen.

A mounted officer displayed the furious anger of a spoiled child. He raged with his head, his arms, and his legs.

Another, the commander of the brigade, was galloping about bawling. His hat was gone and his clothes were awry. He resembled a man who has come from bed to go to a fire. The hoofs of his horse often threatened the heads of the running men, but they scampered with singular fortune. In this rush they were apparently all deaf and blind. They heeded not the largest and longest of the oaths that were thrown at them from all directions.

Frequently over this tumult could be heard the grim jokes of the critical veterans; but the retreating men apparently were not even conscious of the presence of an audience.

The battle reflection that shone for an instant in the faces on the mad current made the youth feel that forceful hands from heaven would not have been able to have held him in place if he could have got intelligent control of his legs.

There was an appalling imprint upon these faces. The struggle in the smoke had pictured an exaggeration of itself on the bleached cheeks and in the eyes wild with one desire.

The sight of this stampede exerted a floodlike force that seemed able to drag sticks and stones and men from the ground. They of the reserves had to hold on. They grew pale and firm, and red and quaking.

The youth achieved one little thought in the midst of this chaos. The composite monster which had caused the other troops to flee had not then appeared. He resolved to get a view of it, and then, he thought he might very likely run better than the best of them.

Sam R. Watkins

On an Incident at Missionary Ridge

The 1st Tennessee's Private Watkins sees battle at Chattanooga in November 1863 from the sidelines, as recorded in his memoir, Co. Aytch.

One morning Theodore Sloan, Hog Johnson, and I were standing picket at the little stream that runs along at the foot of Lookout Mountain. In fact, I would be pleased to name our Captain, Fulcher, and Lieutenant Lansdown, of the guard on this occasion, because we acted as picket for the whole three days' engagement without being relieved, and haven't been relieved yet. But that battle has gone into history. We heard a Yankee call "O, Johnny, Johnny Reb!" I started out to meet him as formerly, when he hallooed out, "Go back, Johnny, go back; we are ordered to fire on you." "What is the matter? Is your army going to advance on us?" "I don't know; we are ordered to fire." I jumped back into the picket post, and a minnie ball ruined the only hat I had; another and another followed in quick succession, and the dirt flew up in our faces off our little breastworks. Before night the picket line was engaged from one end to the other. If you had only heard it, dear reader. It went like ten thousand wood-choppers, and an occasional boom of a cannon would remind you of a tree falling. We could hear Colonels giving commands to their regiments, and could see very plainly the commotion and hubbub, but what was up, we were unable to tell. The picket line kept moving to our right. The second night found us near the tunnel, and right where two railroads cross each other, or rather one runs over the other high enough for the cars to pass under. We could see all over Chattanooga, and it looked like myriads of blue coats swarming. . . .

I know nothing about the battle; how Grant, with one wing, went up the river, and Hooker's corps went down Wills Valley, etc. I heard fighting and commanding and musketry all day long, but I was still on picket. Balls were passing over our heads, both coming and going. I could not tell whether I was standing picket for Yankees or Rebels. I knew that the Yankee line was between me and the Rebel line, for I could see the battle right over the tunnel. We had been placed on picket at the foot of Lookout Mountain, but we were five miles from that place now. If I had tried to run in I couldn't. I had got separated from Sloan and Johnson somehow; in fact, was waiting either for an advance of the Yankees, or to be called in by the captain of the picket. I could see the blue coats fairly lining Missionary Ridge in my rear. The Yankees were swarming everywhere. They were passing me all day with their dead and wounded, going back to Chattanooga. No one seemed to notice me; they were passing to and fro, cannon, artillery, and everything. I was willing to be taken prisoner, but no one seemed disposed to do it. I was afraid to look at them, and I was afraid to hide, for fear some one's attention would be attracted toward me. I wished I could make myself invisible. I think I was invisible. I felt that way anyhow. I felt like the boy who wanted to go to the wedding, but had no shoes. . . .

About two or three o'clock, a column of Yankees advancing to the attack swept right over where I was standing. I was trying to stand aside to get out of their way, but the more I tried to get out of their way, the more in their way I got. I was carried forward, I knew not whither. We soon arrived at the foot of the ridge, at our old breastworks. I recognized Robert Brank's old corn stalk house, and Alf Horsley's fort, an old log house called Fort Horsley. I was in front of the enemy's line, and was afraid to run up the ridge, and afraid to surrender. They were ordered to charge up the hill. There was no firing from the Rebel lines in our immediate front. They kept climbing and pulling and scratching until I was in touching distance of the old Rebel breastworks, right on the very apex of Missionary Ridge. I made one jump, and I heard Captain Turner, who had the very four Napoleon guns we had captured at Perryville, halloo out, "Number Four, solid!" and then a roar. The next order was, "Limber to the rear." The Yankees were cutting and slashing, and the cannoneers were running in every direction. I saw Day's brigade throw down their guns and break like quarter horses. Bragg was trying to rally them. I heard him say, "Here is your commander," and the soldiers hallooed back, "Here is your mule."

The whole army was routed. I ran on down the ridge, and there was our regiment, the First Tennessee, with their guns stacked, and drawing rations as if nothing was going on. Says I, "Colonel Field, what's the matter? The whole army is routed and running; hadn't you better be getting away from here? The Yankees are not a hundred yards from here. Turner's Battery has surrendered, Day's brigade has thrown down their arms; and look yonder, that is the Stars and Stripes." He remarked very coolly, "You seem to be demoralized. We've whipped them here. We've captured two thousand prisoners and five stands of colors."

Just at this time General Bragg and staff rode up. Bragg had joined the Church at Shelbyville, but he had back-slid at Missionary Ridge. He was cursing like a sailor. Says he, "What's this? Ah, ha, have you stacked your arms for a surrender?" "No, sir," says Field. "Take arms, shoulder arms, by the right flank, file right, march," just as cool and deliberate as if on dress parade. Bragg looked scared. He had put spurs to his horse, and was running like a scared dog before Colonel Field had a chance to answer him. Every word of this is a fact. We at once became the rear guard of the whole army.

I felt sorry for General Bragg. The army was routed, and Bragg looked so scared. Poor fellow, he looked so hacked and whipped and mortified and chagrined at defeat, and all along the line, when Bragg would pass, the soldiers would raise the yell, "Here is your mule;" "Bully for Bragg, he's h—l on retreat."

Bragg was a good disciplinarian, and if he had cultivated the love and respect of his troops by feeding and clothing them better than they were, the result would have been different. More depends on a good General than the lives of many privates. The private loses his life, the General his country.

Robert Penn Warren

FROM WILDERNESS, A TALE OF THE CIVIL WAR

On Grant's Arrival

It is spring 1864, and the Army of the Potomac has a new general; from the novel by Pulitzer prize winner Robert Penn Warren.

————————————

One evening, toward sunset, Adam walked into the open fields to the north. At least, fields had once been there. Now the fences were gone, rails and stakes long since burned in campfires, broken in the attempt to pry a caisson wheel from the mud, used as supports for the roof of a hut. But brush, or a heavier growth of weeds showed, here and there, the old patterns of demarcation, and under foot the parallel corrugations of old plowing, sinking now into the level of earth, told where rows had, long ago, run. How long ago? Adam asked himself that. Only three years, he decided. It might have been fifty, he thought, staring across the fields at the charred ruin of a house fallen between two tall stone chimneys.

He moved toward the ruin. There had once been an approach, too modest to be called an avenue, lined with trees. Now there were stumps, and grass had grown over the old lane. Three or four trees yet stood near the ruin. They, however, were blackened. They put forth no leaf.

He looked westward across the land. The late light washed toward him from the reddening sky. He thought of the grass coming back over the fields, the weeds coming back. The land was beautiful in the light, glimmering with that pale new green. To the north a patch of woodland showed the red mist of leafing oak, the gold of maple. He sat on a stump by the ruined lane, and let his heart be at peace. He wondered how he would feel when he was old. Would he move in a peace like this?

He wondered how this land would be when it was old.

He rose and walked toward the camp. He had just crossed a track of rutted earth when, looking westward, he saw a body of horsemen approaching. The hooves made no sound on the soft earth. But when they were still some distance he could hear the soft creaking of leather. He stood by the road facing northward and waited, while the mounts footed soberly past him.

Three men rode in front, silent, eyes fixed ahead but seemingly seeing nothing, all thought turned inward from the dimming land. Next came a lone horseman, young, heroic, gauntleted fist on hip, yellow hair, worn long, showing from beneath the cant of the cavalryman's black hat. He was, Adam could see, a captain. The captain did not see

Adam. He did not seem to see anything. His eyes were fixed ahead, and in that pose of heroic solitude, or indifference, he drew steadily away.

Next came the guidon-bearer, riding on the left side of the track, supporting upright the staff, set in a kind of cup, or fewter, attached to the right stirrup. The guidon hung listless, scarcely stirred by the motion. But once, in an unexpected shift of air, it lifted, displaying for an instant its swallowtail shape and a glint of red.

Then, in pairs, troopers moved past, erect, faces blank and eyes veiled, the only sign of life the faint motion of hips absorbing the motion of the mount into the portentous immobility of the human torso. They slipped by in their visionary silence, the hooves soundless. But the leather creaked. Now and then one of the beasts snorted softly.

The troop moved off, in that evenly paced, remorseless process, and the leveling rays of sunset fell calmly on their backs;

The last pair of troopers had moved a few rods down the track before Adam realized what he had seen. Then he saw, in the fresh memory more sharply than he had in fact, the figure of the second of the three men riding in front, a smallish, lumpish, bearded man between two gold-gleaming warriors, a man who, despite his limpishness, sat his mount well, a man with a hat pulled low on his brow, no insignia on his coat. The coat was unbuttoned and hung without tidiness. Adam realized that he had seen, under that unbuttoned coat, a gold sash bound over the incipient paunch of middle-age.

He watched the horsemen dwindle into distance. Then he turned and walked toward the camp. . . .

Men said: "It won't be long now."

Walt Whitman
"A GLIMPSE OF WAR'S HELL-SCENES"
On the Guerrilla War

An incident in Confederate guerrilla leader John S. Mosby's "Confederacy," in Virginia. Whitman called it "a glimpse of war's hell-scenes."

In one of the late movements of our troops in the valley (near Upperville, I think), a strong force of Mosby's guerrillas attacked a train of wounded and the guard of cavalry convoying them. The ambulances contained about sixty wounded, quite a number of them officers of rank. The Rebels were in strength, and the capture of the train and its partial guard after a short snap was effectually accomplished. No sooner had our men surrendered, the Rebels instantly commenced robbing the train and murdering their prisoners, even the wounded. Here is the scene or a sample of it—ten minutes after.

Among the wounded officers in the ambulances were one, a lieutenant of regulars, and another, of higher rank. These two were dragged out on the ground on their backs and were now surrounded by the guerrillas, a demoniac crowd, each member of which was stabbing them in different parts of their bodies. One of the officers had his feet pinned firmly to the ground by bayonets stuck through them and thrust into the ground. These two officers, as afterwards found on examination, had received about twenty such thrusts, some of them through the mouth, face, etc. The wounded had all been dragged (to give a better chance for plunder) out of their wagons; some had been effectually dispatched, and their bodies were lying there lifeless and bloody. Others, not yet dead but horribly mutilated, were moaning or groaning. Of our men who surrendered, most had been thus maimed or slaughtered.

At this instant, a force of our cavalry, who had been following the train at some interval, charged suddenly upon the Secesh captors, who proceeded at once to make the best escape they could. Most of them got away, but we gobbled two officers and seventeen men in the very acts just described. The sight was one which admitted of little discussion, as may be imagined. The seventeen captured men and two officers were put under guard for the night, but it was decided there and then that they should die.

The next morning the two officers were taken in the town—separate places—put in the centre of the street and shot. The seventeen men were taken to an open ground a little to one side. They were placed in a h. 'low square, half encompassed by two of our cavalry regiments, one of which regiments had three days before found the bloody corpses of three of their men hamstrung and hung up by the heels to limbs of trees by Mosby's guerrillas; and the other had not long before had twelve men, after surrendering, shot and then hung by the neck to limbs of trees, and jeering inscriptions pinned to the breast of one of the corpses, who had been a sergeant.

Those three, and those twelve, had been found, I say, by these environing regiments. Now, with revolvers, they formed the grim cordon of the seventeen prisoners. The latter were placed in the midst of the hollow square, unfastened, and the ironical remark made to them that they were now to be given "a chance for themselves." A few ran for it. But

ALFRED R. WAUD. *A Guerilla.* ca. 1863.
Drawing. Library of Congress, Washington, D.C.

what use? From every side the deadly pills came. In a few minutes the seventeen corpses strewed the hollow square.

I was curious to know whether some of the Union soldiers, some few (some one or two at least of the youngsters), did not abstain from shooting on the helpless men. Not one. There was no exultation, very little said—almost nothing—yet every man there contributed his shot.

Multiply the above by scores, aye hundreds; verify it in all the forms that different circumstances, individuals, places could afford; light it with every lurid passion—the wolf's, the lion's lapping thirst for blood; the passionate, boiling volcanoes of human revenge for comrades, brothers slain; with the light of burning farms and heaps of smutting, smouldering black embers—and in the human heart everywhere, black, worse embers—and you have an inkling of the war.

Alexander Hunter
On Trading Across the River

Trading with the enemy in Virginia in 1863, remembered by a man in the 17th Virginia in his Johnny Reb and Billy Yank.

The next day our squad, Sergeant Joe Reid in command, sauntered down the bank, but seeing no one we lay at length under the spreading trees, smoking as solemnly and meditatively as the redoubtable Wilhelmus Kraft and all the Dutch Council, over the affairs of state.

The Rappahannock, which was at this place about two hundred yards wide, flowing slowly oceanward, its bosom reflecting the roseate-hued morn, was as lovely a body of water as the sun ever shone upon. The sound of the gentle ripple of its waves upon the sand was broken by a faint "halloo" which came from the other side.

"Johnny Reb; I say, J-o-h-n-n-y R-e-b, don't shoot!"

Joe Reid shouted back, "All right!"

"What command are you?"

The spoken words floated clear and distinct across the water, "The Black Horse Cavalry. Who are you?"

"The Second Michigan Cavalry."

"Come out on the bank," said our spokesman, "and show yourselves; we won't fire."

"On your honor, Johnny Reb?"

"On our honor, Billy Yank."

In a second a large squad of blue-coats across the way advanced to the water's brink. The Southerners did the same; then the former put the query.

"Have you any tobacco?"

"Plenty of it," went out our reply.

"Any sugar and coffee?" they questioned.

"Not a taste nor a smell."

"Let's trade," was shouted with eagerness.

"Very well," was the reply. "We have not much with us, but we will send to Fredericksburg for more, so meet us here this evening."

"All right," they answered; then added, "Say, Johnny, want some newspapers?"

"Y-e-s!"

"Then look out, we are going to send you some."

"How are you going to do it?"

"Wait and see."

The Rebs watched the group upon the other side curiously, wondering how even Yankee ingenuity could devise a way for sending a batch of papers across the river two hundred yards wide, and in the meantime each man had his own opinion.

"They will shoot arrows over," said Martin.

"Arrows, the devil!" replied the sergeant; "there never was a bow bent which could cast an arrow across this river."

"Maybe they will wrap them around a cannon ball and shoot them across; we'd better get away from here," hastily answered a tall, slim six-footer, who was rather afraid of big shots.

A roar of laughter followed this suggestion, but the originator was too intent on his own awakened fears to let the slightest movement of the enemy pass unscanned. Eagerly he watched while the others were having all the fun at his expense. Presently he shouted:

"Here they come!" and then in a tone of intense admiration, "I'll be doggoned if these Yanks are not the smartest people in the world."

On the other side were several miniature boats and ships — such as schoolboys delight in — with sails set; the gentle breeze impelled the little crafts across the river, each freighted with a couple of newspapers. Slowly, but surely, they headed for the opposite bank as if some spirit Oberon or Puck sat at the tiller; and in a few minutes had accomplished their voyage and were drawn up to await a favorable wind to waft them back.

Drawing lots, Joe Boteler, who found luck against him, started to town, with a muttered curse, to buy tobacco, leaving his comrades to seek some shady spot, and with pipes in our mouths sink deep in the latest war news from the enemy's standpoint, always interesting reading.

It was a cloudless day, — a day to dream, — and with a lazy *sans souci* manner and half-shut eyes, enjoy to the soul the deep loveliness of the scene which lay around us like some fair creation of the fancy, listening the while to the trills of the blue-bird which sat on the top of a lofty tree industriously practicing his notes like a prima donna getting a new opera by heart.

Joe returned in the evening with a box of plug tobacco about a foot square; but how to get it across was the question. The miniature boats could not carry it, and we shouted over to the Yanks that we had about twenty pounds of cut plug, and asked them what we must do? They hallooed back to let one of us swim across, and declared that it was perfectly safe. We held a council of war, and it was found that none of the Black Horse could swim beyond a few rods. Then I volunteered. Having lived on the banks of the Potomac most of my life, I was necessarily a swimmer.

Sergeant Reid went to a house not far off and borrowed a bread trough, and placing it on a plank, the box of tobacco was shipped, and disrobing I started, pushing my queer craft in front of me. As I approached the shore the news of my coming had reached camp, and nearly all the Second Michigan were lined up along the bank.

I felt a little queer, but I had perfect faith in their promise and kept on without missing a stroke until my miniature scow grounded on the beach. The blue-coats crowded around me and gave me a hearty welcome, and relieving the trough of its load, heaped the craft with offerings of sugar, coffee, lemons, and even candy, till I cried out that they would sink my transport. I am sure they would have filled a rowboat to the gunwhale had I brought one.

There was no chaffing or banter, only roistering welcomes.

Bidding my friends the enemy good-by, I swam back with the precious cargo, and we had a feast that night.

John W. De Forest
"FORCED MARCHES"
On Amusing the Enemy

Best known for his 1867 novel Miss Ravenel's Conversion from Secession to Loyalty, *John De Forest served in the 12th Connecticut throughout the war. In the magazine* Galaxy, *in 1868, he describes an incident along the lower Mississippi in April of 1863.*

The Teche country was to the war in Louisiana what the Shenandoah Valley was to the war in Virginia. It was a sort of back alley, parallel to the main street wherein the heavy fighting must go on; and one side or the other was always running up or down the Teche with the other side in full chase after it. There the resemblance ends, for the Teche country is a long flat, hemmed in by marshes and bayous, which, as everybody but a blind man can see, is a very different thing from a rolling valley bordered by mountains. . . .

My first adventure in this region was in January, 1863. Weitzel dashed up to the confluence of the Teche and Atchafalaya with five or six regiments, scared Mouton out of his position there, smashed the Confederates' new iron-clad gunboat *Cotton*, and returned next morning. Although pestered with cold and hunger, our march homeward was as hilarious as a bacchanal procession. It was delightful to have beaten the enemy, and it was delightful to be on the way back to our comfortable quarters. The expedition was thus brief because it had fulfilled its object, which was to weaken the Confederate naval power on the Teche, and thus enable Banks to take the back alley in his proposed advance on Port Hudson.

But why should he go by the back alley of the Teche instead of by the main street of the Mississippi? Because it was necessary to destroy the army of Mouton, or, at least, to drive it northward as far as possible, in order to incapacitate it from attacking New Orleans while we should be engaged with the fortress of the bluffs. The story ran in our brigade that this sensible plan originated in the head of our own commandant, Weitzel. I believed it then, and I have learned no better since, although I can affirm nothing. The reader will please to remember that there is a great deal of uncertainty in war, not only before but after.

About the middle of April, 1863, I was once more at the confluence of the Teche and the Atchafalaya. This time Mouton was there in strong force, posted behind entrenchments which seemed to me half a mile in length, with an impassable swamp on his right and armored gunboats on his left. Banks's army was far superior in numbers and, supported as it was by a sufficient fleet of gunboats, could doubtless have carried the position; but the desirable thing to do was of course, not so much to beat Mouton as to bag him, and so finish the war in this part of Louisiana. Accordingly, by mysterious waterways of which I know nothing, Grover's division was transported to Irish Bend, in Mouton's rear, while Emory's and Weitzel's divisions should amuse him in front.

And here I am tempted . . . to describe this same amusement. The first part of the joke was to push up Weitzel's brigade to draw the enemy's fire. In a single long line, stretching from the wood on the left well toward the river on the right, the brigade advanced directly toward the enemy's works, prostrating or climbing fences, and struggling amid horrible labyrinths of tangled sugar cane. Rush through a mile of Indian corn, taking the furrows diagonally, then imagine yourself three times as tired and breathless as you are, and you will form some conception of what it is to move in line through a canefield. At first you valiantly push aside the tough green obstacles; then you ignominiously dodge under or around them; at last you fall down with your tongue out. The ranks are broken; the regiment tails off into strings, the strongest leading; the ground is strewn with panting soldiers; the organization disappears.

The cane once passed, stragglers began to come up and find their places; the ranks counted off anew while advancing, and we had once more a regiment. Now we obtained a full view of the field of projected amusement. Before us lay a long and comparatively narrow plain, bounded by forests rising out of swamps, and decorated by a long low earthwork, a third of a mile ahead of us, and barely visible to the naked eye. Away to our right were two half-demolished brick sugar-houses, near which there was a scurrying of dust to and fro, bespeaking a skirmishing of cavalry. Otherwise the scene was one of perfect quietness and silence and desertion.

Of a sudden *bang, bang, bang*, roared an unseen battery, and *jiz, jiz, jiz*, screeched the shells over our heads. Evidently the enemy was too much amused to keep his mouth shut. Then our own batteries joined in with their *bang, bang, bang, jiz, jiz, jiz*, and for twenty minutes or more it was as disgusting as a Fourth of July. The shelling did not hurt us a bit, and consequently did not scare us much, for we were already accustomed to this kind of racket, and only took it hard when it was mingled with the cries of the wounded. I never assisted, as the French phrase it, at a noisier or a more harmless bout of cannonading. Not a man in my regiment was injured, although the shells hummed and cracked and fought each other in flights over our heads, dotting the sky with the little globes of smoke which marked their explosions, and sending buzzing fragments in all directions.

Meantime our point was gained; the enemy had defined his position. There was a battery in the swampy wood on his right, which would enfilade an attacking column, while on his left the same business would be performed by his armored gunboats in the Teche. Now came an order to take the brigade to the rear. A greenhorn of an aide, shrieking with excitement, galloped up to our commander and yelled: "Colonel, double-quick your men out of range. Double-quick!"

I remember the wrath with which I heard this order. Run? Be shot if I would run or let a man of my company run. The regiment, hearing the command, had faced about and was going to the rear at a pace which threatened confusion and panic. I rushed through the ranks, drew my sword, ordered, threatened, and brought my own company from a double-quick down to the ordinary marching step. Every other officer, from the colonel downward, instinctively did the same; and the regiment moved off in a style which we considered proper for the Twelfth Connecticut.

That night we bivouacked with mosquitoes, who drew more blood than the cannonade of the afternoon. Next morning the heavy guns of the opposing gunboats opened a game of long bowls, in which the Parrotts of the Twenty-first Indiana took a part, sending loud-whispering shells into the farthest retreats of the enemy. At ten, the whole army, three lines deep and stretching across the river—a fine martial spectacle—advanced slowly through the canefields toward the entrenchments. Marching in my preferred position, in the front rank of my company and next to the regimental colors, I felt myself to be an undesirably conspicuous person, as we came out upon the open ground in view of the enemy, and received the first discharge of their artillery. It is a grand thing to take the lead in battle, but all the same it is uncomfortable. The first cannon shot which I noticed struck the ground sixty or eighty feet in front of our color guard, threw up the ploughed soil in a little cloud, leaped a hundred feet behind the regiment, and went bounding off to the rear.

"That's bad for the fellows behind us," I said to my men, with that smile which a hero puts on when he makes the best he can of battle, meantime wishing himself at home.

The next shot struck within thirty feet of the line, and also went jumping and whistling rearward. They were evidently aiming at the colors, and that was nearly equivalent to aiming at me.

"You'll fetch him next time," I thought, grimly; and so, doubtless, thought hundreds of others, each for himself.

But at this moment one of our own batteries opened with great violence and evidently shook the nerves of the enemy's gunners, for their next shot screeched over the colors and first struck the ground far in rear of the regiment, and thereafter they never recovered their at first dangerously accurate range. Now came an order to the infantry to halt and lie down, and no veteran will need to be told that we obeyed it promptly. I never knew that order to be disregarded on a field of battle, not even by the most inexperienced and insubordinate of troops, unless, indeed, they were already running.

The battle of Camp Beaseland was an artillery duel of fifteen or twenty pieces on a side, lasting hotly from eleven in the morning till six in the evening, with a dash of infantry charging and heavy musketry on either flank, and a dribble of skirmishing along the whole line. Where we were, it was all artillery and skirmishing, noisy and lively enough, but by no means murderous. Bainbridge's regular battery on our right pitched into a Louisiana battery on our left front, and a little beyond it a battery of the Twenty-first Indiana pounded away at the Confederate gunboats and at an advanced earthwork. The loud metallic spang of the brass howitzers, the dull thud of the iron Parrotts, and the shrieking and cracking of the enemy's shells made up a *charivari* long to be remembered.

Meantime, companies moved out here and there from the line of infantry, deployed as skirmishers, advanced to within two or three hundred yards of the breastworks, and opened fire. This drew the Rebel musketry and made things hotter than ever. The order to lie low passed along, and we did the best we could with the cane-hills, wishing that they were bigger. As I lay on my side behind one of these six-inch fortifications, chewing the hardtack which was my only present creature comfort, several balls cut the low weeds which overhung me. Yet, notwithstanding the stunning racket and the quantity of lead and iron flying about, our loss was very small.

Nor could the enemy have suffered more severely, except on our left. There the Seventy-fifth and 114th New York, drawn up in the swampy wood which at that point separated the two armies, repulsed with a close volley of musketry a swarm of Texans who attempted to ford the morass and turn our flank. There, too, the heaviest fire of our batteries was concentrated and made havoc, as I afterward heard, of the enemy's artillery. An officer of one of our skirmishing companies, whose position enabled him to see this part of the enemy's line, assured me, with a jocose exaggeration founded on fact, that "the air was full of horses' tails and bits of harness." But, in a general way, there was very little slaughter for the amount of powder expended. We were not fighting our hardest; we were merely amusing the enemy. The only serious work done was to smash one or two of his gunboats. Meanwhile, it was hoped that Grover was gaining Mouton's rear and so posting himself as to render escape impossible. . . .

About five o'clock an order arrived to move out of range of fire. The skirmishers came in; the men rose and took their places in line; and we marched slowly back to our position of the morning. During the night we fought mosquitoes, not with the idea of amusing them, but in deadly earnest. During the night, also, the colonel in charge of the pickets, a greenhorn of some nine-months' regiment, distinguished himself by an exhibition of the minimum of native military genius. Early in the morning he reported to Weitzel that the enemy had vacated their position.

"How do you know?" demanded the startled general.

"I heard their artillery going off about two o'clock."

"Good God, sir! why didn't you inform me of it immediately?"

"Why, General, I thought you wanted them to clear out; and I didn't like to disturb you after such a hard day's work."

Thus collapsed the plan by which we were to stick like a burr to the enemy and pitch into his rear whenever he should attempt to force his way through Grover.

J. B. Polley

Letter on Truce-Making at Chickamauga 1863

Polley, of Hood's Texas Brigade, explains the mysterious ways of truce-making with the Yankees in Tennesssee, from his A Soldier's Letters to Charming Nellie.

. . . Soon afterward, a truce along the picket lines in front of the Texans was arranged; that is, there was to be no more shooting at each other's pickets—the little killing and wounding done by the practice never compensating for the powder and shot expended, and the discomfort of being always on the alert, night and day.

But the South Carolinians, whose picket line began at our left, their first rifle-pit being within fifty feet of the last one of the First Texas, could make no terms whatever. The Federals charge them with being the instigators and beginners of the war, and, as I am informed, always exclude them from the benefit of truces between the pickets. It is certainly an odd spectacle to see the Carolinians hiding in their rifle-pits and not daring to show their heads, while, not fifty feet away, the Texans sit on the ground playing poker, in plain view and within a hundred yards of the Yankees. Worse than all, the palmetto fellows are not even permitted to visit us in daylight, except in disguise—their new uniforms of gray always betraying them wherever they go. One of them is not only very fond of, but successful at, the game of poker, concluded the other day to risk being shot for the chance of winning the money of the First Texas, and, divesting himself of his

ARTIST UNKNOWN.
*Camp Las Moras,
Texas, March, 1861.*
1861. Pencil.
Library of Congress,
Washington, D.C.

coat, slipped over to the Texas pit an hour before daylight, and by sunrise was giving his whole mind to the noble pastime.

An hour later a keen-sighted Yankee sang out, "Say, you Texas Johnnies! ain't that fellow playing cards, with his back to a sapling, one of them d—d South Carolina secessionists? Seems to me his breeches are newer'n they ought to be." This direct appeal for information placed the Texans between the horns of a dilemma; hospitality demanded the protection of their guest—prudence, the observance of good faith toward the Yankees. The delay in answering obviated the necessity for it by confirming the inquirer's suspicions, and, exclaiming, "D—n him, I just know it is!" he raised his gun quickly to his shoulder and fired. The South Carolinian was too active, though; at the very first movement of the Yankee, he sprang ten feet and disappeared into a gulch that protected him from further assault.

Walt Whitman

Letter of Condolence to a Union Soldier's Parents August 10, 1863

For three years, Whitman was a volunteer nurse in Washington's military hospitals. As one of his nursing duties, he wrote letters of condolence.

Dear Friends: I thought it would be soothing to you to have a few lines about the last days of your son Erastus Haskell, of Company K 141st New York Volunteers—I write in haste, but I have no doubt anything about Erastus will be welcome.

STAUCH. *Kentucky Cavalryman with a Gangrene Infection after Amputation at the Lower Arm.* 1863. Pencil. 8 x 10″. Armed Forces Institute of Pathology, Washington, D.C. Otis Historical Archives, National Museum of Health and Medicine.

From the time he came into Armory-Square, until he died, there was hardly a day but I was with him a portion of the time—if not in the day, then at night (I am merely a friend visiting the wounded and sick soldiers). From almost the first I felt somehow that Erastus was in danger, or at least was much worse then they supposed in the hospital. As he made no complaint, they thought him nothing so bad. I told the doctor of the ward over and over again he was a very sick boy, but he took it lightly, and said he would certainly recover; he said: "I know more about these fever cases than you do—he looks very sick to you, but I shall bring him out all right."

Probably the doctor did his best; at any rate, about a week before Erastus died, he got really alarmed, and after that he and all the doctors tried to help him, but it was too late. Very possibly it would not have made any difference. I think he was broken down before he came to hospital here.

I believe he came here about July 11th; I took to him. He was a quiet young man, behaved always so correct and decent, said little. I used to sit on the side of his bed. I said once, jokingly, "You don't talk much, Erastus, you leave me to do all the talking." He only answered quietly, "I was never much of a talker."

The doctor wanted every one to cheer him up very lively; I was always pleasant and cheerful with him, but never tried to be lively. Only I tried once to tell him amusing narratives, etc., but after I had talked a few minutes, I saw that the effect was not good, and after that I never tried it again. I used to sit by the side of his bed, generally silent. He was oppressed for breath and with the heat, and I would fan him. Occasionally he would want a drink; some days he dozed a good deal; sometimes when I would come in, he woke up, and I would lean down and kiss him. He would reach out his hand and pat my hair and beard as I sat on the bed and leaned over him—it was painful to see the working in his throat to breathe. . . .

One thing was that he could not talk very comfortably at any time—his throat and chest were bad. I have no doubt he had some complaint beside the typhoid. In my limited talks with him, he told me about his brothers and sisters and his parents; wished me to write to them and send them all his love. I think he told me about his brothers being away, living in New York City or elsewhere. . . .

I was very anxious he should be saved, and so were they all; he was well used by attendants; he was tanned and looked well in the face when he came; was in pretty good flesh; never complained; behaved manly and proper. I assure you I was attracted to him very much.—Some nights I sat by his cot till far into the night. The lights would be put out and I sat there silently hour after hour. He seemed to like to have me sit there, but he never cared much to talk.

I shall never forget those nights, in the dark hospital. It was a curious and solemn scene, the sick and wounded lying all around, and this dear young man close by me, lying on what proved to be his deathbed. I do not know his past life, but what I saw and know of, he behaved like a noble boy. I feel if I could have seen him under right circumstances of health, etc., I should have got much attached to him. He made no display or talk; he met his fate like a man. I think you have reason to be proud of such a son and all his relatives have cause to treasure his memory.

He is one of the thousands of our unknown American young men in the ranks about whom there is no record or fame, no fuss made about their dying unknown, but who are the real precious and royal ones of this land, giving up—aye even their young and precious lives—in the country's cause. Poor dear son, though you were not my son, I felt to love you as a son what short time I saw you, sick and dying there.

But it is well as it is—perhaps better. Who knows whether he is not far better off, that patient and sweet young soul, to go, than we are to stay? Farewell, deary boy, it was my opportunity to be with you in your last days. I had no chance to do much for you; nothing could be done—only you did not lay there among strangers without having one near who loved you dearly, and to whom you gave your dying kiss.

Mr. and Mrs. Haskell, I have thus written rapidly whatever came up about Erastus, and must now close. Though we are strangers and shall probably never see each other, I send you and all Erastus' brothers and sisters my love. I live when at home in Brooklyn, New York, in Portland Avenue, fourth floor, north of Myrtle.

SOLDIER LIFE

Abner R. Small
"PORTRAIT OF A PRIVATE"

In his memoirs, Major Small of the 16th Maine offers a pen portrait of the typical Civil War enlisted man.

The ideal picture of a soldier makes a veteran smile. Be a man never so much a man, his importance and conceit dwindle when he crawls into an unteaseled shirt, trousers too short and very baggy behind, coat too long at both ends, shoes with soles like firkin covers, and a cap as shapeless as a feed bag. Let me recall how our private looked to me in the army, in the ranks, a position he chose from pure patriotism. I can see him exactly as I saw him then. He is just in front of me trying to keep his balance and his temper, as he spews from a dry mouth the infernally fine soil of Virginia, and with his hands—he hasn't a handkerchief—wipes the streaks of dirty sweat that make furrows down his unshaven face. No friend of civilian days would recognize him in this most unattractive and disreputable-looking fellow, bowed under fifty-eight pounds of army essentials, and trying to suck a TD.

His suit is a model one, cut after the regulation pattern, fifty thousand at a time, and of just two sizes. If he is a small man, God pity him; and if he is a big man, God pity him still more; for he is an object of ridicule. His forage cap, with its leather visor, when dry curls up, when wet hangs down, and usually covers one or both ears. His army brogans, nothing can ever make shine or even black. Perhaps the coat of muddy blue can be buttoned in front, and it might be lapped and buttoned behind. The tailor never bushels army suits, and he doesn't crease trousers, although he is always generous in reënforcing them with the regulation patch.

The knapsack (which is cut to fit, in the engraving) is an unwieldy burden with its rough, coarse contents of flannel and sole leather and sometimes twenty rounds of am-

BRADY STUDIO, WASHINGTON, D.C.
A Union Volunteer of 1861.
Photograph. Library of Congress,
Washington, D.C.

120

COLORPLATE 33

WINSLOW HOMER. *In Front of Yorktown.* 1862. Oil on canvas. 13¼ × 19½″.
Yale University Art Gallery, New Haven. Gift of Samuel R. Betts, B.A., 1875.

COLORPLATE 34

D. JAMES. *Winter Quarters, Culpeper, Virginia*. 1864. Oil on canvas. 12 × 18″. Virginia Museum of Fine Arts, Richmond. Gift of Edgar William and Bernice Chrysler Garbisch. Photo copyright © 1991 Virginia Museum of Fine Arts.

COLORPLATE 35 *(opposite)*

WILLIAM LUDWELL SHEPPARD. *A Newspaper in the Trenches*. 1901. Watercolor on paper. 11¼ × 8″. Museum of the Confederacy, Richmond. Eleanor S. Brockenbrough Library. Photo by Larry Sherer, copyright © 1985 Time-Life Books, Inc.

COLORPLATE 36

WINSLOW HOMER. *A Rainy Day in Camp.* 1871. Oil on canvas. 19⅞ × 36″.
Metropolitan Museum of Art, New York. Gift of Mrs. William F. Milton, 1923.

Winslow Homer
1871

COLORPLATE 37

SANFORD ROBINSON GIFFORD. *Preaching to the Troops.* 1861.
Oil on canvas. 16 × 30″. Union League Club, New York.

COLORPLATE 38 *(opposite)*

WILLIAM LUDWELL SHEPPARD. *Reveille.* Watercolor on paper. 11¼ × 8″. Museum of the
Confederacy, Richmond. Eleanor S. Brockenbrough Library. Photo by Katherine Wetzel.

COLORPLATE 39

WINSLOW HOMER. *Pitching Horseshoes.* 1865. Oil on canvas. $26\frac{3}{4} \times 53\frac{11}{16}''$.
Harvard University Art Museums, Cambridge. Gift of Mr. and Mrs. Frederic H. Curtiss.

munition extra. Mixed in with these regulation essentials, like beatitudes, are photographs, cards, huswife, Testament, pens, ink, paper, and oftentimes stolen truck enough to load a mule. All this is crowned with a double wool blanket and half a shelter tent rolled in a rubber blanket. One shoulder and the hips support the "commissary department"—an odorous haversack, which often stinks with its mixture of bacon, pork, salt junk, sugar, coffee, tea, desiccated vegetables, rice, bits of yesterday's dinner, and old scraps husbanded with miserly care against a day of want sure to come.

Loaded down, in addition, with a canteen, full cartridge-box, belt, cross belt, and musket, and tramping twenty miles in a hurry on a hot day, our private was a soldier, but not just then a praiser of the soldier's life. I saw him multiplied by thousands. A photograph of any one of them, covered with yellow dust or mosaics of mud, would have served any relation, North or South, and ornamented a mantel, as a true picture of "Our Boy.". . .

Carlton McCarthy

FROM DETAILED MINUTIAE OF SOLDIER LIFE IN THE ARMY OF NORTHERN VIRGINIA

On the Volunteer

A private in the Richmond Howitzers offers these details of the soldier's uniform and gear in this perfectly titled account.

The volunteer of 1861 made extensive preparations for the field. Boots, he thought, were an absolute necessity, and the heavier the soles and longer the tops the better. His pants were stuffed inside the tops of his boots, of course. A double-breasted coat, heavily wadded, with two rows of big brass buttons and a long skirt, was considered comfortable. A small stiff cap, with a narrow brim, took the place of the comfortable "felt," or the shining and towering tile worn in civil life.

Then over all was a huge overcoat, long and heavy, with a cape reaching nearly to the waist. On his back he strapped a knapsack containing a full stock of underwear, soap, towels, comb, brush, looking-glass, tooth-brush, paper and envelopes, pens, ink, pencils, blacking, photographs, smoking and chewing tobacco, pipes, twine string, and cotton strips for wounds and other emergencies, needles and thread, buttons, knife, fork, and spoon, and many other things as each man's idea of what he was to encounter varied. On the outside of the knapsack, solidly folded, were two great blankets and a rubber or oil-cloth. This knapsack, etc., weighed from fifteen to twenty five pounds, sometimes more. All seemed to think it was impossible to have on too heavy clothes, or to have too many conveniences, and each had an idea that to be a good soldier he must be provided against every possible emergency.

In addition to the knapsack, each man had a haversack, more or less costly, some of cloth and some of fine morocco, and stored with provisions always, as though he expected any moment to receive orders to march across the Great Desert, and supply his own wants on the way. A canteen was considered indispensable, and at the outset it was thought prudent to keep it full of water. Many, expecting terrific hand-to-hand encounters, carried revolvers, and even bowie-knives. Merino shirts (and flannel) were thought to be the right thing, but experience demonstrated the contrary. Gloves were also thought to be very necessary and good things to have in winter time, the favorite style being buck gauntlets with long cuffs.

In addition to each man's private luggage, each mess, generally composed of from five to ten men, drawn together by similar tastes and associations, had *its* outfit, consisting of a large camp chest containing skillet, frying pan, coffee boiler, bucket for lard, coffee box, salt box, meal box, flour box, knives, forks, spoons, plates, cups, etc., etc. These chests were so large that eight or ten of them filled up an army wagon, and were so heavy that two strong men had all they could do to get one of them into the wagon. In addition to the chest each mess owned an axe, water bucket, and bread tray. Then the tents of each company, and little sheet-iron stoves, and stove pipe, and the trunks and valises of the company officers, made an immense pile of stuff, so that each company had a small wagon train of its own.

All thought money to be absolutely necessary, and for a while rations were disdained and the mess supplied with the best that could be bought with the mess fund. Quite a large number had a "boy" along to do the cooking and washing. Think of it! a Confederate soldier with a body servant all his own, to bring him a drink of water, black his boots, dust his clothes, cook his corn bread and bacon, and put wood on his fire. . . .

Experience soon demonstrated that boots were not agreeable on a long march. They were heavy and irksome, and when the heels were worn a little one-sided, the wearer would find his ankle twisted nearly out of joint by every unevenness of the road. When thoroughly wet, it was a laborious undertaking to get them off, and worse to get them on in time to answer the morning roll-call. And so, good, strong brogues or brogans, with broad bottoms and big, flat heels, succeeded the boots, and were found much more comfortable and agreeable, easier put on and off, and altogether the more sensible.

A short-waisted and single-breasted jacket usurped the place of the long-tailed coat, and became universal. The enemy noticed this peculiarity, and called the Confederates gray jackets, which name was immediately transferred to those lively creatures which were the constant admirers and inseparable companions of the Boys in Gray and in Blue.

Caps were destined to hold out longer than some other uncomfortable things, but they finally yielded to the demands of comfort and common sense, and a good soft felt hat was worn instead. A man who has never been a soldier does not know, nor indeed can know, the amount of comfort there is in a good soft hat in camp, and how utterly useless is a "soldier hat" as they are generally made. Why the Prussians, with all their experience, wear their heavy, unyielding helmets, and the French their little caps, is a mystery to a Confederate who has enjoyed the comfort of an old slouch.

Overcoats an inexperienced man would think an absolute necessity for men exposed to the rigors of a northern Virginia winter, but they grew scarcer and scarcer; they were found to be a great inconvenience. The men came to the conclusion that the trouble of carrying them on hot days outweighed the comfort of having them when the cold day arrived. Besides they found that life in the open air hardened them to such an extent that changes in the temperature were not felt to any degree. Some clung to their overcoats to the last, but the majority got tired lugging them around, and either discarded them altogether, or trusted to capturing one about the time it would be needed. Nearly every overcoat in the army in the latter years was one of Uncle Sam's captured from his boys.

The knapsack vanished early in the struggle. It was inconvenient to "change" the underwear too often, and the disposition not to change grew, as the knapsack was found to gall the back and shoulders, and weary the man before half the march was accomplished. The better way was to dress out and out, and wear that outfit until the enemy's knapsacks, or the folks at home supplied a change. Certainly it did not pay to carry around clean clothes while waiting for the time to use them.

Very little washing was done, as a matter of course. Clothes once given up were parted with forever. There were good reasons for this: cold water would not cleanse them or destroy the vermin, and hot water was not always to be had. One blanket to each man was found to be as much as could be carried, and amply sufficient for the severest weather. This was carried generally by rolling it lengthwise, with the rubber cloth outside, tying the ends of the roll together, and throwing the loop thus made over the left shoulder with the ends fastened together hanging under the right arm.

The haversack held its own to the last, and was found practical and useful. It very seldom, however, contained rations, but was used to carry all the articles generally carried in the knapsack; of course the stock was small. Somehow or other, many men managed to do without the haversack, and carried absolutely nothing but what they wore and had in their pockets.

The infantry threw away their heavy cap boxes and cartridge boxes, and carried their caps and cartridges in their pockets. Canteens were very useful at times, but they were as a general thing discarded. They were not much used to carry water, but were found useful when the men were driven to the necessity of foraging, for conveying buttermilk, cider, sorghum, etc., to camp. A good strong tin cup was found better than a canteen, as it was easier to fill at a well or spring, and was serviceable as a boiler for making coffee when the column halted for the night. . . .

Strong cotton was adopted in place of flannel and merino, for two reasons: first, because easier to wash; and second, because the vermin did not propagate so rapidly in cotton as in wool. Common white cotton shirts and drawers proved the best that could be used by the private soldier.

Gloves to any but a mounted man were found useless, worse than useless. With the gloves on, it was impossible to handle an axe, buckle harness, load a musket, or handle a rammer at the piece. Wearing them was found to be simply a habit, and so, on the principle that the less luggage the less labor, *they* were discarded.

The camp-chest soon vanished. The brigadiers and major-generals, even, found them too troublesome, and soon they were left entirely to the quarter-masters and commissar-

TIMOTHY H. O'SULLIVAN.
*Noncommissioned Officers
Mess of Company D,
93rd New York Infantry,
Bealton, Virginia.* August,
1863. Photograph.
Library of Congress,
Washington, D.C.

ies. One skillet and a couple of frying pans, a bag for flour or meal, another bag for salt, sugar, and coffee, divided by a knot tied between served the purpose as well. The skillet passed from mess to mess. Each mess generally owned a frying pan, but often one served a company. The oil-cloth was found to be as good as the wooden tray for making up the dough. The water bucket held its own to the last!

Tents were *rarely seen*. All the poetry about the *"tented field"* died. Two men slept together, each having a blanket and an oil-cloth; one oil-cloth went next to the ground. The two laid on this, covered themselves with two blankets, protected from the rain with the second oil-cloth on top, and slept very comfortably through rain, snow or hail, as it might be.

Very little money was seen in camp. The men did not expect, did not care for, or often get any pay, and they were not willing to deprive the old folks at home of their little supply, so they learned to do without any money. . . .

Reduced to the minimum, the private soldier consisted of one man, one hat, one jacket, one shirt, one pair of pants, one pair of drawers, one pair of shoes, and one pair of socks. His baggage was one blanket, one rubber blanket, and one haversack. The haversack generally contained smoking tobacco and a pipe, and a small piece of soap, with temporary additions of apples, persimmons, blackberries, and such other commodities as he could pick up on the march.

The company property consisted of two or three skillets and frying pans, which were sometimes carried in the wagon, but oftener in the hands of the soldiers. The infantrymen generally preferred to stick the handle of the frying pan in the barrel of a musket, and so carry it.

The wagon trains were devoted entirely to the transportation of ammunition and commissary and quartermaster's stores, which had not been issued. Rations which had become company property, and the baggage of the men, when they had any, was carried by the men themselves. If, as was sometimes the case, three days' rations were issued at one time and the troops ordered to cook them, and be prepared to march, they did cook them, *and eat them if possible,* so as to avoid the labor of carrying them. It was not such an undertaking either, to eat three days' rations in one, as frequently none had been issued for more than a day, and when issued were cut down one half.

The infantry found out that bayonets were not of much use, and did not hesitate to throw them, with the scabbard, away.

The artillerymen, who started out with heavy sabres hanging to their belts, stuck them up in the mud as they marched, and left them for the ordnance officers to pick up and turn over to the cavalry.

The cavalrymen found sabres very tiresome when swung to the belt, and adopted the plan of fastening them to the saddle on the left side, with the hilt in front and in reach of the hand. Finally sabres got very scarce even among the cavalrymen, who relied more and more on their short rifles.

No soldiers ever marched with less to encumber them, and none marched faster or held out longer.

John D. Billings

FROM HARDTACK AND COFFEE

On Army Rations

In his memoir, a Massachusetts soldier displays his perfect memory for the staples of an army diet.

I will now give a complete list of the rations served out to the rank and file, as I remember them. They were salt pork, fresh beef, salt beef, rarely ham or bacon, hard bread, soft bread, potatoes, an occasional onion, flour, beans, split pease, rice, dried apples, dried peaches, desiccated vegetables, coffee, tea, sugar, molasses, vinegar, candles, soap, pepper, and salt.

It is scarcely necessary to state that these were not all served out at one time. There was but one kind of meat served at once, and this, to use a Hibernianism, was usually pork. When it was hard bread, it wasn't *soft* bread or flour, and when it was pease or beans it wasn't rice.

Here is just what a single ration comprised, that is, what a soldier was entitled to have in one day. He should have had twelve ounces of pork or bacon, *or* one pound four ounces of salt or fresh beef; one pound six ounces of soft bread or flour, *or* one pound of hard bread, *or* one pound four ounces of corn meal. With every hundred such rations there should have been distributed one peck of beans or pease; ten pounds of rice or hominy; ten pounds of green coffee, *or* eight pounds of roasted and ground, *or* one pound eight ounces of tea; fifteen pounds of sugar; one pound four ounces of candles; four pounds of soap; two quarts of salt; four quarts of vinegar; four ounces of pepper; a half bushel of potatoes when practicable, and one quart of molasses. Desiccated potatoes or desiccated compressed vegetables might be substituted for the beans, pease, rice, hominy, or fresh potatoes. Vegetables, the dried fruits, pickles, and pickled cabbage were occasionally issued to prevent scurvy, but in small quantities. . . .

I will speak of the rations more in detail, beginning with the hard bread, or, to use the name by which it was known in the Army of the Potomac, *Hardtack*. What was hardtack? It was a plain flour-and-water biscuit. Two which I have in my possession as mementos measure three and one-eighth by two and seven-eighths inches, and are nearly half an inch thick. Although these biscuits were furnished to organizations by weight, they were dealt out to the men by number, nine constituting a ration in some regiments, and ten in others; but there were usually enough for those who wanted more, as some men would not draw them. While hardtack was nutritious, yet a hungry man could eat his ten in a short time and still be hungry. When they were poor and fit objects for the soldiers' wrath, it was due to one of three conditions: First, they may have been so hard that they could not be bitten; it then required a very strong blow of the fist to break them. The cause of this hardness it would be difficult for one not an expert to determine. This variety certainly well deserved their name. They could not be *soaked* soft, but after a time took on the elasticity of gutta-percha.

The second condition was when they were mouldy or wet, as sometimes happened, and should not have been given to the soldiers. I think this condition was often due to their having been boxed up too soon after baking. It certainly was frequently due to exposure to the weather. It was no uncommon sight to see thousands of boxes of hard bread piled up at some railway station or other place used as a base of supplies, where they were only imperfectly sheltered from the weather, and too often not sheltered at all. The failure of inspectors to do their full duty was one reason that so many of this sort reached the rank and file of the service.

The third condition was when from storage they had become infested with maggots and weevils. These weevils were, in my experience, more abundant than the maggots. They were a little, slim, brown bug an eighth of an inch in length, and were great *bores* on a small scale, having the ability to completely riddle the hardtack. I believe they never interfered with the hardest variety. . . .

But hardtack was not so bad an article of food, even when traversed by insects, as may be supposed. Eaten in the dark, no one could tell the difference between it and hardtack that was untenanted. It was no uncommon occurrence for a man to find the surface of his pot of coffee swimming with weevils, after breaking up hardtack in it, which had come out of the fragments only to drown; but they were easily skimmed off, and left no distinctive flavor behind. If a soldier cared to do so, he could expel the weevils by heating the bread at the fire. The maggots did not budge in that way. . . .

Having gone so far, I know the reader will be interested to learn of the styles in which this particular article was served up by the soldiers. I say *styles* because I think there must have been at least a score of ways adopted to make this simple *flour tile* more edible. Of course, many of them were eaten just as they were received—hardtack *plain*; then I have already spoken of their being crumbed in coffee, giving the "hardtack and coffee." Probably more were eaten in this way than in any other, for they thus frequently furnished the soldier his breakfast and supper. But there were other and more appetizing ways of preparing them. Many of the soldiers, partly through a slight taste for the business but more from force of circumstances, became in their way and opinion experts in the art of cooking the greatest variety of dishes with the smallest amount of capital.

Some of these crumbed them in soups for want of other thickening. For this purpose they served very well. Some crumbed them in cold water, then fried the crumbs in the juice and fat of meat. A dish akin to this one, which was said to "make the hair curl," and certainly was indigestible enough to satisfy the cravings of the most ambitious dyspeptic, was prepared by soaking hardtack in cold water, then frying them brown in pork fat, salting to taste. Another name for this dish was "skillygalee." Some liked them toasted, either to crumb in coffee, or, if a sutler was at hand whom they could patronize, to butter. The toasting generally took place from the end of a split stick, and if perchance they dropped out of it into the camp-fire, and were not recovered quickly enough to prevent them from getting pretty well charred, they were not thrown away on that account, being then thought good for weak bowels.

Sidney Lanier
Letter on Life in Winter Camp 1861

The Georgia writer reports to his brother on life in camp near Norfolk, Virginia, during the first winter of the war.

———————

You would not think, my dear Cliff, that I was a soldier, enduring the frowns of "grim-visaged war," if you could see me with slippers and smoking-cap on, pipe in months, writing to you on a real pine table, surrounded by ten noisy boys, in a room with ten sleeping-bunks built against its walls, and a "great and glorious" fire blazing in the fireplace—I can hardly realize that I am in a *house*, but find myself continually asking myself if it is not some delightful dream; it is impossible for you to imagine with what delight I hail a real, bona-fide *room* as a habitation for the winter, unless you had, as I have, shivered in cold tents for the last few months, which the rains beat through and the winds blew down at every available opportunity (and oh pluvial Gods! with what astonishing frequency the said availables *did* occur!): unless you had become accustomed, 1st, to going to sleep with the expectation that your tent would blow down and the rains wet you to the skin before you could get your clothes on; and, 2nd, to having the said expectations *realized* in the most satisfactory manner; unless you had been in the habit of eating in a drenching rain which diluted your coffee (without any sugar)

CONRAD WISE CHAPMAN. *Scene Near Corinth, Mississippi, May 10, 1862.* 1862. Oil on board. 5½ x 9¼". Valentine Museum, Richmond.

before you could drink it, and made mush of your biscuit before you could eat it; unless you had customarily made your ablutions in a mud puddle (which you had previously caused a swine to vacate for that purpose); unless you had, in short, been as horribly uncomfortable as it is possible for a man to be.—The room, which so excites my delight, is the one which my mess occupies in our winter-quarters, which we have been actively engaged in building for two weeks past—; and, by the way, you ought to have seen me carpentering: I have hammered, sawed, filed, planed, toted bricks and mortar in a hod (real Irish style), built partitions, bunks and gun-racks, shingled roofs, and done various and sundry feats in the house carpentering line.

We had snow night before last, which is yet on the ground; and the rest of the night was occupied with a terrible storm of wind and sleet, which had nearly blown down our winter quarters; had we been in tents we would have suffered severely.

Tell Uncle William that I took the breech-loading carbine, which he gave me, to a gunsmith in Norfolk; who hummed and hawed about it, until he made me mad, when I took the gun back to my tent and, after three days of incessant work, got the breech-chamber open! It then took me about a week to clean it out; it was the rustiest affair I have ever seen; I succeeded, however, at length, in getting it in order; and made some very good shots with it, at a quarter of a mile's distance.

It is rumored in camp that our Battalion may possibly be discharged in January, tho' I am not disposed to attach much importance to the rumor.

A steamboat came up to Norfolk from Fortress Monroe yesterday, under a flag of truce; among other items, she brought news that England has formally demanded of the Federal Government a full apology, or a fight, on account of the Mason and Slidell affair—. If the news be true, I think it extremely probable that we will have peace in the Spring.

John D. Billings

FROM HARDTACK AND COFFEE

On the Ironclad Warriors and the Steel-Armor Enterprise

In the industrial North, at least, it appeared possible to be a live hero. The use of body armor by Yankee soldiers peaked during the Peninsula campaign of 1862.

There was another invention that must have been sufficiently popular to have paid the manufacturer a fair rate on his investment, and that was the steel-armor enterprise. There were a good many men who were anxious to be heroes, but they were particular. They preferred to be *live* heroes. They were willing to go to war and fight as never man fought before, if they could only be insured against bodily harm. They were not willing to assume all the risks which an enlistment involved, without securing something in the shape of a drawback. Well, the iron tailors saw and appreciated the situation and sufferings of this class of men, and came to the rescue with a vest of steel armor, worth, as I remember it, about a dozen dollars, and greaves. The latter, I think, did not find so ready a market as the vests, which were comparatively common. These iron-clad warriors admitted that when panoplied for the fight their sensations were much as they might be if they were dressed up in an old-fashioned air-tight stove; still, with all the discomforts of this casing, they felt a little safer with it on than off in battle, and they reasoned that it was the right and duty of every man to adopt all honorable measures to assure his safety in the line of duty. This seemed solid reasoning, surely; but, in spite of it all, a large number of these vests never saw Rebeldom. Their owners were subjected to such a storm of ridicule that they could not bear up under it. It was a stale yet common joke to remind them that in action these vests must be worn behind. Then, too, the ownership of one of them was taken as evidence of faint-heartedness. Of this the owner was often reminded; so that when it came to the packing of the knapsack for departure, the vest, taking as it did considerable space, and adding no small weight to his already too heavy burden, was in many cases left behind. The officers, whose opportunity to take baggage along was greater, clung to them longest; but I think that they were quite generally abandoned with the first important reduction made in the luggage.

John Hampden Chamberlayne
Letter Describing a Party
September 6, 1862

On the march to Second Bull Run in August 1862, Jackson's men captured Yankee general John Pope's main supply base, as described by a Confederate artillery officer in a letter home; from Ham Chamberlayne—Virginian.

FREDERICK CITY, FREDERICK CO. MARYLAND

Saturday Sept. 6th 1862

My dear Mother

I am brimful of matter, as an egg of meat. Since my letter, date unknown, from camp in Orange, near Raccoon Ford—there has been no chance to send a letter & therefore I have not written; & now I am at a loss to tell when I can send this. . . .

Now comes the great wonder. Starting up the bank of the River we marched through Amosville in Rappahannock Co., still farther up, crossed the Rappahannock within ten miles of the Blue Ridge, marched by strange country paths, across open fields & comfortable homesteads, by a little town called Orleans in Fauquier on & on as if we would never cease—to Salem on the Manassas Gap R. R. reaching it after midnight; up again by day & still on, along the Manassas Gap R. R. meeting crowds along the road, all welcoming, cheering staring with blank amazement, so all day Tuesday the 26th through White plains, Haymarket Thoroughfare Gap in Bull Run Mountains, Gainesville to Bristow Station on the Orange & Alexandria R. R., making the distance from Amosville to Bristow (between 45 & 50 miles) within the 48 hours. We burned up at Bristow 2 or three Railway trains & moved on to Manassas Junction on Wednesday taking our prisoners with us. Ewells Division brought up the rear, fighting all the way a force that Pope had sent up from Warrenton supposing us a cavalry party.

Upon reaching the Junction we met a Brigade the 1st New Jersey which had been sent from Alex^ia on the same supposition, we at once & of course they even were fools enough to send in a flag demanding our surrender; at once & of course we scattered the Brigade, taking several hundred prisoners, killing & wounding many & among them the Brig-Gen. Taylor, who has since died.

TIMOTHY H. O'SULLIVAN. *Railroad Rolling Stock at Manassas Junction Destroyed by Jackson's Men.* August, 1862. Photograph. Library of Congress, Washington, D.C.

At the Junction was a large store depôt, 5 or six pieces of artillery, two trains containing probably 200 large cars loaded down with many millions worth of qr mr. & Commissary stores; beside these there were very large sutlers depôts full of everything; in short there was collected there in a square mile an amount & variety of property such as I had never conceived of (I speak soberly). Twas a curious sight to see our ragged & famished men helping themselves to every imaginable article of luxury or necessity whether of clothing, food or what not; for my part I got a tooth brush, a box of candles, a quantity of lobster salad, a barrel of coffee & other things wh. I forget. But I must hurry on for I have not time to tell the hundredth part & the scene utterly beggars description.

A part of us hunted that Brigade like scattered partridges over the hills just to the right of the Battlefield of the 18th July /61 while the rest were partly plundering partly fighting the forces coming on us from Warrenton. Our men we had been living on roasted corn since crossing Rappahannock, & we had brought no new wagons so we could carry little away of the riches before us. But the men could eat for one meal at least, so they were marched up and as much of everything eatable served out as they could carry To see a starving man eating lobster salad & drinking wine rhine wine, barefooted & in tatters was curious; the whole thing is indescribable, I'll tell you sometime may be. . . .

Norwood Penrose Hallowell

On Training the 54th Massachusetts

A Massachusetts officer, in his Letters and Papers, *describes the approach of Robert Gould Shaw, a white officer, to his regiment, the all-black 54th Massachusetts.*

Colonel Robert Gould Shaw was not a sentimentalist. He imposed the strict discipline of the Second Regiment, from which he came, upon the Fifty-fourth. The men of a slave regiment required, and in the case of the First South Carolina received treatment very different from that required by mixed regiments like the Fifty-fourth and Fifty-fifth. In a slave regiment the harsher forms of punishment were, or ought to have been, unknown, so that every suggestion of slavery might be avoided. This was Colonel T. W. Higginson's enlightened method—the method of kindness, and it was successful. Colonel Shaw's method was the method of coercion, and it too was successful. The unruly members of the Fifty-fourth and Fifty-fifth were stood on barrels, bucked, gagged and, if need be, shot; in fact, treated as white soldiers were in all well-disciplined regiments. The squads of recruits which arrived at Readville for the Fifty-fifth could hardly at first sight have been called picked men. They were poor and ragged. Upon arrival they were marched to the neighboring pond, disrobed, washed and uniformed. Their old clothes were burnt. The transformation was quite wonderful. The recruit was very much pleased with the uniform. He straightened up, grew inches taller, lifted, not shuffled, his feet, began at once to try, and to try hard, to take the position of the soldier, the facings and other preliminary drill, so that his ambition to carry "one of those muskets" might be gratified. When finally he was entrusted with the responsible duties of a guard, there was nothing quite so magnificent and, let me add, quite so reliable, as the colored volunteer. The effect of camp discipline on his character was very marked. His officers were gentlemen who understood the correct orthography and pronunciation of the word "negro." For the first time in his life he found himself respected, and entrusted with duties, for the proper performance of which he would be held to a strict accountability. Crossing the camp lines by connivance of the guard was almost unknown. "Running guard" was an experiment too dangerous to try. The niceties of guard-mounting and guard-duty, the absolute steadiness essential to a successful dress-parade, were all appreciated and faithfully observed. The cleanliness of the barracks and camp grounds at Readville was a delight. Not a scrap of loose floating paper or stuff of any kind was permitted. The muskets, the accoutrements, were kept clean and polished. Every one was interested, every one did his best. The Sunday morning inspections discovered a degree of perfection that received much praise from several regular as well as veteran volunteer officers. It is not extravagant to say that thousands of strangers who visited the camp were instantly converted by what they saw. The aptitude of the colored volunteer to learn the manual of arms, to execute readily the orders for company and regimental movements, and his apparent inability to march out of time at once arrested the attention of every officer. His power of imitation was great, his memory for such movements was good, and his ear for time or cadence perfect. You may call the imitative power a sign of inferiority, or what you will. We have now to do with the negro as a soldier, and as such it may be accurately said that the average colored soldier adapts himself more readily to the discipline of a camp, and acquires what is called the drill, in much less time than the average white soldier. These characteristics stand out clear and are undisputed by those who have had experience in both kinds of regiments. Treated kindly and respectfully, the average col-

Guard Detail, 107th U.S. Colored Infantry, Fort Corcoran, Washington, D.C. 1864. Photograph. Library of Congress, Washington, D.C.

ored citizen is the most inoffensive of persons. He prefers to get out of rather than in your way. Innately he is a gentleman. Instinctively he touches his hat when passing. The requirements of military discipline were very favorable for the full development of these traits, so much so that in the matter of etiquette and polite manners one felt that he was in command of a regiment of a thousand men—each man a possible Lord Chesterfield.

William Stillwell
A Soldier's Letter to His Wife
March 23, 1864

A Georgia soldier writes home.

Greenville, Tennessee : March 23, 1864

My dearest Mollie:

Although I have received but one letter from you since my return and that has been answered long ago, yet I feel like writing and of the abundance of the heart the mouth speakest. And as you are the light, love and pleasure of my life, I know you will excuse me for writing so often to one whose presence can give happiness and pleasure.

I dreamed a most delightful dream last night. I went to sleep after commending you and our sweet children to God. I was thinking how sweetly you were lying in bed, perhaps not asleep but resting your weary body and thinking of the one on earth most dear, with one [child] on each side. Oh, how sweet! Thus I was thinking when I fell asleep. I thought we were together and had walked into a garden of flowers. Oh, it was so beautiful! We had been walking hand in hand. We came to a pretty bunch of flowers and stopped

WINSLOW HOMER. *Reveille.* 1865. Oil on canvas. 13¼ x 9½". Photo courtesy of Wildenstein & Co., New York.

to look at them, one on either side. I thought you raised your head up to see what I was doing. I looked at you and you smiled. It pleased me to the heart. I sprang over the flowers to catch you around the waist and just as I caught at you, someone called my name and you vanished from my sight and was gone. I awoke. Someone was calling me. Oh, to think that you would treat me so, if you had just stayed until I could have kissed you once more! I would not take anything for my dream.

Your spirits must have been hovering around me here. Yet it was so lovely and sweet. I was so much delighted and happy. But to think that you would leave me thus without allowing me to embrace you or to kiss your hand! Say what made you do me so, you loving creature! I would have been happy all day if you had just given me one kiss. Oh, don't do me so no more, my dearest Wife! Leave me not thus in anguish and pain but again when we walk among the flowers, let me embrace thee and kiss thy loving brow and be not scared off by anyone that calls my name! I wish they had been somewhere else and then I could have kissed you and been happy once more. I thank [the] God of dreams, for thus making me happy once and hope he will give me another visit soon, and, if so, I hope no one will interfere with my happiness. For I don't have those blessed opportunities often. Still, I am happy today to think that I once more was by thy side amidst flowers and did see thee smile once more, one of those bewitching smiles which only those that love can give. Oh, my dearest, do smile once more upon your unworthy Husband, one of those sweet smiles that only you can give. Forgive me, my dear, if I cause you to shed a tear. If I do, I know it will be a tear of love and not of grief. Oh, Mollie, I have loved as never man loved almost. Come tonight and let me kiss you, dear!

WAR AT SEA

James Keenan

Letter on the Success of the Merrimack

A Georgia soldier describes for his wife the historic contest between the ironclad Merrimack *and the Federal wooden warships in Hampton Roads on March 8, 1862. The next day, the "ironclad battery" of the Federals—the* Monitor—*fought the* Merrimack *to a draw.*

Norfolk, Virginia : March 11, 1862

Dear:

Your favor of the 6th came to hand two or three days ago, but I restrained my first impulse to answer immediately until the present, in anticipation of the stirring events of the 9th and 10th, of which you have been already informed by the papers. As what I saw may prove interesting, I will write briefly. I told you in a former letter, "The *Merrimack* is a success." So I now have the pleasure of verifying my prospective opinion by actual observation. Fortunately, I went to town Saturday morning, and at eleven o'clock a gun was fired at the Navy Yard, which appeared to be the signal for something. In an instant the whole city was in an uproar. Women, children, men on horseback and on foot were running down towards the river from every conceivable direction, shouting, "The

Merrimack is going down." And sure enough, upon approaching the river, I saw the huge monster swung loose from her moorings and making her way down the river with the gun boats *Beaufort* and *Raleigh* a little piece in the rear. The morning was unusually fine, in pleasing contrast with the miserable weather that we have been tortured with so long. A good portion of her crew were on top and received the enthusiastic cheers from the excited populace without a single response. Everything betokened serious business, for the heaviest ships of the enemy lay but a few miles below, like sullen bull-dogs ready to seize man or beast by the throat at the slightest provocation. Just imagine a house 150 feet long, sunk three feet below the eaves, pierced about one-half way up for three guns on each side and three portholes at bow and stern through which last two pivot guns worked, and you have an exact picture of the *Merrimack*, now called the *Virginia*.

Although Hampton Roads is a large expanse of water, yet it is not navigable for vessels of such draft as the *Merrimack*, consequently she had to traverse 14 to 15 miles in keeping the channel running down until opposite Sewell's Point and then turning up the James River channel and making for the blockading vessels of Newport News. So quietly did the *Merrimack* go that we could not observe any stir either among the ships or at Newport News batteries, until one of our little gunboats took a short cut and fired at the *Cumberland*. Then some stir was observable on board both the *Cumberland* and *Congress*. Both vessels cleared their decks for action and coolly waited for the nondescript. The *Merrimack* never halted nor fired a gun in reply to the *Cumberland*, which was firing away with desperation. You may be able to partly imagine the great anxiety which prevailed along the shore, now lined with thousands of anxious spectators. Everyone said, "Why don't the *Merrimack* fire? The *Cumberland* will sink her &c. &c." But she kept steadily on making directly for her adversary. When she came within a few yards, she fired her bow gun, which went clear through the other and, yet continuing on her course, drove her iron prow right into the *Cumberland*'s side, crushing all before her. The crew fought as the vessel went down. Their last guns were fired as the men stood knee deep in water. After the collision, the *Merrimack* backed out and started for the *Congress*. This vessel fired rapidly, but seeing the fate of its consort she started to run ashore. This she did. But in the meantime she was so riddled with shot that she became perfectly useless and struck her colors. The *Beaufort* then went up to her to take off the

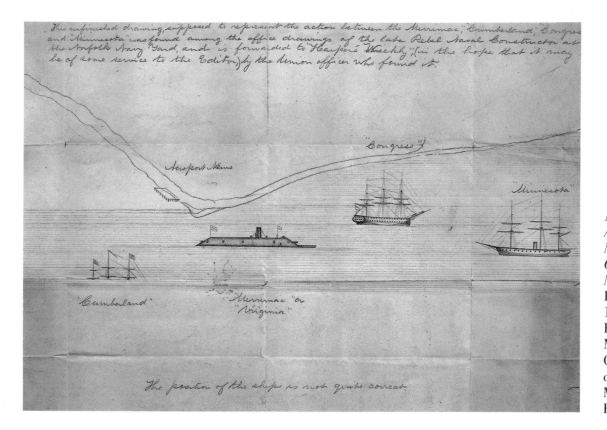

wounded and crew. The sight on board was sickening. Arms, legs and mutilated bodies were lying in every direction on this vessel. While our men were assisting, the enemy fired with minié muskets at friend and foe, killing several of their own men and ours. When Captain Buchanan saw this, he commenced firing hot shot into the already surrendered *Congress*. At this the survivors raised white handkerchiefs as a protection against the murderous fire of the *Merrimack*. During the engagement between the ships, the enemy shore batteries were hammering away at the *Merrimack* but without avail. When the *Cumberland* was sinking, her captain walked out on the bowsprit and directed the movements of his crew. The captain of the *Beaufort* ran up in speaking distance and asked him to surrender so that he might make some effort to save him and crew. But he shook his head and said, "No, never!" and went down waving the U.S. colors in his hand. Out of a crew of over four hundred, very few survived. After dark, a boat's crew went aboard the *Congress* and set her on fire. About 12 o'clock, her magazine exploded with a terrific noise, shaking houses for many miles around. While this engagement was going on, the *Minnesota*, *St. Lawrence* and *Roanoke* started from Old Point to Newport News. Passing Sewell's Point, the battery opened on them and fired guns which had never been fired before. It is quite certain that some damage was done them at this point, but not enough to stop them. The *Minnesota* mistook the right channel and got aground, and the *Merrimack* paid her compliments to her by moonlight. Thus ended Saturday's conflict: two splendid ships destroyed, another aground and the *Roanoke* backed down to Fortress Monroe.

Sunday morning, we all repaired to the shore three miles distant and stood watching the movements. At 8 o'clock A.M. the *Merrimack* started out from under Sewell's Point and attacked two tugs which were going up to get the *Minnesota* off. One shell exploded over one of the tugs and sunk her immediately. About 11 o'clock A.M., the *Merrimack* got aground, and an ironclad battery from Fortress Monroe gave her some heavy blows. But after awhile she got off and tried to run this iron steamer down. This, it is supposed, would have destroyed her, but it was then discovered that she had lost the iron prow in the engagement with the *Cumberland* the day previous. This collision caused the *Merrimack* to leak considerably, at the same time injuring the other much, for it withdrew towards Old Point. The *Merrimack* steamed up to this city and goes into the dock for repairs. Her armor shows signs of rough handling. Still, everyone is rejoiced at the great success of the day. Our total loss in killed and wounded does not exceed seventeen, while eight hundred will hardly cover theirs.

Nathaniel Hawthorne
FROM "CHIEFLY ABOUT WAR MATTERS"
On a New Kind of Naval Warfare

Visiting the union fleet in Hampton Roads in 1862, New England man-of-letters Hawthorne reflects, for the Atlantic Monthly, *on the revolution in naval warfare, fought now "with only the clank and smash of iron."*

The waters around Fortress Monroe were thronged with a gallant array of ships of war and transports, wearing the Union flag—"Old Glory," as I hear it called in these days.

A little withdrawn from our national fleet lay two French frigates, and in another direction an English sloop, under that manner which always makes itself visible, like a red portent in the air, wherever there is strife.

In pursuance of our official duty (which had no ascertainable limits), we went on board the flagship, and were shown over every part of her, and down into her depths, inspecting her gallant crew, her powerful armament, her mighty engines, and her furnaces, where the fires are always kept burning, as well at midnight as at noon, so that it would require only five minutes to put the vessel under full steam. This vigilance has been felt necessary ever since the "Merrimac" made that terrible dash from Norfolk. Splendid as she is, however, and provided with all but the very latest improvements in naval armament, the "Minnesota" belongs to a class of vessels that will be built no more, nor ever fight another battle—being as much a thing of the past as any of the ships of Queen Elizabeth's time, which grappled with the galleons of the Spanish Armada.

On her quarter deck, an elderly flag officer was pacing to-and-fro, with a self-conscious dignity to which a touch of the gout or rheumatism perhaps contributed a little additional stiffness. He seemed to be a gallant gentleman, but of the old, slow and pompous school of naval worthies, who have grown up amid rules, forms and etiquette which were adopted full-blown from the British navy into ours, and are somewhat too cumbrous for the quick spirit of today.

This order of nautical heroes will probably go down, along with the ships in which they fought valourously and strutted most intolerably. How can an admiral condescend to go to sea in an iron pot? What space and elbow room can be found for quarter-deck

JAMES F. GIBSON.
Effect of the Fire from the C. S. S. Virginia on the Turret of the U. S. S. Monitor. July, 1862. Photograph. Library of Congress, Washington, D.C.

COLORPLATE 40

WINSLOW HOMER. *The Briarwood Pipe*. 1864. Oil on canvas. 16⅞ × 14¾".
The Cleveland Museum of Art. Mr. and Mrs. William H. Marlatt Fund, 44.524.

COLORPLATE 41

WINSLOW HOMER. *Punishment for Intoxication.* 1863. Oil on canvas. 17 × 13″.
Canajoharie Library and Art Gallery, Canajoharie, New York.

COLORPLATE 42

WINSLOW HOMER. *Playing Old Soldier.* 1863. Oil on canvas. 16 × 12″. Museum of Fine Arts, Boston. Ellen Kalleran Gardner Fund. Photo copyright © 1985 Museum of Fine Arts, Boston.

COLORPLATE 43

JAMES HOPE. *The Army of the Potomac.* 1865. Oil on canvas. 17¾ × 41¾″. Museum of Fine Arts, Boston. M. and M. Karolik Collection. Photo copyright © 1991 Museum of Fine Arts, Boston. *Soldier-artist Hope pictured McClellan's army at Cumberland Landing during the Peninsula campaign.*

COLORPLATE 44

WINSLOW HOMER. *The Bright Side.* 1865. Oil on canvas. 13¼ × 17½".
The Fine Arts Museums of San Francisco. Gift of Mr. and Mrs. John D. Rockefeller, 3rd.

COLORPLATE 45 *(opposite, above)*

GIOVANNI PONTICELLI. *The Mud March.* ca. 1863. Oil on canvas. 24 × 42¾". West Point
Museum, United States Military Academy, West Point, New York. *A Federal advance in January
1863 stymied by the elements.*

COLORPLATE 46 *(opposite, below)*

DAVID GILMOUR BLYTHE. *General Abner Doubleday Watching His Troops Cross the Potomac.*
No date. Oil on canvas. 31 × 41". National Baseball Library, Cooperstown, New York.

COLORPLATE 47

EDWIN FORBES. *Marching in the Rain After Gettysburg.* No date. Oil on canvas.
13¹³⁄₁₆ × 29¾". Library of Congress, Washington, D.C.

COLORPLATE 48

JAMES WALKER. *Union Cavalry Near Lookout Mountain.* 1863-1864. Oil on canvas.
20 × 40". American National Bank and Trust Company, Chattanooga.

dignity in the cramped look-out of the "Monitor," or even in the twenty-feet diameter of her cheese-box?

All the pomp and splendor of naval warfare are gone by. Henceforth there must come up a race of enginemen and smoke-blackened canoneers, who will hammer away at their enemies under the direction of a single pair of eyes; and even heroism—so deadly a grip is Science laying on our noble possibilities—will become a quality of very minor importance, when its possessor cannot break through the iron crust of his own armament and give the world a glimpse of it.

At no great distance from the "Minnesota" lay the strangest-looking craft I ever saw. It was a platform of iron, so nearly level with the water that the swash of waves broke over it, under the impulse of a very moderate breeze; and, on this platform was raised a circular structure, likewise of iron, and rather broad and capacious, but of no great height. It could not be called a vessel at all; it was a machine—and I have seen one of somewhat similar appearance employed in cleaning out the docks; or for lack of a better similitude, it looked like a gigantic rattrap; it was ugly, questionable, suspicious, evidently mischievous—nay, I will allow myself to call it devilish; for this was the new war fiend, destined, along with others of the same breed, to annihilate whole navies and batter down old supremacies.

The wooden walls of Old England cease to exist, and a whole history of naval renown reaches its period, now that the "Monitor" comes smoking into view; while the billows dash over what seems her deck, and storms bury even her turret in green water, as she burrows and snorts along, oftener under the surface than above. The singularity of the object has betrayed me into a more ambitious vein of description than I often indulge, and, after all, I might as well have contented myself with simply saying that she looked very queer. . . .

The inaccessibility, the apparent impregnability, of this submerged iron fortress are most satisfactory; the officers and crew get down through a little hole in the deck, hermetically seal themselves, and go below; and until they see fit to reappear, there would seem to be no power given to man whereby they can be brought to light. A storm of cannonshot damages them no more than a handful of dried peas. We saw the shot marks made by the great artillery of the "Merrimac" on the outer casing of the iron tower; they were about the breadth and depth of shallow saucers, almost imperceptible dents, with no corresponding bulge on the interior surface. In fact, the thing looked altogether too safe, though it may not prove quite an agreeable predicament to be thus boxed up in impenetrable iron, with the possibility, one would imagine, of being sent to the bottom of the sea, and, even there, not drowned, but stifled.

Nothing, however, can exceed the confidence of the officers in this new craft. It was a pleasure to see their benign exultation in her powers of mischief, and the delight with which they exhibited the circumvolutory movement of the tower, the quick thrusting forth of the immense guns to deliver their ponderous missiles, and then the immediate recoil, and the security behind the closed portholes. Yet even this will not long be the last and most terrible improvement in the science of war. Already we hear of vessels the armament of which is to act entirely beneath the surface of the water; so that, with no other external symptoms than a great bubbling and foaming, and gush of smoke, and belch of smothered thunder out of the yeasty waves, there shall be a deadly fight going on below—and, by and by, a sucking whirlpool, as one of the ships goes down.

The "Monitor" was certainly an object of great interest; but on our way to Newport News, whither we went next, we saw a spectacle that affected us with far profounder emotion. It was the sight of the few sticks that are left of the frigate "Congress," stranded near the shore—and still more, the masts of the "Cumberland" rising midway out of the water, with a tattered rag of a pennant fluttering from one of them. The invisible hull of the latter ship seems to be careened over, so that the three masts stand slantwise; the rigging looks quite unimpaired, except that a few ropes dangle loosely from the yards. The flag (which never was struck, thank Heaven!) is entirely hidden under the waters of the bay, but is still doubtless waving in its old place, although it floats to and fro with the swell and reflux of the tide, instead of rustling on the breeze. A remnant of the dead crew still man the sunken ship, and sometimes a drowned body floats up to the surface.

That was a noble fight. When was ever a better word spoken than that of Commodore Smith, the father of the "Congress," when he heard that his son's ship was surrendered? "Then Joe's dead!" said he; and so it proved. Nor can any warrior be more certain of enduring renown than the gallant Morris, who fought so well the final battle of the old system of naval warfare, and won glory for his country and himself out of inevitable disaster and defeat.

That last gun from the "Cumberland," when her deck was half submerged, sounded the requiem of many sinking ships. Then went down all the navies of Europe, and our own, "Old Ironsides" and all, and Trafalgar and a thousand other fights became only a memory, never to be acted over again; and thus our brave countrymen come last in that long procession of heroic sailors that includes Blake and Nelson, and so many mariners of England, and other mariners as brave as they, whose renown is our native inheritance.

There will be other battles, but no more such tests of seamanship and manhood as the battles of the past; and, moreover, the Millennium is certainly approaching, because human strife is to be transferred from the heart and personality of man into cunning contrivances of machinery, which by and by will fight out our wars with only the clank and smash of iron, strewing the field with broken engines, but damaging nobody's little finger, except by accident. Such is the tendency of modern improvement.

But, in the meanwhile, so long as manhood retains any part of its pristine value, no country can afford to let gallantry like that of Morris and his crew, any more than that of the brave Worden, pass unhonored and unrewarded. If the Government do nothing, let the people take the matter into their own hands, and cities give him swords, gold boxes, festivals of triumph, and, if he needs it, heaps of gold. Let poets brood upon the theme, and make themselves sensible how much of the past and future is contained within its compass, till its spirit shall flash forth in the lightning of a song!

Alfred W. Ellet
"THE STEAM-RAMS AT MEMPHIS"
On the River War at Memphis

The second-in-command of the victorious Federal flotilla of steam rams records the naval clash on the Mississippi at Memphis on June 6, 1862. The author's brother, Colonel Charles Ellet, commanded the flotilla.

After leaving Fort Randolph the ram-fleet proceeded without incident to within about twenty-five miles of Memphis, where they all rounded to and tied up for the night, with orders of sailing issued to each commander; instructions to be ready to round out at the signal from the flag-ship, and that "each boat should go into the anticipated fight in the same order they maintained in sailing." At the first dawn of day (June 6th) the fleet moved down the river, and at sunrise the flag-ship rounded the bend at "Paddy's Hen and Chickens," and immediately after came in sight of the Federal gun-boats anchored in line across the river, about a mile above Memphis. Colonel Ellet promptly signaled

his vessels to tie up on the Arkansas shore, in the order of their sailing, as he desired to confer with Flag-Officer Davis before passing further.

The *Queen of the West* came to, first, followed by the *Monarch* and other rams in regular succession. The *Queen of the West* had made the land, and passed out line to make fast; the *Monarch* was closing in just above, but had not yet touched the shore. At this moment, and as the full orb of the sun rose above the horizon, the report of a gun was heard from around the point and down the river. It was the first gun from the Confederate River Defense Fleet moving to attack us. Colonel Ellet was standing on the hurricane-deck of the *Queen of the West*. He immediately sprang forward, and, waving his hat to attract my attention, called out: "It is a gun from the enemy! Round out and follow me! Now is our chance!" Without a moment's delay, the *Queen* moved out gracefully, and the *Monarch* followed. By this time our gun-boats had opened their batteries, and the reports of guns on both sides were heavy and rapid.

The morning was beautifully clear and perfectly still; a heavy wall of smoke was formed across the river, so that the position of our gun-boats could only be seen by the flashes of their guns. The *Queen* plunged forward, under a full head of steam, right into this wall of smoke and was lost sight of, her position being known only by her tall pipes which reached above the smoke. The *Monarch*, following, was greeted, while passing the gun-boats, with wild huzzas from our gallant tars. When freed from the smoke, those of us who were on the *Monarch* could see Colonel Ellet's tall and commanding form still standing on the hurricane-deck, waving his hat to show me which one of the enemy's vessels he desired the *Monarch* to attack,—namely, the *General Price*, which was on the right wing of their advancing line. For himself he selected the *General Lovell* and directed the *Queen* straight for her, she being about the middle of the enemy's advancing line. The two vessels came toward each other in most gallant style, head to head, prow to prow; and had they met in that way, it is most likely that both vessels would have gone down. But at the critical moment the *General Lovell* began to turn; and that moment sealed her fate. The *Queen* came on and plunged straight into the *Lovell's* exposed broadside; the vessel was cut almost in two and disappeared under the dark waters in less time than it takes to tell the story. The *Monarch* next struck the *General Price* a glancing blow which cut her starboard wheel clean off, and completely disabled her from further participation in the fight.

As soon as the *Queen* was freed from the wreck of the sinking *Lovell*, and before she

THEODORE R. DAVIS.
*Building Gunboats and
Mortar Boats.* 1886.
Pen and wash.
6⅝ x 11⅝".
Century Collection,
New York.

could recover headway, she was attacked on both sides by the enemy's vessels, the *Beauregard* on one side and the *Sumter* on the other. In the *mêlée* one of the wheels of the *Queen* was disabled so that she could not use it, and Colonel Ellet, while still standing on the hurricane-deck to view the effects of the encounter with the *General Lovell*, received a pistol-ball in his knee, and, lying prone on the deck, gave orders for the *Queen* to be run on her one remaining wheel to the Arkansas shore, whither she was soon followed by the *General Price* in a sinking condition. Colonel Ellet sent an officer and squad of men to meet the *General Price* upon her making the shore, and received her entire crew as prisoners of war. By this time consternation had seized upon the enemy's fleet, and all had turned to escape. The fight had drifted down the river, below the city.

The *Monarch*, as soon as she could recover headway after her conflict with the *General Price*, drove down upon the *Beauregard*, which vessel, after her encounter with the *Queen of the West*, was endeavoring to escape. She was thwarted by the *Monarch* coming down upon her with a well-directed blow which crushed in her side and completely disabled her from further hope of escape. Men on the deck waved a white flag in token of surrender, and the *Monarch* passed on down to intercept the *Little Rebel*, the enemy's flag-ship. She had received some injury from our gun-boats' fire, and was making for the Arkansas shore, which she reached at the moment when the *Monarch*, with very slight headway, pushed her hard and fast aground; her crew sprang upon shore and ran into the thick woods, making their escape. Leaving the *Little Rebel* fast aground, the *Monarch* turned her attention to the sinking *Beauregard*, taking the vessel in tow, and making prisoners of her crew. The *Beauregard* was towed by the *Monarch* to the bar, where she sank to her boiler-deck and finally became a total loss.

The others of the enemy's fleet were run ashore and fired by the crews before they escaped into the adjoining Arkansas swamps. The *Jeff. Thompson* burned and blew up with a tremendous report; the *General Bragg* was secured by our gun-boats before the fire gained headway, and was saved. The *Van Dorn* alone made her escape, and was afterward burned by the enemy at Liverpool Landing, upon the approach of two of our rams in Yazoo River, in order to prevent her from falling into our hands. Two other rebel boats were burned at the same time,—the *Polk* and the *Livingston*.

Author Unknown

On the Fight between the Alabama *and the U. S. S.* Hatteras

An unidentified officer aboard the Confederate commerce raider Alabama *records her battle with the U.S.S.* Hatteras *off Galveston, Texas.*

Sunday, 11th—Fine moderate breeze from the eastward. Read Articles of War. Noon: Eighteen miles from Galveston. As I write this some are discussing the probability of a fight before morning. 2.25 P.M.: Light breeze; sail discovered by the look-out on the bow. Shortly after, three, and at last five, vessels were seen; two of which were reported to be steamers. Every one delighted at the prospect of a fight, no doubt whatever existing as to their being war-vessels—blockaders we supposed. The watch below came on deck, and of their own accord began preparing the guns, &c., for action. Those whose watch it was on deck were engaged in getting the propeller ready for lowering; others were bending a cable to a kedge and putting it over the bow—the engineers firing up for steam, officers looking to their side-arms, &c., and discussing the size of their expected adversary or adversaries. At 2.30 shortened sail and tacked to the southward. 4 P.M.: A steamer reported standing out from the fleet towards us. Backed main-topsail and lowered propeller. 4.50: Everything reported ready for action. Chase bearing N.N.E., distant ten miles. Twilight set in about 5.45. Took in all sail. At 6.20 beat up to quarters, manned the starboard battery, and loaded with fine second shell; turned round, stood for the steamer, having previously made her out to be a two-masted side-wheel, of apparent 1200 tons, though at the distance she was before dark we could not form any correct estimate of her size, &c.

At 6.30 the strange steamer hailed and asked: "What steamer is that?" We replied (in order to be certain who he was), "Her Majesty's ship Petrel! What steamer is that?" Two or three times we asked the question, until we heard, "This is the United States steamer—," not hearing the name. However, United States steamer was sufficient. As no doubt existed as to her character, we said, at 6.35, that this was the "Confederate States steamer, Alabama," accompanying the last syllable of our name with a shell fired over him. The signal being given, the other guns took up the refrain, and a tremendous volley from our whole broadside given to him, every shell striking his side, the shot striking being distinctly heard on board our vessels, and thus found that she was iron.

The enemy replied, and the action became general. A most sharp spirited firing was kept up on both sides, our fellows peppering away as though the action depended on each individual. And so it did. Pistols and rifles were continually pouring from our quarter-deck messengers most deadly, the distance during the hottest of the fight not being more than forty yards! It was a grand, though fearful sight, to see the guns belching forth, in the darkness of the night, sheets of living flame, the deadly missiles striking the enemy with a force that we could *feel*. Then, when the shells struck her side, and especially the percussion ones, her whole side was lit up, and showing rents of five or six feet in length. One shot had just struck our smoke-stack, and wounding one man in the cheek, when the enemy ceased his firing, and fired a lee gun; then a second, and a third. The order was given to "Cease firing." This was at 6.52. A tremendous cheering commenced, and it was not till everybody had cleared his throat to his own satisfaction, that silence could be obtained. We then hailed him, and in reply he stated that he had surrendered, was on fire, and also that he was in a sinking condition. He then sent a boat on board, and surrendered the U. S. gun-boat, Hatteras, nine guns, Lieutenant-Commander Blake, 140 men. Boats were immediately lowered and sent to his assistance, when an alarm was given that another steamer was bearing down for us. The boats were recalled and hoisted up, when it was found to be a false alarm. The order was given, and the boatswain and his mates piped "All hands out boats to save life;" and soon the prisoners were transferred to our ship—the officers under guard on the quarter-deck, and the men in single irons. The boats were then hoisted up, the battery run in and secured, and the main brace spliced. All hands piped down, the enemy's vessel sunk, and we steaming quietly away by 8.30, all having been done in less than two hours. . . .

From conversation with her First-Lieutenant, I learnt that as soon as we gave our name and our first broadsides, the whole after division on board her left the guns, apparently paralyzed; it was some time before they recovered themselves. The conduct of one of her officers was cowardly and disgraceful in the extreme. Some of our shells went completely through her before exploding, others burst inside her, and set her on fire in three places. One went through her engines, completely disabling her; another exploding in her steam chest, scalding all within reach. Thus was fought, twenty-eight miles from Galveston, a battle, though small, yet the first yard arm action between two steamers at sea.

James Morris Morgan

On an Incident at Sea between the Georgia *and the* Bold Hunter

In Recollections of a Rebel Reefer, *a midshipman aboard the Confederate raider* Georgia *describes her encounter with the* Bold Hunter, *and its unexpected consequences, October 9, 1863.*

On October 9, 1863, in a light breeze and after a lively chase we brought to, with our guns, the splendid American full-rigged ship *Bold Hunter*, of Boston, from Dundee, bound to Calcutta with a heavy cargo of coal. We hove to leeward of her and brought her captain and crew over to our ship, where as usual the crew were placed in irons and below decks. Being short of coal and provisions we proceeded to supply our wants from the prize. This was easy so far as the provisions were concerned, but when it came to carrying the coal from one ship to the other in our small boats, in something of a seaway, that was another matter. After half a dozen trips one of our boats came very near being swamped, and the wind and sea rapidly rising, we gave it up as a bad job. This was about two bells (1 P.M.) in the afternoon watch. We signalled our prize-master to set fire to the *Bold Hunter* and also to come aboard the *Georgia* at once, which he did.

We had hardly finished hoisting our boats to the davits when a great cloud of smoke burst from the hatches of the *Bold Hunter*, coming from the thousands of tons of burning coal in her hold. The wind had by this time increased to a gale and the sea was running very high. As before mentioned, the wind was very light when we captured the ship and she had hove to with all sail set, even to her royals. The flames leaped from her deck to her tarry rigging and raced up the shrouds and backstays and burned away her braces—her yards swung around, her sails filled, and the floating inferno, like a mad bull, bore down on us at full speed, rushing through the water as though she was bent on having her revenge.

To avoid a collision, the order was given on the *Georgia* to go ahead at full speed. The gong in the engine-room sounded, the engine turned the screw, and the screw began to churn the water under our counter. The engine made two or three revolutions—then there was a crash—followed by yells as the engineers and oilers rushed on to the deck accompanied by a shower of lignum-vitae cogs and broken glass from the engine-room windows. The order to make sail was instantly given, but before the gaskets which confined the furled sails to the yardarms could be cast off, the burning ship was upon us.

She had come for us with such directness that one could easily have imagined that she was being steered by some demon who had come out of the inferno which was raging in her hold. We stood with bated breath awaiting the catastrophe which seemingly was about to overtake us. The *Bold Hunter* was rated at over three thousand tons, and had inside her a burning cargo of coal of even greater weight—the *Georgia* was scarcely one-sixth her size. Onward rushed the blazing ship, presenting an awesome spectacle, with the flames leaping about her sails and rigging, while a huge mass of black smoke rolled out of her hatches. High above our heads her long, flying jib-boom passed over our poop deck as she arose on a great wave and came down on our quarter, her cutwater cleaving through the *Georgia's* fragile plates as cleanly as though they had been made out of cheese. The force of the impact pushed the *Georgia* ahead, and for a moment we congratulated ourselves that we had escaped from the fiery demon whose breath was scorching us.

But the *Bold Hunter* was not yet satisfied with the injuries she had inflicted. Recovering from the recoil she again gathered way and struck us near the place she had previously damaged, but fortunately this was a glancing blow which had the effect only of wrenching off our port quarter davits and reducing the boat which was slung to them to kindling wood.

Not yet satisfied, the apparently infuriated inanimate object made a third attempt to destroy the *Georgia*, this time, fortunately, missing her mark and passing a few yards to leeward of us. Her sails having burned, she soon lost headway and helplessly lay wallowing in the trough of the sea while the fire ate through her sides, and her tall masts, one after the other, fell with a great splash into the sea. Before she went down surrounded by a cloud of steam, we had a good view through the great holes burned in her sides of the fire raging inside her. I imagine it was a very realistic imitation of what hell looks like when the forced draughts are turned on in honour of the arrival of a distinguished sinner.

John McIntosh Kell
"CRUISE AND COMBATS OF THE *ALABAMA*"
On the Great Naval Duel – the Alabama *vs. the* Kearsarge

The most famous naval duel of the war, as reported by the Alabama's *executive officer, June, 1864. In cruises that took her as far as the Indian Ocean, the raider* Alabama, *captained by Raphael Semmes, had taken sixty-four Yankee prizes before this fateful encounter with the* Kearsarge.

We therefore set our course for Europe, and on the 11th of June, 1864, entered the port of Cherbourg, and applied for permission to go into dock. There being none but national docks, the Emperor had first to be communicated with before permission could be granted, and he was absent from Paris. It was during this interval of waiting, on the third day after our arrival, that the *Kearsarge* steamed into the harbor, for the purpose, as we learned, of taking on board the prisoners we had landed from our last two prizes. Captain Semmes, however, objected to this on the ground that the *Kearsarge* was adding to her crew in a neutral port. The authorities conceding this objection valid, the *Kearsarge* steamed out of the harbor, without anchoring. During her stay we examined her closely with our glasses, but she was keeping on the opposite side of the harbor, out of the reach of a very close scrutiny, which accounts for our not detecting the boxing to her chain armor. After she left the harbor Captain Semmes sent for me to his cabin, and said: "I am going out to fight the *Kearsarge*; what do you think of it?" We discussed the battery, and especially the advantage the *Kearsarge* had over us in her 11-inch guns. She was built for a vessel of war, and we for speed, and though she carried one gun less, her battery was more effective at point-blank range. While the *Alabama* carried one more gun, the *Kearsarge* threw more metal at a broadside; and while our heavy guns were more effective at long range, her 11-inch guns gave her greatly the advantage at close range. She also had a slight advantage in her crew, she carrying 163, all told, while we

WALTON TABER.
"Kearsarge" Gun Crew.
1886. Pen and crayon.
8½ x 13¾".
Century Collection,
New York.

carried 149. Considering well these advantages, Captain Semmes communicated through our agent to the United States consul that if Captain Winslow would wait outside the harbor he would fight him as soon as we could coal ship.

Accordingly, on Sunday morning, June 19th, between 9 and 10 o'clock, we weighed anchor and stood out of the western entrance of the harbor, the French iron-clad frigate *Couronne* following us. The day was bright and beautiful, with a light breeze blowing. Our men were neatly dressed, and our officers in full uniform. The report of our going out to fight the *Kearsarge* had been circulated, and many persons from Paris and the surrounding country had come down to witness the engagement. With a large number of the inhabitants of Cherbourg they collected on every prominent point on the shore that would afford a view seaward. As we rounded the breakwater we discovered the *Kearsarge* about seven miles to the northward and eastward. We immediately shaped our course for her, called all hands to quarters, and cast loose the starboard battery. Upon reporting to the captain that the ship was ready for action, he directed me to send all hands aft, and mounting a gun-carriage, he made the following address:

"Officers and Seamen of the 'Alabama': You have at length another opportunity of meeting the enemy—the first that has been presented to you since you sank the *Hatteras!* In the meantime you have been all over the world, and it is not too much to say that you have destroyed, and driven for protection under neutral flags, one-half of the enemy's commerce, which at the beginning of the war covered every sea. This is an achievement of which you may well be proud, and a grateful country will not be unmindful of it. The name of your ship has become a household word wherever civilization extends! Shall that name be tarnished by defeat? The thing is impossible! Remember that you are in the English Channel, the theater of so much of the naval glory of our race, and that the eyes of all Europe are at this moment upon you. The flag that floats over you is that of a young Republic, which bids defiance to her enemy's whenever and wherever found! Show the world that you know how to uphold it! Go to your quarters."

In about forty-five minutes we were somewhat over a mile from the *Kearsarge*, when she headed for us, presenting her starboard bow. At a distance of a mile we commenced the action with our 100-pounder pivot-gun from our starboard bow. Both ships were now approaching each other at high speed, and soon the action became general with broadside batteries at a distance of about five hundred yards. To prevent passing, each ship used a strong port helm. Thus the action was fought around a common center, gradually drawing in the circle. At this range we used shell upon the enemy. Captain Semmes, standing on the horse-block abreast the mizzen-mast with his glass in hand, observed the effect of our shell. He called to me and said: "Mr. Kell, use solid shot; our shell strike the enemy's side and fall into the water." We were not at this time aware of the chain armor of the enemy, and attributed the failure of our shell to our defective ammunition. After using solid shot for some time, we alternated shell and shot. The enemy's 11-inch shells were now doing severe execution upon our quarter-deck section. Three of them successively entered our 8-inch pivot-gun port: the first swept off the forward part of the gun's crew; the second killed one man and wounded several others; and the third struck the breast of the gun-carriage, and spun around on the deck till one of the men picked it up and threw it overboard. Our decks were now covered with the dead and the wounded, and the ship was careening heavily to starboard from the effects of the shot-holes on her water-line.

Captain Semmes ordered me to be ready to make all sail possible when the circuit of fight should put our head to the coast of France; then he would notify me at the same time to pivot to port and continue the action with the port battery, hoping thus to right the ship and enable us to reach the coast of France. The evolution was performed beautifully, righting the helm, hoisting the head-sails, hauling aft the fore try-sail sheet, and pivoting to port, the action continuing almost without cessation.

This evolution exposed us to a raking fire, but, strange to say, the *Kearsarge* did not take advantage of it. The port side of the quarter-deck was so encumbered with the mangled trunks of the dead that I had to have them thrown overboard, in order to fight the after pivot-gun. I abandoned the after 32-pounder, and transferred the men to fill up the vacancies at the pivot-gun under the charge of young Midshipman Anderson, who in the midst of the carnage filled his place like a veteran. At this moment the chief engineer came on deck and reported the fires put out, and that he could no longer work the engines. Captain Semmes said to me, "Go below, sir, and see how long the ship can float." As I entered the ward-room the sight was indeed appalling. There stood Assistant-Surgeon Llewellyn at his post, but the table and the patient upon it had been swept away from him by an 11-inch shell, which opened in the side of the ship an aperture that was fast filling the ship with water.

It took me but a moment to return to the deck and report to the captain that we could not float ten minutes. He replied to me, "Then, sir, cease firing, shorten sail, and haul down the colors; it will never do in this nineteenth century for us to go down, and the decks covered with our gallant wounded." The order was promptly executed. . . .

I now gave the order for every man to jump overboard with a spar and save himself from the sinking ship. To enforce the order, I walked forward and urged the men overboard. As soon as the decks were cleared, save of the bodies of the dead, I returned to the stern-port, where stood Captain Semmes with one or two of the men and his faithful steward, who, poor fellow! was doomed to a watery grave, as he could not swim. The *Alabama's* stern-port was now almost at the water's edge. Partly undressing, we plunged into the sea, and made an offing from sinking ship, Captain Semmes with a life-preserver and I on a grating.

The *Alabama* settled stern foremost, launching her bows high in the air. Graceful even in her death-struggle, she in a moment disappeared from the face of the waters. . . .

John C. Kinney

"FARRAGUT AT MOBILE BAY"

Admiral David Farragut challenges Rebel forts, mines (torpedoes), and the powerful ironclad Tennessee *in the Battle of Mobile Bay, August 5, 1864. Signalman John Kinney of the flagship* Hartford *tells the story in* Farragut at Mobile Bay.

———————

It was a quarter of six o'clock before the fleet was in motion. Meantime a light breeze had scattered the fog and left a clear, sunny August day. The line moved slowly, and it was an hour after starting before the opening gun was fired. This was a 15-inch shell from the *Tecumseh*, and it exploded over Fort Morgan. Half an hour afterward the fleet came within range and the firing from the starboard vessels became general, the fort and the Confederate fleet replying. . . . Gradually the fleet came into close quarters with Fort Morgan, and the firing on both sides became terrific. The wooden vessels moved more rapidly than the monitors, and as the *Brooklyn* came opposite the fort, and approached the torpedo line, she came nearly alongside the rear monitor. To have kept on would have been to take the lead, with the ram *Tennessee* approaching and with the unknown danger of the torpedoes underneath. At this critical moment the *Brooklyn* halted and began backing and signaling with the army signals. The *Hartford* was immediately behind and the following vessels were in close proximity, and the sudden stopping of the *Brooklyn* threatened to bring the whole fleet into collision. . . .

Owing to the *Hartford's* position, only her few bow guns could be used, while a deadly rain of shot and shell was falling on her, and her men were being cut down by scores, unable to make reply. The sight on deck was sickening beyond the power of words to portray. Shot after shot came through the side, mowing down the men, deluging the decks with blood, and scattering mangled fragments of humanity so thickly that it was difficult to stand on the deck, so slippery was it. The old expressions of the "scuppers running blood," "the slippery deck," etc., give but the faintest idea of the spectacle on the *Hartford*. The bodies of the dead were placed in a long row on the port side, while the wounded were sent below until the surgeons' quarters would hold no more. . . .

Soon after the fight began, Admiral Farragut, finding that the low-hanging smoke from the guns interfered with his view from the deck, went up the rigging of the mainmast as far as the futtock-shrouds, immediately below the maintop. The pilot, Martin Freeman, was in the top directly overhead, and the fleet-captain was on the deck below. Seeing the admiral in this exposed position, where, if wounded, he would be killed by falling to the deck, Fleet-Captain Drayton ordered Knowles, the signal-quartermaster, to fasten a rope around him so that he would be prevented from falling.

Finding that the *Brooklyn* failed to obey his orders, the admiral hurriedly inquired of the pilot if there was sufficient depth of water for the *Hartford* to pass to the left of the *Brooklyn*. Receiving an affirmative reply, he said: "I will take the lead," and immediately ordered the *Hartford* ahead at full speed. As he passed the *Brooklyn* a voice warned him of the torpedoes, to which he returned the contemptuous answer, "Damn the torpedoes." This is the current story, and may have some basis of truth. But as a matter of fact, there was never a moment when the din of the battle would not have drowned any attempt at conversation between the two ships, and while it is quite probable that the admiral made the remark it is doubtful if he shouted it to the *Brooklyn*.

Then was witnessed the remarkable sight of the *Hartford* and her consort, the *Metacomet*, passing over the dreaded torpedo ground and rushing ahead far in advance of the rest of the fleet. . . .

The *Tennessee*, after remaining near Fort Morgan while the fleet had made its way four miles above to its anchorage,—certainly as much as half an hour,—had suddenly decided to settle at once the question of the control of the bay. Single-handed she came on to meet the whole fleet, consisting now of ten wooden vessels and the three monitors. At that time the *Tennessee* was believed to be the strongest vessel afloat, and the safety with which she carried her crew during the battle proved that she was virtually invulnerable. . . .

Because of the slowness of the monitors, Admiral Farragut selected the fastest of the wooden vessels to begin the attack. While the navy signals for a general attack of the enemy were being prepared, the *Monongahela* (Captain Strong) and the *Lackawanna* (Captain Marchand) were ordered by the more rapid signal system of the army to "run down the ram," the order being immediately repeated to the monitors.

The *Monongahela*, with her prow already somewhat weakened by the previous attempt to ram, at once took the lead, as she had not yet come to anchor. The ram from the first headed for the *Hartford*, and paid no attention to her assailants, except with her guns. The *Monongahela*, going at full speed, struck the *Tennessee* amidships—a blow that would have sunk almost any vessel of the Union navy, but which inflicted not the slightest damage on the solid iron hull of the ram. (After the surrender it was almost impossible to tell where the attacking vessel had struck.) Her own iron prow and cutwater were carried away, and she was otherwise badly damaged about the stern by the collision.

The *Lackawanna* was close behind and delivered a similar blow with her wooden bow, simply causing the ram to lurch slightly to one side. As the vessels separated the *Lackawanna* swung alongside the ram, which sent two shots through her and kept on her course for the *Hartford*, which was now the next vessel in the attack. The two flag-ships approached each other, bow to bow, iron against oak. It was impossible for the *Hartford*, with her lack of speed, to circle around and strike the ram on the side; her only safety was in keeping pointed directly for the bow of her assailant. The other vessels of the fleet were unable to do anything for the defense of the admiral except to train their guns on the ram, on which as yet they had not the slightest effect.

It was a thrilling moment for the fleet, for it was evident that if the ram could strike the *Hartford* the latter must sink. But for the two vessels to strike fairly, bows on, would probably have involved the destruction of both, for the ram must have penetrated so far into the wooden ship that as the *Hartford* filled and sank she would have carried the ram under water. Whether for this reason or for some other, as the two vessels came together the *Tennessee* slightly changed her course, the port bow of the *Hartford* met the port bow of the ram, and the ships grated against each other as they passed. The *Hartford* poured her whole port broadside against the ram, but the solid shot merely dented the side and bounded into the air. The ram tried to return the salute, but owing to defective primers only one gun was discharged. This sent a shell through the berth-deck, killing five men and wounding eight. The muzzle of the gun was so close to the *Hartford* that the powder blackened her side.

The admiral stood on the quarter-deck when the vessels came together, and as he saw the result he jumped on to the port-quarter rail, holding to the mizzen-rigging, a position from which he might have jumped to the deck of the ram as she passed. Seeing him in this position, and fearing for his safety, Flag-Lieutenant Watson slipped a rope around him and secured it to the rigging, so that during the fight the admiral was twice "lashed to the rigging," each time by devoted officers who knew better than to consult him before acting. . . .

The *Tennessee* now became the target for the whole fleet, all the vessels of which were making toward her, pounding her with shot, and trying to run her down. As the *Hartford* turned to make for her again, we ran in front of the *Lackawanna*, which had already turned and was moving under full headway with the same object. She struck us on our starboard side, amidships, crushing halfway through, knocking two port-holes into one, upsetting one of the Dahlgren guns, and creating general consternation. . . .

The unfortunate *Lackawanna*, which had struck the ram a second blow, was making for her once more, and, singularly enough, again came up on our starboard side, and another collision seemed imminent. And now the admiral became a trifle excited. He had no idea of whipping the rebels to be himself sunk by a friend, nor did he realize at the moment that the *Hartford* was as much to blame as the *Lackawanna*. Turning to the writer he inquired. "Can you say 'For God's sake' by signal?"

"Yes, sir," was the reply.

"Then say to the *Lackawanna*, 'For God's sake get out of our way and anchor!'". . . .

The remainder of the story is soon told. As the *Tennessee* left the *Hartford* she became the target of the entire fleet, and at last the concentration of solid shot from so many guns began to tell. The flag-staff was shot away, the smoke-stack was riddled with holes, and finally disappeared. The monitor *Chickasaw*, Lieutenant-Commander Perkins, succeeded in coming up astern and began pounding away with 11-inch solid shot, and one shot from a 15-inch gun of the *Manhattan* crushed into the side sufficiently to prove that a few more such shots would have made the casemate untenable. Finally, one of the *Chickasaw's* shots cut the rudder-chain of the ram and she would no longer mind her helm. At this time, as Admiral Farragut says in his report, "She was sore beset. The *Chickasaw* was pounding away at her stern, the *Ossipee* was approaching her at full speed, and the *Monongahela*, *Lackawanna*, and this ship were bearing down upon her, determined upon her destruction." From the time the *Hartford* struck her she did not fire a gun. Finally the Confederate admiral, Buchanan, was severely wounded by an iron splinter or a piece of shell, and just as the *Ossipee* was about to strike her the *Tennessee* displayed a white flag, hoisted on an improvised staff through the grating over her deck. The *Ossipee* (Captain Le Roy) reversed her engine, but was so near that a harmless collision was inevitable.

Suddenly the terrific cannonading ceased, and from every ship rang out cheer after cheer, as the weary men realized that at last the ram was conquered and the day won.

William B. Cushing

"THE DESTRUCTION OF THE *ALBEMARLE*"

The daring attack on the Confederate ram Albemarle *in the Roanoke River, October 27, 1864, described by the commander of the attacking party.*

Impossibilities are for the timid: we determined to overcome all obstacles. On the night of the 27th of October we entered the river, taking in tow a small cutter with a few men, whose duty was to dash aboard the wreck of the *Southfield* at the first hail, and prevent a racket from being ignited.

We passed within thirty feet of the pickets without discovery, and neared the vessel. I now thought that it might be better to board her, and "take her alive," having in the two boats twenty men well armed with revolvers, cutlasses, and hand-grenades. To be sure, there were ten times our number on the ship and thousands near by; but a surprise is everything, and I thought if her fasts were cut at the instant of boarding, we might overcome those on board, take her into the stream, and use her iron sides to protect us afterward from the forts. Knowing the town, I concluded to land at the lower wharf, creep around, and suddenly dash aboard from the bank; but just as I was sheering in close to the wharf, a hail came, sharp and quick, from the iron-clad, and in an instant was repeated. I at once directed the cutter to cast off, and go down to capture the guard left in our rear, and, ordering all steam, went at the dark mountain of iron in front of us. A heavy fire was at once opened upon us, not only from the ship, but from men stationed on the shore. This did not disable us, and we neared them rapidly. A large fire now blazed upon the bank, and by its light I discovered the unfortunate fact that there was a circle of logs around the *Albemarle*, boomed well out from her side, with the very intention of preventing the action of torpedoes. To examine them more closely, I ran alongside until amidships, received the enemy's fire, and sheered off for the purpose of turning, a hundred yards away, and going at the booms squarely, at right angles, trusting to their having been long enough in the water to have become slimy — in which case my boat, under full headway, would bump up against them and slip over into the pen with the ram. This was my only chance of success, and once over the obstruction my boat would never get out again. As I turned, the whole back of my coat was torn out by buckshot, and the sole of my shoe was carried away. The fire was very severe.

In a lull of the firing, the captain hailed us, again demanding what boat it was. All my men gave comical answers, and mine was a dose of canister from the howitzer. In another instant we had struck the logs and were over, with headway nearly gone, slowly

J. O. Davidson. *The Destruction of the "Albemarle."* 1886. Drawing. North Carolina Division of Archives and History, Raleigh.

forging up under the enemy's quarter-port. Ten feet from us the muzzle of a rifle gun looked into our faces, and every word of command on board was distinctly heard.

My clothing was perforated with bullets as I stood in the bow, the heel-jigger in my right hand and the exploding-line in the left. We were near enough then, and I ordered the boom lowered until the forward motion of the launch carried the torpedo under the ram's overhang. A strong pull of the detaching-line, a moment's waiting for the torpedo to rise under the hull, and I hauled in the left hand, just cut by a bullet.

The explosion took place at the same instant that 100 pounds of grape, at 10 feet range, crashed among us, and the dense mass of water thrown out by the torpedo came down with choking weight upon us.

Twice refusing to surrender, I commanded the men to save themselves; and, throwing off sword, revolver, shoes, and coat, struck out from my disabled and sinking boat into the river. It was cold, long after the frosts, and the water chilled the blood, while the whole surface of the stream was plowed up by grape and musketry, and my nearest friends, the fleet, were twelve miles away; but anything was better than to fall into rebel hands, so I swam for the opposite shore. . . .

As soon as it became known that I had returned, rockets were thrown up and all hands were called to cheer ship; and when I announced success, all the commanding officers were summoned on board to deliberate upon a plan of attack. In the morning I was well again in every way, with the exception of hands and feet, and had the pleasure of exchanging shots with the batteries that I had inspected the day before. I was sent in the *Valley City* to report to Admiral Porter at Hampton Roads, and soon after Plymouth and the whole district of the Albemarle, deprived of the iron-clad's protection, fell an easy prey to Commander Macomb and our fleet.

LANDSCAPE OF WAR

Walt Whitman

On Washington, and the Soldiers' Return from Bull Run

A recollection of the war coming to Washington in the wake of the First Battle of Bull Run, in July 1861; from Whitman's Specimen Days.

(All battles, and their results, are far more matters of accident than is generally thought; but this was throughout a casualty, a chance. One [side] had, in point of fact, just the same right to be routed as the other. By a fiction, or series of fictions, the national forces at the last moment exploded in a panic and fled from the field.) The defeated troops commenced pouring into Washington over the Long Bridge at daylight on Monday, 22nd—day drizzling all through with rain.

The Saturday and Sunday of the battle (20th, 21st) had been parched and hot to an extreme—the dust, the grime, and smoke in layers, sweated in, followed by other layers again sweated in, absorbed by those excited souls—their clothes all saturated with the clay-powder filling the air, stirred up everywhere on the dry roads and trodden fields by the regiments, swarming wagons, artillery, etc.—all the men with this coating of murk and sweat and rain, now recoiling back, pouring over the Long Bridge—a horrible march of twenty miles—returning to Washington, baffled, humiliated, panic-struck.

Where are your banners and your bands of music and your ropes to bring back your prisoners? Well, there isn't a band playing, and there isn't a flag but clings ashamed and lank to its staff.

The sun rises but shines not. The men appear, at first sparsely and shamefaced enough, then thicker, in the streets of Washington; appear in Pennsylvania Avenue and on the steps and basement entrances. They come along in disorderly mobs; some in squads, stragglers, companies. Occasionally a rare regiment, in perfect order, with its officers (some gaps, dead—the true braves), marching in silence, with lowering faces—stern, weary to sinking, all black and dirty, but every man with a big musket and stepping alive; but these are the exceptions.

Sidewalks of Pennsylvania Avenue, Fourteenth Street, etc. crowded, jammed with citizens, darkies, clerks, everybody, lookers-on; women in the windows; curious expressions from faces, as those swarms of dirt-covered returned soldiers there (will they never end?) move by; but nothing said, no comments; (half our lookers-on Secesh of the most venomous kind—they say nothing, but the devil snickers in their faces). During the forenoon Washington gets all over motley with these defeated soldiers—queer-looking objects—strange eyes and faces, drenched (the steady rain drizzles all day) and fearfully worn, hungry, haggard, blistered in the feet.

Good people (but not over-many of them either) hurry up something for their grub. They put wash-kettles on the fire for soup, for coffee. They set tables on the sidewalks, wagonloads of bread are purchased, swiftly cut in stout chunks. Here are two aged ladies, beautiful, the first in the city for culture and charm—they stand with store of eating and

THOMAS NAST. *Ladies' Parlor at Willard's Hotel, Washington, March 6, 1861.* 1861. Pencil and wash. 9½ x 14″. Library of Congress, Washington, D.C.

drink at an improvised table of rough plank, and give food and have the store replenished from their house every half-hour all that day; and there in the rain they stand, active, silent, white-haired, and give food, though the tears stream down their cheeks almost without intermission the whole time.

Amid the deep excitement, crowds and motion and desperate eagerness, it seems strange to see many, very many of the soldiers sleeping—in the midst of all—sleeping sound. They drop down anywhere—on the steps of houses, up close by the basements or fences, on the sidewalk, aside on some vacant lot—and deeply sleep. A poor seventeen- or eighteen-year-old boy lies there on the stoop of a grand house; he sleeps so calmly, so profoundly. Some clutch their muskets firmly even in sleep. Some in squads— comrades, brothers, close together—and on them, as they lay, sulkily drips the rain.

As afternoon passed and evening came, the streets, the barrooms, knots everywhere—listeners, questioners, terrible yarns, bugaboo, masked batteries, "our regiment all cut up," and so on—stories and storytellers, windy, bragging, vain centers of street crowds. Resolution, manliness, seem to have abandoned Washington.

The principal hotel, Willard's, is full of shoulder-straps. (I see them and must have a word with them. There you are, shoulder straps!—But where are your companies? Where are your men? Incompetents! Never tell me of chance of battle, of getting strayed, and the like. I think this is your work, this retreat, after all. Sneak, blow, put on airs there in Willard's sumptuous parlors and barrooms or anywhere—no explanation shall save you. Bull Run is your work; had you been half or one-tenth worthy your men, this never would have happened.)

Meantime in Washington, among the great persons and their entourage, a mixture of awful consternation, uncertainty, rage, shame, helplessness, and stupefying disappointment. The worst is not only imminent but already there. In a few hours—perhaps before the next meal—the Secesh generals, with their victorious hordes, will be upon us. The dream of humanity, the vaunted Union we thought so strong, so impregnable—lo! it seems already smashed like a china plate.

One bitter, bitter hour—perhaps proud America will never again know such an hour. . . .

Nathaniel Hawthorne
FROM "CHIEFLY ABOUT WAR MATTERS"

The celebrated New England novelist reports for readers of the Atlantic Monthly *on his tour of the seat of war in Virginia in March of 1862.*

On our way we heard many rumors of the war, but saw few signs of it. The people were staid and decorous, according to their ordinary fashion; and business seemed about as brisk as usual—though I suppose it was considerably diverted from its customary channels into war-like ones. In the cities, especially in New York, there was a rather prominent display of military goods at the shop windows—such as swords with gilded scabbards and trappings, epaulets, carabines, revolvers, and sometimes a great iron cannon at the edge of the pavement, as if Mars had dropped one of his pocket pistols there, while hurrying to the field. . . .

Beyond Philadelphia there was a much greater abundance of military people. Between Baltimore and Washington a guard seemed to hold every station along the railroad;

COLORPLATE 49

Artist Unknown. *Siege of Vicksburg.* No date. Oil on canvas. 24¼ × 30″. The American Museum in Britain, Bath, England. *Bundles of wood called fascines shield a Federal approach to the enemy lines.*

COLORPLATE 50

WILLIAM MacLEOD. *Maryland Heights: Siege of Harper's Ferry.* 1863. Oil on canvas.
30 × 40″. The Corcoran Gallery of Art, Washington, D.C. Gift of Genevieve Plummer,
1954. Photo copyright © Corcoran Gallery of Art.

COLORPLATE 51 *(opposite, above)*

PRINCE DE JOINVILLE. *Federal Cavalrymen Fording Bull Run.* 1862. Watercolor on paper.
4¾ × 6¾″. Fondation Saint-Louis, Amboise, France.

COLORPLATE 52 *(opposite, below)*

PRINCE DE JOINVILLE. *The Army of the Potomac Landing at Fort Monroe.* 1862.
Watercolor on paper. 4¾ × 6¾″. Fondation Saint-Louis, Amboise, France.

COLORPLATE 53

SANFORD ROBINSON GIFFORD. *The Evening Meal of the Seventh Regiment New York in Camp near Frederick, Maryland, 1863.* 1864. Oil on canvas. 18 × 30″. The Seventh Regiment Fund, Inc., New York. Photo courtesy Metropolitan Museum of Art, New York.

COLORPLATE 54

SANFORD ROBINSON GIFFORD. *Night Bivouac of the Seventh Regiment New York at Arlington Heights, Virginia.* 1861. Oil on canvas. 18 × 30″. The Seventh Regiment Fund, Inc., New York. Photo courtesy Metropolitan Museum of Art, New York.

COLORPLATE 55

Artist Unknown. *Blue in Bivouac, on Lookout Mountain, Tennessee.* 1863. Watercolor. 9¾ ×
12⅛″. Museum of Fine Arts, Boston. M. and M. Karolik Collection. Photo copyright © 1991
Museum of Fine Arts, Boston.

COLORPLATE 56

EDWARD LAMSON HENRY. *The Old Westover Mansion.* 1869. Oil on panel. 11¼ × 14⅝″.
Corcoran Gallery of Art, Washington, D.C. Gift of the American Art Association. Photo
copyright © Corcoran Gallery of Art.

and frequently, on the hillsides, we saw a collection of weather-beaten tents, the peaks of which, blackened with smoke, indicated that they had been made comfortable by stove heat throughout the winter. At several commanding positions we saw fortifications, with the muzzles of cannon protruding from the ramparts, the slopes of which were made of the yellow earth of that region.

Our stopping-places were thronged with soldiers, some of whom came through the cars asking for newspapers that contained accounts of the battle between the Merrimac and Monitor, which had been fought the day before. A railway train met us, conveying a regiment out of Washington to some unknown point; and reaching the capitol, we filed out of the station between lines of soldiers, with shouldered muskets, putting us in mind of similar spectacles at the gates of European cities. It was not without sorrow that we saw the free circulation of the nation's lifeblood (at the very heart, moreover) clogged with such strictures as these, which have caused chronic diseases in almost all countries save our own.

Among other excursions to camps and places of interest in the neighborhood of Washington, we went, one day, to Alexandria. In peaceful times it no doubt bore an aspect of decorous quietude and dullness; but it was now thronged with the Northern soldiery, whose stir and bustle contrasted strikingly with the many closed warehouses, the absence of citizens from their customary haunts, and the lack of any symptom of healthy activity, while army wagons trundled heavily over the pavements, and sentinels paced the side-walks, and mounted dragoons dashed to and fro on military errands.

I tried to imagine how very disagreeable the presence of a Southern army would be in a sober town of Massachusetts; and the thought considerably lessened my wonder at the cold and shy rewards that are cast upon our troops, the gloom, the sullen demeanor, the declared or scarcely hidden sympathy with rebellion, which are so frequent here. It is a strange thing in human life that the greatest errors both of men and women often spring from their sweetest and most generous qualities; and so, undoubtedly thousands of warm-hearted, sympathetic, and impulsive persons have joined the Rebels, not from any real zeal for the cause, but because, between two conflicting loyalties, they chose that which necessarily lay nearest the heart.

There never existed any other government against which treason was so easy, and could defend itself by such plausible arguments, as against that of the United States. The anomaly of two allegiances (of which that of the State comes nearest home to a man's feelings, and includes the altar and the hearth, while the General Government claims his devotion only to an airy mode of law, and has no symbol but a flag) is exceedingly mischievous in this point of view; for it has converted crowds of honest people into traitors, who seem to themselves not merely innocent, but patriotic, and who die for a bad cause with as quiet a conscience as if it were the best.

Driving out of Alexandria, we stopped on the edge of the city to inspect an old slave pen, which is one of the lions of the place, but a very poor one. Reaching the open country, we saw forts and camps on all sides, some of the tents being placed immediately on the ground, while others were raised over a basement of logs, laid lengthwise, like those of a circle—thus forming a solid wall, the chinks closed up with Virginia mud, and above it the pyramidal shelter of the tent.

Here were in progress all the occupations, and all the idleness, of the soldier in the tented field; some were cooking the company rations in pits hung over fires in the open air; some played at ball, or developed their muscular power by gymnastic exercise; some read newspapers; some smoked cigars or pipes; and many were cleaning their arms and accoutrements—the more carefully, perhaps, because their division was to be reviewed by the Commander-in-Chief that afternoon; others sat on the ground while their comrades cut their hair—it being a soldierly fashion (and for excellent reasons) to crop it within an inch of the skull; others, finally, lay asleep in breast-high tents, with their legs protruding into the open air.

We paid a visit to Fort Ellsworth, and from its ramparts (which have been heaped up out of the muddy soil within the last few months, and will require still a year or two to make them verdant) we had a beautiful view of the Potomac, a truly majestic river, and the surrounding country. The fortifications, so numerous in all this region, and now so unsightly with their bare, precipitous sides, will remain as historic monuments, grass-grown and picturesque memorials of an epoch of terror and suffering.

Even in an aesthetic point of view, however, the war has done a great deal of enduring mischief, by causing the devastation of great tracts of woodland scenery, in which this part of Virginia would appear to have been very rich. Around all the encampments and everywhere along the road, we saw the bare sites of what had evidently been tracts of hardwood forest, indicated by the unsightly stumps of well-grown trees, not smoothly felled by regular ax-men, but hacked, haggled, and unevenly amputated, as by a sword or other miserable tool, in an unskillful hand. Fifty years will not repair this desolation.

The carcasses of horses were scattered along the wayside.

One very pregnant token of a social system thoroughly disturbed was presented by a party of contrabands, escaping out of the mysterious depths of Secessia; and its strange-ness consisted in the leisurely delay with which they trudged forward as dreading no pursuer, and encountering nobody to turn them back. . . .

So rudely were they attired—as if their garb had grown upon them spontaneously; so picturesquely natural in manners; and wearing such a crust of primeval simplicity (which is quite polished away from the Northern black man), that they seemed a kind of creature by themselves, not altogether human, but quite as good, and akin to the fauns and rustic deities of olden times. I wonder whether I shall excite anybody's wrath by saying this. It is no great matter.

At all events, I felt most kindly towards these poor fugitives, but knew not precisely what to wish in their behalf, nor in the least how to help them. For the sake of the

manhood which is latent in them, I would not have turned them back; but I should have felt almost as reluctant, on their own account, to hasten them forward to the stranger's land; and I think my prevalent idea was, that, whoever may be benefited by the results of this war, it will not be the present generation of Negroes, the childhood of whose race is now gone forever, and who must henceforth fight a hard battle with the world, on very unequal terms. On behalf of my own race, I am glad and can only hope that an inscrutable Providence means good to both parties. . . .

Another of our excursions was to Harper's Ferry. . . . Immediately on the shore of the Potomac, and extending back towards the town, lay the dismal ruins of the United States arsenal and armory, consisting of piles of broken bricks and a waste of shapeless demolition, amid which we saw gun barrels in heaps of hundreds together. They were relics of the conflagration, bent with the heat of the fire and rusted with the wintry rain to which they had since been exposed. The brightest sunshine could not have made the scene cheerful, nor taken away the gloom from the dilapidated town; for, besides the natural shabbiness, and decayed, unthrifty look of a Virginian village, it has an inexpressible forlornness resulting from the devastation of war and its occupation by both armies alternately.

There was a small shop, which appeared to have nothing for sale. A single man and one or two boys were all the inhabitants in view, except the Yankee sentinels and soldiers, belonging to Massachusetts regiments, and who were scattered about pretty numerously. A guard house stood on the slope of the hill; and in the level street at its base were the offices of the Provost Marshall and other military authorities, to whom we forthwith reported ourselves.

The Provost Marshall kindly sent a corporal to guide us to the little building which John Brown seized upon as his fortress, and which, after it was stormed by the United States Marines, became his temporary prison. It is an old engine house, rusty and shabby, like every other work of man's hands in the God-forsaken town, and stands fronting upon the river, only a short distance from the bank, nearly at the point where the pontoon bridge touches the Virginia shore. In its front wall, on each side of the door, are two or three ragged loopholes, which John Brown perforated for his defense, knocking out merely a brick or two, so as to give himself and his garrison a sight over their rifles. Through these orifices the sturdy old man dealt a good deal of deadly mischief among his assailants, until they broke down the door by thrusting against it with a ladder, and tumbled headlong in upon him.

From these and various excursions, and a good many others (including one to Manassas), we gained a pretty lively idea of what was going on; but, after all, if compelled to pass a rainy day in the hall and parlors of Willard's Hotel, it proved about as profitably spent as if we had floundered through miles of Virginia mud, in quest of interesting matter. This hotel, in fact, may be much more justly called the centre of Washington and the Union than either the Capitol, the White House, or the State Department. Everybody may be seen there.

It is the meeting place of the true representatives of the country—not such as are chosen blindly and amiss by electors who take a folded ballot from the hand of a local politician, and thrust it into the ballot box unread, but men who gravitate or are attracted hither by real business, or a native impulse to breathe the intensest atmosphere of the nation's life, or a genuine anxiety to see how this life-and-death struggle is going to deal with us. Nor these only, but all manner of loafers. Never, in any other spot, was there such a miscellany of people. You exchange nods with governors of sovereign States; you elbow illustrious men, and tread on the toes of generals; you hear statesmen and orators speaking in their familiar tones. You are mixed up with office-seekers, wire-pullers, inventors, artists, poets, prosers (including editors, army correspondents, attachés of foreign journals, and long-winded talkers), clerks, diplomatists, mail contractors, railway directors, until your own identity is lost among them.

We saw at Willard's many who had thus found out for themselves that, when Nature gives a young man no other utilizable faculty, she must be understood as intending him for a soldier. The bulk of the army had moved out of Washington before we reached the city; yet it seemed to us that at least two thirds of the guests and idlers at the hotel wore one or another token of the military profession. Many of them, no doubt, were self-commissioned officers, and put on the buttons and the shoulder straps, and booted themselves to the knees, merely because captain, in these days, is so good a travelling name. The majority, however, had been duly appointed by the President, but might be none the better warriors for that. It was pleasant, occasionally, to distinguish a grizzly veteran among this crowd of carpet-knights—the trained soldier of a lifetime, long ago from West Point, who had spent his prime upon the frontier, and very likely could show an Indian bullet-mark on his breast—if such decorations, won in an obscure warfare, were worth the showing now.

The question often occurred to me—and, to say the truth, it added an indefinable piquancy to the scene—what proportion of all these people, whether soldiers or civilians, were true at heart to the Union; and what part were tainted, more or less, with treasonable sympathies and wishes, even if such had never blossomed into purpose. Traitors there were among them—no doubt of that —civil servants of the public, very reputable persons, who yet deserved to dangle from a cord; or men who unbuttoned military coats over their breasts, hiding perilous secrets there, which might bring the gallant officer to stand pale-faced before a file of musketeers, with his open grave behind him.

But, without insisting upon such picturesque criminality and punishment as this, an observer, who kept both his eyes and heart open, would find it by no means difficult to discern that many residents and visitors of Washington so far sided with the South as to desire nothing more nor better than to see everything re-established a little worse than its former basis. If the cabinet of Richmond were transferred to the Federal city, and the North awfully snubbed, at least, and driven back within its old political limits, they would deem it a happy day. . . .

Sallie Putnam

On the Confederate Army in the Streets of Richmond

It is April 1862, and a Richmond woman records the passage of the South's Army of the Potomac—soon to be better known as the Army of Northern Virginia—to the battlefields of the Virginia Peninsula, in her memoir, Richmond During the War.

The day of the passage of the Army of the Potomac through Richmond will long be remembered by those who were then in the city. It was known that they were on their way to the Peninsula, and for days they had been expected to march through the streets of the capital. The greatest interest and excitement prevailed. The morning was bright and beautiful in the early spring, balmy with the odors of the violet and the hyacinth, and the flaunting narcissus, the jonquil, and myriads of spring flowers threw on their parti-colored garments to welcome the army of veterans as they passed.

From an early hour until the sun went down in the West the steady tramp of the soldier was heard on the streets. Continuous cheers went up from thousands of voices;

from every window fair heads were thrust, fair hands waved snowy handkerchiefs, and bright eyes beamed "welcome!" Bands of spirit-stirring music discoursed the favorite airs,—Dixie's Land, My Maryland, the Bonny Blue Flag, and other popular tunes—and as the last regiments were passing we heard the strains of "Good-Bye," and tears were allowed to flow, and tender hearts ached as they listened to the significant tune. Soldiers left the ranks to grasp the hands of friends in passing, to receive some grateful refreshment, a small bouquet, or a whispered congratulation. Officers on horseback raised their hats, and some of the more gallant ventured to waft kisses to the fair ones at the doors and windows. We shall never forget the appearance of General Longstreet, the sturdy fighter, the obstinate warrior, as he dashed down Main street surrounded by his splendid staff.

Through other streets poured our cavalry, under their gallant chieftain, the pink of Southern chivalry,—the gay, rollicking, yet bold, daring and venturous "Jeb." Stuart. As we saw him then, sitting easily on the saddle, as though he was born to it, he seemed every inch the cavalier. His stout yet lithe figure, his graceful bearing, his broad, well-formed chest and shoulders, on which was gracefully poised his splendid head, his bright, beaming countenance, lighted up with a smile as pleasant as a woman's, his dark red hair and flowing beard, with his lower limbs encased in heavy cavalry boots, made up the *tout ensemble* of this brave son of Maryland. His genial temperament made him the idol and companion of the most humble of his men, and his deeds of daring and heroic courage made him respected as their leader.

As they swept through our streets on that beautiful morning, with their horses in good order, their own spirits buoyant and cheerful, many of them wearing in their caps bouquets of the golden daffodils of early spring, cheered on by the ringing sounds of the bugle, we thought never to see them pass again with worn-out horses and weary, listless spirits, as they spurred on their broken-down steeds; but so it was.

The Sumter Light Guards, Company K of the 4th Regiment Georgia Volunteer Infantry. April, 1861. Photograph. Georgia Department of Archives & History, Atlanta.

George Washington Cable
On the Fall of New Orleans

The Southern writer recalls the day in his youth, in the spring of 1862, when the Yankees came to the Crescent City.

In the spring of 1862, we boys of Race, Orange, Magazine, Camp, Constance, Annunciation, Prytania, and other streets had no game. Nothing was "in"; none of the old playground sports that commonly fill the school-boy's calendar. We were even tired of drilling. Not one of us between seven and seventeen but could beat the drum, knew every bugle-call, and could go through the manual of arms and the facings like a drill-sergeant. We were *blasé* old soldiers—military critics.

Who could tell us anything? I recall but one trivial admission of ignorance on the part of any lad. On a certain day of grand review, when the city's entire defensive force was marching through Canal street, there came along, among the endless variety of good and bad uniforms, a stately body of tall, stalwart Germans, clad from head to foot in velveteen of a peculiarly vociferous fragrance, and a boy, spelling out the name upon their banner, said:

"H-u-s-s-a-r-s: what's them?"

"Aw, you fool!" cried a dozen urchins at once, "them's the Hoosiers. Don't you smell 'em?"

But that was earlier. The day of grand reviews was past. Hussars, Zouaves, and numberless other bodies of outlandish name had gone to the front in Tennessee and Virginia. Our cultivated eyes were satisfied now with one uniform that we saw daily. Every afternoon found us around in Coliseum Place, standing or lying on the grass watching the dress parade of the "Confederate Guards." Most of us had fathers or uncles in the long, spotless, gray, white-gloved ranks that stretched in such faultless alignment down the hard, harsh turf of our old ball-ground.

This was the flower of the home guard. The merchants, bankers, underwriters, judges, real-estate owners, and capitalists of the Anglo-American part of the city were "all present or accounted for" in that long line. Gray heads, hoar heads, high heads, bald heads. Hands flashed to breast and waist with a martinet's precision at the command of "Present arms,"—hands that had ruled by the pen—the pen and the dollar—since long before any of us young spectators was born, and had done no harder muscular work than carve roasts and turkeys these twenty, thirty, forty years. Here and there among them were individuals who, unaided, had clothed and armed companies, squadrons, battalions, and sent them to the Cumberland and the Potomac. A good three-fourths of them had sons on distant battle-fields, some living, some dead.

We boys saw nothing pathetic in this array of old men. To us there was only rich enjoyment in the scene. If there was anything solemn about it, why did the band play polkas? Away down to the far end of the line and back again, the short, stout German drum-major—holding his gaudy office in this case by virtue of his girth, not height (as he had himself explained)—flourished his big stick majestically, bursting with rage at us for casually reiterating at short intervals in his hearing that "he kot it mit his size."

In those beautiful spring afternoons there was scarcely a man to be found, anywhere, out of uniform. Down on the steamboat landing, our famous Levee, a superb body of Creoles drilled and paraded in dark-blue uniform. The orders were given in French; the manual was French; the movements were quick, short, nervy. Their "about march" was four sharp stamps of their neatly shod feet—*un, deux, trois, quatre*—that brought them face about and sent them back, tramp, tramp, tramp, over the smooth white pavement of powdered oyster-shells. Ah, the nakedness of that once crowded and roaring mart!

And there was a "Foreign Legion." Of course, the city had always been full of foreigners; but now it was a subject of amazement, not unmixed with satire, to see how many whom every one had supposed to be Americans or "citizens of Louisiana" bloomed out as British, or French, or Spanish subjects. But, even so, the tremendous pressure of popular sentiment crowded them into the ranks and forced them to make every show of readiness to "hurl back the foe," as we used to call it. And they really served for much. Merely as a gendarmerie they relieved just so many Confederate soldiers of police duty in a city under martial law, and enabled them to man forts and breastworks at short notice whenever that call should come.

But the public mind was at a transparent heat. Everybody wanted to know of everybody else, "Why don't you go to the front?" Even the gentle maidens demanded tartly, one of another, why their brothers or lovers had not gone long ago, though, in truth, the laggards were few indeed. The very children were fierce. For now even we, the uninformed, the lads and women, knew the enemy was closing down upon us. Of course we confronted the fact very valorously, we boys and mothers and sisters—and the newspapers. Had we not inspected the fortifications ourselves? Was not every man in town ready to rush into them at the twelve taps of the fire-alarm bells? Were we not ready to man them if the men gave out? Nothing afloat could pass the forts. Nothing that walked could get through our swamps. The *Mississippi*—and, in fact, she was a majestically terrible structure, only let us *complete* her—would sweep the river clean!

But there was little laughter. Food was dear; the destitute poor were multiplying terribly; the market men and women, mainly Germans, Gascon-French, and Sicilians, had lately refused to take the shinplaster currency, and the city authority had forced them to accept it. There was little to laugh at. The Mississippi was gnawing its levees and threatening to plunge in upon us. The city was believed to be full of spies.

I shall not try to describe the day the alarm-bells told us the city was in danger and called every man to his mustering-point. The children poured out from the school-gates and ran crying to their homes, meeting their sobbing mothers at their thresholds. The men fell into ranks. I was left entirely alone in charge of the store in which I was employed. Late in the afternoon, receiving orders to close it, I did so, and went home. But I did not stay. I went to the river-side. There until far into the night I saw hundreds of drays carrying cotton out of the presses and yards to the wharves, where it was fired. The glare of those sinuous miles of flame set men and women weeping and wailing thirty miles away on the farther shore of Lake Pontchartrain. But the next day was the day of terrors. During the night fear, wrath, and sense of betrayal had run through the people as the fire had run through the cotton. You have seen, perhaps, a family fleeing with lamentations and wringing of hands out of a burning house: multiply it by thousands upon thousands; that was New Orleans, though the houses were not burning. The firemen were out; but they cast fire on the waters, putting the torch to the empty ships and cutting them loose to float down the river.

Whoever could go was going. The great mass, that had no place to go to or means to go with, was beside itself. "Betrayed! betrayed!" it cried, and ran in throngs from street to street, seeking some vent, some victim for its wrath. I saw a crowd catch a poor fellow at the corner of Magazine and Common streets, whose crime was that he looked like a stranger and might be a spy. He was the palest living man I ever saw. They swung him to a neighboring lamp-post, but the Foreign Legion was patroling the town in strong squads, and one of its lieutenants, all green and gold, leaped with drawn sword, cut the rope, and saved the man. This was but one occurrence: there were many like it. I stood in the rear door of our store, Canal street, soon after reopening it. The junior of the firm was within. I called him to look toward the river. The masts of the cutter *Washington* were slowly tipping, declining, sinking—down she went. The gun-boat moored next to her began to smoke all over and then to blaze. My employers fell into ranks and left the city—left their goods and their affairs in the hands of one mere lad (no stranger would

J. O. DAVIDSON.
*Union Fleet Passing
Burning "Governor
Moore."* 1886.
Century Collection,
New York.

have thought I had reached fourteen) and one big German porter. I closed the doors, sent the porter to his place in the Foreign Legion, and ran to the levee to see the sights.

What a gathering! The riff-raff of the wharves, the town, the gutters. Such women — such wrecks of women! And all the juvenile rag-tag. The lower steamboat landing, well covered with sugar, rice, and molasses, was being rifled. The men smashed; the women scooped up the smashings. The river was overflowing the top of the levee. A rain-storm began to threaten. "Are the Yankee ships in sight?" I asked of an idler. He pointed out the tops of their naked masts as they showed up across the huge bend of the river. They were engaging the batteries at Camp Chalmette — the old field of Jackson's renown. Presently that was over. Ah, me! I see them now as they come slowly round Slaughterhouse Point into full view, silent, grim, and terrible; black with men, heavy with deadly portent; the long-banished Stars and Stripes flying against the frowning sky. Oh, for the *Mississippi!* the *Mississippi!* Just then she came down upon them. But how? Drifting helplessly, a mass of flames.

The crowds on the levee howled and screamed with rage. The swarming decks answered never a word; but one old tar on the *Hartford*, standing with lanyard in hand beside a great pivot-gun, so plain to view that you could see him smile, silently patted its big black breech and blandly grinned.

And now the rain came down in sheets. About 1 or 2 o'clock in the afternoon (as I remember), I being again in the store with but one door ajar, came a roar of shoutings and imprecations and crowding feet down Common street. "Hurrah for Jeff Davis! Hurrah for Jeff Davis! Shoot them! Kill them! Hang them!" I locked the door on the outside, and ran to the front of the mob, bawling with the rest, "Hurrah for Jeff Davis!" About every third man there had a weapon out. Two officers of the United States navy were walking abreast, unguarded and alone, looking not to right or left, never frowning, never flinching, while the mob screamed in their ears, shook cocked pistols in their faces, cursed and crowded, and gnashed upon them. So through the gates of death those two men walked to the City Hall to demand the town's surrender. It was one of the bravest deeds I ever saw done.

Later events, except one, I leave to other pens. An officer from the fleet stood on the City Hall roof about to lower the flag of Louisiana. In the street beneath gleamed the bayonets of a body of marines. A howitzer pointed up and another down the street. All around swarmed the mob. Just then Mayor Monroe—lest the officer above should be fired upon, and the howitzers open upon the crowd—came out alone and stood just before one of the howitzers, tall, slender, with folded arms, eying the gunner. Down sank the flag. Captain Bell, tall and stiff, marched off with the flag rolled under his arm, and the howitzers clanking behind. Then cheer after cheer rang out for Monroe. And now, I dare say, every one is well pleased that, after all, New Orleans never lowered her colors with her own hands.

N. J. Brooks

Letter on the Battlefields of Richmond July 4-5, 1862

A Georgia cavalryman views the carnage and suffering of the Seven Days' Battles.

Richmond, Virginia : July 4, 1862

Dear Mother and all:

I take the present opportunity to write to you. I expect you are mad because I had not written sooner, but I think if you knew what I have been through and how sick I have been and am now you would excuse me. It is with great effort that I make this attempt, but I must write as much as I can and rest and try it again. To write all I have seen and know would take a volume. I will sketch at a few things. The great battle near Richmond commenced yesterday evening a week ago and is still continuing. They have fought every day and night since it began. I did not hear any fighting yesterday. I was on picket the day it began. They began skirmishing in half a mile of my post. Late in the evening I was relieved and went back to camp. I concluded to follow on and get with them, accordingly next morning I started. They were fighting at Mechanicsville about five miles below here. I got there in time to see them wind up the show and start the Yankees to running. Soon after the fight was over they began to bring in the wounded, and I went in among them and began to give them water. While doing this, I turned sick at the sight of the blood. While there I saw two dying, one a Christian undoubtedly, for he was praying, saying, "Oh! my Jesus, sweet Jesus, come, take me home!" and many other such like expressions he used. The other was not saying a word but holding up his hands.

After staying a while with these sufferers I went on, on the way the Yanks retreated, inquiring for my legion. The route was strewn with a heap of Yankee plunder. Many dead and wounded horses were seen by the wayside and occasionally a dead man. Trees were cut up by cannon balls and the road filled with ambulances, ordnance wagons, worn out soldiers and ordnance and equipment. I went on 'till I came to a mill, where the North Carolinians charged the enemy's entrenchments through brush and an old millpond place and drove them away and lost many a life. This happened the day before. They were lying very thick on both sides of the road. They were lying in every position you could think, some holding up their hands, looking very pitiful, some across their guns. I saw two that were killed with cannon balls, one's head shot off, the other his face, leaving his hollow skull attached to his body. While looking at these dead, I thought I saw Joe Ford. Thinks I, poor Joe, here you lie! I spurred my horse up to him and soon perceived that he was a larger man than Joe and that he was a North Carolinian.

After awhile I went on in the direction of the firing, hunting for my legion and Pink's Brigade and got in three-fourth miles of where they were bombing each other with all fury. I stood off on an eminence and beheld the scene, which was awful and terrible beyond the power of human tongue to tell or pen to describe. After fighting some time, the Yanks retreated, leaving many valuable things behind, such as ammunitions, boats and boat wagons, which they carried along to cross rivers with, provided the bridges should be burnt. They went on and took another position and began to fight most desperately. I hurried on, thinking I would find somebody that I knew, for I had not seen a man that I knew the whole day. I passed an ordnance wagon, which the Yanks broke down and set afire. The bombs were bursting and powder exploding, making as much noise as a little battle. I was soon on the battlefield and saw the contending parties engaged. It was Yankee infantry fighting our artillery. They were about 100 yards apart and pour into each other a most deadly fire. I could see the men falling. The Yanks fought bravely, keeping a good line and holding their ground very well while I stayed. I looked around for cavalry to get with but saw none. I had 20 cartridges I wanted to fire into the enemy lines, but, seeing no cavalry nor anybody I knew, I did not venture in reach of their small arms. I was in reach, too, but not in their range. I was in range of some of their cannons, for several balls passed me while I was watching the fight. I thought it best for me not to get in, as there were no cavalry to go with nor friend to know what, became of me, provided I should get killed or wounded.

Winslow Homer. *Wounded Soldier Being Given a Drink from a Canteen.* 1864. Charcoal, white chalk on green paper. 14⅜ x 19¾". Cooper-Hewitt National Museum of Design, Smithsonian Institution / Art Resource, New York.

I feel very unwell this morning but will try and finish this letter. While on the field I saw a heart-rending sight. The wounded getting off of the battlefield, some hobbling alone, some with broken arms dangling by their sides, some with bloody heads, one his whiskers and hair burnt in a crisp by the explosion of powder. Some that were wounded in arms were helping those that were wounded in the legs. I saw poor fellow who was trying to get another one who was shot through the ankle. He had him up astride of his neck. The fellow was so sick he was reeling every way, wearying his companion a great deal. I told him I would take him away on my horse. He said he would be glad I would. I got him up behind me. As I was leaving with him, I heard a cannon ball coming right behind me. I thought it was going to take my head off, and I could not help dodging, the only ball I ever dodged. And I had heard many whiz before but not so close. It passed right over a man's head, the wind of it knocking him nearly off of his horse, and struck the ground, tearing large hole. I brought my man back towards Richmond. He came very near fainting several times. I'd give him water, and he would revive. At last he gave out and said he could not stand it. I got a man to help me down with him and lay him by the roadside. I stayed with him 'till an ambulance came along and put him in it and sent him to Richmond.

As I came along, I passed a hospital for wounded, where I heard a woman weeping and wailing like one in deepest despair. I thought that if all the women, North and South, would come upon the hills and valleys around Richmond and could see at once the many slain of their fathers, husbands, sons, brothers and lovers, that their weeping and wailing would be such that it would wring tears from angelic eyes and that there would be a ten-fold greater clamor for peace among them than there ever was for war. Men love to fight too well to ever need the example and persuasion of women to excite them to war. I tell you of a truth, a battlefield is awful when you see thousands of angry warriors rushing upon each other, yelling like so many hell hounds from the infernal regions, with glittering steel and brazen guns, eager for each other's destruction. And when you see hundreds of bombs bursting and men falling, horses running away, killing themselves and riders, cannons firing, clouds of smoke and dust rising, cannon balls tearing up the earth and cutting down timber, ambulances and men running hither and thither getting the wounded away, many wounded getting themselves and other wounded away as bloody as butchered hogs. . . .

Herman Melville
"MALVERN HILL"

Novelist Melville commemorates Malvern Hill, the last battle of the Seven Days' Battles, fought on July 1, 1862.

———————

Ye elms that wave on Malvern Hill
      In prime of morn and May,
Recall ye how McClellan's men
      Here stood at bay?
While deep within yon forest dim
      Our rigid comrades lay—
Some with the cartridge in their mouth,

Others with fixed arms lifted South—
                    Invoking so
the cypress glades? Ah wilds of woe!

The spires of Richmond, late behold
                    Through rifts in musket-haze
Were closed from view in clouds of dust
                    on leaf-walled ways,
Where streamed our wagons in caravan;
                    And the Seven Nights and Days
Of march and fast, retreat and fight,
Pinched our grimed faces to ghastly plight—
                    Does the elm wood
Recall the haggard beards of blood?

The battle-smoked flag, with stars eclipsed,
                    We followed (it never fell)—
In silence husbanded our strength—
                    Received their yell;
Till on this slope we patient turned
                    With cannon ordered well;
Reverse we proved was not defeat;
But ah, the sod what thousands met!—
                    Does Malvern wood
Bethink itself, and muse and brood?

We elms of Malvern Hill
                    Remember every thing;
But sap the twig will fill:
Wag the world how it will,
                    Leaves must be green in Spring.

William Thompson Lusk
Letter from a Union Soldier
September 6, 1862

In the aftermath of the Second Bull Run campaign, in August of 1862, a Federal soldier reflects bitterly on the state of affairs.

HEADQUARTERS 1ST DIVISION, 9TH ARMY CORPS,
MERIDIAN HILL, WASHINGTON, D. C.

Sept. 6th, 1862.

My dear Mother:

Now that our General is dead, a Colonel commands the old Division temporarily, and I continue to superintend the office, running the old machine along until different arrangements can be made, when I suppose I shall be set adrift with no pleasant prospects

EDWIN FORBES. *Union Forces, 2nd Bull Run. Retreat of the Army of the Rappahannock, August 28, 1862.* Pencil and wash. 5⅝ x 14⅞". Library of Congress, Washington, D.C.

before me. I would resign, were I permitted to do so, and would gladly return to my medical studies this winter, tired as I am of the utter mismanagement which characterizes the conduct of our public affairs. Disheartened by the termination of a disastrous campaign—disasters which every one could and did easily foresee from the course pursued—we find as a consolation, that our good honest old President has told a new story apropos of the occasion, and the land is ringing with the wisdom of the rail-splitting Solomon. Those who were anxious and burning to serve their country, can only view with sullen disgust the vast resources of the land directed not to make our arms victorious, but to give political security to those in power. Men show themselves in a thousand ways incompetent, yet still receive the support of the Government. Politicians, like Carl Schurz, receive high places in the army without a qualification to recommend them. Stern trusty old soldiers like Stevens are treated with cold neglect. The battle comes—there is no head on the field—the men are handed over to be butchered—to die on inglorious fields. Lying reports are written. Political Generals receive praises where they deserve execration. Old Abe makes a joke. The army finds that nothing has been learned. New preparations are made, with all the old errors retained. New battles are prepared for, to end in new disasters. Alas, my poor country! The army is sadly demoralized. Men feel that there is no honor to be gained by the sword. No military service is recognized unless coupled with political interest. The army is exhausted with suffering—its enthusiasm is dead. Should the enemy attack us here however, we should be victorious. The men would never yield up their Capitol. There is something more though than the draft needed to enable us to march a victorious host to the Gulf of Mexico. Well, I have been writing freely enough to entitle me to accommodations in Fort Lafayette, but I can hardly express the grief and indignation I feel at the past. God grant us better things in future.

I had said my own prospects are somewhat gloomy. When the changes are made in this command, and new hands shall take charge of it, I will have to return to the 79th Regiment—a fate at which I shudder. The Regiment has been in five large battles, and in ten or twelve smaller engagements. While adding on each occasion new luster to its own reputation, it has never taken part in a successful action. The proud body that started from the city over a thousand strong, are now a body of cripples. The handful (230) that remains are foreigners whose patriotism misfortunes have quenched. The *morale* is destroyed—discipline relaxed beyond hope of restoration. The General and all the true friends of the Regiment were of the opinion that it should be mustered out of the service. After performing hard duties in the field for fifteen months I find there is nothing left me, but to sink into disgrace with a Regiment that is demoralized past hope of restoration. This for a reward. I am writing this from the old scene of the mutiny of last year. A strange year it has been. God has marvellously preserved my life through every danger.

May he be merciful to my mother in the year to come. My old friend Matteson is dead. He was a Major in Yates' Regiment of Sharpshooters which distinguished itself at Corinth. He died at Rosecrans' Headquarters, of typhoid fever.

We are going to move from here to-morrow, but your safest direction will be Capt. W. T. Lusk, A. A. A. G., 1st Div. 9th Army Corps, Washington (or elsewhere). All the letters sent me since I left Fredericksburg have miscarried, and I am very anxious for news.

Affec'y.,
WILL.

Oliver Wendell Holmes
"MY HUNT AFTER THE CAPTAIN"
On the Search for His Wounded Son

In an essay for the Atlantic Monthly, *the Autocrat of the Breakfast Table writes of his search for his son, Oliver Wendell Holmes, Jr., the future Supreme Court justice, wounded at Antietam on September 17, 1862.*

In the dead of the night which closed upon the bloody field of Antietam, my household was startled from its slumbers by the loud summons of a telegraphic messenger. The air had been heavy all day with rumors of battle, and thousands and tens of thousands had walked the streets with throbbing hearts, in dread anticipation of the tidings any hour might bring.

We rose hastily, and presently the messenger was admitted. I took the envelope from his hand, opened it, and read:

Hagerstown 17th

To [Oliver Wendell] H[olmes]
Capt H[olmes] was wounded shot through the neck thought not mortal at Keedysville

WILLIAM G LEDUC

Through the neck—no bullet left in wound. Windpipe, foodpipe, carotid, jugular, half a dozen smaller, but still formidable, vessels, a great braid of nerves, each as big as a lamp-wick, spinal cord—ought to kill at once, if at all. *Thought not* mortal, or *not thought* mortal—which was it? The first; that is better than the second would be;— "Keedysville, a post office, Washington Co, Maryland." Leduc? Leduc? Don't remember that name. The boy is waiting for his money. A dollar and thirteen cents. Has nobody got thirteen cents? Don't keep that boy waiting—how do we know what messages he has got to carry?

The boy *had* another message to carry. It was to the father of Lieutenant Colonel Wilder Dwight, informing him that his son was grievously wounded in the same battle, and was lying at Boonesborough, a town a few miles this side of Keedysville. This I learned the next morning from the civil and attentive officials at the Central Telegraph Office.

Calling upon this gentleman, I found that he meant to leave in the quarter past two o'clock train, taking with him Dr. George H. Gray, an accomplished and energetic surgeon, equal to any difficult question or pressing emergency. I agreed to accompany them, and we met in the cars. I felt myself peculiarly fortunate in having companions whose society would be a pleasure, whose feelings would harmonize with my own, and whose assistance I might, in case of need, be glad to claim.

I set out with a full and heavy heart, though many times chilled with what were perhaps needless and unwise fears, though I broke through all my habits without thinking about them, which is almost as hard in certain circumstances as for one of our young fellows to leave his sweetheart and go into a Peninsular campaign. . . .

There was nothing worthy of special note in the trip to Frederick, except our passing a squad of Rebel prisoners, whom I missed seeing as they flashed by, but who were said to be a most forlorn-looking crowd of scarecrows. Arrived at the Monacacy River, about three miles this side of Frederick, we came to a halt, for the railroad bridge had been blown up by the Rebels, and its iron pillars and arches were lying in the bed of the river. The unfortunate wretch who fired the train was killed by the explosion, and lay buried hard by, his hands sticking out of the shallow grave into which he had been huddled.

There was a great confusion of carriages and wagons at the stopping place of the train, so that it was a long time before I could get anything that would carry us. At last I was lucky enough to light on a sturdy wagon, drawn by a pair of serviceable bays, and driven by James Grayden with whom I was destined to have a somewhat continued acquaintance. . . .

Frederick looked cheerful for a place that had so recently been in an enemy's hands. There and there a house or shop was shut up, but the national colors were waving in all directions, and the general aspect was peaceful and contented. I saw no bullet marks or other signs of the fighting which had gone on in the streets. The Colonel's lady was taken in charge by a daughter of that hospitable family to which we had been commended, and I proceeded to inquire for wounded officers at the various temporary hospitals.

At the United States Hotel, where many were lying, I heard mention of an officer in an upper chamber, and, going there, found Lieutenant Abbot, of the Twentieth Massachusetts Volunteers, lying ill with what looked like typhoid fever. While there, who should come in but the almost ubiquitous Lieutenant Wilkins, of the same Twentieth, whom I had met repeatedly before on errands of kindness or duty, and who was just from the battle ground. He was going to Boston in charge of the body of the lamented Dr. Revere, the Assistant Surgeon of the regiment, killed on the field.

From his lips, I learned something of the mishaps of the regiment. My Captain's wound he spoke of as less grave than at first thought; but he mentioned incidentally having heard a story recently that he was *killed*—a fiction, doubtless—a mistake—a palpable absurdity—not to be remembered or made any account of. Oh, no! but what dull ache is this where the nervous centre called the *semilunar ganglion* lies unconscious of itself until a great grief or a mastering anxiety reaches it through all the non-conductors which isolate it from ordinary impressions?

I talked awhile with Lieutenant Abbot, who lay prostrate, feeble, but soldier-like and uncomplaining, carefully waited upon by a most excellent lady, a captain's wife, New England born, loyal as the Liberty on a golden ten-dollar piece, and of lofty bearing enough to have sat for that Goddess's portrait. She had stayed in Frederick through the Rebel inroad, and kept the star-spangled banner where it would be safe, to unroll it as the last Rebel hoofs clattered off from the pavement of the town.

And now, as we emerged from Frederick, we struck at once upon the trail from the great battle-field. The road was filled with straggling and wounded soldiers. All who could travel on foot—multitudes with slight wounds of the upper limbs, the head, or face—were told to take up their beds—a light burden or none at all—and walk. Just as the battlefield sucks everything into its red vortex for the conflict, so does it drive everything off in long, diverging rays after the fierce centripetal forces have met and neutralized each other.

For more than a week there had been sharp fighting all along this road. Through the streets of Frederick, through Crampton's Gap, over South Mountain, sweeping at last the hills and the woods that skirt the windings of the Antietam, the long battle had travelled, like one of those tornadoes which tear their path through our fields and villages. The slain of higher condition, "embalmed" and iron-cased, were sliding off on the railways to their far homes; the dead of the rank and file were being gathered up and committed hastily to the earth; the gravely wounded were cared for hard by the scene of conflict, or pushed a little way along to the neighboring villages; while those who could walk were meeting us, as I have said, at every step in the road.

It was a pitiable sight, truly pitiable, yet so vast, so far beyond the possibility of relief, that many single sorrows of small dimensions have wrought upon my feelings more than the sight of this great caravan of maimed pilgrims. The companionship of so many seemed to make a joint stock of their suffering; it was next to impossible to individualize it, and so bring it home, as one can do with a single broken limb or aching wound. Then they were all of the male sex, and in the freshness or the prime of their strength. Though they tramped so wearily along, yet there was rest and kind nursing in store for them. These wounds they bore would be the medals they would show children and grandchildren by and by. Who would not rather wear his decorations beneath his uniform than on it?

Yet among them were figures which arrested our attention and sympathy. Delicate boys, with more spirit than strength, flushed with fever or pale with exhaustion or haggard with suffering, dragged their weary limbs along as if each step would exhaust their slender store of strength. At the roadside sat or lay others, quite spent with their journey. Here and there was a house at which the wayfarers could stop, in the hope, I fear often vain, of getting refreshment; and in one place was a clear, cool spring, where the little hands of the long procession halted for a few moments, as the trains that traverse the desert rest by its fountains. . . .

At intervals, a dead horse lay by the roadside, or in the fields unburied, not grateful to gods or men; I saw no bird of prey, no ill-omened fowl, on my way to the carnival of death, or at the place where it had been held . . . no black wing was spread over these animal ruins, and no call to the banquet pierced through the heavy-laden and sickening air. . . .

On Sunday morning, the twenty-first, having engaged James Grayden and his team, I set out with the Chaplain and the Philanthropist for Keedysville. Our track lay through the South Mountain Gap, and led us first to the town of Boonesborough, where, it will be remembered Colonel Dwight had been brought after the battle. We saw the positions occupied in the battle of South Mountain, and many traces of the conflict. In one situation a group of young trees was marked with shot, hardly one having escaped. . . .

A ride of some three hours brought us to Boonesborough, where I roused the unfortunate army surgeon who had charge of the hospitals, and who was trying to get a little sleep after his fatigues and watchings. He bore his cross very creditably, and helped me to explore all places where my soldier might be lying among the crowds of wounded. After the useless search, I resumed my journey, fortified with a note of introduction to Dr. Letterman; also with a bale of oakum which I was to carry to that Gentleman, this substance being employed as a substitute for lint. We were obliged also to procure a pass to Keedysville from the Provost Marshal of Boonesborough. As we came near the place, we learned that General McClellan's headquarters had been removed from this village some miles farther to the front.

On entering the small settlement of Keedysville, there were some thousands of wounded in the place, he told me, scattered about everywhere. It would be a long job to hunt up my Captain; the only way would be to go to every house and ask for him. Just then a medical officer came up.

"Do you know anything of Captain H. of the Massachusetts Twentieth?"

"Oh yes; he is staying in that house. I saw him there, doing very well."

A chorus of hallelujahs arose in my soul, but I kept them to myself. Now, then, for our twice-wounded volunteer, our young centurion whose double-barred shoulder straps

COLORPLATE 57

JOHN GADSBY CHAPMAN. *Charleston Bay and City.* 1864. Oil on board. 11½ × 15½″.
Museum of the Confederacy, Richmond. Photo by Katherine Wetzel.

COLORPLATE 58

EDWARD LAMSON HENRY. *City Point, Virginia: Headquarters of General Grant.* 1872. Oil on canvas.
29½ × 60½". Addison Gallery of American Art, Phillips Academy, Andover, Massachusetts.
Photo copyright © Addison Gallery of Art.

COLORPLATE 59

EARL OF DUNMORE. *Blockade Runner Nashville and Escorts, April 24, 1862.*
Watercolor. 11¼ × 15½". The Mariner's Museum, Newport News, Virginia.

COLORPLATE 60

WILLIAM TORGERSON. *Confederate Blockade Runners at St. George's, Bermuda.* 1881. Oil on canvas. 29¾ × 48″. West Point Museum, United States Military Academy, West Point, New York.

COLORPLATE 61

D. J. **KENNEDY.** *The Blockade Runner Ashore.* 1864. Watercolor. 10¼ × 16¾″. Franklin D. Roosevelt Library, Hyde Park, New York.

COLORPLATE 62

D. McFarlane.
*C. S. S. Nashville
Burning the Ship
Harvey Birch.*
1864. Oil on
canvas. 23½ ×
35½″. Peabody
Museum of Salem,
Massachusetts.

COLORPLATE 63

ALEXANDER SIMPLOT. *The Great Naval Battle at Memphis, June 1862.* 1862.
Oil on canvas. 30¼ × 42⅛″. Chicago Historical Society.

COLORPLATE 64

EDOUARD MANET. *Alabama and Kearsarge.* ca. 1865. Oil on canvas. 54¼ × 50¾″.
Philadelphia Museum of Art. The John G. Johnson Collection.

COLORPLATE 65

JAMES HOPE. *Burnside's Bridge.* ca. 1885. Oil on canvas. 144 × 66″.
Antietam National Battlefield, Sharpsburg, Maryland. Photo by Edward Owen.

COLORPLATE 66

JAMES HOPE. *Dunker Church.* ca. 1885. Oil on canvas. 144 × 66″.
Antietam National Battlefield, Sharpsburg, Maryland. Photo by Edward Owen.

we have never yet looked upon. Let us observe the proprieties, however; no swelling upward of the mother—no *hysterica passio*—we do not like scenes. A calm salutation—then swallow and hold hard. That is about the programme.

A cottage of squared logs, filled in with plaster, and white-washed. A little yard before it, with a gate swinging. The door of the cottage ajar—no one visible as yet. I push open the door and enter. An old woman, Margaret Kitxmuller her name proves to be, is the first person I see.

"Captain H. here?"

"Oh no, sir—he left yesterday morning for Hagerstown—in a milk-cart."

But there was the great battle-field only about three miles from Keedysville.

We followed the road through the village for a space, then turned off to the right, and wandered somewhat vaguely, for want of precise directions, over the hills. Inquiring as we went, we forded a wide creek in which soldiers were washing their clothes, the name of which we did not then know, but which must have been the Antietam. At one point we met a party, women among them, bringing off various trophies they had picked up on the battlefield. Still wandering along, we were at last pointed to a hill in the distance, a part of the summit of which was covered with Indian corn. There, we were told, some of the fiercest fighting of the day had been done. The fences were taken down so as to make a passage across the fields, and the tracks worn within the last few days looked like old roads. We passed a fresh grave under a tree near the road. A board was nailed to the tree, bearing the name, as well as I could make it out, of Gardiner, of a New Hampshire regiment.

On coming near the brow of the hill, we met a party carrying picks and spades. "How many?" "Only one." The dead were nearly all buried, then, in this region of the field of strife. We stopped the wagon, and, getting out, began to look around us. Hard by was a large pile of muskets, scores, if not hundreds, which had been picked up, and were guarded for the Government. A long ridge of fresh gravel rose before us. A board stuck up in front of it bore this inscription, the first part of which was, I believe, not correct: "The Rebel General Anderson and 80 Rebels are buried in this hole."

Other smaller ridges were marked with the number of dead lying under them. The whole ground was strewn with fragments of clothing, haversacks, canteens, cap boxes, bullets, cartridges, scraps of paper, portions of bread and meat. I saw two soldiers' caps that looked as though their owners had been shot through the head. In several places I noticed dark red patches where a pool of blood had curdled and caked, as some poor fellow poured his life out on the sod. I then wandered about in the cornfield. It surprised me to notice, that, though there was every mark of hard fighting having taken place here, the Indian corn was not generally trodden down.

One of our cornfields is a kind of forest, and even when fighting, men avoid the tall stalks as if they were trees. At the edge of this cornfield lay a gray horse, said to have belonged to a Rebel colonel, who was killed near the same place. Not far off were two dead artillery horses in their harness. Another had been attended to by a burying-party, who had thrown some earth over him; but his last bedclothes were too short, and his legs stuck out stark and stiff from beneath the gravel coverlet.

It was a great pity that we had no intelligent guide to explain to us the position of that portion of the two armies which fought over this ground. There was a shallow trench before we came to the cornfield, too narrow for a road, as I should think, too elevated for a watercourse, and which seemed to have been used as a rifle pit. At any rate, there had been hard fighting in and about it. This and the cornfield may serve to identify the part of the ground we visited, if any who fought there should ever look over this paper. The opposing tides of battle must have blended their waves at this point, for portions of gray uniform were mingled with the "garments rolled in blood" torn from our own dead and wounded soldiers.

I picked up a Rebel canteen, and one of our own—but there was something repulsive about the trodden and stained relics of the stale battlefield. It was like the table of some hideous orgy left uncleared, and one turned away disgusted from its broken fragments and muddy heeltaps. A bullet or two, a button, a brass plate from a soldier's belt served well enough for mementos of my visit, with a letter, which I picked up directed to Richmond, Virginia, its seal unbroken. "N. C., Cleveland County, E. Wright to J. Wright." On the other side, "A few lines from W. L. Vaughn," who has just been writing for the wife to her husband and continues on his own account. The postscript, "tell John that nancy's folks are all well and has a very good little Crop of corn a growing."

I wonder, if, by one of those strange chances of which I have seen so many, this number or leaf of the "Atlantic" will not sooner or later find its way to Cleveland County, North Carolina, and E. Wright, widow of James Wright, and Nancy's folks, get from these sentences the last glimpse of husband and friend as he threw up his arms and fell in the bloody cornfield of Antietam? I will keep this stained letter for them until peace comes back, if it comes in my time.

Lieutenant P—, of the Pennsylvania—th, was a very fresh, bright-looking young man, lying in bed from the effects of a recent injury received in action. A grape-shot, after passing through a post and a board, had struck him in the hip, bruising, but not penetrating or breaking. He had good news for me.

That very afternoon, a party of wounded officers had passed through Harrisburg, going East. He had conversed in the bar-room of this hotel with one of them, who was wounded about the shoulder (it might be the lower part of the neck), and had his arm in a sling. He belonged to the Twentieth Massachusetts; the Lieutenant saw that he was a Captain, by the two bars on his shoulder strap. His name was my family name; he was tall and youthful, like my Captain. At four o'clock he had left in the train for Philadelphia. . . .

What more could I ask to assure me of the Captain's safety? As soon as the telegraph office opens to-morrow morning we will send a message to our friends in Philadelphia, and get a reply, doubtless, which will settle the whole matter.

The hopeful morrow dawned at last, and the following reply was received:

"Phil Sept 24 I think the report you have heard that W has gone East must be an error we have not seen or heard of him here MLH"

ALEXANDER GARDNER.
*Burial Detail on
the Miller Farm.*
September 19, 1862.
Photograph. Library
of Congress,
Washington, D.C.

He *could* not have passed through Philadelphia without visiting the house called Beautiful, where he had been so tenderly cared for after his wound at Ball's Bluff, and where those whom he loved were lying in grave peril of life or limb. Yet *did* he pass through Harrisburg, going East, going to Philadelphia, on his way home? Ah, this is it! He must have taken the late night train from Philadelphia for New York, in his impatience to reach home. There is such a train, not down in the guide book, but we are assured of the fact at the Harrisburg depot.

By and by came the reply from Dr. Wilson's telegraphic message: nothing had been heard of the Captain at Chambersburg. Still later, another message came from our Philadelphia friend, saying he was last seen at the house of Mrs. K, a well-known Union lady in Hagerstown. . . . A telegram was at once sent to Mrs. K.—asking information. But when the answer would be received was uncertain, as the Government almost monopolized the line. . . .

Ten o'clock in the evening was approaching. The telegraph office would presently close, and as yet there were no tidings from Hagerstown. Let us step over and see for ourselves. A message! A message!

"*Captain H. still here* leaves tomorrow for Harrisburg Penna Is doing well

Mrs H K

A note from Dr. Cuyler to the same effect came soon afterwards to the hotel. . . . We shall sleep well tonight. . . .

The time approached for the train to arrive from Hagerstown, and we went to the station.

The expected train came in so quietly that I was almost startled to see it on the track. Let us walk calmly through the cars, and look around us.

In the first car, on the fourth seat to the right, I saw my Captain; there saw I him, even my first-born, whom I had sought through many cities.

"How are you, Boy?"

"How are you, Dad?"

Such are the proprieties of life, as they are observed among us Anglo-Saxons of the nineteen century, decently disguising those natural impulses. . . . But the hidden cisterns of the soul may be filling fast with sweet tears, while the windows through which it looks are undimmed by a drop or a film of moisture. . . .

Heros Von Borcke

On Jeb Stuart's Ball

In September 1862, during the Maryland campaign, the Confederate cavalry stages an interlude from war; from Memoirs of the Confederate War for Independence, *by one of Jeb Stuart's staff officers.*

———————————

We were indulging in the dreamy sentiment natural to the hour, when the gay voice of Stuart broke in—"Major, what a capital place for us to give a ball in honour of our arrival in Maryland! don't you think we could manage it?" To this there was a unanimous response in the affirmative, which was especially hearty on the part of the ladies. It was at once agreed that the ball should be given. I undertook to make all necessary arrangements for the illumination and decoration of the hall, the issuing of the cards of invita-

tion, &c., leaving to Stuart the matter of the music, which he gladly consented to provide.

A soldier's life is so uncertain, and his time is so little at his own disposal, that in affairs of this sort delays are always to be avoided; and so we determined on our way home, to the great joy of our fair companions, that the ball should come off on the following evening.

There was great stir of preparation at headquarters on the morning of the 8th. Invitations to the ball were sent out to all the families in Urbana and its neighbourhood, and to the officers of Hampton's brigade. The large halls of the Academy were aired and swept and festooned with roses, and decorated with battle flags borrowed from the different regiments. At seven in the evening all was complete, and already the broad avenue was filled with our fair guests, proceeding to the scene of festivity according to their social rank and fortune—some on foot, others in simple light "rockaways," others again in stately family coaches, driven by fat Negro coachmen who sat upon the box with great dignity. Very soon the sound of distant bugles announced the coming of the band of the 18th Mississippi Infantry, the Colonel and Staff of the regiment, who had been invited as an act of courtesy, leading the way, and the band playing in excellent style, the well-known air of Dixie. Amid the loud applause of the numerous invited and uninvited guests, we now made our grand *entrée* into the large hall, which was brilliantly lighted with tallow candles. . . .

Louder and louder sounded the instruments, quicker and quicker moved the dancers, and the whole crowded room, with its many exceedingly pretty women and its martial figures of officers in their best uniforms, presented a most striking spectacle of gaiety and enjoyment.

Suddenly enters an orderly covered with dust, and reports in a loud voice to General Stuart that the enemy have surprised and driven in our pickets and are attacking our camp in force, while at the same moment the sound of shots in rapid succession is distinctly borne to us on the midnight air.

The excitement which followed this announcement I cannot undertake to describe. The music crashed into a *concordia discors*. The officers rushed to their weapons and called for their horses, panic-stricken fathers and mothers endeavoured in a frantic way to collect around them their bewildered children, while the young ladies ran to and fro in most admired despair. General Stuart maintained his accustomed coolness and composure. Our horses were immediately saddled, and in less than five minutes we were in rapid gallop to the front. Upon arriving there we found, as is usually the case in such sudden alarms, that things were by no means so desperate as they had been represented.

Colonel Baker, with the splendid 1st North Carolina regiment, had arrested the bold forward movement of the Yankees. Pelham, with his guns in favourable position, was soon pouring a rapid fire upon their columns. The other regiments of the command were speedily in the saddle. The line of battle having been formed, Stuart gave the order for a general attack, and with great rage and fury we precipitated ourselves upon the foe, who paid, with the loss of many killed and wounded, and a considerable number of prisoners for their unmannerly interruption of our social amusement. They were pursued in their headlong flight for several miles by the 1st North Carolina, until, a little past midnight, they got quite out of reach, and all was quiet again.

It was about one o'clock in the morning when we got back to the Academy, where we found a great many of our fair guests still assembled, awaiting with breathless anxiety the result of the conflict. As the musicians had never dispersed, General Stuart ordered them again to strike up; many of our pretty fugitives were brought back by young officers who eagerly volunteered for that commendable purpose; and as everybody was determined that the Yankees should not boast of having completely broken up our party, the dancing was resumed in less than half an hour, and kept up till the first glimmer of dawn. At this time the ambulances laden with the wounded of last night's engagement were slowly approaching the Academy, as the only building at Urbana that was at all suited to the purposes of an hospital. Of course the music was immediately stopped and the dancing ceased, and our lovely partners in the quadrille at once became "ministering angels" to the sufferers.

Alexander K. McClure
On the Rebel Occupation of Chambersburg

A Pennsylvania newspaper editor recalls the day in October 1862 when Jeb Stuart's cavalry occupied Chambersburg.

The committee went through the form of a grave but brief consultation, somewhat expedited, perhaps, by the rain, and we then solemnly and formally surrendered the town upon the terms proposed. . . . So rebel rule began at Chambersburgh. They marched in very orderly, and most of their force started out different roads to procure horses, forage, and provisions.

I started in advance of them for my house, but not in time to save the horses. I confidently expected to be overrun by them, and to find the place one scene of desolation in the morning. I resolved, however, that things should be done soberly, if possible, and I had just time to destroy all the liquors about the house. As their pickets were all around me, I could not get it off. A barrel of best old rye, which Senator Finney had sent me to prove the superiority of the Crawford County article over that of Franklin, was quietly rolled out of a cellar side-door, and a good-sized hole bored into it. A keg of Oberholtzer's best, sent me several years ago, but never tapped, followed Finney's testimonial to Craword County distillation; and a couple cases of Presbury's best Girard House importation had the necks of the bottles taken off summarily, and the contents given to the angry storm. I finished just in time, for they were soon out upon me in force, and every horse in the barn—ten in all—was promptly equipped and mounted by a rebel cavalryman. They passed on towards Shippensburgh, leaving a picket-force on the road.

In an hour they returned with all the horses they could find, and dismounted to spend the night on the turnpike in front of my door. It was now midnight, and I sat on the porch observing their movements. They had my best corn-field beside them, and their horses fared well. In a little while, one entered the yard, came up to me, and, after a profound bow, politely asked for a few coals to start a fire. I supplied him, and informed him as blandly as possible where he would find wood conveniently, as I had dim visions of camp-fires made of my palings. I was thanked in return, and the mild-mannered villain proceeded at once to strip the fence and kindle fires. Soon after, a squad came and asked permission to get some water. I piloted them to the pump, and again received a profusion of thanks.

Communication having thus been opened between us, squads followed each other closely for water, but each called and asked permission before getting it, and promptly left the yard. I was somewhat bewildered at this uniform courtesy, and supposed it but a prelude to a general movement upon every thing eatable in the morning. . . .

About one o'clock, half a dozen officers came to the door and asked to have some coffee made for them, offering to pay liberally for it in confederate scrip. After concluding a treaty with them on behalf of the colored servants, coffee was promised them, and they then asked for a little bread with it. They were wet and shivering, and seeing a bright, open wood-fire in the library, they asked permission to enter and warm themselves until their coffee should be ready, assuring me that under no circumstances should any thing in the house be disturbed by their men. I had no alternative but to accept them as my guests until it might please them to depart, and I did so with as good grace as possible.

Once seated around the fire, all reserve seemed to be forgotten on their part, and they opened a general conversation on politics, the war, the different battles, the merits of generals in both armies, etc. They spoke with entire freedom upon every subject but their movement into Chambersburgh. Most of them were men of more than ordinary intelligence and culture, and their demeanor was in all respects eminently courteous. I took a cup of coffee with them, and have seldom seen any thing more keenly relished. They said they had not tasted coffee for weeks before, and then they had paid from six dollars to ten dollars per pound for it. When they were through, they asked whether there was any coffee left, and finding that there was some, they proposed to bring some more officers and a few privates who were prostrated by exposure to get what was left. They were, of course, as welcome as those present, and on they came in squads of five or more, until every grain of browned coffee was exhausted. They then asked for tea, and that was served to some twenty more.

In the mean time, a subordinate officer had begged of me a little bread for himself and few men, and he was supplied in the kitchen. He was followed by others in turn, until nearly an hundred had been supplied with something to eat or drink. All, however, politely asked permission to enter the house, and behaved with entire propriety. They did not make a single rude or profane remark, even to the servants. In the mean time, the officers, who had first entered the house, had filled their pipes from the box of Killickinick on the mantel—after being assured that smoking was not offensive—and we had another hour of free talk on matters generally. When told that I was a decided Republican, they thanked me for being candid. . . .

Herman Melville
"THE WILDERNESS"

*The armies enter Virginia's Wilderness in 1864, and find relics from the battle of the
year before.*

———————

In glades they meet skull after skull
Where pine cones lay—the rusted gun.
Green shoes full of bones, the mouldering coat
And cuddled-up skeleton;
And scores of such. Some start as in dreams.
And comrades lost bemoan:
By the edge of those wilds Stonewall had charged—
But the year and the Man were gone.

*Bones of Dead Soldiers
in the Wilderness.
1864. Photograph.
Library of Congress,
Washington, D.C.*

George Augustus Sala
On a New Kind of War

In his diary, entitled My Diary in America in the Midst of War, *a correspondent for the* London Telegraph *portrays the war in America as something new under the sun.*

A more painful account of what civilians imagine to be a scene of bustle, cheering, drumming, and trumpeting, "fights for the standard" after the style of Mr. Ansdell's picture, and hand-to-hand combats à la Coburg melodrama, I heard from an officer who was actively engaged in the dreadful fight of Spottsylvania Court House. All day long the corps to which he belonged was posted on the skirts of a wood. From hour to hour whole regiments were sent into this wood. Reinforcement succeeded reinforcement. A dull booming sound of cannonading never ceased; and, as the doomed men went in, fatigue parties continued to come out, bearing shattered and mutilated forms on stretchers. Was not this going into the jaws of Death and the mouth of Hell? There was no excitement, no sensational melodrama. When your time came you went in to be killed. "And the dead in that wood," added my informant, "have never been buried." To have stood firm through that awful day, "waiting for death," and calmly obeying the grim summons when it came, argues the possession, I think, of a higher grade of personal bravery than is displayed in rushing, amidst the applause of one's comrades, into the embrasure of a fort, or even heading a forlorn hope. The truth is that, since the introduction of arms of precision and artillery of long range, fighting under cover has become the almost invariable rule in America, as it must become when—God avert the evil day!—war breaks out in Europe. The slaughter, even in ambush, is frightful enough; but in the open—as after the explosion of the mine at Petersburg—it would be aggravated to a perfect *battue*. And here let it be sorrowfully noted that an illusion long entertained by the fanatics for Peace—of whom the subscriber hopes that he is one; the humblest, but not the least earnest—has been dispelled. It was long represented that the perfection of offensive weapons—of Miniés, and Armstrongs, and Whitworths—must have a tendency gradually but surely to discourage war; and, at last, by increasing the chances of mutual destruction in a ratio too frightful for contemplation, render war impossible, and abrogate it altogether. When each side could do no more in devising means of annihilation—when the irresistable force met the immovable body—the result was to be inertia. But the Devil is not to be so easily outflanked. His resources are infinite. In proportion as weapons are becoming more formidable, defenses against them are becoming stronger. Whole fleets and armies go into panoply of proof. The loss of human life is much greater than of yore, but it is not in excess of proportion to the means of destruction brought to bear. An average army in the last generation, which, fighting a hundred miles from its base, had lost ten thousand men, was virtually ruined; but now, within a dozen hours, a dozen railway trains can reinforce it to twice the amount of its casualties. Like a witch's prayer—a saintly orison read backwards—the phenomena of modern warfare present a horrible parody of the doctrine of compensation. More men can be killed than in the old time; but more men can be procured to be killed, and they can hold out much longer before they *are* killed. Soldiers are fain to become earthclads, as, on the ocean, sailors trust in ironclads. Analogically, the difference is very slight between plating the sides of your ship and burrowing in the earth like a mole. Almost the first proceeding of an advancing corps is to throw up earth-works, and these, the tools being carried with them, are constructed with wonderful speed. The opposing force has done the same, and then both parties "blaze away." If one side can't stand the fire,

JAMES F. GIBSON.
*Mortar Battery #4,
Yorktown.* May, 1862.
Photograph.
Library of Congress,
Washington, D.C.

they retire, and entrench themselves somewhere else; the other side feel their way into the abandoned pits; this is called "carrying the earthworks in gallant style." The movements of the cavalry are as mysterious as those of the infantry. The real use of the American dragoons is for the marauding expeditions known as raids. For burning houses, cutting railroads, gutting stores, and destroying crops, they are invaluable; but very little employment can be found for them in a pitched battle, and nothing is more common than to dismount them, leaving their horses picketed in charge of a few of their number, and send them into ambuscade to "blaze away." The sabre they are scarcely ever called upon to use.

I have now done my best to describe what, at the risk of paradox, I may term the indescribability of Transatlantic warfare, in which the opposing elements are not only angry and resolute men, but Dahlgrens and Parrotts, Sharps' rifles, and mounds of earth. And these elements, I apprehend, conspire to make scientific warfare more venomous and more persistent than the old hand-to-hand fighting. No little David can come out to the Philistine front to challenge Goliath of Gath to the duello. The "gentlemen of the guard" fire first, and whenever they have an opportunity, without waiting for an invitation. The slaughter of human beings has come to be a mere matter of settled calculation and mute volition. The Engineers of Murder are only called upon to make the working drawings, and draw out the specifications of bloodshed. Tinkle a bell, touch a wire, and our enemy is dead.

Walt Whitman
"ASHES OF SOLDIERS"

For Whitman, the war went on and endlessly on, and he was haunted by "the memories of all dead soldiers."

Ashes of soldiers South or North,
As I muse retrospective murmuring a chant in thought,
The war resumes, again to my sense your shapes,
And again the advance of the armies.

Noiseless as mists and vapors,
From their graves in the trenches ascending,
From cemeteries all through Virginia and Tennessee,
From every point of the compass out of the countless graves,
In wafted clouds, in myriads large, or squads of twos or threes or single ones they come,
And silently gather round me.

Now sound no note O trumpeters,
Not at the head of my cavalry parading on spirited horses,
With sabres drawn and glistening, and carbines by their thighs, (ah my brave horsemen!
My handsome tan-faced horsemen! what life, what joy and pride,
With all the perils were yours.)

Nor you drummers, neither at reveillé at dawn,
Nor the long roll alarming the camp, nor even the muffled beat for a burial,
Nothing from you this time O drummers bearing my warlike drums.
But aside from these and the marts of wealth and the crowded promenade,
Admitting around me comrades close unseen by the rest and voiceless.

Graves of Confederate Soldiers, Hollywood Cemetery, Richmond, Virginia. 1865. Photograph. Library of Congress, Washington, D.C.

The slain elate and alive again, the dust and debris alive,
I chant this chant of my silent soul in the name of all dead soldiers.

Faces so pale with wondrous eyes, very dear, gather closer yet,
Draw close, but speak not.

Phantoms of countless lost,
Invisible to the rest henceforth become my companions,
Follow me ever—desert me not while I live.

Sweet are the blooming cheeks of the living—sweet are the musical voices sounding,
But sweet, ah sweet, are the dead with their silent eyes.

Dearest comrades, all is over and long gone,
But love is not over—and what love, O comrades
Perfume from battle-fields rising, up from the foetor arising.

Perfume therefore my chant, O love, immortal love,
Give me to bathe the memories of all dead soldiers,
Shroud them, embalm them, cover them all over with tender pride.

Perfume all—make all wholesome,
Make these ashes to nourish and blossom,
O love, solve all, fructify all with the last chemistry.

Give me exhaustless, make me a fountain,
That I exhale love from me wherever I go like a moist perennial dew,
For the ashes of all dead soldiers South or North.

DAYS OF BATTLE

Elisha Hunt Rhodes

On the Fighting at Bull Run

The Civil War's first battle, at Bull Run, July 21, 1861, from the diary of a private in the 2nd Rhode Island volunteer infantry who would rise to the command of his regiment.

July 21, 1861—About two o'clock this morning we left "Bush Camp," and marching down the hill, through Centreville, found the woods obstructed by wagons and troops that had failed to start on time. Soon the Second left the main road and struck off to the right, through a wood path that had been much obstructed. As we led the Brigade the task of clearing the road fell to us, and hard work we found it. About nine o'clock in the forenoon we reached Sudley church, and a distant gun startled us, but we did not realize that our first battle was so near at hand. We now took a side road that skirted a piece of woods and marched for some distance, the men amusing themselves with laughter and jokes, with occasional stops for berries. On reaching a clearing, separated from our left

ARTIST UNKNOWN. *Panic on the Road Between Bull Run and Centreville.* July, 1861. Pencil. 9⅞ x 13¼″. Museum of Fine Arts, Boston. M. and M. Karolik Collection. Photo copyright © 1991 Museum of Fine Arts, Boston.

flank by a rail fence, we were saluted with a volley of musketry, which, however, was fired so high that all the bullets went over our heads. I remember that my first sensation was one of astonishment at the peculiar whir of the bullets, and that the Regiment immediately laid down without waiting for orders. Colonel Slocum gave the command: "By the left flank—MARCH!" and we commenced crossing the field. One of our boys by the name of Webb fell off of the fence and broke his bayonet. This caused some amusement, for even at this time we did not realize that we were about to engage in battle.

As we crossed the fence, the Rebels, after firing a few scattering shots, fled down a slope to the woods. We followed to the brow of the hill and opened fire. Our Battery came into position on our right and replied to the Rebel artillery, which was sending their shell into our line. On what followed I have very confused ideas. I remember that my smooth bore gun became so foul that I was obliged to strike the ramrod against a fence to force the cartridge home, and soon exchanged it for another. There was a hay stack in front of our line, and some of the boys sheltered themselves behind it. A shell from the enemy striking covered the men with hay, from which they emerged and retook their places in line. About this time, Private Thomas Parker of Co. "D" captured a prisoner, a member of the Louisiana Tiger Regiment, and as he brought him back to the line was spoken to by Colonel Slocum. . . .

The second Regiment was engaged about thirty minutes without support, when the balance of the Brigade was brought on to the field and the battle became general. The Eighth Georgia Regiment was in our immediate front, and received the benefit of our fire. Shot and shell were continually striking in or near our line and the troops became much scattered. Losing my own Company I joined Company "F", under command of Lieutenant William B. Sears, and remained with them until the battle ceased and we withdrew to replenish our ammunition.

About three o'clock in the afternoon the enemy disappeared in our front and the firing ceased. We considered that a victory had been won. The wounded were cared for and then orders came for us to retire to a piece of woods in our rear and fill our boxes with ammunition. We found the First Rhode Island in the woods with arms stacked and some of the men cooking. I met friends in the First Regiment and congratulated them on our victory, little expecting the finale of our day's fighting.

The firing, which had gradually receded, now seemed to be nearer, and soon a shell fired into the woods told us that the enemy had returned the combat. I cannot explain the causes of what followed. The woods and roads were soon filled with fleeing men and our Brigade was ordered to the front to cover the retreat, which it was now evident could not be stopped. Lieutenant-Colonel Frank Wheaton who on the fall of Colonel Slocum, had assumed command, posted the Regiment to the left of our first position and behind a fence. The field was soon clear of troops, excepting our Brigade, all of which except the Second Rhode Island, were posted farther back from the brow of the hill. The Rebels came on in a splendid order, pushing two light field guns to the front of them. We received their fire and held them in check until the Brigade had taken up their march, when we followed—the last to leave the field. The Rebels followed us for a short distance, shelling our rear, and then we pursued our march unmolested, until we reached the vicinity of the bridge that crosses Cub Run. Here a Rebel battery opened upon us from a corner of the woods, and the stampede commenced. The bridge was soon rendered impassible by the teams that obstructed it, and we here lost five of the guns belonging to our battery. Many men were killed and wounded at this point, and a panic seemed to seize upon every one. As our Regiment was now broken, I looked for a place to cross the stream, not daring to try the bridge. I jumped into the run and holding my gun above my head struggled across with the water up to my waist. After crossing, the Regiment gradually formed again, and we continued our march to Centreville where we found Blenker's troops posted across the road to protect the retreat. We passed through their ranks, and entered our old grounds, "Bush Camp," supposing the retreat to be at an end.

Tired, hungry and wet, we laid down, only to be awakened about eleven o'clock that night to resume the march towards Washington, in the midst of a rain storm. The Regiment filed out of camp and marched to Fairfax Court House in good order and rested in the streets. Crowds of soldiers were hurrying by and the streets were blocked with trains. After halting a few minutes we started again and soon, in the darkness, rain and crowd, became broken up to some extent. Of the horrors of that night, I can give you no adequate idea. I suffered untold horrors from thirst and fatigue but struggled on, clinging to my gun and cartridge box. Many times I sat down in the mud determined to go no further, and willing to die to end my misery. But soon a friend would pass and urge me to make another effort, and I would stagger on a mile further. At daylight we could see the spires of Washington, and a welcome sight it was. About eight o'clock I reached Fort Runyon, near Long Bridge, and giving my gun to an officer who was collecting them, I entered a tent and was soon asleep. . . .

Shelby Foote

FROM THE CIVIL WAR: A NARRATIVE

On Confederate General Albert Sidney Johnston at Shiloh

Historian Foote traces the ill-starred course of General Albert Sidney Johnston, Confederate army commander, in "the first great modern battle," at Shiloh in western Tennessee on April 6-7, 1862.

Beauregard had taken over the log church called Shiloh, and from this headquarters he performed for the army commander the service the other Johnston had performed for him at Manassas, exercising control of the rear area and forwarding reinforcements to those points where additional strength was needed. Thus Johnston was left free to move up and down the line of battle, encouraging the troops, and this he did. Some he sought to steady by speaking calmly. "Look along your guns, and fire low," he told them. Others he sought to inspirit with fiercer words: "Men of Arkansas, they say you boast of your prowess with the bowie knife. Today you wield a nobler weapon: the bayonet. Employ it well!" Whichever he did, or whether he did neither, but merely rode among them, tall and handsome on his tall, handsome horse, the men cheered at the sight of their commander exposing himself to the dangers he was requiring them to face. This was indeed his hour of vindication.

His men swept forward, overrunning the enemy's front-line camps and whooping with elation as they took potshots at the backs of fleeing Yankees. Where resistance stiffened, as along the ridge where Sherman's tents were pitched, they matched valor against determination and paid in blood for the resultant gain. Not that there were no instances of flinching at the cost. An Arkansas major reported angrily that a Tennessee regiment in front of his own "broke and ran back, hallooing 'Retreat, retreat,' which being mistaken by our own men for orders of their commander, a retreat was made by them and some confusion ensued." No sooner was this corrected than the same thing happened again, only this time the major had an even more shameful occurrence to report: "They were in such great haste to get behind us that they ran over and trampled in the mud our brave color-bearer." There were other, worse confusions. The Orleans Guard battalion, the elite organization with Beauregard's name on its muster roll, came into battle wearing dress-blue uniforms, which drew the fire of the Confederates they were marching to support. Promptly they returned the volley, and when a horrified staff officer came galloping up to tell them they were shooting at their friends: "I know it," the Creole colonel replied. "But dammit, sir, we fire on everybody who fires on us!"

Such mishaps and mistakes could be corrected or even overlooked by the high command. More serious were the evils resulting from straggling, caused mainly by hunger and curiosity. When some Northerners later denied that they had been surprised at Shiloh, a Texan who had scalded his arm in snatching a joint of meat from a bubbling pot as he charged through one of the Federal camps replied that if Grant's army had not been surprised it certainly had "the most devoted mess crews in the history of warfare."

HENRI LOVIE. *Troops at Pittsburg Landing.* April, 1862. Pencil. New York Public Library, New York. Miriam and Ira D. Wallach Division of Art, Prints, and Photographs. Astor, Lenox and Tilden Foundations.

Sunday breakfasts, spread out on tables or still cooking over campfires, were more than the hungry Confederates could resist. Many sat down, then and there, to gorge themselves on white bread and sweet coffee. Others explored the Yankee tents, foraging among the departed soldiers' belongings, including their letters, which they read with interest to find out what northern girls were like. Hundreds, perhaps thousands, were lost thus to their comrades forging ahead, and this also served to blunt the impetus of the attack which in its early stages had rolled headlong over whatever got in its way.

Most serious of all, though, were the flaws that developed when the attack plan was exposed to prolonged strain. Neatly efficient as the thing had looked on paper, it was turning out quite otherwise on the rugged plateau with its underbrush and gullies and its clusters of stubborn blue defenders. Attacking as directed—three corps in line from creek to creek, one behind another, each line feeding its components piecemeal into the line ahead—brigades and regiments and even companies had become so intermingled that unit commanders lost touch with their men and found themselves in charge of strangers who never before had heard the sound of their voices. Coördination was lost. By noon, when the final reserves had been committed, the army was no longer a clockwork aggregation of corps and divisions; it was a frantic mass of keyed-up men crowded into an approximate battle formation to fight a hundred furious skirmishes strung out in a crooked line. Confusing as all this was to those who fought thus to the booming accompaniment of two hundred guns, it was perhaps even more confusing to those who were trying to direct them. And indeed how should they have understood this thing they had been plunged into as if into a cauldron of pure hell? For this was the first great modern battle. It was Wilson's Creek and Manassas rolled together, quadrupled, and compressed into an area smaller than either. From the inside it resembled Armageddon.

Attempting to regain control, the corps commanders divided the front into four sectors, Hardee and Polk on the left, Bragg and Breckinridge on the right. Coördination was lacking, however, and all the attacks were frontal. Besides, compliance with Johnston's original instructions—"Every effort will be made to turn the left flank of the enemy, so as to cut off his line of retreat to the Tennessee River and throw him back on [Snake] Creek, where he will be forced to surrender"—was being frustrated by Prentiss, who stood fast along the sunken road. "It's a hornets' nest in there!" the gray-clad soldiers cried, recoiling from charge after charge against the place. When Sherman and McClernand gave way, taking up successive rearward positions, the Confederate left outstripped the right, which was stalled in front of the Hornets Nest, and thus presented Johnston with the reverse of what he wanted. He rode toward the far right to correct this, carrying in his right hand a small tin cup which he had picked up in a captured camp. Seeing a lieutenant run out of one of the tents with an armload of Yankee souvenirs, Johnston told him sternly: "None of that, sir. We are not here for plunder." Then, observing that he had hurt the young man's feelings, which after all was a poor reward for the gallantry shown in the capture, by way of apology he leaned down without dismounting and took the tin cup off a table. "Let this be my share of the spoils today," he said, and from then on he had used it instead of a sword to direct the battle. He used it so now, his index finger hooked through the loop of the handle, as he rode toward the right where his advance had stalled.

At this end of the battle line, on the far flank of the Hornets Nest, there was a ten-acre peach orchard in full bloom. Hurlbut had a heavy line of infantry posted among the trees, supported by guns whose smoke lazed and swirled up through the branches sheathed in pink, and a bright rain of petals fell fluttering like confetti in the sunlight as bullets clipped the blossoms overhead. Arriving just after one of Breckinridge's brigades had recoiled from a charge against the orchard, Johnston saw that the officers were having trouble getting the troops in line to go forward again. "Men! they are stubborn; we must use the bayonet," he told them. To emphasize his meaning he rode among them and touched the points of their bayonets with the tin cup. "These must do the work," he said. When the line had formed, the soldiers were still hesitant to reënter the smoky uproar. So Johnston did what he had been doing all that morning, all along the line of battle. Riding front and center, he stood in the stirrups, removed his hat, and called back over his shoulder: "I will lead you!" As he touched his spurs to the flanks of his horse, the men surged forward, charging with him into the sheet of flame which blazed to meet them there among the blossoms letting fall their bright pink rain.

This time the charge was not repulsed; Hurlbut's troops gave way, abandoning the orchard to the cheering men in gray. Johnston came riding back, a smile on his lips, his teeth flashing white beneath his mustache. There were rips and tears in his uniform and one bootsole had been cut nearly in half by a minie bullet. He shook his foot so the dangling leather flapped. "They didn't trip me up that time," he said, laughing. His battle blood was up; his eyes were shining. Presently, however, as the general sat watching his soldiers celebrate their capture of the orchard and its guns, Governor Isham Harris of Tennessee, who had volunteered to serve as his aide during the battle, saw him reel in the saddle.

"General—are you hurt?" he cried.

"Yes, and I fear seriously," Johnston said.

None of the rest of his staff was there, the general having sent them off on various missions. Riding with one arm across Johnston's shoulders to prevent his falling, Harris guided the bay into a nearby ravine, where he eased the pale commander to the ground and began unfastening his clothes in an attempt to find the wound. He had no luck until he noticed the right boot full of blood, and then he found it: a neat hole drilled just above the hollow of the knee, marking where the femoral artery had been severed. This called for a knowledge of tourniquets, but the governor knew nothing of such things. The man who knew most about them, Johnston's staff physician, had been ordered by the general to attend to a group of Federal wounded he encountered on his way to the far right. When the doctor protested, Johnston cut him off: "These men were our enemies a moment ago. They are our prisoners now. Take care of them." So Harris alone was left to do what he could to staunch the bright red flow of blood.

He could do little. Brandy might help, he thought, but when he poured some into the hurt man's mouth it ran back out again. Presently a colonel, Johnston's chief of staff, came hurrying into the ravine. But he could do nothing either. He knelt down facing the general. "Johnston, do you know me? Johnston, do you know me?" he kept asking, over and over, nudging the general's shoulder as he spoke.

But Johnston did not know him. Johnston was dead.

Henry Ropes
Letter on the Battle at Fair Oaks
June 3, 1862

In a letter home, Lieutenant Ropes, 20th Massachusetts, reports on his baptism of fire at the Battle of Fair Oaks, on the Virginia Peninsula on May 31, 1862.

————————————

Camp near Fair Oaks Station, Va.
4 P.M. Tuesday June 3rd, 1862

My Dear Father,

I take the first opportunity to inform you of my safety, that a Kind Providence has mercifully preserved me in battle, and above all that I was enabled to do my duty there.

COLORPLATE 67

HUNT P. WILSON. *Battle of Pea Ridge, Arkansas.* 1885. Oil on canvas. 29½ × 44½".
Museum of the Confederacy, Richmond. Photo by Katherine Wetzel.

COLORPLATE 68

DAVID GILMOUR BLYTHE. *Battle of Gettysburg.* 1863-1865. Oil on canvas. 26 × 34¼″. Museum of
Fine Arts, Boston. Bequest of Maxim Karolik. Photo copyright © 1982 Museum of Fine Arts, Boston.

COLORPLATE 69 *(opposite above)*

Artist Unknown. *Grant's First Attack at Vicksburg, May 19, 1863.* 1863. Pencil and watercolor. 20 × 32½″.
Museum of Fine Arts, Boston. M. & M. Karolik Collection.

COLORPLATE 70 *(opposite below)*

Artist Unknown. *Attack at Seminary Ridge, Gettysburg.* 1863. Pastel on prepared board. 20 × 28½″.
Museum of Fine Arts, Boston. M. & M. Karolik Collection.

COLORPLATE 71

PAUL PHILIPPOTEAUX.
Grant at Fort Donelson.
1870-1875. Oil on
canvas. 18 × 25″.
Chicago Historical
Society.

COLORPLATE 72

JAMES WALKER (after John Badger Bachelder). *The Battle of Gettysburg: Repulse of Longstreet's Assault, July 3, 1863.* 1870. Oil on canvas. 24½ × 59½". New Hampshire Historical Society, Concord.

COLORPLATES 73-76 *(overleaf)*

Paul Philippoteaux and Others. *Cyclorama of Gettysburg.* 1881. Oil on canvas. 30 × 370′. Gettysburg National Military Park / Eisenhower National Historic Site, Gettysburg. Photo courtesy United States Department of the Interior, National Park Service, Washington, D.C.

COLORPLATE 77

HARRY J. KELLOGG. *Battle of Kelly's Field, Chickamauga*. 1890. Oil on canvas. 34 × 58".
Minnesota Historical Society, St. Paul.

227

COLORPLATE 78

JAMES WALKER. *The Battle of Chickamauga, September 19, 1863.* Oil on canvas. 13½ × 40″. U.S. Army Center of Military History, Washington, D.C. Photo by Larry Sherer, copyright © 1985 Time-Life Books, Inc.

COLORPLATE 79

JAMES WALKER. *The Battle of Lookout Mountain. November 24, 1863.* U.S. Army Center of Military History, Washington, D.C. Photo by Larry Sherer, copyright © 1985 Time-Life Books, Inc.

COLORPLATE 80

JAMES WALKER. *General Hooker at Lookout Mountain*, 1864-1874. Oil on Canvas. 156 × 360".
Chickamauga - Chattanooga National Military Park and Eastern National Park and Monument
Association, Ft. Oglethorpe, Georgia.

COLORPLATE 81

WINSLOW HOMER. *A Skirmish in the Wilderness*. 1864. Oil on board. 18 × 26″.
New Britain Museum of American Art, New Britain, Connecticut.

On Saturday last, May 31st, we had not the slightest idea of danger being near till about noon when very heavy firing broke out from the woods west of us and at one time approached very near. We were ordered under arms, but I had no particular expectation of a battle, for we have been often called out in the same way before. The firing ceased, and we heard a report that Casey had been repulsed, but we did not know what to believe. At about 4 o'cl. orders came to fall in with one day's rations and we marched from camp, and crossed the Chickahominy on the log bridge built by the Mich. regiment. We came out on a low meadow where our artillery was stuck in the mud. The 19th Mass. was on picket behind us, the Tammany Regt. we left here, and the 7th Mich. and we pushed on alone. After passing the meadow we ascended a small hill and found the country dry and hilly in front. Soon we halted, loaded and primed and then marched on again. In a few minutes we heard guns ahead, and we pushed on rapidly, crossed a stream knee deep and took the double quick, for musketry and artillery were now heard in front, rapidly increasing. We drove forward out of breath and very hot, saw the smoke rising over the trees, and soon the road turned from along the edge of the woods, and we saw at the farther end of a large field our artillery firing with the greatest rapidity, the infantry forming, all hid in smoke. We again took the double quick step and ran through deep mud and pools of water toward the battle. The whole field in the rear of the line of firing was covered with dead; and wounded men were coming in great numbers, some walking, some limping, some carried in stretchers and blankets, many with shattered limbs exposed and dripping with blood.

In a moment we entered the fire. The noise was terrific, the balls whistled by us and the shells exploded over us and by our side; the whole scene dark with smoke and lit up by the streams of fire from our battery and from our infantry in line on each side. We were carried to the left and formed in line, and then marched by the left flank and advanced to the front and opened fire. Our men behaved with the greatest steadiness and stood up and fired and did exactly what they were told. The necessary confusion was very great, and it was as much as all the officers could do to give the commands and see to the men. We changed position 2 or 3 times under a hot fire. Donnelly and Chase of my company fell not 2 feet from me. The shell and balls seemed all around us, and yet few seemed to fall.

We kept up this heavy firing for some time, when the enemy came out of the woods in front and made a grand attack on the battery. They were met by grape and canister and a tremendous fire of the infantry. They faltered and fell back. Some regiments

ALFRED R. WAUD.
Sumner Crossing Chichahominey, Battle of Seven Pines, May 31, 1862. 1862. Pencil. Library of Congress, Washington, D.C.

charged on them; the whole Rebel line was now in front of us, and Genl. Sumner ordered our whole line to advance. We rushed with tremendous cheers, the whole together at a charge. The Rebels did not wait for the bayonets but broke and fled. Our regiment came over a newly ploughed field and sank to the knee. We drove them to the edge of the woods and opened a tremendous fire for a few moments. . . . We were then ordered back, and by the left flank and again charged the Rebels in a field on the left where they had rallied. We drove them and halted in the middle of the field and gave them a few final volleys. It was then dark. We staid there that night. Ground covered with their killed and wounded. We took many prisoners. I will write more fully when I have more time.

Stephen Vincent Benét

FROM "JOHN BROWN'S BODY"

On the Army of the Potomac

The Army of the Potomac was the North's principal army in the war's first great campaign, on the Virginia Peninsula in 1862; from Benét's Pulitzer Prize winning epic poem.

———————————

        The roads are sticky and soft,
There are forts at Yorktown and unmapped rivers to cross.
He has many more men than Johnston or John Magruder
But the country hinders him, and he hinders himself
By always thinking the odds on the other side
And that witches of ruin haunt each move he makes.
But even so—he has boarded that jutting deck
That is the Peninsula, and his forces creep
Slowly toward Richmond, slowly up to the high
Defended captain's cabin of the great ship.
—There was another force that came from its ships
To take a city set on a deck of land,
The cause unlike, but the fighting no more stark,
The doom no fiercer, the fame no harder to win.
There are no gods to come with a golden smoke
Here in the mud between the York and the James
And wrap some high-chinned hero away from death.
There are only Bibles and buckles and cartridge belts
That sometimes stop a bullet before it kills
But oftener let it pass.
        And when Sarpedon
Falls and the heavy darkness stiffens his limbs
They will let him lie where he fell, they will not wash him
In the running streams of Scamander, the half-divine,
They will bury him at a shallow and cumbered pit.
But, if you would sing of fighters, sing of these men
Sing of Fair Oaks and the battered Seven Days,

Not of the raging of Ajax, the cry of Hector,
These men were not gods nor shielded by any gods,
They were men of our shape: they fought as such men may fight
With a mortal skill: when they died it was as men die.
Army of the Potomac, advancing army,
Alloy of a dozen disparate, alien States,
City-boy, farm-hand, bounty-man, first volunteer,
Old regular, drafted recruit, paid substitute,
Men who fought through the war from First Bull Run,
And other men, nowise different in look or purpose,
Whom the first men greeted at first with a ribald cry
"Here they come! Two hundred dollars and a ka-ow!"
Rocks from New England and hickory-chunks from the West,
Bowery boy and clogging Irish adventurer,
Germans who learnt their English under the shells
Or didn't have time to learn it before they died.
Confused, huge weapon, forged from such different metals,
Misused by unlucky swordsmen till you were blunt
And then reforged with anguish and bloody sweat
To be blunted again by one more unlucky captain
Against the millstone of Lee. . . .

Rufus R. Dawes

On the Fighting in Miller's Cornfield

*Major Dawes was with the 6th Wisconsin in the charge and countercharge through the Miller cornfield at Antietam—known ever after as **the** Cornfield. He wrote of this in his memoir,* Service with the Sixth Wisconsin Volunteers.

We had marched ten rods, when whiz-z-z! bang! burst a shell over our heads; then another; then a percussion shell struck and exploded in the very center of the moving mass of men. It killed two men and wounded eleven. It tore off Captain David K. Noyes's foot, and cut off both arms of a man in his company. This dreadful scene occurred within a few feet of where I was riding, and before my eyes. The column pushed on without a halt, and in another moment had the shelter of a barn. Thus opened the first firing of the great battle of Antietam, in the early morning of September 17th, 1862. The regiment continued moving forward into a strip of woods, where the column was deployed into line of battle. The artillery fire had now increased to the roar of an hundred cannon. Solid shot and shell whistled through the trees above us, cutting off limbs which fell about us. In front of the woods was an open field; beyond this was a house, surrounded by peach and apple tress, a garden, and out-houses. The rebel skirmishers were in this cover, and they directed upon us a vigorous fire. But company "I" deployed as skirmishers, under command of Captain John A. Kellogg, dashed across the field at a full run and drove them out, and the line of the regiment pushed on over the green open field, the air above our heads filled with the screaming missiles of the contending batteries. The right of the regiment was now on the Sharpsburg and Hagerstown Turnpike. The left wing was obstructed in its advance by the picket fence around the garden before mentioned. As the right wing passed on, I ordered the men of the left wing to take hold all together and pull down the fence. They were unable to do so. I had, therefore, to pass the left wing by the flank through a gate with the utmost haste, and form again in the garden. Here Captain Edwin A. Brown, of company "E," was instantly killed. There is in my mind as I write, the spectacle of a young officer, with uplifted sword, shouting in a loud imperative voice the order I had given him, "Company 'E,' on the right by file into line!" A bullet passes into his open mouth, and the voice is forever silent. I urged the left wing forward with all possible speed. The men scrambled over briars and flower-beds in the garden. Beyond the garden, we entered a peach orchard. I hurried forward to a rail fence skirting the front edge of the orchard, where we overtook the right wing. Before us was a strip of open-field, beyond which on the left-hand side of the turnpike, was rising ground, covered by a large cornfield, the stalks standing thick and high. The rebel skirmishers ran into the corn as we appeared at the fence. Owing to our headlong advance, we were far ahead of the general lines of battle. They were in open fields, and we had the cover of the houses and orchard. Colonel Bragg, however, with his usual battle ardor, ordered the regiment forward. We climbed the fence, moved across the open space, and pushed on into the corn-field. The three right companies of the regiment were crowded into an open field on the right-hand side of the turnpike. Thus we pushed up the hill to the middle of the corn-field. . . .

Our lines on the left now came sweeping forward through the corn and the open fields beyond. I ordered my men up to join in the advance, and commanded: "Forward—guide left—march!" We swung away from the turnpike, and I sent the sergeant-major (Howard J. Huntington) to Captain Kellogg, commanding the companies on the turnpike, with this order: "If it is practicable, move forward the right companies, aligning with the left wing." Captain Kellogg said: "Please give Major Dawes my compliments, and say it is impracticable; the fire is murderous."

As we were getting separated, I directed Sergeant Huntington to tell Captain Kellogg that he could get cover in the corn, and to join us, if possible. Huntington was struck by a bullet, but delivered the order. Kellogg ordered his men up, but so many were shot that he ordered them down again at once. While this took place on the turnpike, our companies were marching forward through the thick corn, on the right of a long line of battle. Closely following was a second line. At the front edge of the corn-field was a low Virginia rail fence. Before the corn were open fields, beyond which was a strip of woods surrounding a little church, the Dunkard church. As we appeared at the edge of the corn, a long line of men in butternut and gray rose up from the ground. Simultaneously, the hostile battle lines opened a tremendous fire upon each other. Men, I can not say fell; they were knocked out of the ranks by dozens. But we jumped over the fence, and pushed on, loading, firing, and shouting as we advanced. There was, on the part of the men, great hysterical excitement, eagerness to go forward, and a reckless disregard of life, of every thing but victory. Captain Kellogg brought his companies up abreast of us on the turnpike.

The Fourteenth Brooklyn Regiment, red legged Zouaves, came into our line, closing the awful gaps. Now is the pinch. Men and officers of New York and Wisconsin are fused into a common mass, in the frantic struggle to shoot fast. Every body tears cartridges, loads, passes guns, or shoots. Men are falling in their places or running back into the corn. The soldier who is shooting is furious in his energy. The soldier who is shot looks around for help with an imploring agony of death on his face. After a few rods of advance, the line stopped and, by common impulse, fell back to the edge of the corn and lay down on the ground behind the low rail fence. Another line of our men came up through the corn. We all joined together, jumped over the fence, and again pushed out into the open field. There is a rattling fusilade and loud cheers. "Forward" is the word. The men are loading and firing with demoniacal fury and shouting and laughing hysterically, and the whole field before us is covered with rebels fleeing for life, into the woods. Great numbers of them are shot while climbing over the high post and rail fences along the turnpike.

We push on over the open fields half way to the little church. The powder is bad, and the guns have become very dirty. It takes hard pounding to get the bullets down, and our firing is becoming slow. A long and steady line of rebel gray, unbroken by the fugitives who fly before us, comes sweeping down through the woods around the church. They raise the yell and fire. It is like a scythe running through our line. "Now, save, who can." It is a race for life that each man runs for the cornfield. A sharp cut, as of a switch, stings the calf of my leg as I run. Back to the corn, and back through the corn, the headlong flight continues. At the bottom of the hill, I took the blue color of the state of Wisconsin, and waving it, called a rally of Wisconsin men. Two hundred men gathered around the flag of the Badger state. Across the turnpike just in front of the haystacks, two guns of Battery "B," 4th U. S. artillery were in action. The pursuing rebels were upon them. General John Gibbon, our brigade commander, who in regular service was captain of this battery, grimed and black with powder smoke in himself sighting these guns of his old battery, comes running to me, "Here, major, move your men over, we must save these guns." I commanded "Right face, forward march," and started ahead with the colors in my hand into the open field, the men following. As I entered the field, a report as of a thunderclap in my ear fairly stunned me. This was Gibbon's last shot at the advancing rebels. The cannon was double charged with canister. The rails of the fence flew high in the air. A line of union blue charged swiftly forward from our right across the field in front of the battery, and into the corn-field. They drove back the rebels who were firing upon us. It was our own gallant 19th Indiana, and here fell dead their leader, Lieutenant Colonel A. F. Bachman; but the youngest captain in their line, William W. Dudley, stepped forward and led on the charge. I gathered my men on the turnpike, reorganized them, and reported to General Doubleday, who was himself there. He ordered me to move back to the next woods in the rear, to remain and await instruction. Bullets, shot, and shell, fired by the enemy in the corn-field, were still flying thickly around us, striking the trees in this woods, and cutting off the limbs. I placed my men under the best shelter I could find, and here we figured up, as nearly as we could, our dreadful losses in the battle. Three hundred and fourteen officers and men had marched with us into battle. There had been killed and wounded, one hundred and fifty-two. Company

ALEXANDER GARDNER.
Confederate Dead along the Hagerstown Pike.
September 19, 1862.
Photograph.
Library of Congress, Washington, D.C.

"C" under Captain Hooe, thirty-five men, was not in the fight in front of the corn-field. That company was on skirmish duty farther to our right. In this service they lost two men. Of two hundred and eighty men who were at the corn-field and turnpike, one hundred and fifty were killed or wounded. This was the most dreadful slaughter to which our regiment was subjected in the war. We were joined in the woods by Captain Ely, who reported to me, as the senior officer present, with the colors and eighteen men of the second Wisconsin. They represented what remained for duty of that gallant regiment.

The roar of musketry to the front about the corn-field and the Dunkard church had again become heavy. Stragglers and wounded streamed in troops toward the rear. This tide growing momentarily stronger, General Gibbon directed me to form a line of the whole brigade, perhaps five hundred men present, to drive back, at the point of the bayonet, all men who were fit for duty at the front. But, soon, the troops engaged about the Dunkard church fell back, and the whole line was formed in rear of batteries, planted on the ridge near Poffenberger's house. We were on the ground from which, at the early dawn, our regiment had moved forward to begin the battle.

Michael Shaara

FROM THE KILLER ANGELS

On the Fight for Little Round Top

The novelist writes of Colonel Joshua Chamberlain and the 20th Maine when they take a desperate measure to save their position on the second day at Gettysburg.

He limped along the line. Signs of exhaustion. Men down, everywhere. He thought: we cannot hold.

Looked up toward the crest. Fire still hot there, still hot everywhere. Down into the dark. They are damned good men, those Rebs. Rebs, I salute you. I don't think we can hold you.

He gathered with Spear and Kilrain back behind the line. He saw another long gap, sent Ruel Thomas to this one. Spear made a count.

"We've lost a third of the men, Colonel. Over a hundred down. The left is too thin."

"How's the ammunition?"

"I'm checking."

A new face, dirt-stained, bloody: Homan Melcher, Lieutenant, Company F, a gaunt boy with buck teeth.

"Colonel? Request permission to go pick up some of our wounded. We left a few boys out there."

"Wait," Chamberlain said.

Spear came back, shaking his head. "We're out." Alarm stained his face, a grayness in his cheeks.

"Some of the boys have nothing at all."

"Nothing," Chamberlain said.

Officers were coming from the right. Down to a round or two per man. And now there was a silence around him. No man spoke. They stood and looked at him, and then looked down into the dark and then looked back at Chamberlain. One man said, "Sir, I guess we ought to pull out."

Chamberlain said, "Can't do that."

Spear: "We won't hold 'em again. Colonel, you know we can't hold 'em again."

Chamberlain: "If we don't hold, they go right on by and over the hill and the whole flank caves in."

He looked from face to face. The enormity of it, the weight of the line, was a mass too great to express. But he could see it as clearly as in a broad wide vision, a Biblical dream: If the line broke here, then the hill was gone, all these boys from Pennsylvania, New York, hit from behind, above. Once the hill went, the flank of the army went. Good God! He could see troops running; he could see the blue flood, the bloody tide.

Kilrain: "Colonel, they're coming."

Chamberlain marveled. But we're not so bad ourselves. One recourse: Can't go back. Can't stay where we are. Result: inevitable.

The idea formed.

"Let's fix bayonets," Chamberlain said.

For a moment no one moved.

"We'll have the advantage of moving downhill," he said.

Spear understood. His eyes saw; he nodded automatically. The men coming up the hill stopped to volley; weak fire came in return. Chamberlain said, "They've got to be tired, those Rebs. They've got to be close to the end. Fix bayonets. Wait. Ellis, you take the left wing. I want a right wheel forward of the whole Regiment."

Lieutenant Melcher said, perplexed, "Sir, excuse me, but what's a 'right wheel forward'?"

Ellis Spear said, "He means 'charge,' Lieutenant, 'charge.'"

Chamberlain nodded. "Not quite. We charge, swinging down to the right. We straighten out our line. Clarke hangs onto the Eighty-third, and we swing like a door, sweeping them down the hill. Understand? Everybody understand? Ellis, you take the wing, and when I yell you go to it, the whole Regiment goes forward, swinging to the right."

"Well," Ellis Spear said. He shook his head. "Well."

"Let's go." Chamberlain raised his saber, bawled at the top of his voice, "Fix bayonets!"

He was thinking: We don't have two hundred men left. Not two hundred. More than that coming at us. He saw Melcher bounding away toward his company, yelling, waving. Bayonets were coming out, clinking, clattering. He heard men beginning to shout, Maine men, strange shouts, hoarse, wordless, animal. He limped to the front, toward the great boulder where Tozier stood with the colors, Kilrain at his side. The Rebs were in plain view, moving, firing. Chamberlain saw clearly a tall man aiming a rifle at him. At *me*. Saw the smoke, the flash, but did not hear the bullet go by. Missed. Ha! He stepped out into the open, balanced on the gray rock. Tozier had lifted the colors into the clear. The Rebs were thirty yards off. Chamberlain raised his saber, let loose the shout that was the greatest sound he could make, boiling the yell up from his chest: *Fix bayonets! Charge! Fix bayonets! Charge! Fix bayonets! Charge!* He leaped down from the boulder, still screaming, his voice beginning to crack and give, and all around him his men were roaring animal screams, and he saw the whole Regiment rising and pouring over the wall and beginning to bound down through the dark bushes, over the dead and dying and wounded, hats coming off, hair flying, mouths making sounds, one man firing as he ran, the last bullet, last round. Chamberlain saw gray men below stop, freeze, crouch, then quickly turn. The move was so quick he could not believe it. Men were turning and running. Some were stopping to fire. There was the yellow flash and then they turned. Chamberlain saw a man drop a rifle and run. Another. A bullet plucked at Chamberlain's coat, a hard pluck so that he thought he had caught a thorn but looked down and saw the huge gash. But he was not hit. He saw an officer: handsome full-bearded man in gray, sword and revolver. Chamberlain ran toward him, stumbled, cursed the bad foot, looked up and aimed and fired and missed, then held aloft the saber. The officer turned, saw him coming, raised a pistol, and Chamberlain ran toward it downhill, unable to stop, stumbling downhill seeing the black hole of the pistol turning toward him, not anything else but the small hole yards away, feet away, the officer's face a blur behind it and no thought, a moment of gray suspension rushing silently, soundlessly toward the black hole . . . and the gun did not fire; the hammer clicked down on an empty shell, and Chamberlain was at the man's throat with the saber and the man was handing him his sword, all in one motion, and Chamberlain stopped.

"The pistol too," he said.

The officer handed him the gun: a cavalry revolver, Colt.

"Your prisoner, sir." The face of the officer was very white, like old paper. Chamberlain nodded.

He looked up to see an open space. The Rebs had begun to fall back; now they were running. He had never seen them run; he stared, began limping forward to see. Great cries, incredible sounds, firing and yelling. The Regiment was driving in a line, swinging to the fight, into the dark valley. Men were surrendering. He saw masses of gray coats, a hundred or more, moving back up the slope to his front, in good order, the only ones not running, and thought: If they form again we're in trouble, desperate trouble, and he began moving that way, ignoring the officer he had just captured. At that moment a new wave of firing broke out on the other side of the gray mass. He saw a line of white smoke erupt, the gray troops waver and move back this way, stop, rifles begin to fall, men begin to run to the right, trying to get away. Another line of fire—Morrill. B Company. Chamberlain moved that way. A soldier grabbed his Reb officer, grinning, by the arm. Chamberlain passed a man sitting on a rock, holding his stomach. He had been bayoneted. Blood coming from his mouth. Stepped on a dead body, wedged between rocks. Came upon Ellis Spear, grinning crazily, foolishly, face stretched and glowing with a wondrous light.

"By God, Colonel, by God, by God," Spear said. He pointed. Men were running off down the valley. The Regiment was moving across the front of the 83rd Pennsylvania. He looked up the hill and saw them waving and cheering. Chamberlain said, aloud, "I'll be damned."

The Regiment had not stopped, was chasing the Rebs down the long valley between the hills. Rebs had stopped everywhere, surrendering. Chamberlain said to Spear, "Go on up and stop the boys. They've gone far enough."

"Yes, sir. But they're on their way to Richmond."

"Not today," Chamberlain said. "They've done enough today."

Michael Shaara

FROM THE KILLER ANGELS
On General Lee at Gettysburg

The fateful decision, on the third day at Gettysburg, seen through a novelist's eye.

At last Lee turned, summoned Longstreet. Longstreet came up. Lee said, "General, we will attack the center."

He paused. Longstreet took a long breath, let it go.

"You will have Pickett's Division. But I think you are right about the flank. Leave

ALLEN C. REDWOOD.
*Stewart's Brigade at
Culp's Hill.* 1886.
Watercolor. 11⅞ x 16½".
Century Collection,
New York.

Hood and McLaws where they are. I will give you Heth's Division. It was not engaged yesterday. And Pender's."

Longstreet nodded.

"You will have three divisions. Your objective will be that clump of trees . . . there."

He pointed. The center of the Union line, the center of the ridge. The clump of trees was clear, isolated. In the center of the clump was one large tree shaped like an umbrella. Unmistakable. Longstreet nodded, listened, tried not to think.

"Your attack will be preceded by massed artillery fire. *A feu d'enfer.* We will concentrate all our guns on that small area. When the artillery has had its effect, your charge will break the line. The rest of Hill's people will be waiting. Stuart has already gone round to the rear."

Lee turned. Now the excitement was in his eyes. He leaned forward, gazing at Longstreet, hoping to strike fire, but Longstreet said nothing, stood listening, head bowed.

Lee said, "Those three divisions . . . will give you fifteen thousand men."

Longstreet said, "Yes, sir." He stared at the ridge. He said suddenly, "Hancock is up there."

Lee nodded. "Yes, that's the Second Corps."

Longstreet said, "Hard on Armistead."

Lee said, "You can begin at any time. But plan it well, plan it well. We stake everything on this."

"Sir?" Longstreet thought: I can't. "Sir," Longstreet said, "you are giving me two of Hill's divisions, only one of mine. Most of the troops will be Hill's. Wouldn't it be better to give the attack to Hill?"

Lee shook his head. He said, "General, I want *you* to make this attack." Longstreet took another deep breath. Lee said, "General, I need you."

Longstreet said, "Sir, with your permission."

Lee waited. Longstreet spoke and did not want to look him in the face, but did, spoke looking at the weary face, the ancient eyes, the old man who was more than father of the army, symbol of war. "Sir, I have been a soldier all my life. I have served from the ranks on up. You know my service. I have to tell you now, sir, that I believe this attack will fail. I believe that no fifteen thousand men ever set for battle could take that hill, sir."

Lee raised a hand. Longstreet had seen the anger before, had never seen it turned toward him. It was as if Longstreet was betraying him. But Longstreet went on: "It is a distance of more than a mile. Over open ground. As soon as we leave the trees we will be under the fire of their artillery. From all over the field. At the top of the hill are Hancock's boys—"

Lee said, "That's enough."

He turned away. He called Taylor. For a long moment Longstreet thought: he is relieving me. But Lee was sending for someone. Longstreet thought: he should relieve me. He should give it to A. P. Hill. But he knew Hill could not take it, no one could take it; there was no one else Lee could rely on, nothing else to do. It was all set and fated like the coming of the bloody heat, the damned rising of the damned sun, and nothing to do, no way to prevent it, my weary old man, God help us, what are you doing?

Not thinking clearly any more, Longstreet composed himself. Lee came back. Lee said calmly, "General, do you have any question?"

Longstreet shook his head. Lee came to him, touched his arm.

"General, we all do our duty. We do what we have to do."

"Yes, sir," Longstreet said, not looking at him.

"Alexander is handling the artillery. He is very good. We will rely on him to break them up before Pickett gets there."

"Yes, sir."

"Heth is still too ill for action. I am giving his division to Johnston Pettigrew. Is that satisfactory to you?"

Longstreet nodded.

"Pender is out of action, too. Who would you suggest for the command there?"

Longstreet could not think. He said, "Anyone you choose."

"Well," Lee meditated. "How about Isaac Trimble? No one in the army has more fight in him than Trimble."

"Yes," Longstreet said.

"Good. Then that's agreed. Pettigrew, Pickett, and Trimble. The new commanders won't really matter, in an attack of this kind. The men will know where to go."

He went over the plan again. He wanted to be certain, this day, that it all went well, laying it all out like the tracks of a railroad. He was confident, excited, the blood was up. He thought the army could do anything. Longstreet felt the weariness, the heat of the day. The objective was clear. All fifteen thousand men would concentrate, finally, on a small stone wall perhaps a hundred yards wide. They might break through. It was possible.

Lee said, "The line there is not strong. Meade has strengthened both his flanks; he must be weak in the center. I estimate his strength in the center at not much more than five thousand men. The artillery barrage will upset them."

"Yes, sir."

"Is there anything you need? Take whatever time you need."

"I have always been slow," Longstreet said.

"There is no one I trust more."

"If the line can be broken . . ." Longstreet said.

"It can. It will." Lee paused, smiled.

"If it can be done, those boys will do it." Longstreet moved back formally, saluted.

Lee returned the salute, tall, erect, radiating faith and confidence. He said slowly, the voice of the father, "General Longstreet, God go with you."

William Faulkner

FROM INTRUDER IN THE DUST

The southern writer captures a moment, on a July afternoon in 1863, and suspends it in time; and it hasn't happened yet . . .

'It's all *now* you see. Yesterday wont be over until tomorrow and tomorrow began ten thousand years ago. For every Southern boy fourteen years old, not once but whenever he wants it, there is the instant when it's still not yet two o'clock on that July afternoon in 1863, the brigades are in position behind the rail fence, the guns are laid and ready in the woods and the furled flags are already loosened to break out and Pickett himself with his long oiled ringlets and his hat in one hand probably and his sword in the other looking up the hill waiting for Longstreet to give the word and it's all in the balance, it hasn't happened yet, it hasn't even begun yet, it not only hasn't begun yet but there is still time for it not to begin against that position and those circumstances which made more men than Garnett and Kemper and Armstead and Wilcox look grave yet it's going to begin, we all know that, we have come too far with too much at stake and that moment doesn't need even a fourteen-year-old boy to think *This time. Maybe this time* with all this much to lose and all this much to gain: Pennsylvania, Maryland, the world, the golden dome of Washington itself to crown with desperate and unbelievable victory the desperate gamble, the cast made two years ago. . . .'

Stephen Vincent Benét

FROM "JOHN BROWN'S BODY"
On the Army of Northern Virginia

Benét writes of Lee's army, an army of legend.

Army of Northern Virginia, fabulous army,
Strange army of ragged individualists,
The hunters, the riders, the walkers, the savage pastorals,
The unmachined, the men come out of the ground,
Still for the most part, living close to the ground
As the roots of the cow-pea, the roots of the jessamine,
The lazy scorners, the rebels against the wheels,
The rebels against the steel combustion-chamber
Of the half-born new age of engines and metal hands.
The fighters who fought for themselves in the old clan-fashion.
Army of planters' sons and rusty poor-whites,
Where one man came to war with a haircloth trunk

Full of fine shirts and a body-servant to mend them,
And another came with a rifle used at King's Mountain
And nothing else but his pants and his sun-cracked hands,
Aristo-democracy armed with a forlorn hope,
Where a scholar turned the leaves of an Arabic grammar
By the campfire-glow, and a drawling mountaineer
Told dirty stories old as the bawdy world,
Where one of Lee's sons worked a gun with the Rockbridge Battery
And two were cavalry generals.
                    Praying army,
Full of revivals, as full of salty jests,
Who debated on God and Darwin and Victor Hugo,
Decided that evolution might do for Yankees
But that Lee never came from anything with a tail,
And called yourselves "Lee's miserables faintin'"
When the book came out that tickled your sense of romance,
Army of improvisators of peanut-coffee
Who baked your bread on a ramrod stuck through the dough,
Swore and laughed and despaired and sang "Lorena,"
Suffered, died, deserted, fought to the end.
Sentimental army, touched by "Lorena,"
Touched by all lace-paper-valentines of sentiment,
Who wept for the mocking-bird on Hallie's grave
When you had better cause to weep for more private griefs,
Touched by women and your tradition-idea of them,
The old, book-fed, half-queen, half-servant idea,
False and true and expiring.
                    Starving army,
Who, after your best was spent and your Spring lay dead,
Yet held the intolerable lines of Petersburg
With deadly courage.
                    You too are a legend now. . . .

Benjamin Abbott
Letter on the Confederate Victory at Chickamauga September 26, 1863

An aide to General Henry Benning of Georgia records incidents at Chickamauga, the Confederacy's greatest victory in the West.

The good result of this splendid dash can hardly be estimated. It had done the work, for Rosecrans's center was broken where Hood's division had struck it. His army was literally cut in two. In a short while the enemy began to be demoralized. Presently, we heard that 1500 of his men had surrendered on our right. We advanced, I guess about 100 yards, and our brigade was halted. Nearby were the artillery horses, and General Benning and I got one each. While waiting I saw a large mound of knapsacks which belonged to various Federal regiments and the 8th Indiana battery. I searched a number of them for the stationery and found some of the paper of that battery with the Indiana coat of arms and their battery name on it, by which I judged we had captured the guns belonging to it. I have some of the paper now and use it in making reports, &c. Among the stationery found, some of the letter paper contained captions of pictures of valiant Federals in magnificent array, carrying the stars-and-stripes grandly over their heads, storming Confederate earthworks and fortifications. I send you a specimen.

This is highly picturesque, but as history, it is lacking in one important ingredient, truth. But I digress. Shouts began to go up from the right, and we knew it was our boys. It soon spread along the whole line. The enemy was firing away all along the line. On the left, musketry was heavy but retiring, the cannon seeming to play a small part in it. The yell of victory became louder and fiercer as the sun declined. There seemed to be no enemy in our front. General Benning ordered me to go forward a short distance to see what was in front. We had become afraid of firing into our own men and being fired into by them. I went as ordered and came to the Chattanooga road. I was sure I saw the enemy sending men across attempting to reinforce their left. I rode back and told what I had seen. General Benning suggested artillery and sent a courier to the division commander for it. In a few minutes a number of pieces were sending shell down that road like lightning. I watched from behind one of the guns and saw with intense excitement the shot as it would rise, curve over and explode at the very spot aimed among the demoralized Federals. Why were we not pressed forward then? Evidently they were broken and would leave the field, perhaps were leaving then. Incompetent fools were allowing the fruits of a great victory to fly from us. I can see now how we idled and waited.

ALFRED R. WAUD.
Battle of Chickamauga.
1863. Drawing.
Library of Congress,
Washington, D.C.

After a while, we advanced by the flank to the road. The artillery had gone. We stopped near a log hut.

Around us the enemy's dead and wounded lay very thick. I walked among them, while we waited for orders. I came upon a young officer and found he was mortally wounded and suffering very much. I saw at once he would die and asked if I could do anything for him. He replied, "I am dying. Wash me clean and bury me decently." I promised him all I could under the circumstances and asked his name. His answer was, "Lieutenant Colonel D. J. Hall of Chicago." I had him moved in the hut and in less than an hour he died. As far as I could I complied with his request and marked his grave with a board on which I carved his name with my knife. I also talked with another officer who was mortally wounded, and he asked me to communicate, if I could, and tell his wife of his death. His name was Captain Barnett. As soon as I found Hall suffering so much, I took from my pocket a small vial of *morphia* and gave him about half a grain, and he was relieved very soon of pain and died easily and rationally. I had carried this little vial during all my service, fearing I might be wounded and left suffering on the field. It had never served me, but it was now to relieve an enemy.

These little incidents I relate to you as they may prove interesting, while they might be considered only personal history. They serve to show, in philosophizing over these sad days, that we cannot yet be barbarians. In my own heart before the battle I felt very bitter against these men who had invaded our soil, as I believe against every principle of right, and yet in the hour of victory we soldiers were touched with pity for these wounded and dying enemies. It was not the place to discuss right and wrong: it was simply a question of humanity. . . .

Sam R. Watkins

On the Confederate Defeat at Franklin

The battle at Franklin, Tennessee, November 30, 1864, as witnessed by Sam Watkins, Co. H, 1st Tennessee, from his memoir, Co. Aytch.

Kind reader, right here my pen, and courage, and ability fail me. I shrink from butchery. Would to God I could tear the page from these memoirs and from my own memory. It is the blackest page in the history of the war of the Lost Cause. It was the bloodiest battle of modern times in any war. It was the finishing stroke to the independence of the Southern Confederacy. I was there. I saw it. My flesh trembles, and creeps, and crawls when I think of it to-day. My heart almost ceases to beat at the horrid recollection. Would to God that I had never witnessed such a scene!

I cannot describe it. It beggars description. I will not attempt to describe it. I could not. The death-angel was there to gather its last harvest. It was the grand coronation of death. Would that I could turn the page. But I feel, though I did so, that page would still be there, teeming with its scenes of horror and blood. I can only tell of what I saw.

Our regiment was resting in the gap of a range of hills in plain view of the city of Franklin. We could see the battle-flags of the enemy waving in the breeze. Our army had been depleted of its strength by a forced march from Spring Hill, and stragglers lined the road. Our artillery had not yet come up, and could not be brought into action. Our cavalry was across Harpeth river, and our army was but in poor condition to make an assault. While resting on this hill-side, I saw a courier dash up to our commanding

John Bell Hood. Photograph. Valentine Museum, Richmond. Cook Collection.

General, B. F. Cheatham, and the word, "Attention!" was given. I knew then that we would soon be in action. Forward, march. We passed over the hill and through a little skirt of woods.

The enemy were fortified right across the Franklin pike, in the suburbs of the town. Right here in these woods a detail of skirmishers was called for. Our regiment was detailed. We deployed as skirmishers, firing as we advanced on the left of the turnpike road. If I had not been a skirmisher on that day, I would not have been writing this today, in the year of our Lord 1882.

It was four o'clock on that dark and dismal December day when the line of battle was formed, and those devoted heroes were ordered forward, to

"Strike for their altars and their fires,
For the green graves of their sires,
For God and their native land."

As they marched on down through an open field toward the rampart of blood and death, the Federal batteries began to open and mow down and gather into the garner of death, as brave, and good, and pure spirits as the world ever saw. The twilight of evening had begun to gather as a precursor of the coming blackness of midnight darkness that was to envelop a scene so sickening and horrible that it is impossible for me to describe it. "Forward, men," is repeated all along the line. A sheet of fire was poured into our very faces, and for a moment we halted as if in despair, as the terrible avalanche of shot and shell laid low those brave and gallant heroes, whose bleeding wounds attested that the struggle would be desperate. Forward, men! The air loaded with death-dealing missiles. Never on this earth did men fight against such terrible odds. It seemed that the very elements of heaven and earth were in one mighty uproar. Forward, men! And the blood spurts in a perfect jet from the dead and wounded. The earth is red with blood. It runs in streams, making little rivulets as it flows. Occasionally there was a little lull in the storm of battle, as the men were loading their guns, and for a few moments it seemed as if night tried to cover the scene with her mantle. The death-angel shrieks and laughs and old father Time is busy with his sickle, as he gathers in the last harvest of death, crying, More, more, more! while his rapacious maw is glutted with the slain.

But the skirmish line being deployed out, extending a little wider than the battle did—passing through a thicket of small locusts, where Brown, Orderly Sergeant of Company B, was killed—we advanced on toward the breast-works, on and on. I had made up my mind to die—felt glorious. We pressed forward until I heard the terrific roar of battle open on our right. Cleburne's division was charging their works. I passed on until I got their works, walked up the ascent, and got over on their (the Yankees') side. But in fifty yards of where I was the scene was lit up by fires that seemed like hell itself. It appeared to be but one line of streaming fire. Our troops were upon one side of the breast-works, and the Federals on the other. I ran up on the line of works, where our men were engaged. Dead soldiers filled the entrenchments. The firing was kept up until after midnight, and gradually died out. We passed the night where we were. But when the morrow's sun began to light up the eastern sky with its rosy hues, and we looked over the battle-field. O, my God! what did we see! It was a grand holocaust of death. Death had held high carnival there that night. The dead were piled the one on the other all over the ground. I never was so horrified and appalled in my life. Horses, like men, had died game on the gory breast-works. Gen. Adams' horse had his fore feet on one side of the works and his hind feet on the other, dead. The General seems to have been caught so that he was held to the horse's back, sitting almost as if living, riddled, and mangled, and torn with balls. Gen. Cleburne's mare had her fore feet on top of the works, dead in that position. Gen. Cleburne's body was pierced with forty-nine bullets, through and through. Gen. Strahl's horse lay by the roadside and the General by his side, both dead, and all his staff. Gen. Gist, a noble and brave cavalier from South Carolina, was lying with his sword reaching across the breast-works still grasped in his hand. He was lying there dead. Gen. Granberry, from Texas, and his horse were seen, horse and rider, right on top of the breast-works, dead. All dead! They sleep in the graveyard yonder at Ashwood, almost in sight of my home, where I am writing to-day. They sleep the sleep of the brave. We love and cherish their memory. They sleep beneath the ivy-mantled walls of St. John's church, where they expressed a wish to be buried. The private soldier sleeps where he fell, piled in one mighty heap. Four thousand five hundred privates! all lying side by side in death! Thirteen Generals were killed and wounded. Four thousand five hundred men slain, all piled and heaped together at one place. I cannot tell the number of others killed and wounded. God alone knows that. We'll all find out on the morning of the final resurrection.

COLORPLATE 82

SAMUEL J. READER. *The Battle of the Blue, October 22, 1864.* 1895.
Pastels. 8½ × 18⅛″. Kansas State Historical Society, Topeka.

COLORPLATE 83

Artist Unknown. *Howard's Grove Hospital, Richmond.* 1862-1864.
Oil on canvas. 21 × 30⅛″. Chicago Historical Society.

COLORPLATE 84

EASTMAN JOHNSON. *The Letter Home.* 1867. Oil on composition board. 23 × 27½″.
Museum of Fine Arts, Boston. M. and M. Karolik Collection.

COLORPLATE 85

WINSLOW HOMER. *Prisoners from the Front*. 1866. Oil on canvas. 24 × 38″.
Metropolitan Museum of Art, New York. Gift of Mrs. Frank B. Porter, 1922.

COLORPLATE 86

SAMUEL J. READER. *Captured by Price's Confederate Raiders.* 1865.
Watercolor and ink. 7⅞ × 9⅞". Kansas State Historical Society, Topeka.

COLORPLATE 87

FRANK VIZETELLY. *Union Soldiers Attacking Confederate Prisoners in the Streets of Washington.*
1861. Pencil, watercolor, ink on paper. 6⅞ × 9⅝″. Harvard College Library, Cambridge.

COLORPLATE 88

DAVID GILMOUR BLYTHE. *Libby Prison.* 1863. Oil on canvas. 24 × 36″. Museum of Fine
Arts, Boston. M. and M. Karolik Collection. *Captured federal officers were confined in Libby's
warehouse in Richmond.*

TOLL OF BATTLE

Constance Cary Harrison
"RICHMOND SCENES IN '62"
On the Streets of Richmond after the Battle of Seven Pines

A Richmond woman recalls the city's ordeal after Seven Pines, or Fair Oaks, fought on the Virginia Peninsula on May 31 and June 1, 1862.

And now we come to the 31st of May, 1862, when the eyes of the whole continent turned to Richmond. On that day Johnston assaulted the Federals who had been advanced to Seven Pines. In face of recent reverses, we in Richmond had begun to feel like the prisoner of the Inquisition in Poe's story, cast into a dungeon of slowly contracting walls. With the sound of guns, therefore, in the direction of Seven Pines, every heart leaped as if deliverance were at hand. And yet there was no joy in the wild pulsation, since those to whom we looked for succor were our own flesh and blood, barring the way to a foe of superior numbers, abundantly provided, as we were not, with all the equipments of modern warfare, and backed by a mighty nation as determined as ourselves to win. Hardly a family in the town whose father, son, or brother was not part and parcel of the defending army.

When on the afternoon of the 31st it became known that the engagement had begun, the women of Richmond were still going about their daily vocations quietly, giving no sign of the inward anguish of apprehension. There was enough to do now in preparation for the wounded; yet, as events proved, all that was done was not enough by half. Night brought a lull in the cannonading. People lay down dressed upon beds, but not to sleep, while the weary soldiers slept upon their arms. Early next morning the whole town was on the street. Ambulances, litters, carts, every vehicle that the city could produce, went and came with a ghastly burden; those who could walk limped painfully home, in some cases so black with gunpowder they passed unrecognized. Women with pallid faces flitted bareheaded through the streets searching for their dead or wounded. The churches were thrown open, many people visiting them for a sad communion-service or brief time of prayer; the lecture-rooms of various places of worship were crowded with ladies volunteering to sew, as fast as fingers could fly, the rough beds called for by the surgeons. Men too old or infirm to fight went on horseback or afoot to meet the returning ambulances, and in some cases served as escort to their own dying sons. By afternoon of the day following the battle, the streets were one vast hospital. To find shelter for the sufferers a number of unused buildings were thrown open. I remember, especially, the St. Charles Hotel, a gloomy place, where two young girls went to look for a member of their family, reported wounded. We had tramped in vain over pavements burning with the intensity of the sun, from one scene of horror to another, until our feet and brains alike seemed about to serve us no further. The cool of those vast dreary rooms of the St. Charles was refreshing; but such a spectacle! Men in every stage of mutilation lying on the bare boards, with perhaps a haversack or an army blanket beneath their heads,—some dying, all suffering keenly, while waiting their turn to be attended to. To be there empty-handed and impotent nearly broke our hearts. We passed from one to the other, making such slight additions to their comfort as were possible, while looking in every upturned face in dread to find the object of our search. This sorrow, I may add, was spared, the youth arriving at home later with a slight flesh-wound. The condition of things at this and other improvised hospitals was improved next day by the offerings from many churches of pew-cushions, which, sewn together, served as comfortable beds; and for the remainder of the war their owners thanked God upon bare benches for every "misery missed" that was "mercy gained." To supply food for the hospitals the contents of larders all over town were emptied into baskets; while cellars long sealed and cobwebbed, belonging to the old Virginia gentry who knew good Port and Madeira, were opened by the Ithuriel's spear of universal sympathy. There was not much going to bed that night, either; and I remember spending the greater part of it leaning from my window to seek the cool night air, while wondering as to the fate of those near to me. There was a summons to my mother about midnight. Two soldiers came to tell her of the wounding of one close of kin; but she was already on duty elsewhere, tireless and watchful as ever. Up to that time the younger girls had been regarded as superfluities in hospital service; but on Monday two of us found a couple of rooms where fifteen wounded men lay upon pallets around the floor, and, on offering our services to the surgeons in charge, were proud to have them accepted and to be installed as responsible nurses, under direction of an older and more experienced woman. The constant activity our work entailed was a relief from the strained excitement of life after the battle of Seven Pines. When the first flurry of distress was over, the residents of those pretty houses standing back in gardens full of roses set their cooks to work, or, better still, went themselves into the kitchen, to compound delicious messes for the wounded, after the appetizing old Virginia recipes. Flitting about the streets in the direction of the hospitals were smiling, white-jacketed negroes, carrying silver trays with dishes of fine porcelain under napkins of thick white damask, containing soups, creams, jellies, thin biscuit, eggs *à la crême*, boiled chicken, etc., surmounted by clusters of freshly gathered flowers. A year later we had cause to pine after these culinary glories when it came to measuring out, with sinking hearts, the meager portions of milk and food we could afford to give our charges.

Walt Whitman

On the Military Hospitals in Washington

Whitman reports to the New York Times, *on February 26, 1863, on how the wounded are handled in Washington.*

The military hospitals, convalescent camps, etc. in Washington and its neighborhood sometimes contain over fifty thousand sick and wounded men. Every form of wound (the mere sight of some of them having been known to make a tolerably hardy visitor faint away), every kind of malady—like a long procession, with typhoid, and diarrhoea at the head as leaders—are here in steady motion. The soldiers' hospital! How many sleepless nights, how many women's tears, how many long and waking hours and days of suspense from every one of the Middle, Eastern, and Western states have concentrated here! Our own New York, in the form of hundreds and thousands of her young men, may consider herself here; Pennsylvania, Ohio, Indiana, and all the West and Northwest the same, and all the New England States the same!

Upon a few of these hospitals I have been almost daily calling on a mission, on my own account, for the sustenance and consolation of some of the most needy cases of sick and dying men for the last two months. One has much to learn to do good in these places. Great tact is required. These are not like other hospitals. By far the greatest proportion (I should say five sixths) of the patients are American young men, intelligent, of independent spirit, tender feelings, used to a hardy and healthy life; largely the farmers are represented by their sons—largely the mechanics and workingmen of the cities. Then they are soldiers. All these points must be borne in mind.

People through our Northern cities have little or no idea of the great and prominent feature which these military hospitals and convalescent camps make in and around

WINSLOW HOMER. *"From Richmond."* 1862. Watercolor, graphite. 6⅛ x 4⅞". Cooper-Hewitt National Museum of Design, Smithsonian Institution / Art Resource, New York.

Washington. There are not merely two or three or a dozen, but some fifty of them of different degrees of capacity. Some have a thousand and more patients. The newspapers here find it necessary to print every day a directory of the hospitals—a long list something like what a directory of the churches would be in New York, Philadelphia, or Boston.

The government (which really tries, I think, to do the best and quickest it can for these sad necessities) is gradually settling down to adopt the plan of placing the hospitals in clusters of one-story wooden barracks, with their accompanying tents and sheds for cooking and all needed purposes. Taking all things into consideration, no doubt these are best adapted to the purpose, better than using churches and large public buildings like the Patent Office. These sheds now adopted are long, one-story edifices, sometimes ranged along in a row with their heads to the street, and numbered either alphabetically—Wards A or B, C, D, and so on; or Wards 1, 2, 3, etc. The middle one will be marked by a flagstaff, and is the office of the establishment, with rooms for the ward surgeons, etc. One of these sheds or wards will contain sixty cots; sometimes, on an emergency, they move them close together and crowd in more. Some of the barracks are larger, with, of course, more inmates. Frequently there are tents—more comfortable here than one might think—whatever they may be down in the army.

Each ward has a ward-master and generally a nurse for every ten or twelve men. A ward surgeon has, generally, two wards—although this varies. Some of the wards have a woman nurse; the Armory-Square wards have some very good ones. The one in Ward E is one of the best. . . .

Of course, there are among these thousands of prostrated soldiers in hospital here all sorts of individual cases. On recurring to my notebook, I am puzzled which cases to select to illustrate the average of these young men and their experiences. I may say here, too, in general terms, that I could not wish for more candor and manliness among all their sufferings than I find among them.

Take this case in Ward 6, Campbell Hospital, a young man from Plymouth County, Massachusetts; a farmer's son, aged about twenty or twenty-one—a soldierly, American young fellow, but with sensitive and tender feelings. Most of December and January last he lay very low, and for quite a while I never expected he would recover. He had become prostrated with an obstinate diarrhoea; his stomach would hardly keep the least thing down; he was vomiting half the time. But that was hardly the worst of it. Let me tell you his story—it is but one of thousands.

He had been some time sick with his regiment in the field, in front, but did his duty as long as he could; was in the battle of Fredericksburg; soon after was put in the regimental hospital. He kept getting worse—could not eat anything they had there; the doctor told him nothing could be done for him there. The poor fellow had fever also; received (perhaps it could not be helped) little or no attention; lay on the ground getting worse. Toward the latter part of December, very much enfeebled, he was sent up from the front, from Falmouth Station, in an open platform car (such as hogs are transported upon North), and dumped with a crowd of others on the boat at Aquia Creek. . . .

Arrived at Washington, he was brought ashore and again left on the wharf or above it, amid the great crowds, as before, without any nourishment, not a drink for his parched mouth; no kind hand had offered to cover his face from the forenoon sun. Conveyed at last some two miles by the ambulance to the hospital and assigned a bed (Bed 49, Campbell Hospital, January and February, 1863), he fell down exhausted upon the bed. But the ward-master (he has since been changed) came to him with a growling order to get up; the rules, he said, permitted no man to lie down in that way with his own clothes on; he must sit up—must first go to the bathroom, be washed, and have his clothes properly changed. (A very good rule, properly applied.) He was taken to the bathroom and scrubbed well with cold water. The attendants, callous for a while, were soon alarmed, for suddenly the half-frozen and lifeless body fell limpsy in their hands, and they hurried it back to the cot, plainly insensible, perhaps dying. . . .

As luck would have it, at this time I found him. I was passing down Ward No. 6 one day about dusk (4th January, I think), and noticed his glassy eyes, with a look of despair and hopelessness, sunk low in his thin, pallid-brown young face. One learns to divine quickly in the hospital, and as I stopped by him and spoke some commonplace remark (to which he made no reply), I saw as I looked that it was a case for ministering to the affection first and other nourishment and medicines afterward.

I sat down by him without any fuss; talked a little; soon saw that it did him good; led him to talk a little himself; got him somewhat interested; wrote a letter for him to his folks in Massachusetts (to L. H. Campbell, Plymouth County); soothed him down, as I saw he was getting a little too much agitated and tears in his eyes; gave him some small gifts and told him I should come again soon. (He has told me since that this little visit, at that hour, just saved him; a day more and it would have been perhaps too late.)

Of course I did not forget him, for he was a young fellow to interest anyone. He remained very sick—vomiting much every day, frequent diarrhoea, and also something like bronchitis, the doctor said. For a while, I visited him almost every day, cheered him up, took him some little gifts, and gave him small sums of money (he relished a drink of new milk when it was brought through the ward for sale). For a couple of weeks his condition was uncertain; sometimes I thought there was no chance for him at all, but of late he is doing better—is up and dressed and goes around more and more (February 21) every day. He will not die but will recover.

The other evening, passing through the ward, he called me—he wanted to say a few words, particular. I sat down by his side on the cot in the dimness of the long ward, with the wounded soldiers there in their beds, ranging up and down. H. told me I had saved his life. He was in the deepest earnest about it. It was one of those things that repay a soldiers' hospital missionary a thousandfold—one of the hours he never forgets. . . .

John Esten Cooke

FROM OUTLINES FROM THE OUTPOST

On the Death of John Pelham

A Virginian commemorates "the Gallant Pelham," Lee's great artillerist, killed at the Battle of Kelly's Ford in March 1863.

Thus passed away a noble, lofty soul; thus ended a career, brief, it is true, but among the most arduous, glorious and splendid which the history of this war contains. Young, but immortal; a boy in years, but heir to undying fame—he was called away from the scene of his triumphs and glory, to a brighter world, where neither wars nor rumors of wars, can come, and wounds and pain and suffering are unknown; where

"Malice domestic, foreign levy, nothing
Can touch him further!"

To him who writes these lines, the death of this noble youth has been inexpressibly saddening. It has cast a shadow on the very sunlight; and the world seems, somehow, colder and more dreary since he went away. It was but yesterday almost, that he was in this tent, and I looked into his frank, brave eyes, and heard his kind, honest voice. There is the seat he occupied as we conversed—the bed where he so often slept with me,

Major John Pelham.
May 1861. Photograph.
United States Military
Academy Archives,
West Point, New York.

prolonging his gay talk deep into the night. There are the books he read—the papers which he wrote; at this table he once sat, and here where my own hand rests, has rested the hand of the Dead! Every object thus recalls him, even as he lived and moved beside me, but a few days ago. His very words seem still echoing in the air, and the dreary camp is full of his presence!

Nor am I the only one whose heart has bled for the young soldier. All who knew him loved him for his gay, sweet temper, as they admired him for his unshrinking courage. I have seen no face over which a sort of shadow did not pass at the announcement "Pelham is dead!"

"Pelham is dead!"

It is only another mode of saying "honor is dead! courage is dead! modesty, kindness, courtesy, the inborn spirit of the true and perfect gentleman, the nerve of the soldier, the gayety of the good companion, the kindly heart and the resolute soul—all dead, and never more to revisit us in his person!"

These words are not dictated by a blind partiality, or mere personal regard for the brave youth who has fallen in front of the foe, in defence of the sacred liberties of the South. Of his matchless daring, his unshrinking nerve and utter coolness in the hour of deadliest peril, let the name of "the gallant Pelham," given him by General Lee at Fredericksburg, bear witness. Of his noble, truthful nature, those who knew him best will speak.

He had made for himself a "great immortal name," and he was only twenty-four when he died!

Emily Dickinson
On a Union Casualty

War news reaches Amherst, Massachusetts, and Emily Dickinson mourns young Frazer Stearns, 21st Massachusetts, dead on the North Carolina coast.

You have done more for me—'tis least that I can do, to tell you of brave Frazer—"killed at Newbern," darlings. His big heart shot away by a "minie ball."

I had read of those—I didn't think that Frazer would carry one to Eden with him. Just as he fell, in his soldier's cap, with his sword at his side, Frazer rode through Amherst. Classmates to the right of him, and classmates to the left of him, to guard his narrow face! He fell by the side of Professor Clark, his superior officer—lived ten minutes in a soldier's arms, asked twice for water—murmured just, "My God!" and passed! Sanderson, his classmate, made a box of boards in the night, put the brave boy in, covered with a blanket; rowed six miles to reach the boat—so poor Frazer came. They tell that Colonel Clark cried like a little child when he missed his pet, and could hardly resume his post. They loved each other very much. Nobody here could look on Frazer— not even his father. The doctors would not allow it.

The bed on which he came was enclosed in a large casket shut entirely, and covered from head to foot with the sweetest flowers. He went to sleep from the village church. Crowds came to tell him good-night, choirs sang to him, pastors told how brave he was— early-soldier heart. And the family bowed their heads, as the reeds the wind shakes.

So our part in Frazer is done, but you must come next summer and we will mind ourselves of this young crusader—too brave that he could fear to die. We will play his tunes—maybe he can hear them; we will try to comfort his broken-hearted Ella, who, as the clergyman said, "gave him peculiar confidence." . . . Austin is stunned completely. Let us love better, children, it's most that's left to do.

Austin is chilled—by Frazer's murder—he says—his Brain keeps saying over "Frazer is killed—Frazer is killed," just as Father told it—to him. Two or three words of lead—that dropped so deep, they keep weighing—

Walt Whitman

On the Wounded from Chancellorsville

It is May 1863, and the wounded from the new campaign begin arriving in Washington.

As I write this, wounded have begun to arrive from Hooker's command from bloody Chancellorsville. I was down among the first arrivals. The men in charge told me the bad cases were yet to come. If that is so, I pity them—for these are bad enough. You ought to see the scene of the wounded arriving at the landing here at the foot of Sixth Street at night. Two boatloads came about half-past seven last night. A little after eight, it rained a long and violent shower. The pale, helpless soldiers had been debarked, and lay around on the wharf and neighborhood anywhere. The rain was probably grateful to them; at any rate, they were exposed to it. The few torches light up the spectacle.

All around—on the wharf, on the ground, out on side places—the men are lying on blankets, old quilts, etc., with bloody rags bound 'round heads, arms, and legs. The attendants are few, and at night few outsiders also; only a few hard-worked transportation men and drivers. (The wounded are getting to be common, and people grow callous.)

The men, whatever their condition, lie there and patiently wait till their turn comes to be taken up. Nearby, the ambulances are now arriving in clusters, and one after another is called to back up and take its load. Extreme cases are sent off on stretchers. The men generally make little or no ado, whatever their sufferings. A few groans that cannot be suppressed and occasionally a scream of pain, as they lift a man into the ambulance. Today, as I write, hundreds more are expected, and tomorrow and the next day more, and so on for many days. Quite often they arrive at the rate of one thousand a day.

Washington Military Hospital. 1864. Photograph. National Archives, Washington, D.C.

Stephen Vincent Benét
FROM "JOHN BROWN'S BODY"
On Stonewall Jackson

Stonewall Jackson—Mighty Stonewall—dead at Chancellorsville.

In the dense heart of the thicketed Wilderness,
Stonewall Jackson lies dying for four long days.
They have cut off his arm, they have tried such arts as they know,
But no arts now can save him.
                              When he was hit
By the blind chance bullet-spatter from his own lines,
In the night, in the darkness, they stole him off from the field
To keep the men from knowing, but the men knew.
The dogs in the house will know when there's something wrong.
You do not have to tell them.
                              He marched his men
That grim first day across the whole Union front
To strike a sleepy right wing with a sudden stone
And roll it up—it was his old trick of war
That Lee and he could play like finger and thumb!
It was the last time they played so.
                              When the blue-coated
Unprepared ranks of Howard saw that storm,
Heralded by wild rabbits and frightened deer,
Burst on them yelling, out of the whispering woods,
They could not face it. Some men died where they stood,
The storm passed over the rest. It was Jackson's storm,
It was his old trick of war, for the last time played.
He must have known it. He loosed it and drove it on,
Hearing the long yell shake like an Indian cry
Through the dense black oaks, the clumps of second-growth pine,
And the red flags reel ahead through the underbrush.
It was the hour he did not stop to taste,
Being himself. He saw it and found it good,
But night was falling, the Union centre still held,
Another attack would end it. He pressed ahead
Through the dusk, pushing Little Sorrel, as if the horse
Were iron, and he were iron, and all his men
Not men but iron, the stalks of an iron broom
Sweeping a dire floor clean—and yet, as he rode,
A canny captain, planning a ruthless chess
Skilfully as night fell. The night fell too soon.
It is hard to tell your friend from your enemy
In such a night. So he rode too far in advance
And, turning back toward his lines, unrecognized,
Was fired upon in the night, in the stumbling darkness,
By his own men. He had ridden such rides before
Often enough and taken the chance of them,
But this chance was his bane. . . .

Ambrose Bierce
"CHICKAMAUGA"
On the Debris of Battle

The scene in September 1863 when the guns fell silent. Bierce fought in the Union army in the bloodiest battles in the western theater, including Chickamauga.

————————

They were men. They crept upon their hands and knees. They used their hands only, dragging their legs. They used their knees only, their arms hanging idle at their sides. They strove to rise to their feet, but fell prone in the attempt. They did nothing naturally, and nothing alike, save only to advance foot by foot in the same direction.

Singly, in pairs, and in little groups, they came on through the gloom, some halting now and again while others crept slowly past them, then resuming their movement. They came by dozens and by hundreds; as far on either hand as one could see in the deepening gloom they extended and the black wood behind them appeared to be inexhaustible. The very ground seemed in motion toward the creek. Occasionally one who had paused did not again go on, but lay motionless. He was dead. Some, pausing, made strange gestures with their hands, erected their arms and lowered them again, clasped their heads; spread their palms upward, as men are sometimes seen to do in public prayer.

. . . These were men, yet crept like babies. Being men, they were terrible, though unfamiliarly clad. . . . All their faces were singularly white and many were streaked and gouted with red. . . . But on and ever on they crept, these maimed and bleeding men. . . . one of the crawling figures . . . turned . . . a face that lacked a lower jaw—from the upper teeth to the throat was a great red gap fringed with hanging shreds of flesh and splinters of bone. The unnatural prominence of nose, the absence of chin, the fierce eyes, gave this man the appearance of a great bird of prey crimsoned in throat and breast by the blood of its quarry. . . .

And so the clumsy multitude dragged itself slowly and painfully along in hideous pantomime—moved forward down the slope like a swarm of great black beetles with never a sound of going—in silence profound, absolute.

Instead of darkening, the haunted landscape began to brighten. Through the belt of trees beyond the brook shone a strange red light, the trunks and branches of the trees making a black lacework against it. It struck the creeping figures and gave them monstrous shadows, which caricatured their movements on the lit grass. It fell upon their faces, touching their whiteness with a ruddy tinge, accentuating the stains with which so many of them were freaked and maculated. It sparkled on buttons and bits of metal in their clothing.

Scattered about upon the ground now slowly narrowing by the encroachment of this awful march to the water, were certain articles . . . : an occasional blanket, tightly rolled lengthwise, doubled and the ends bound together with a string; a heavy knapsack here, and there a broken rifle—such things, in short, as are found in the rear of retreating troops, the "spoor" of men flying from their hunters. Everywhere near the creek, which here had a margin of lowland, the earth was trodden into mud by the feet of men and horses . . . footprints pointed in both directions; the ground had been twice passed over—in advance and in retreat. A few hours before, these desperate, stricken men, with their more fortunate and now distant comrades, had penetrated the forest in thousands. Their successive battalions, breaking into swarms and reforming in lines. . . . They had fought a battle. . . .

WINSLOW HOMER.
The Walking Wounded.
1861–1862. Pen and
brown ink, graphite.
4¾ x 7⅜".
Cooper-Hewitt
National Museum of
Design, Smithsonian
Institution / Art
Resource, New York.

The fire beyond the belt of woods on the farther side of the creek, reflected to earth from the canopy of its own smoke, was now suffusing the whole landscape. It transformed the sinuous line of mist to the vapor of gold. The water gleamed with dashes of red, and red, too, were many of the stones protruding above the surface. But that was blood; the less desperately wounded had stained them in crossing. . . .

The advance was arriving at the creek. The stronger had already drawn themselves to the brink and plunged their faces into the flood. Three or four who lay without motion appeared to have no heads. . . . After slaking their thirst these men had not the strength to back away from the water, nor to keep their heads above it. They were drowned. In the rear of these, the open spaces of the forest showed . . . many formless figures . . . ; but not nearly so many were in motion. . . .

Walt Whitman

On the Release of Union Prisoners

Whether Union or Confederate, no experience of the Civil War was more harrowing than that of prisoners of war. Whitman's account, in Specimen Days, *was written at war's end.*

The released prisoners of war are now coming up from the Southern prisons. I have seen a number of them; the sight is worse than any sight of battlefields or any collection of wounded, even the bloodiest.

There was (as a sample) one large boatload of several hundreds brought about the 25th to Annapolis; and, out of the whole number, only three individuals were able to walk from the boat. The rest were carried ashore and laid down in one place or another.

WILLIAM WAUD.
Returned Prisoners of
War Exchanging Their
Rags, Charleston, S.C.
December, 1864.
Pencil, wash, and
chinese white on
paper. 9⅝ x 13⅞″.
Library of Congress,
Washington, D.C.

Can these be *men*—these little, livid brown, ash-streaked, monkey-looking dwarfs? Are they really not mummied, dwindled corpses? They lay there, most of them quite still, but with a horrible look in their eyes and skinny lips—often with not enough flesh to cover their teeth. Probably no more appalling sight was ever seen on this earth.

(There are deeds, crimes, that may be forgiven; but this is not among them. It steeps its perpetrators in blackest, escapeless, endless damnation. Over fifty thousand have been compelled to die the death of starvation—reader, did you ever try to realize what *starvation* actually is?—in those prisons—and in a land of plenty!) An indescribable meanness, tyranny, aggravating course of insults—almost incredible—was evidently the rule of treatment through all the Southern military prisons. The dead there are not to be pitied as much as some of the living that come from there—if they can be called living—many of them are mentally imbecile and will never recuperate. . . .

S. S. Boggs
On Andersonville

Sergeant Boggs of the 21st Illinois remembers his arrival at Andersonville, the infamous prisoner-of-war camp in Georgia, in his memoir Eighteen Months a Prisoner Under the Rebel Flag.

We learned that this was Andersonville. We were taken from the cars to an open piece of ground just east of the station, looking east about a quarter of a mile, we could see an immense stockade. The last few days of our journey we had no water, and were suffering from thirst. The car that I was in had been used as a lime car, and had a half-inch of lime dust on the floor when they loaded us in at Petersburg; they put about seventy-five men in each car; any moving around would stir up the dust. Our lips and tongues seemed parched and cracked. Two died in our car on the trip. There was a small brook within two rods of us; the guard line was between us and the water. I was pleading with the guard to let us to the water, when a little grinny-faced Rebel captain, on a sway-backed gray horse, rode up and shook a revolver in my face and said: "You Got tam Yankee! you youst vait, and you got so much vater voy you drown in booty quick!" He rode around us several times, bouncing high in his saddle, flourishing a revolver and swearing at the guards and us alternately. After satisfying himself that we did not have any thing worth robbing us of, he proceeded to form us into nineties and detachments. One of our sergeants was put over each ninety, and one over each detachment. By this time we learned that this was Captain Wirz, the commander of the interior of the prison.

We were ordered forward toward the big stockade, moving quietly and painfully along, our spirits almost crushed within us, urged on by the double file of guards on either side of our column of ragged, lousy, skeletons, who scarce had strength to run away if given the opportunity. We neared the wall of great squared logs and the massive wooden gates that were to shut out hope and life from nearly all of us forever. The uncheerful sight, near the gate, of a pile of ghastly dead—the eyes of whom shone with a stony glitter, the faces black with a smoky grime, and pinched with pain and hunger, the long matted hair and almost fleshless frame swarming with lice—gave us some idea that a like fate awaited us on the inside. The rebels knowing our desperation, used every precaution to prevent a break; the artillerymen stood with lanyard in hand at their cannister-shotted guns, which were trained to sweep the gates. All being ready, the huge bolts were drawn, the gate swung open on its massive iron hinges, and as we moved into that hell on earth we felt that we were cut off from the world and completely at the mercy of our cruel keepers.

The creek which ran through the pen was pointed out to us. A rush was made for it, as we were famishing from thirst. The water soon became cloudy; two comrades, to get the water just above the "dead line," and not knowing the danger, reached beyond it, and both dropped dead in the water, shot by the guards on the wall. We dared not move their bodies until ordered to do so by a Rebel officer, who was some time in getting around. The water running red with our comrades' blood, stopped the drinking until the bodies were removed. We had not been in the stockade ten minutes until two of our number were ready to be put on the dead pile we had seen just outside the gate, but the poor fellows missed the horrible torture which was planned for them and us, and which if I knew I had to pass through again I would cross the "dead line" and ask the guard

WALTON TABER.
Weary Hours,
Andersonville. 1890.
Pen. 4½ x 11⅜".
Century Collection,
New York.

to show me mercy by tearing my body through with the ball and buckshot from his old Queen Anne musket. . . .

The spot of ground we were to occupy was pointed out to the sergeant of our detachment, who guided us to near the northeast corner of the pen, where we arranged in rows, north and south, leaving a narrow alley between each ninety. We then commenced fixing our bedding-place, or, rather, "spooning-ground." There was yet some debris left from cutting and hewing the palisade timbers. The prisoners who had been there, some of them more than a month, had consumed nearly all of the refuse for fuel, for making huts and "dug outs." Some, with a view of speculation, had stored by many of the best poles and sticks. However, there were yet some small poles and sticks to be had along the edge of the swamp; with these, and sun-dried bricks, we made a temporary shelter, which would do in dry weather, but when it rained it seemed to rain more in the hut than it did outside and our brick generally had to be made anew.

Our rations now consisted of a pint of coarse corn-meal and about a *gill* of stock peas per day. . . .

CIVILIANS AT WAR

Constance Cary Harrison
"VIRGINIA SCENES IN '61"

A Virginia woman remembers the first summer of the war.

The only association I have with my old home in Virginia that is not one of unmixed happiness relates to the time immediately succeeding the execution of John Brown at Charlestown. Our homestead was in Fairfax County, at some distance from the theater of that tragic episode; and, belonging as we did to a family among the first in the State to manumit slaves,—our grandfather having set free those that came to him by inheritance, and the people who served us being hired from their owners and remaining in our employ through years of kindliest relations,—there seemed to be no especial reason for us to share in the apprehension of an uprising of the blacks. But there was the fear—unspoken, or pooh-poohed at by the men who were mouth-pieces for our community—dark, boding, oppressive, and altogether hateful. I can remember taking it to bed with me at night, and awaking suddenly oftentimes to confront it through a vigil of nervous terror, of which it never occurred to me to speak to any one. The notes of whip-poor-wills in the sweet-gum swamp near the stable, the mutterings of a distant thunder-storm, even the rustle of the night wind in the oaks that shaded my window, filled me with nameless dread. In the daytime it seemed impossible to associate suspicion with those familiar tawny or sable faces that surrounded us. We had seen them for so many years smiling or saddening with the family joys or sorrows; they were so guileless, so patient, so satisfied. What subtle influence was at work that should transform them into tigers thirsting for our blood? The idea was preposterous. But when evening came again, and with it the hour when the colored people (who in summer and autumn weather kept astir half the night) assembled themselves together for dance or prayer-meeting, the ghost that refused to be laid was again at one's elbow. Rusty bolts were drawn and rusty fire-arms loaded. A watch was set where never before had eye or ear been lent to such a service. In short, peace had flown from the borders of Virginia.

Although the newspapers were full of secession talk and the matter was eagerly discussed at our tables, I cannot remember that, as late as Christmastime of the year 1860, coming events had cast any definite shadow on our homes. The people in our neighborhood, of one opinion with their dear and honored friend, Colonel Robert E. Lee, of Arlington, were slow to accept the startling suggestion of disruption of the Union. At any rate, we enjoyed the usual holiday gathering of kinsfolk in the usual fashion. The old Vaucluse house, known for many years past as a center of cheerful hospitality in the county, threw wide open its doors to receive all the members who could be gathered there of a large family circle.

My first vivid impression of war-days was during a ramble in the neighboring woods one Sunday afternoon in spring, when the young people in a happy band set out in search of wild flowers. Pink honeysuckles, blue lupine, beds of fairy flax, anemones, and ferns in abundance sprung under the canopy of young leaves on the forest boughs, and the air was full of the song of birds and the music of running waters. We knew every mossy path far and near in those woods; every tree had been watched and cherished by those who went before us, and dearer than any other spot on earth was our tranquil, sweet Vaucluse. Suddenly the shrill whistle of a locomotive struck the ear, an unwonted sound on Sunday. "Do you know what that means?" said one of the older cousins who accompanied the party. "It is the special train carrying Alexandria volunteers to Manassas, and to-morrow I shall follow with my company." Silence fell upon our little band. A cloud seemed to come between us and the sun. It was the beginning of the end too soon to come.

The story of one broken circle is the story of another at the outset of such a war. Before the week was over, the scattering of our household, which no one then believed to be more than temporary, had begun. Living as we did upon ground likely to be in the track of armies gathering to confront each other, it was deemed advisable to send the children and young girls into a place more remote from chances of danger. Some weeks later the heads of the household, two widowed sisters whose sons were at Manassas, drove away from their home in their carriage at early morning, having spent the previous night in company with a half-grown lad digging in the cellar hasty graves for the interment of two boxes of old English silver-ware, heirlooms in the family, for which there was no time to provide otherwise. Although the enemy were long encamped immediately above it after the house was burnt the following year, this silver was found there when the war had ended; it was lying loose in the earth, the boxes having rotted away.

The point at which our family reunited within the Confederate lines was Bristoe, the station next beyond Manassas, a cheerless railway inn; a part of the premises was used as a country grocery store; and there quarters were secured for us with a view to being near the army. By this time all our kith and kin of fighting age had joined the volunteers. One cannot picture accommodations more forlorn than these eagerly taken for us and for other families attracted to Bristoe by the same powerful magnet. The summer sun poured its burning rays upon whitewashed walls unshaded by a tree. Our bedrooms were almost uninhabitable by day or night, our fare the plainest. From the windows we beheld only a flat, uncultivated country, crossed by red-clay roads, then ankle-deep in dust. We learned to look for all excitement to the glittering lines of railway track, along which continually thundered trains bound to and from the front. It was impossible to allow such a train to pass without running out upon the platform to salute it, for in this way we greeted many an old friend or relative buttoned up in the smart gray uniform, speeding with high hope to the scene of coming conflict. Such shouts as went up from sturdy throats while we stood waving hands, handkerchiefs, or the rough woolen garments we were at work upon! Then fairly awoke the spirit that made of Southern women the inspiration of Southern men throughout the war. Most of the young fellows we knew and were cheering onward wore the uniform of privates, and for the right to wear it had left homes of ease and luxury. To such we gave our best homage; and from that time forth the youth who was lukewarm in the cause or unambitious of military glory fared uncomfortably in the presence of the average Confederate maiden.

Thanks to our own carriage, we were able during those rallying days of June to drive frequently to visit "the boys" in camp, timing the expeditions to include battalion drill and dress parade, and taking tea afterward in the different tents. Then were the gala days of war, and our proud hosts hastened to produce home dainties dispatched from the far-away plantations — tears and blessings interspersed amid the packing, we were sure; though I have seen a pretty girl persist in declining other fare, to make her meal upon raw biscuit and huckleberry pie compounded by the bright-eyed amateur cook of a well-beloved mess. Feminine heroism could no farther go.

And so the days wore on until the 17th of July, when a rumor from the front sent an electric shock through our circle. The enemy were moving forward! On the morning of the 18th those who had been able to sleep at all awoke early to listen for the first guns of the engagement of Blackburn's Ford. Deserted as the women at Bristoe were by every male creature old enough to gather news, there was, for us, no way of knowing the progress of events during the long, long day of waiting, of watching, of weeping, of praying, of rushing out upon the railway track to walk as far as we dared in the direction whence came that intolerable booming of artillery. The cloud of dun smoke arising over Manassas became heavier in volume as the day progressed. Still, not a word of tidings, till toward afternoon there came limping up a single, very dirty, soldier with his arm in a sling. What a heaven-send he was, if only as an escape-valve for our pent-up sympathies! We seized him, we washed him, we cried over him, we glorified him until the man was fairly bewildered. Our best endeavors could only develop a pin-scratch of a wound on his right hand; but when our hero had laid in a substantial meal of bread and meat, we plied him with trembling questions, each asking news of some staff or regiment or company. It has since occurred to me that he was a humorist in disguise. His invariable reply, as he looked from one to the other of his satellites, was: "The — Virginia, marm? Why, of coase. They warn't no two ways o' thinkin' 'bout that ar reg'ment. They just *kivered* tharselves with glory!"

A little later two wagon-loads of slightly wounded claimed our care, and with them came authentic news of the day. Most of us received notes on paper torn from a soldier's pocket-book and grimed with gunpowder, containing assurance of the safety of our own. At nightfall a train carrying more wounded to the hospitals at Culpeper made a halt at Bristoe; and, preceded by men holding lanterns, we went in among the stretchers with milk, food, and water to the sufferers. One of the first discoveries I made, bending over in that fitful light, was a young officer whom I knew to be a special object of solicitude with one of my comrades in the search; but he was badly hurt, and neither he nor she knew the other was near until the train had moved on. The next day, and the next, were full of burning excitement over the impending general engagement, which people then said would decide the fate of the young Confederacy. Fresh troops came by with every train, and we lived only to turn from one scene to another of welcome and farewell. On Saturday evening arrived a message from General Beauregard, saying that early on Sunday an engine and car would be put at our disposal, to take us to some point more remote from danger. We looked at one another, and, tacitly agreeing the gallant general had sent not an order but a suggestion, declined his kind proposal.

Another unspeakably long day, full of the straining anguish of suspense. Dawning bright and fair, it closed under a sky darkened by cannon-smoke. The roar of guns seemed never to cease. First, a long sullen boom; then a sharper rattling fire, painfully distinct; then stragglers from the field, with varying rumors; at last, the news of victory; and, as before, the wounded, to force our numbed faculties into service. One of our group, the mother of an only son barely fifteen years of age, heard that her boy, after

COLORPLATE 89

EDOUARD ARMAND DUMARESQ. *Mosby's Rangers Returning from a Raid.* ca. 1868. Oil on canvas. 17¾ × 26¾". Museum of the Confederacy, Richmond. Photo by Katherine Wetzel.

COLORPLATE 90

ALBERT MOYER. *Northern Prison Camp, Camp Douglas, Chicago.* 1864. Oil on canvas. 16⅞ × 22¼″. Chicago Historical Society. *A camp for Confederate prisoners of war, painted by one of the guards.*

COLORPLATE 91

EASTMAN JOHNSON. *A Ride for Liberty - The Fugitive Slaves*. 1862. Oil on board.
22 × 26¼″. The Brooklyn Museum. Gift of Miss Gwendolyn O. L. Conkling.

COLORPLATE 92

THOMAS MORAN. *Slaves Escaping Through the Swamp*. 1863.
Oil on canvas. 32½ × 43″. Philbrook Art Center, Tulsa.

COLORPLATE 93

C. Giroux. *Cotton Plantation.* 1850-1865. Oil on canvas. 22 × 36″.
Museum of Fine Arts, Boston. M. and M. Karolik Collection.

COLORPLATE 94

WILLIAM D. WASHINGTON. *Burial of Latané.* 1874. Oil on canvas. 48 × 55″. From the
Collection of Judge John E. DeHardit, Gloucester, Virginia. Photo by Larry Sherer, copyright
© 1984 Time-Life Books, Inc. *Captain William Latané, 9th Virginia Cavalry, was killed in
Jeb Stuart's "Ride Around McClellan" on the Peninsula in 1862.*

COLORPLATE 95

D. E. Henderson. *Petersburg Refugee Family.* 1865. Oil on canvas. 25 × 30". Gettysburg National Military Park Museum / Eisenhower National Historic Site, Gettysburg. Photo by Larry Sherer, copyright © 1984 Time-Life Books, Inc.

COLORPLATE 96

GEORGE CALEB BINGHAM. *Order No. 11*. ca. 1865-1870. Oil on canvas. 55½ × 78½″.
Cincinnati Art Museum. The Edwin and Virginia Irwin Memorial, 1958.515 *A Federal army
order of 1863 evicted some 20,000 Missouri civilians from their homes for aiding Confederate
guerrillas.*

being in action all the early part of the day, had through sheer fatigue fallen asleep upon the ground, where he was found resting peacefully amidst the roar of the guns.

A few days later we rode over the field. The trampled grass had begun to spring again, and wild flowers were blooming around carelessly made graves. From one of these imperfect mounds of clay I saw a hand extended; and when, years afterward, I visited the tomb of Rousseau beneath the Pantheon in Paris, where a sculptured hand bearing a torch protrudes from the sarcophagus, I thought of that mournful spectacle upon the field of Manassas. Fences were everywhere thrown down; the undergrowth of the woods was riddled with shot; here and there we came upon spiked guns, disabled gun-carriages, cannon-balls, blood-stained blankets, and dead horses. We were glad enough to turn away and gallop homeward.

Julia Ward Howe

On Writing "The Battle Hymn of the Republic"

In her Reminiscences *the author recalls the inspiration for writing the most famous song of the Civil War, the "Battle Hymn of the Republic," first published in the* Atlantic Monthly *in February 1862.*

We returned to the city very slowly, of necessity, for the troops nearly filled the road. My dear minister was in the carriage with me, as were several other friends. To beguile the rather tedious drive, we sang from time to time snatches of the army songs so popular at that time, concluding, I think, with:

John Brown's body lies a-moldering in the ground;
    His soul is marching on.

The soldiers seemed to like this and answered back, "Good for you!" Mr. Clark said, "Mrs. Howe, why do you not write some good words for that stirring tune?" I replied that I had often wished to do this but had not as yet found in my mind any leading toward it.

I went to bed that night as usual and slept, according to my wont, quite soundly. I awoke in the gray of the morning twilight, and as I lay waiting for the dawn, the long lines of the desired poem began to twine themselves in my mind. Having thought out all the stanzas, I said to myself, "I must get up and write these verses down, lest I fall asleep again and forget them." So with a sudden effort I sprang out of bed and found in the dimness an old stump of a pen which I remembered to have used the day before. I scrawled the verses almost without looking at the paper. I had learned to do this when, on previous occasions, attacks of versification had visited me in the night and I feared to have recourse to a light lest I should wake the baby, who slept near me. I was always obliged to decipher my scrawl before another night should intervene, as it was only legible while the matter was fresh in my mind. At this time, having completed my writing, I returned to bed and fell asleep, saying to myself, "I like this better than most things that I have written."

THE BATTLE HYMN OF THE REPUBLIC

Mine eyes have seen the glory of the coming of the Lord:
He is trampling out the vintage where the grapes of wrath are stored;

He hath loosed the fateful lightning of his terrible swift sword:
His truth is marching on.

I have seen Him in the watch fires of a hundred circling camps;
They have builded Him an altar in the evening dews and damps;
I can read His righteous sentence by the dim and flaring lamps.
His day is marching on.

I have read a fiery gospel writ in burnished rows of steel:
"As ye deal with my contemners, so with you my grace shall deal;
Let the Hero, born of woman, crush the serpent with his heel,
Since God is marching on."

He has sounded forth the trumpet that shall never call retreat;
He is sifting out the hearts of men before his judgment seat:
Oh! be swift, my soul, to answer Him! be jubilant, my feet!
Our God is marching on.

In the beauty of the lilies Christ was born across the sea,
With a glory in His bosom that transfigures you and me:
As He died to make men holy, let us die to make men free,
While God is marching on.

George Augustus Sala
On a War Artist

The London Telegraph's *correspondent in America describes Alfred R. Waud, one of the war artists whose work filled the illustrated newspapers of the day.*

There had galloped furiously by us, backwards and forwards during our journey, a tall man, mounted on a taller horse. Blue-eyed, fair-bearded, strapping and stalwart, full of loud cheery laughs and comic songs, armed to the teeth, jack-booted, gauntleted, slouch-hatted, yet clad in the shooting-jacket of a civilian, I had puzzled myself many times during the afternoon and evening to know what manner of man this might inwardly be. He didn't look like an American; he was too well dressed to be a guerilla. I found him out at last, and struck up an alliance with him. The fair-bearded man was the "war-artist" of *Harper's Weekly* [A. R. Waud]. He had been with the Army of the Potomac, sketching, since its first organisation, and doing for the principal pictorial journal of the United States, that which Mr. Frank Vizetelly, in the South, has done so admirably for the *Illustrated London News*. He had been in every advance, in every retreat, in every battle, and almost in every reconnaissance. He probably knew more about the several campaigns, the rights and wrongs of the several fights, the merits and demerits of the commanders, than two out of three wearers of generals' shoulder-straps. But he was a prudent man, who could keep his own counsel, and went on sketching. Hence he had become a universal favourite. Commanding officers were glad to welcome in their tents the genial companion who could sing and tell stories, and imitate all the trumpet and bugle-calls — who could transmit to posterity, through woodcuts, their features and their exploits — but who was not charged with the invidious mission of commenting in print on their performances. He had been offered, time after time, a staff appointment in the Federal service;

and, indeed, as an aide-de-camp, or an assistant-quartermaster, his minute knowledge of the theatre of war would have been invaluable. Often he had ventured beyond the picket-lines, and been chased by the guerillas; but the speed and mettle of his big brown steed had always enabled him to show these gentry a clean pair of heels. He was continually vaulting on this huge brown horse, and galloping off full split, like a Wild Horseman of the Prairie. The honours of the staff appointment he had civilly declined. The risk of being killed he did not seem to mind; but he had no relish for a possible captivity in the Libby or Castle Thunder. He was, indeed, an Englishman—English to the backbone; and kept his Foreign Office passport in a secure side-pocket, in case of urgent need.

Abraham Lincoln
Letter to Horace Greeley
August 22, 1862

The President responds to a New York Tribune *editorial by Horace Greeley.*

Executive Mansion,
Washington, August 22, 1862.

Hon. Horace Greel[e]y:

Dear Sir

I have just read yours of the 19th. addressed to myself through the New-York Tribune. If there be in it any statements, or assumptions of fact, which I may know to be erroneous, I do not, now and here, controvert them. If there be in it any inferences which I may believe to be falsely drawn, I do not now and here, argue against them. If there be perceptable in it an impatient and dictatorial tone, I waive it in deference to an old friend, whose heart I have always supposed to be right.

As to the policy I "seem to be pursuing" as you say, I have not meant to leave any one in doubt.

I would save the Union. I would save it the shortest way under the Constitution. The sooner the national authority can be restored; the nearer the Union will be "the Union as it was." If there be those who would not save the Union, unless they could at the same time *save* slavery, I do not agree with them. If there be those who would not save the Union unless they could at the same time *destroy* slavery, I do not agree with them. My paramount object in this struggle *is* to save the Union, and is *not* either to save or to destroy slavery. If I could save the Union without freeing *any* slave I would do it, and if I could save it by freeing *all* the slaves I would do it; and if I could save it by freeing some and leaving others alone I would also do that. What I do about slavery, and the colored race, I do because I believe it helps to save the Union; and what I forbear, I forbear because I do *not* believe it would help to save the Union. I shall do *less* whenever I shall believe what I am doing hurts the cause, and I shall do *more* whenever I shall believe doing more will help the cause. I shall try to correct errors when shown to be errors; and I shall adopt new views so fast as they shall appear to be true views.

I have here stated my purpose according to my view of *official* duty; and I intend no modification of my oft-expressed *personal* wish that all men every where could be free. Yours,

A. LINCOLN

New York Times

On a Photographic Exhibit

*A New York Times review, on October 20, 1862, of an exhibit of photographs from the
Antietam battlefield—the work of Alexander Gardner and James Gibson—at the
Mathew Brady Gallery in New York City.*

The dead of the battle-field come up to us very rarely, even in dreams. We see the list
in the morning paper at breakfast, but dismiss its recollection with the coffee. There is
a confused mass of names, but they are all strangers; we forget the horrible significance
that dwells amid the jumble of type. The roll we read is being called over in Eternity,
and pale, trembling lips are answering to it. Shadowy fingers point from the page to a
field where even imagination is loth to follow. Each of these little names that the printer
struck off so lightly last night, whistling over his work, and that we speak with a clip of
the tongue, represents a bleeding, mangled corpse. It is a thunderbolt that will crash
into some brain—a dull, dead, remorseless weight that will fall upon some heart, straining it to the breaking. There is nothing very terrible to us, however, in the list, though
our sensations might be different if the newspaper carrier left the names on the battle-
field and the bodies at our doors instead.

We recognize the battle-field as a reality, but it stands as a remote one. It is like a
funeral next door. The crape on the bell-pull tells there is a death in the house, and in
the close carriage that rolls away with muffled wheels you know there rides a woman to
whom the world is very dark now. But you only see the mourners in the last of the long

line of carriages—they ride very jollily and at their ease, smoking cigars in a furtive and discursive manner, perhaps, and, were it not for the black gloves they wear . . . it might be a wedding for all the world would know. It attracts your attention, but does not enlist your sympathy. But it is very different when the hearse stops at your own door, and the corpse is carried out over your own threshold—you know whether it is a wedding or a funeral then, without looking at the color of the gloves worn. Those who lose friends in battle know what battle-fields are. . . .

Mr. Brady has done something to bring home to us the terrible reality and earnestness of war. If he has not brought bodies and laid them in our door-yards and along streets, he has done something very like it. . . .

These pictures have a terrible distinctness. . . . We would scarce choose to be in the gallery, when one of the women bending over them should recognize a husband, a son, or a brother in the still, lifeless lines of bodies, that lie ready for the gaping trenches. For these trenches have a terror for a woman's heart, that goes far to outweigh all others that hover over the battle-field. How can a mother bear to know that the boy whose slumbers she has cradled, and whose head her bosom pillowed until the rolling drums called him forth—whose poor, pale face, could she reach it, should find the same pillow again . . . when, but for the privilege of touching that corpse, of kissing once more the lips though white and cold, of smoothing back the hair from the brow and cleansing it of blood, stains, she would give all the remaining years of life that Heaven has allotted her—how can this mother bear to know that in a shallow trench, hastily dug, rude hands have thrown him. She would have handled the poor corpse so tenderly, have prized the boon of caring for it so dearly—yet, even the imperative office of hiding the dead from sight has been done by those who thought it trouble, and were only glad when their work ended.

ALEXANDER GARDNER.
*Union Dead of
the Irish Brigade.*
September 19, 1862.
Photograph. Library
of Congress,
Washington, D.C.

Robert Gould Shaw

Letter on a Union Raid on a Small Southern Town
June 9, 1863

The fate of a small town on the Georgia coast, recorded in a letter by an officer of the 54th Massachusetts. Shaw would later die leading the all-black 54th against Battery Wagner at Charleston.

St. Simon's Island, June 9th, 1863

On Wednesday, a steamboat appeared off our wharf, and Colonel Montgomery hailed me from the deck with, "How soon can you get ready to start on an expedition?"

I said, "In a half an hour," and it was not long before we were on board, with eight companies, leaving two for camp-guard.

We steamed down by his camp, where two other steamers, with five companies from his regiment, with two sections of Rhode Island artillery, joined us. A little below there we ran aground and had to wait until midnight for flood-tide, when we got away once more.

At 8 A.M. we were at the mouth of the Altamaha river, and immediately made for Darien. We wound in and out through the creeks, twisting and turning continually, often heading in directly the opposite direction from that which we intended to, and often running aground, thereby losing much time. Besides our three vessels, we were followed by the gunboat *Paul Jones.*

On the way up, Montgomery threw several shells among the plantations, in what seemed to me a very brutal way, for he didn't know how many women and children there might be.

About noon, we came in sight of Darien, a beautiful little town. Our artillery peppered it a little, as we came up, and then our three boats made fast to the wharves, and we landed the troops. The town was deserted, with exception of two white women and two Negroes.

Montgomery ordered all the furniture and movable property to be taken on board the boats. This occupied some time; and, after the town was pretty thoroughly disembowelled, he said to me, "I shall burn this town." He speaks always in a very low tone, and has quite a sweet smile when addressing you. I told him "I did not want the responsibility of it;" and he was only too happy to take it all on his shoulders. So the pretty little place was burnt to the ground, and not a shed remained standing—Montgomery firing the last buildings with his own hand. One of my companions assisted in it, because he ordered them out, and I had to obey. You must bear in mind, that not a shot had been fired at us from this place, and that there were evidently very few men left in it. All the inhabitants (principally women and children) had fled on our approach, and were, no doubt, watching the scene from a distance. Some of our grapeshot tore the skirt of one of the women whom I saw. Montgomery told her that her house and property should be spared; but it went down with the rest.

The reasons he gave me for destroying Darien were, that the Southerners must be made to feel that this was a real war, and that they were to be swept away by the hand of God, like the Jews of old. In theory, it may seem all right to some, but when it comes to being made the instrument of the Lord's vengeance, I myself don't like it. Then he says "We are outlawed, and, therefore, not bound by the rules of regular warfare." But that makes it none the less revolting to wreak our vengeance on the innocent and defenceless.

By the time we had finished this dirty piece of business, it was too dark to go far down the narrow river, where our boat sometimes touched both sides at once: so we lay at anchor until daylight, occasionally dropping a shell at a stray house. The *Paul Jones* fired a few guns as well as we.

I reached camp at about 2 P.M., to-day, after as abominable a job as I ever had a share in.

Remember not to breathe a word of what I have written about this raid, for I have not yet made up my mind what I ought to do. Besides my own distaste for this barbarous sort of warfare, I am not sure that it will not harm very much the reputation of black troops and of those connected with them. For myself, I have gone through the war so far without dishonor, and I do not like to degenerate into a plunderer and robber—and the same applies to every officer in my regiment. . . .

Author Unknown
On the Siege of Vicksburg

The diary of an unidentified Southern woman living in Vicksburg, Mississippi, describes a city under siege in 1863.

May 17.—Hardly was our scanty breakfast over this morning when a hurried ring drew us both to the door. Mr. J., one of H.'s assistants, stood there in high excitement. "Well, Mr. L., they are upon us: the Yankees will be here by this evening."

"What do you mean?"

"That Pemberton has been whipped at Baker's Creek and Big Black, and his army are running back here as fast as they can come, and the Yanks after them, in such numbers nothing can stop them.". . .

What struck us both was the absence of that concern to be expected, and a sort of relief or suppressed pleasure. After twelve some worn-out-looking men sat down under the window.

"What is the news?" I inquired.

"Ritreat, ritreat!" they said, in broken English—they were Louisiana Acadians.

About three o'clock the rush began. I shall never forget that woeful sight of a beaten, demoralized army that came rushing back,—humanity in the last throes of endurance. Wan, hollow-eyed, ragged, foot-sore, bloody, the men limped along unarmed, but followed by siege-guns, ambulances, gun-carriages, and wagons in aimless confusion. At twilight two or three bands on the court-house hill and other points began playing "Dixie," "Bonnie Blue Flag," and so on, and drums began to beat all about; I suppose they were rallying the scattered army.

May 28.—Since that day the regular siege has continued. We are utterly cut off from the world, surrounded by a circle of fire. Would it be wise like the scorpion to sting ourselves to death? The fiery shower of shells goes on day and night. H.'s occupation, of course, is gone; his office closed. Every man has to carry a pass in his pocket. People do nothing but eat what they can get, sleep when they can, and dodge the shells. There are three intervals when the shelling stops, either for the guns to cool or for the gunners' meals, I suppose,—about eight in the morning, the same in the evening, and at noon. In that time we have both to prepare and eat ours. Clothing cannot be washed or anything else done. On the 19th and 22d, when the assaults were made on the lines, I watched the soldiers cooking on the green opposite. The half-spent balls coming all the way from those lines were flying so thick that they were obliged to dodge at every turn. At all the caves I could see from my high perch, people were sitting, eating their poor suppers at the cave doors, ready to plunge in again. As the first shell again flew they dived, and not a human being was visible. The sharp crackle of the musketry-firing was a strong contrast to the scream of the bombs. I think all the dogs and cats must be killed or starved: we don't see any more pitiful animals prowling around. . . .

I am so tired of corn-bread, which I never liked, that I eat it with tears in my eyes. We are lucky to get a quart of milk daily from a family near who have a cow they hourly expect to be killed. I send five dollars to market each morning, and it buys a small piece of mule-meat. Rice and milk is my main food; I can't eat the mule-meat. We boil the rice and eat it cold with milk for supper. Martha runs the gauntlet to buy the meat and milk once a day in a perfect terror. The shells seem to have many different names: I hear the soldiers say, "That's a mortar-shell. There goes a Parrott. That's a rifle-shell." They are all equally terrible. A pair of chimney-swallows have built in the parlor chimney. The concussion of the house often sends down parts of their nest, which they patiently pick up and reascend with. . . .

July 4.—It is evening. All is still. Silence and night are once more united. I can sit at the table in the parlor and write. Two candles are lighted. I would like a dozen. We have had wheat supper and wheat bread once more. H. is leaning back in the rocking-chair; he says:

"G., it seems to me I can hear the silence, and feel it, too. It wraps me like a soft garment; how else can I express this peace?"

THEODORE R. DAVIS.
Effects of Shellfire,
Vicksburg. 1886.
Pen. 6⅞ x 8¾".
Century Collection,
New York.

But I must write the history of the last twenty-four hours. About five yesterday afternoon, Mr. J., H.'s assistant, who, having no wife to keep him in, dodges about at every change and brings us the news, came to H. and said:

"Mr. L., you must both come to our cave to-night. I hear that to-night the shelling is to surpass everything yet. An assault will be made in front and rear. You know we have a double cave; there is room for you in mine, and mother and sister will make a place for Mrs. L. Come right up; the ball will open about seven."

We got ready, shut up the house, told Martha to go to the church again if she preferred it to the cellar, and walked up to Mr. J.'s. When supper was eaten, all secure, and ladies in their cave night toilet, it was just six, and we crossed the street to the cave opposite. As I crossed a mighty shell flew screaming right over my head. It was the last thrown into Vicksburg. We lay on our pallets waiting for the expected roar, but no sound came except the chatter from neighboring caves, and at last we dropped asleep. I woke at dawn stiff. A draft from the funnel-shaped opening had been blowing on me all night. Every one was expressing surprise at the quiet. We started for home and met the editor of the "Daily Citizen." H. said:

"This is strangely quiet, Mr. L."

"Ah, sir," shaking his head gloomily, "I'm afraid the last shell has been thrown into Vicksburg."

"Why do you fear so?"

"It is surrender. At six last evening a man went down to the river and blew a truce signal; the shelling stopped at once."

George Templeton Strong
On the Draft Riots

In his diary, a New Yorker records the rioting in protest against military conscription in New York City in July 1863.

July 13, MONDAY. A notable day. Stopped at the Sanitary Commission office on my way downtown to endorse a lot of checks that had accumulated during my absence, and heard there of rioting in the upper part of the city. As Charley is at Newport and Bidwell in Berkshire County, I went to Wall Street nevertheless; but the rumors grew more and more unpleasant, so I left it at once and took a Third Avenue car for uptown. At the Park were groups and small crowds in more or less excitement (which found relief afterwards, I hear, in hunting down and maltreating sundry unoffending niggers), but there was nothing to indicate serious trouble. The crowded car went slowly on its way, with its perspiring passengers, for the weather was still of this deadly muggy sort with a muddy sky and lifeless air. At Thirteenth Street the track was blocked by a long line of stationary cars that stretched indefinitely up the Avenue, and I took to the sidewalk. Above Twentieth Street all shops were closed, and many people standing and staring or strolling uptown, not riotously disposed but eager and curious. Here and there a rough could be heard damning the draft. No policemen to be seen anywhere. Reached the seat of war at last, Forty-sixth Street and Third Avenue. Three houses on the Avenue and two or three on the street were burned down: engines playing on the ruins—more energetically, I'm told, than they did when their efforts would have been useful.

The crowd seemed just what one commonly sees at any fire, but its nucleus of riot was concealed by an outside layer of ordinary peaceable lookers-on. Was told they had beat off a squad of police and another of "regulars" (probably the Twelfth Militia). At last, it opened and out streamed a posse of perhaps five hundred, certainly less than one thousand, of the lowest Irish day laborers. The rabble was perfectly homogeneous. Every brute in the drove was pure Celtic—hod-carrier or loafer. They were unarmed. A few carried pieces of fence-paling and the like. They turned off west into Forty-fifth Street and gradually collected in front of two three-story dwelling houses on Lexington Avenue, just below that street, that stand alone together on a nearly vacant block. Nobody could tell why these houses were singled out. Some said a drafting officer lived in one of them, others that a damaged policeman had taken refuge there. The mob was in no hurry; they had no need to be; there was no one to molest them or make them afraid. The beastly ruffians were masters of the situation and of the city. After a while sporadic paving-stones began to fly at the windows, ladies and children emerged from the rear and had a rather hard scramble over a high board fence, and then scudded off across the open, Heaven knows whither. Then men and small boys appeared at rear windows and began smashing the sashes and the blinds and shied out light articles, such as books and crockery, and dropped chairs and mirrors into the back yard; the rear fence was demolished and loafers were seen marching off with portable articles of furniture. And at last a little smoke began to float out of the windows and I came away. I could endure the disgraceful, sickening sight no longer, and what could I *do*?

The fury of the low Irish women in that region was noteworthy. Stalwart young vixens and withered old hags were swarming everywhere, all cursing the "bloody draft" and egging on their men to mischief.

Omnibussed down to No. 823, where is news that the Colored Half Orphan Asylum on Fifth Avenue, just above the reservoir, is burned. "*Tribune* office to be burned to-night." Railroad rails torn up, telegraph wires cut, and so on. If a quarter one hears be true, this is an organized insurrection in the interest of the rebellion and Jefferson Davis rules New York today.

Attended to business. Then with Wolcott Gibbs to dinner at Maison Dorée. During our symposium, there was an alarm of a coming mob, and we went to the window to see. The "mob" was moving down Fourteenth Street and consisted of just thirty-four lousy, blackguardly Irishmen with a tail of small boys. Whither they went, I cannot say, nor can I guess what mischief the handful of *canaille* chose to do. A dozen policemen would have been more than a match for the whole crew, but there were no policemen in sight.

Walked uptown with Wolcott Gibbs. Large fire on Broadway and Twenty-eighth Street. Signs of another to the east, said to be on Second Avenue. Stopped awhile at Gibbs's in Twenty-ninth Street, where was madame, frightened nearly to death, and then to St. Nicholas Hotel to see the mayor and General Wool. We found a lot of people with them. There were John Jay and George W. Blunt and Colonel Howe and John Austin Stevens, Jr., all urging strong measures. But the substantial and weighty and influential men were not represented; out of town, I suppose. Their absence emboldened Gibbs and myself to make pressure for instant action, but it was vain. We begged that martial law might be declared. Opdyke said that was Wool's business, and Wool said it was Opdyke's, and neither would act. "Then, Mr. Mayor, issue a proclamation calling on all loyal and law-abiding citizens to enroll themselves as a volunteer force for defense of life and property." "Why," quoth Opdyke, "that is *civil war* at once." Long talk with Colonel Cram, Wool's chief of staff, who professes to believe that everything is as it should be and sufficient force on the ground to prevent further mischief. Don't believe it. Neither Opdyke nor General Wool is nearly equal to this crisis. Came off disgusted. Went to Union League Club awhile. No comfort there. Much talk, but no one ready to do anything whatever, not even to telegraph to Washington.

We telegraphed, two or three of us, from General Wool's rooms, to the President, begging that troops be sent on and stringent measures taken. The great misfortune is that nearly all our militia regiments have been despatched to Pennsylvania. All the military force I have seen or heard of today were in Fifth Avenue at about seven P.M. There were two or three feeble companies of infantry, a couple of howitzers, and a squadron or two of unhappy-looking "dragoons."

These wretched rioters have been plundering freely, I hear. Their outbreak will either destroy the city or damage the Copperhead cause fatally. Could we but catch the scoundrels who have stirred them up, what a blessing it would be! God knows what tonight or tomorrow may bring forth. We may be thankful that it is now (quarter past twelve) raining briskly. Mobs have no taste for the effusion of cold water. I'm thankful, moreover, that Ellie and the children are out of town. I sent Johnny off to Cornwall this afternoon in charge of John the waiter.

Gurdon Grovenor

On the Sack of Lawrence, Kansas

William Quantrill and his Confederate guerrilla band descend on Lawrence, Kansas, in August 1863, as reported in Quantrill and the Border Wars *by one of the few survivors.*

Just then a party of a half dozen of the raiders came riding towards the house from the north, and seeing my enemy, hallooed to him "Don't shoot that man." They rode up to the gate and told me to come there; I did so and my would be murderer came up to me and placed the muzzle of his revolver in my ear. It was not a pleasant place to be in, but the leader of the new crowd told him not to shoot, but to let me alone until he could inquire about me, so he asked me if I had ever been down in Missouri stealing niggers or horses; I told him "No that I never had been in Missouri, except to cross the state going and coming from the east." This seemed to be satisfactory so he told my old enemy to let me alone and not to kill me. This seemed to make him very angry, and he cursed me terribly, but I ventured to put my hand up and push away his revolver. The leader

SHERMAN ENDERTON. *Quantrill's Raid on Lawrence, August 21, 1863.* 1863. Pencil. 9½ x 16". Kansas State Historical Society, Topeka.

of the party then told me if I did not expect to get killed, I must get out of sight, that they were all getting drunk, and would kill everybody they saw; I told him that that was what I had wanted to do all the morning, but I could not; "Well," he says, "you must hide or get killed." And they all rode away.

After they had gone I told my wife that I would go into the cellar, and stay until the fire reached me, and if any more of the raiders inquired for me to tell them that I had been taken a prisoner and carried off. Some years ago I read an article in the Sunday School Times, saying that a lie under any circumstances was a sin. I thought then that I should like to see that writer try my experiences at the time of the raid and see what he would think then; I did not feel my lie a sin then and never have since.

The cellar of my house was under the ell and the fire was in the front and in the upper story. There was an outside bulk-head door, where I knew I could get out after the fire had reached the floor above me. I had not been in the cellar long before my wife came and said they had just killed my neighbor across the street.

Soon after the notorious Bill Anderson, passing by the house, saw my wife standing in the yard, stopped and commenced talking with her; told her how many men he had killed that morning, and inquiring where her husband was; she told him that he had been taken prisoner and carried away—was it my wife's duty to tell him the truth, tell him where I was and let him come and shoot me as he would a dog, which he would have done? Awhile after my wife came and said she thought the raiders had all gone, and so I came out of my prison just as the fire was eating through the floor over my head, thankful that I had passed through that dreadful ordeal and was safe.

Such was my experience during those four or five terrible hours. Our home and its contents was in ashes, but so thankful were we that my life was spared that we thought but little of our pecuniary loss. After the raiders had left and the people could get out on the street, a most desolate and sickening sight met their view. The whole business part of the town, except two stores, was in ashes. The bodies of dead men, some of them partly burned away, were laying in all directions. A large number of dwellings were burned to the ground, and the moaning of the grief stricken people was heard from all sides. Gen. Lane, who was in the city at the time, told me that he had been over the battleground of Gettysburg a few days before, but the sight was not so sickening as the one which the burned and sacked city of Lawrence presented. The exact number killed was never known, but it was about 150, many of them of the best citizens.

Bruce Catton

FROM GLORY ROAD

On Commemorating the Dead at Gettysburg

The historian of the Army of the Potomac describes the scene at Gettysburg and how Mr. Lincoln came to be there on November 19, 1863.

———————

An army medical officer was telling no more than the plain truth when he wrote that the ten days immediately after the battle were "the occasion of the greatest amount of human suffering known to this nation since its birth." This country market town of two thousand inhabitants had been presented with some twenty-two thousand wounded men, and the place was swamped with them. They lay on the fields and in ditches, in the woods under trees, in barns and haystacks and homes and churches for miles around. The very fact that the battle had been a victory made the men's lot worse, for instead of remaining on the field where it could care for them the army had marched south in expectation of a new battle and had been able to leave behind it only a fraction of the required number of doctors and hospital attendants.

So appalling was the number of men awaiting attention that the overworked doctors had begun with a grim job of sorting out, separating the men who were bound to die from those whose lives might be saved. In one wood there was a long, pathetic row of semiconscious men who lay on the ground, moaning and twitching fitfully, completely unattended—men who had been shot through the head and whose wounds, upon hasty inspection, had been pronounced mortal and who had simply been put aside to die as quickly as they might. Not far away there was a long table where for an entire week doctors worked from dawn to twilight cutting off arms and legs, with an army wagon standing by to carry off the wreckage and hurry back for a new load. A young woman who came to Gettysburg to help nurse the wounded entered a church which had been hastily converted into a hospital and found that planks had been laid across the tops of the pews so that the entire auditorium was one vast hard bed, jammed with wounded men lying elbow to elbow: "I seemed to stand breast-high in a sea of anguish." Permeating everything in and near the town was the foul, overpowering stench of the unburied dead—an atmosphere which, as this woman said, "robbed the battlefield of its glory, the survivors of their victory, and the wounded of what little chance of life was left to them."

Little by little order was restored, the army working hand in hand with the Sanitary Commission and the Christian Commission. The one railroad leading into Gettysburg had been broken, but Herman Haupt was on the job almost before the battle ended, and as always he made things happen. He found the railroad totally inadequate, even after its breaks had been made good—a country railroad without experienced officers, with no more sidings, water tanks, turntables, or fuel than were needed for its normal traffic of three or four trains a day. It was necessary now to operate thirty trains a day, and he had locomotives and cars sent up from Alexandria. He improvised water tanks, brought in loads of fuel, got repair crews on the job with prefabricated bridges and culverts, and before long he had the railway in shape to move fifteen hundred tons of freight each way every day. The army medical service was telegraphing frantically to Baltimore for immediate shipments of alcohol, creosote, nitric acid, permanganate of potassium, tin cups, buckets, stretchers, bed sacks, and other equipment, and the Sanitary Commission made up a special train of food, tents, clothing, stoves, and bandages which reached the town three days after the battle.

All across the northeast, in the pulpits of hundreds of churches, ministers read appeals for help. Money was needed, and food, and medicines, and the little delicacies sick men need—and, above all, "all females qualified for usefulness in this emergency." Nurses were brought in; regular-army nurses recruited by Miss Dorothea Dix, who sternly refused to accept women who were either young or pretty, considering such persons quite unsuited for work in army hospitals, and women enlisted by the Sanitary Commission, which had agents at railroad stations in the big Eastern cities to interview applicants and organize them into working units. Pennsylvania militia regiments were brought in to guard the place, and as the hospital tents were set up in the groves near the town these soldiers marched all visitors away at four every afternoon so that the nurses might not be exposed to nameless perils. The nurses found themselves far too busy to be in any danger, however. Five days after the battle ambulances were still going about the fields collecting hundreds of men whose wounds had not yet been dressed and who had had nothing to eat except such hardtack as they happened to have in their haversacks.

As these women worked, an ancient tradition quietly died. It had always been supposed that army nursing was strictly a job either for enlisted men or for superannuated trollops who were beyond contamination. But here they were, women precisely like the wives and sisters and mothers the soldiers had left behind, up to their elbows in it and taking no harm whatever. One of them quietly wrote: "I have been for weeks the only lady in a camp of seven hundred men, and have never been treated with more deference, respect, and kindness." Uniformly, these women testified that the men they cared for were nothing less than magnificent, and in a letter to her sister a little New Jersey Quaker wrote: "More Christian fortitude was never witnessed than they exhibit, always say— 'Help my neighbor first, he is worse.'" After some weeks, when the emergency had passed and one group of women prepared to leave, two army bands turned out to escort them to the railroad station.

As rapidly as the men became well enough to be moved they were sent off to permanent hospitals in Baltimore, Washington, York, and Harrisburg, and before long six hospital trains were leaving town every day. Until the army got hold of this business the trips were pretty grim. A medical inspector who looked into matters protested with fury that "the railroad companies, who got the only profit of the battle, and who had the greatest opportunities of ameliorating the sufferings of the wounded, alone stood aloof and rendered no aid." He specified: trains were fearfully unclean, there were no attendants for the wounded, there was no water, there was not even straw for the men to lie upon—"absolutely nothing but the bare cars, filthy from the business of transporting cattle and freight." He cracked down hard, and a medical officer was detailed to accompany each train, water coolers and bedpans and medicines and bandages were provided, and at the first junction point agents of the Christian Commission were alerted to meet the trains and provide any help that might be needed. In the end, things were fairly well organized, and in three weeks sixteen thousand men were sent away. The Gettysburg hospitals still contained four thousand more who were too sick to be moved, but the worst of it was over.

So the wounded were taken care of. There were still the dead. Many bodies had never been buried—the gullies and rocky crannies around Devil's Den contained some horrible relics—and the rains had washed the earth away from bodies imperfectly covered, and there were many unmarked graves. Governor Andrew Curtin visited the place and

*Lincoln at Gettysburg.
November 19, 1863.*
Photograph.
National Archives,
Washington, D.C.
Brady Collection.

appointed a local businessman as his agent to see to it that the state of Pennsylvania did what was necessary, and toward the end of July, at Curtin's request, this agent got in touch with the governors of all of the Northern states whose men had fought at Gettysburg and proposed that they get together to provide a proper cemetery. There were meetings and an exchange of letters, and by mid-August money had been raised and Pennsylvania had bought seventeen acres of land on Cemetery Hill, and the work of establishing a cemetery was under way.

It would be a project for the states, naturally. They had thought of it first, they were putting up the money, their governors were making the arrangements, and anyway, the national government was busy with other matters. As the lifeless bodies were moved up to Cemetery Hill it was agreed that they should be grouped there by states—one plot for New Yorkers, another for Pennsylvanians, and so on down the list—and if from these honored dead each governor could take increased prestige, with visible proof that his state had done its full share, that would be so much the better, because possibly this battle had really been an affair of the separate states from the beginning. As host, Governor Curtin was the man of the hour, and he invited the famous orator, Edward Everett, to do the talking when the cemetery was formally dedicated. He also asked General Meade to attend if he could.

Everett could come, but he would need more time. A speech commemorating the Gettysburg dead could not be put together overnight, and Everett had certain engagements. The date originally selected was October 23, and it would not be possible for him to complete his preparations by that time: could not there be a postponement? Governor Curtin and the others agreed that there could, and the ceremonies were put off until November 19. General Meade sent his regrets, pointing out that military affairs in the state of Virginia would be taking all of his time.

Settled, then, for the nineteenth of November, and the battlefield could be fairly well policed up by that time. There were still a few wounded men around, but by late November it should be possible to get all of them shipped off, and the air was becoming fit to breathe again. The summer wore away, the burial squads were busy, the hilltop was being nicely landscaped, and down below the Potomac the army was maneuvering back and forth, getting into small fights occasionally, losing a few men here and killing a few rebels there, sparring the time away until a new campaign could be begun. The drafted men were coming in to fill the ranks—coming in under guard, with a roll call every two hours, because most of them had very little intention of remaining with the army if they could help it—and the veterans looked forward to their arrival with a certain unholy pleasure. Their attitude was pretty well expressed by a diarist in the 15th Massachusetts, which had been consolidated to four companies because of heavy battle losses, who wrote: "I wish the conscripts were out here now. I want to see them. I want to put some of them through the drill. I want to see them live on salt pork and hard bread. I want to see them carry their knapsacks." Admittedly, the draftees were not very good material but there were men in the army who would see that they became soldiers once they got to camp.

The great day came at last, and there were troops in Gettysburg again, and bands, and special trains bringing distinguished guests, and there was a big parade through the town and up to the hill, with parade marshals in their sashes, horses shying and curvetting affectedly, much pomp and circumstance, and a famous orator with an hour-long speech in his hand. There was also Abraham Lincoln, who had been invited more or less as an afterthought—the invitation went to him on November 2, suggesting that he might honor the occasion by his presence—and Mr. Lincoln was to say a few words after Mr. Everett had made the speech. After the usual fuss and confusion the procession climbed the hill and the honored guests got up on the flag-draped speakers' stand, and eventually a certain degree of quiet was restored. A chaplain offered a prayer, and a glee club sang an ode composed especially for the occasion, and at last the orator got up to make his speech.

An oration was an oration in those days, and it had to have a certain style to it—

COLORPLATE 97

FRANK VIZETELLY. *Confederate Cotton Burners Surprised by Federal Patrol.* No date. Pencil, watercolor, crayon, and Chinese white on light green paper. 9 × 11″. Harvard College Library, Cambridge. *Southerners burning cotton to prevent it from falling into Union hands.*

COLORPLATE 98

Artist Unknown. *Christmas Eve, 1862.* West Point Museum, United States Military
Academy, West Point, New York. *The artist based his work on an engraving by Thomas Nast
in* Harper's Weekly.

COLORPLATE 99

David Gilmour Blythe. *Lincoln Crushing the Dragon of Rebellion*. 1862. Oil on canvas. 18 × 22″. Museum of Fine Arts, Boston. M. and M. Karolik Collection. *In Blythe's allegory the president is fettered by his New York Democratic opponents.*

COLORPLATE 100

EDMUND HAWTHORNE. *Interior of George Hayward's Porter House, New York.* ca. 1863.
Oil on canvas. 33⅓ × 46″. New-York Historical Society, New York.

COLORPLATE 101

LILY MARTIN SPENCER. *The War Spirit at Home - Celebrating the Victory at Vicksburg.* 1866.
Oil on canvas. 30 × 32¾″. Newark Museum. Purchase 1944 Wallace M. Scudder Bequest Fund.

COLORPLATE 102

J. JOFFRAY. *Farragut's Fleet Passing Fort Jackson and Fort St. Philip, Louisiana, April 24, 1862.* ca. 1862. Oil on canvas. 32½ × 39½″. Chicago Historical Society, Chicago. Bequest of Mrs. Lewis L. Coburn. *Farragut's battle fleet passed these forts on the lower Mississippi on the night of April 24, 1862, and took New Orleans the next day.*

COLORPLATE 103 *(opposite, above)*

CONRAD WISE CHAPMAN. *Fort Sumter, Charleston, Dec. 8th, 1863.* 1864. Oil on board. 11½ × 15½″. Museum of the Confederacy, Richmond. Photo by Katherine Wetzel.

COLORPLATE 104 *(opposite, below)*

CONRAD WISE CHAPMAN. *Submarine Torpedo Boat H. L. Hunley, Charleston, Dec. 6, 1863.* 1864. Oil on board. 11½ × 15½″. Museum of the Confederacy, Richmond. Photo by Katherine Wetzel.

COLORPLATE 105

MAURITZ F. H. DEHAAS. *The Battle of New Orleans-Farragut's Fleet Passing the Forts Below New Orleans*. ca. 1867. Oil on canvas. 59 × 105¾″. Historic New Orleans Collection, New Orleans. Photo copyright © 1985 The Historic New Orleans Collection.

classical allusions, a leisurely approach to the subject matter, a carefully phrased recital of the background and history of the occasion, the whole working up to a peroration which would sum everything up in memorable sentences. Mr. Everett was a master of this art form and had been hard at work for many weeks, and he stood up now in the center of the field where five thousand men had died and began his polished cadenced sentences. He recalled how the ancient Greeks commemorated their heroic dead in the days of Pericles. . . .

There were many thousands of people at this ceremony, and among them were certain wounded veterans who had come back to see all of this, and a knot of these wandered away from the crowd around the speakers' stand and strolled down along Cemetery Ridge, pausing when they reached a little clump of trees, and there they looked off toward the west and talked quietly about what they had seen and done there.

In front of them was the wide gentle valley of the shadow of death, brimming now with soft autumn sunlight, and behind them the flags waved lazily about the speakers' stand and the voice droned on, building up toward a literary climax. The valley was a mile wide, and there was the rolling ground where the rebel guns had been ranked, and on the crest of this ridge was the space where a girlish artillery lieutenant had had a sergeant hold him up while he called for the last round of canister, the ground where file closers had gripped hands and dug in their heels to hold a wavering line together, the place where the noise of men desperately fighting had been heard as a great mournful roar; and the voice went on, and the governors looked dignified, and the veterans by the trees looked about them and saw again the fury and the smoke and the killing.

This was the valley of dry bones, waiting for the word, which might or might not come in rhythmic prose that began by describing the customs of ancient Athens. The bones had lain there in the sun and the rain, and now they were carefully arranged state by state under the new sod. They were the bones of men who had exulted in their youth, and some of them had been unstained heroes while others had been scamps who pillaged and robbed and ran away when they could, and they had died here, and that was the end of them. They had come here because of angry words and hot passions in which they had not shared. They had come, too, because the drums had rolled and the bands had blared the swinging deceitful tunes that piped men off to battle . . . three cheers for the red white and blue, here's a long look back at the girl I left behind me, John Brown's body lies a-moldering in the grave but we go marching on, and Yankee Doodle on his spotted pony rides off into the eternal smoky mist of war.

Back of these men were innumerable long dusty roads reaching to the main streets of a thousand youthful towns and villages where there had been bright flags overhead and people on the board sidewalks cheering and crying and waving a last good-by. It had seemed once that there was some compelling reason to bring these men here — something so broad that it would encompass all of the terrible contradictory manifestations of the country's pain and bewilderment, the riots and the lynchings, the hysterical conspiracies with their oaths written in blood, the hard hand that had been laid upon the countryside, the scramble for riches and the scheming for high place, and the burdens carried by quiet folk who wanted only to live at peace by the faith they used to have.

Perhaps there was a meaning to all of it somewhere. Perhaps everything that the nation was and meant to be had come to a focus here, beyond the graves and the remembered echoes of the guns and the wreckage of lives that were gone forever. Perhaps the whole of it somehow was greater than the sum of its tragic parts, and perhaps here on this wind-swept hill the thing could be said at last, so that the dry bones of the country's dreams could take on flesh.

The orator finished, and after the applause had died away the tall man in the black frock coat got to his feet, with two little sheets of paper in his hand, and he looked out over the valley and began to speak.

Frank Wilkeson

On Filling the Ranks

A Union enlistee in 1863 finds himself in bad company, as recorded in Recollections of a Private Soldier in the Army of the Potomac.

———————

The war fever seized me in 1863. All the summer and fall I had fretted and burned to be off. That winter, and before I was sixteen years old, I ran away from my father's high-lying Hudson River valley farm. I went to Albany and enlisted in the Eleventh New York Battery, then at the front in Virginia, and was promptly sent out to the penitentiary building. There, to my utter astonishment, I found eight hundred or one thousand ruffians, closely guarded by heavy lines of sentinels, who paced to and fro, day and night, rifle in hand, to keep them from running away. When I entered the barracks these recruits gathered around me and asked, "How much bounty did you get?" "How many times have you jumped the bounty?" I answered that I had not bargained for any bounty, that I had never jumped a bounty, and that I had enlisted to go to the front and fight. I was instantly assailed with abuse. . . .

Cuffed, prodded with bayonets, and heartily cursed, we fell into line in front of the barracks. An officer stepped in front of us and said in a loud voice that any man who attempted to escape would be shot. A double line of guards quickly took their proper positions around us. We were faced to the right and marched through a room, where the men were paid their bounties. Some men received $500, others less; but I heard of no man who received less than $400. I got nothing. As the men passed through the room they were formed into column by fours. When all the recruits had been paid, and the column formed, we started to march into Albany, guarded by a double line of sentinels. Long before we arrived at State Street three recruits attempted to escape. They dropped their knapsacks and fled wildly. Crack! crack! crack! a dozen rifles rang out, and what had been three men swiftly running were three bloody corpses. The dead patriots lay by the roadside as we marched by. We marched down State Street, turned to the right at Broadway, and marched down that street to the steamboat landing. Previous to my enlistment I had imagined that the population of Albany would line the sidewalks to see the defenders of the nation march proudly by, bound for the front, and that we would be cheered, and would unbend sufficiently to accept floral offerings from beautiful maidens. How was it? No exultant cheers arose from the column. The people who saw us did not cheer. The faces of the recruits plainly expressed the profound disgust they felt at the disastrous outcome of what had promised to be a remunerative financial enterprise. Small boys derided us. Mud balls were thrown at us. One small lad, who was greatly excited by the unwonted spectacle, rushed to a street corner, and after placing his hands to his mouth, yelled to a distant and loved comrade: "Hi, Johnnie, come see de bounty-jumpers!" He was promptly joined by an exasperating, red-headed, sharp-tongued little wretch, whom I desired to destroy long before we arrived at the steamboat landing. Men and women openly laughed at us. Fingers, indicative of derision, were pointed at us. Yes, a large portion of the populace of Albany gathered together to see us; but they were mostly young males, called guttersnipes. They jeered us, and were exceedingly loth to leave us. It was as though the congress of American wonders were parading in the streets preparatory to aërial flights under tented canvas.

Once on the steamboat, we were herded on the lower deck, where freight is usually carried, like cattle. . . .

MULLIGAN'S BRIGADE!

LAST CHANCE TO AVOID THE DRAFT!

$402 BOUNTY!

TO VETERANS!

$302 to all other VOLUNTEERS!

All Able-bodied Men, between the ages of 18 and 45 Years, who have heretofore served not less than nine months, who shall re-enlist for **Regiments in the field, will be deemed Veterans, and will receive one month's pay in advance, and a bounty and premium of $402.** To all other recruits, one month's pay in advance, **and a bounty and premium of $302 will be paid.**
All who wish to join Mulligan's Irish Brigade, now in the field, and to receive the munificent bounties offered by the Government, can have the opportunity by calling at the headquarters of

CAPT. J. J. FITZGERALD

Of the Irish Brigade, 23d Regiment Illinois Volunteers, Recruiting Officer. Chicago, Illinois.

Each Recruit, Veteran or otherwise, will receive

Seventy-five Dollars Before Leaving General Rendezvous,

and the remainder of the bounty in regular instalments till all is paid. **The pay, bounty and premium for three years will average $24 per month, for Veterans; and $21.30 per month for all others.**

If the Government shall not require these troops for the full period of Three Years, and they shall be mustered honor out of the service before the expiration of their term of enlistment, they shall receive, **UPON BEING MUSTERED O the whole amount of BOUNTY remaining unpaid, the same as if the full term been served.**

J. J. FITZGERALD.

Chicago, December, 1863.

Recruiting Officer, corner North Clark & Kenzie Stree

*"Mulligan's Brigade,"
Recruiting Poster.* 1863.
Chicago Historical Society,
Chicago.

George Templeton Strong

On Hiring a Substitute

In 1864 a New Yorker recorded in his diary how he hired a substitute to do his fighting by proxy.

August 29. To office of Provost Marshal of my district this morning (Captain Manierre), where, after waiting an hour, I purveyed myself a substitute, a big "Dutch" boy of twenty or thereabouts, for the moderate consideration of $1,100. Thus do we approach the alms-house at an accelerating rate of speed. My *alter ego* could make a good soldier if he tried. Gave him my address, and told him to write to me if he found himself in the hospital or in trouble, and that I would try to do what I properly could to help him. I got myself exempted at this high price because I felt all day as if some attack of illness were at hand, and as if it might be unsafe to leave my liability to draft unsettled. . . .

Carl Schurz

Letter on Mr. Lincoln and the Conduct of the War October 12, 1864

A politically astute and prophetic Union general, in a letter to a friend, takes a reflective look at the president.

———————————

. . . Now I must give you a little lecture. I do not share your opinion as to what we should not do in the present crisis. You would surely not have judged so if you had shared in the great struggles which are now over. You may have been surprised when I defend[ed] the present Administration in public. But I believe that a few words regarding my way of looking at matters will make things clear to you. Every crisis in human affairs has one principal question to which all minor questions must be subordinated. We are engaged in a war in which the existence of the Nation, indeed, in which everything is involved. A party has risen in this country that threatens to overthrow all the results of the war, and that at a moment at which the final outcome is hardly doubtful, if the policy introduced is firmly adhered to. There can be no doubt that the Government has made great mistakes; persons who are directing the fate of the country are certainly far from ideal statesmen, though not nearly as insignificant as their critics would represent them to be. But that is of minor importance. The most vital thing is that the policy of the party moves in the right direction, that is to say, that the slaveholder be vanquished and slavery abolished. Whether this policy moves in that direction skilfully or awkwardly, slowly or rapidly, is a matter of little consequence in comparison with the question whether a policy should be adopted that would move in another, a wrong and disastrous direction. Accordingly, it was easy for me to choose. I did not hesitate one moment. . . . The signs of the times are now very favorable. The reelection of the President is almost certain unless some great military misfortune overwhelms us and that is not to be expected. The results of the election will determine the results of the war, and the worst will then be over. . . .

I wish to enlighten you on two other points. You are underrating the President. I grant that he lacks higher education and his manners are not in accord with European conceptions of the dignity of a chief magistrate. He is a well-developed child of nature and is not skilled in polite phrases and poses. But he is a man of profound feeling, correct and firm principles and incorruptible honesty. His motives are unquestionable, and he possesses to a remarkable degree the characteristic God-given trait of this people, sound common-sense. Should you read his official documents and his political letters, you would find this verified to a surprising extent. I know him from personal observation as well as anyone, and better than the majority. I am familiar with his motives. I have seen him heroically wage many a terrible struggle and work his way through many a desperate situation with strength born of loyalty to conviction. I have criticised him often and severely, and later I found that he was right. I also know his failings; they are those of a good man. That he has committed great errors in the endless embarrassments of his position, cannot be denied, but it can be explained. Possibly other persons, if in his position, would not have committed the same errors, but they would have committed others. Moreover, Lincoln's personality has a special importance in this crisis. Free from the aspirations of genius, he will never be dangerous to a liberal government. He personifies the people, and that is the secret of his popularity. His Administration is the most representative that the history of the world has ever seen. I will make a prophecy that may now sound peculiar. In fifty years, perhaps much sooner, Lincoln's name will be inscribed close to Washington's on this American Republic's roll of honor. And there it will remain for some time. The children of those who persecute him now, will bless him. . . .

John Hay

On the Election Returns, November 8, 1864

From the diary of Lincoln's secretary, we learn how the president received the tidings that he had defeated General McClellan in the 1864 election.

Nov. 8. The house has been still and almost deserted today. Everybody in Washington, not at home voting, seems ashamed of it and stays away from the President.

I was talking with him to-day. He said, "It is a little singular that I, who am not a vindictive man, should have always been before the people for election in canvasses marked for their bitterness: always but once; when I came to Congress it was a quiet time. But always besides that the contests in which I have been prominent have been marked with great rancor.". . .

During the afternoon few despatches were received.

At night, at 7 o'clock we started over to the War Department to spend the evening. Just as we started we received the first gun from Indianapolis, showing a majority of 8,000 there, a gain of 1,500 over Morton's vote. The vote itself seemed an enormous one for a town of that size and can only be accounted for by considering the great influx since the war of voting men from the country into the State centres where a great deal of Army business is done. There was less significance in this vote on account of the October victory which had disheartened the enemy and destroyed their incentive to work.

The night was rainy, steamy and dark. We splashed through the grounds to the side door of the War Department where a soaked and smoking sentinel was standing in his own vapor with his huddled-up frame covered with a rubber cloak. Inside a half-dozen idle orderlies, up-stairs the clerks of the telegraph. As the President entered they handed him a despatch from Forney claiming ten thousand Union majority in Philadelphia. "Forney is a little excitable." Another comes from Felton, Baltimore, giving us "15,000 in the city, 5,000 in the state. All Hail, Free Maryland." That is superb. A message from Rice to Fox, followed instantly by one from Sumner to Lincoln, claiming Boston by 5,000, and Rice's & Hooper's elections by majorities of 4,000 apiece. A magnificent advance on the chilly dozens of 1862.

WILLIAM WAUD.
*Pennsylvania Soldiers
Voting.* 1864. Pencil,
wash, and chinese
white on paper.
8⅝ x 13⅞". Library
of Congress,
Washington, D.C.

Eckert came in shaking the rain from his cloak, with trousers very disreputably muddy. We sternly demanded an explanation. He had slipped, he said, & tumbled prone, crossing the street. He had done it watching a fellow-being ahead and chuckling at his uncertain footing. Which reminded the Tycoon, of course. The President said, "For such an awkward fellow, I am pretty sure-footed. It used to take a pretty dextrous man to throw me. I remember, the evening of the day in 1858, that decided the contest for the Senate between Mr. Douglas and myself, was something like this, dark, rainy & gloomy. I had been reading the returns, and had ascertained that we had lost the Legislature and started to go home. The path had been work hog-back & was slippery. My foot slipped from under me, knocking the other one out of the way, but I recovered myself & lit square, and I said to myself, 'It's a slip and not a fall.'"

The President sent over the first fruits to Mrs. Lincoln. He said, "She is more anxious than I.". . .

Despatches kept coming in all the evening showing a splendid triumph in Indiana, showing steady, small gains all over Pennsylvania, enough to give a fair majority this time on the home vote. Guesses from New York and Albany which boiled down to about the estimated majority against us in the city, 35,000, and left the result in the State still doubtful.

A despatch from Butler was picked up & sent by Sanford, saying that the City had gone 35,000 McC. & the State 40,000. This looked impossible. The State had been carefully canvassed & such a result was impossible except in view of some monstrous and undreamed of frauds. After a while another came from Sanford correcting former one & giving us the 40,000 in the State.

Sanford's despatches all the evening continued most jubilant: especially when he announced that most startling majority of 80,000 in Massachusetts. . . .

Towards midnight we had supper, provided by Eckert. The President went awkwardly and hospitably to work shovelling out the fried oysters. He was most agreeable and genial all the evening in fact. Fox was abusing the coffee for being so hot—saying quaintly, it kept hot all the way down to the bottom of the cup as a piece of ice staid cold till you finished eating it.

We got later in the evening a scattering despatch from the West, giving us Michigan, one from Fox promising Missouri certainly, but a loss in the first district from that miserable split of Knox & Johnson, one promising Delaware, and one, too good for ready credence, saying Raymond & Dodge & Darling had been elected in New York City.

Capt. Thomas came up with a band about half-past two, and made some music and a small hifalute.

The President answered from the window with rather unusual dignity and effect & we came home. . . .

He [Ward Lamon] took a glass of whiskey and then, refusing my offer of a bed, went out &, rolling himself up in his cloak, lay down at the President's door; passing the night in that attitude of touching and dumb fidelity, with a small arsenal of pistols & bowie knives around him. In the morning he went away leaving my blankets at my door, before I or the President were awake.

SOUTH BESIEGED

Nathaniel Paige

On the Assault on Battery Wagner

A reporter's account for the New York Tribune *of the attack on a fort defending Charleston on July 18, 1863. Leading the assault was the all-black 54th Massachusetts regiment.*

Not in widely extended battle-line, with cavalry and artillery at supporting distances, but in solid regimental column, on the hard ocean beach, for half a mile before reaching the Fort, in plain sight of the enemy, did these three brigades move to their appointed work.

General Strong, who has so frequently since his arrival in this department braved death in its many forms of attack, was assigned to the command of the First brigade. Colonel Putnam of the Seventh New-Hampshire . . . took command of the Second, and General Stevenson the Third, constituting the reserve. The Fifty-fourth Massachusetts, (colored regiment,) Colonel Shaw, was the advanced regiment in the First brigade, and the Second South-Carolina, (Negro,) Colonel Montgomery, was the last regiment of the reserve. . . .

Just as darkness began to close in upon the scene of the afternoon and the evening, General Strong rode to the front and ordered his brigade . . . to advance to the assault. At the instant, the line was seen slowly advancing in the dusk toward the Fort, and before a double-quick had been ordered, a tremendous fire from the barbette guns on Fort

Sumter, from the batteries on Cumming's Point, and from all the guns on Fort Wagner, opened upon it. The guns from Wagner swept the beach, and those from Sumter and Cumming's Point enfiladed it on the left. In the midst of this terrible shower of shot and shell they pushed their way, reached the Fort, portions of the Fifty-fourth Massachusetts, the Sixth Connecticut, and the Forty-eighth New-York dashed through the ditches, gained the parapet, and engaged in a hand-to-hand fight with the enemy, and for nearly half an hour held their ground, and did not fall back until nearly every commissioned officer was shot down. . . .

When the brigade made the assault General Strong gallantly rode at its head. When it fell back, broken, torn, and bleeding, Major Plimpton of the Third New-Hampshire was the highest commissioned officer to command it. General Strong, Colonel Shaw, Colonel Chatfield, Colonel Barton, Colonel Green, Colonel Jackson, all had fallen; and the list I send you will tell how many other brave officers fell with them. . . . It must be remembered, too, that this assault was made in the night—a very dark night—even the light of the stars was obscured by the blackness of a heavy thunder-storm, and the enemy could be distinguished from our own men only by the light of bursting shell and the flash of the howitzer and the musket. The Fifty-fourth Massachusetts, (Negro,) whom copperhead officers would have called cowardly if they had stormed and carried the gates of hell, went boldly into battle, for the second time, commanded by their brave Colonel, but came out of it led by no higher officer than the boy, Lieutenant Higginson.

The First brigade, under the lead of General Strong, failed to take the Fort. It was

FRANK VIZETELLY.
The Appearance of the Ditch the Morning after the Assault on Fort Wagner, July 19, 1863. 1863. Pencil, wash, and chinese white on paper. 9 x 10⅞". Houghton Library, Harvard University, Cambridge.

now the turn of Colonel Putnam, commanding the Second brigade, composed of the Seventh New-Hampshire, the Sixty-second Ohio, Colonel Vorhees, the Sixty-seventh Ohio, Colonel Commager, and the One Hundredth New-York, Colonel Dandy, to make the attempt. But alas! the task was too much for him. Through the same terrible fire he led his men to, over, and into the Fort, and for an hour held one half of it, fighting every moment of that time with the utmost desperation, and, as with the First brigade, it was not until he himself fell killed, and nearly all his officers wounded, and no reënforcements arriving, that his men fell back, and the rebel shout and cheer of victory was heard above the roar of Sumter and the guns from Cumming's Point. . . .

Without a doubt, many of our men fell from our own fire. The darkness was so intense, the roar of artillery so loud, the flight of grape and canister shot so rapid and destructive, that it was absolutely impossible to preserve order in the ranks of individual companies, to say nothing of the regiments.

More than half the time we were in the Fort, the fight was simply a hand-to-hand one, as the wounds received by many clearly indicate. Some have sword-thrusts, some are hacked on the head, some are stabbed with bayonets, and a few were knocked down with the butt-end of muskets, but recovered in time to get away with swollen heads. There was terrible fighting to get into the Fort, and terrible fighting to get out of it. The cowardly stood no better chance for their lives than the fearless. Even if they surrendered, the shell of Sumter were thickly falling around them in the darkness, and, as prisoners, they could not be safe, until victory, decisive and unquestioned, rested with one or the other belligerent.

The battle is over; it is midnight; the ocean beach is crowded with the dead, the dying, and the wounded. It is with difficulty you can urge your horse through to Lighthouse Inlet. Faint lights are glimmering in the sand-holes and rifle-pits to the right, as you pass down the beach. In these holes many a poor wounded and bleeding soldier has lain down to his last sleep. Friends are bending over them to staunch their wounds, or bind up their shattered limbs, but the deathly glare from sunken eyes tells that their kind services are all in vain.

Stephen D. Ramseur

Letter on Disaster in the Valley
October 10, 1864

In a letter to his wife, General Ramseur reports the devastation inflicted on the Shenandoah Valley in 1864 by the Yankees. Nine days after writing this letter Ramseur was mortally wounded in battle in the Valley.

Camp near New Market—Oct 10th '64

I can't help feeling the most intense anxiety & solicitude on your behalf—since our disaster in the Valley, my prospect for a furlough is greatly diminished. I think my duty is plain. I ought not to leave now, even if I could do so—so my Beloved—you must be brave & cheerful without me for awhile—to be separated from you is the hardest trial of my life. . . .

Father writes me that tho discouraged by our late disasters—he is still hopeful as to the final result. I agree with you about your remarks about the "Croakers." I must confess I would be willing to take a musket & fight to the bitter end rather than submit to these miserable Yankees. I feel that they have put themselves beyond the pale of civilization by the course they have pursued in this campaign. This beautiful & fertile valley has been totally destroyed. Sheridan had some of the houses, *all* of the mills & barns, every straw & wheat stack burned. This valley is one great desert. I do not see how these people are to live. We have to haul our supplies from far up the valley. It is rumored that the Yankees are rebuilding the Manassas Gap R. R. If this is true, Sheridan will not give up his hold on the valley, & we will probably remain here for the winter—unless Gen'l Lee becomes so hard pressed that we will have to go to him. My hope now is from Hood. I do hope he may be able to overwhelm Sherman & send reinforcements to our great General Lee. The last private advices I had from Ga. were encouraging. Time is an important element. I believe that Hood can whip Sherman, & I trust he will do it quickly. I have not written you as often recently—because I have been either so constantly occupied or (I must acknowledge it) so much mortified at the recent disasters to our army of the valley that I could not write with any pleasure. There is nothing new to write about right now.

THEODORE R. DAVIS.
Laying Waste the
Shenandoah Valley.
1887. Pen and wash.
9 x 11". Century Collection,
New York.

William Tecumseh Sherman

Letter on Peace, War, and the Evacuation of Atlanta September 12, 1864

General Sherman describes the true face of war to the civilian authorities in Atlanta, which city he had just captured.

Headquarters Military Division of the Mississippi
in the Field, Atlanta, Georgia, September 12, 1864

James M. Calhoun, Mayor, E. E. Rawson and S. C. Wells,
representing City Council of Atlanta.

Gentlemen: I have your letter of the 11th, in the nature of a petition to revoke my orders removing all the inhabitants from Atlanta. I have read it carefully, and give full credit to your statements of the distress that will be occasioned, and yet shall not revoke my orders, because they were not designed to meet the humanities of the case, but to prepare for the future struggles in which millions of good people outside of Atlanta have a deep interest. We must have peace, not only at Atlanta, but in all America. To secure this, we must stop the war that now desolates our once happy and favored country. To stop war, we must defeat the rebel armies which are arrayed against the laws and Constitution that all must respect and obey. To defeat those armies, we must prepare the way to reach them in their recesses, provided with the arms and instruments which enable us to accomplish our purpose. Now, I know the vindictive nature of our enemy, that we may have many years of military operations from this quarter; and, therefore, deem it wise and prudent to prepare in time. The use of Atlanta for warlike purposes is inconsistent with its character as a home for families. There will be no manufactures, commerce, or agriculture here, for the maintenance of families, and sooner or later want will compel the inhabitants to go. Why not go now, when all the arrangements are completed for the transfer, instead of waiting till the plunging shot of contending armies will renew the scenes of the past month? Of course, I do not apprehend any such thing at this moment, but you do not suppose this army will be here until the war is over. I cannot discuss this subject with you fairly, because I cannot impart to you what we propose to do, but I assert that our military plans make it necessary for the inhabitants to go away, and I can only renew my offer of services to make their exodus in any direction as easy and comfortable as possible.

You cannot qualify war in harsher terms than I will. War is cruelty, and you cannot refine it; and those who brought war into our country deserve all the curses and maledictions a people can pour out. I know I had no hand in making this war, and I know I will make more sacrifices to-day than any of you to secure peace. But you cannot have peace and a division of our country. If the United States submits to a division now, it will not stop, but will go on until we reap the fate of Mexico, which is eternal war. The United States does and must assert its authority, wherever it once had power; for, if it relaxes one bit to pressure, it is gone, and I believe that such is the national feeling. This feeling assumes various shapes, but always comes back to that of Union. Once admit the Union, once more acknowledge the authority of the national Government, and, instead of devoting your houses and streets and roads to the dread uses of war, I and this army become at once your protectors and supporters, shielding you from danger, let it come from what quarter it may. I know that a few individuals cannot resist a torrent of error and passion, such as swept the South into rebellion, but you can point out, so that we may know those who desire a government, and those who insist on war and its desolation.

You might as well appeal against the thunder-storm as against these terrible hardships of war. They are inevitable, and the only way the people of Atlanta can hope once more to live in peace and quiet at home, is to stop the war, which can only be done by admitting that it began in error and is perpetuated in pride.

We don't want your Negroes, or your horses, or your houses, or your lands, or any thing you have, but we do want and will have a just obedience to the laws of the United States. That we will have, and if it involves the destruction of your improvements, we cannot help it.

You have heretofore read public sentiment in your newspapers, that live by falsehood and excitement; and the quicker you seek for truth in other quarters, the better. I repeat then that, by the original compact of government, the United States had certain rights in Georgia, which have never been relinquished and never will be; that the South began war by seizing forts, arsenals, mints, custom-houses, etc., etc., long before Mr. Lincoln was installed, and before the South had one jot or tittle of provocation. I myself have seen in Missouri, Kentucky, Tennessee, and Mississippi, hundreds and thousands of women and children fleeing from your armies and desperadoes, hungry and with bleeding feet. In Memphis, Vicksburg, and Mississippi, we fed thousands upon thousands of the families of rebel soldiers left on our hands, and whom we could not see starve. Now that war comes home to you, you feel very different. You deprecate its horrors, but did not feel them when you sent car-loads of soldiers and ammunition, and moulded shells and shot, to carry war into Kentucky and Tennessee, to desolate the homes of hundreds and thousands of good people who only asked to live in peace at their old homes, and under the Government of their inheritance. But these comparisons are idle. I want peace, and

GEORGE N. BARNARD.
The Last Train from Atlanta.
1864. Photograph.
Library of Congress,
Washington, D.C.

believe it can only be reached through union and war, and I will ever conduct war with a view to perfect an early success.

But, my dear sirs, when peace does come, you may call on me for any thing. Then will I share with you the last cracker, and watch with you to shield your homes and families against danger from every quarter.

Now you must go, and take with you the old and feeble, feed and nurse them, and build for them, in more quiet places, proper habitations to shield them against the weather until the mad passions of men cool down, and allow the Union and peace once more to settle over your old homes at Atlanta. Yours in haste,

W. T. SHERMAN, *Major-General commanding*

Herman Melville
"MARCHING TO THE SEA . . . "

Sherman's army cuts a great slash from Atlanta to the sea.

> For behind they left a wailing,
>   A terror and a ban,
> And blazing cinders sailing,
>   And houseless households wan,
> Wide zones of countries paling
>   And towns where maniacs ran.
> Was it Treason's retribution—
>   Necessity the plea?
> They will long remember Sherman
>   And his streaming columns free—
> They will long remember Sherman
>   Marching to the sea.

Mary S. Mallard
On Sherman's Bummers in Georgia

In her journal, Mrs. Mallard describes the descent of Sherman's "bummers" on Montevideo plantation on the Georgia coast in December 1864.

Friday, December 16th. Much to our relief, Prophet came over this morning with a note from Kate to know if we thought she could come to us. Mother wrote her to come imme-

diately, which she did in great fear and trembling, not knowing but that she would meet the enemy on the road. We all felt truly grateful she had been preserved by the way.

About four in the afternoon we heard the clash of arms and noise of horsemen, and by the time Mother and I could get downstairs we saw forty or fifty men in the pantry, flying hither and thither, ripping open the safe with their swords and breaking open the crockery cupboards. Fearing we might not have a chance to cook, Mother had some chickens and ducks roasted and put in the safe for our family. These the men seized whole, tearing them to pieces with their teeth like ravenous beasts. They were clamorous for whiskey, and ordered us to get our keys. One came to Mother to know where her meal and flour were, insisted upon opening her locked pantry, and took every particle. They threw the sacks across their horses. Mother remonstrated and pointed to her helpless family; their only reply was: "We'll take it!"

They flew around the house, tearing open boxes and everything that was closed. They broke open Mother's little worktable with an andiron, hoping to find money or jewelry; it contained principally little mementos that were valuable only to herself. Failing to find treasure, they took the sweet little locks of golden hair that her mother had cut from the heads of her angel children near a half century ago, and scattering them upon the floor trampled them under their feet. A number of them rifled the sideboard, taking away knives, spoons, forks, tin cups, coffeepots, and everything they wished. They broke open Grandfather's old liquor case and carried off two of the large square gallon bottles, and drank up all the blackberry wine and vinegar which was in the case. It was vain to utter a word, for we were completely paralyzed by the fury of these ruffians.

A number of them went into the attic into a little storeroom and carried off twelve bushels of meal Mother had stored there for our necessities. She told them they were taking all she had to support herself and daughter, a friend, and five little children. Scarcely one regarded even the sound of her voice; those who did laughed and said they would leave one sack to keep us from starving. But they only left some rice which they did not want, and poured out a quart or so of meal upon the floor. At other times they said they meant to starve us to death. They searched trunks and bureaus and wardrobes, calling for shirts and men's clothes.

We asked for their officer, hoping to make some appeal to him; they said they were all officers and would do as they pleased. We finally found one man who seemed to make a little show of authority, which was indicated by a whip which he carried. Mother appealed to him, and he came up and ordered the men out. They instantly commenced cursing him, and we thought they would fight one another. They brought a wagon and took another from the place to carry off their plunder.

It is impossible to imagine the horrible uproar and stampede through the house, every room of which was occupied by them, all yelling, cursing, quarreling, and running from one room to another in wild confusion. Such was their blasphemous language, their horrible countenances and appearance, that we realized what must be the association of the lost in the world of eternal woe. Their throats were open sepulchres, their mouths filled with cursing and bitterness and lies. These men belonged to Kilpatrick's cavalry. We look back upon their conduct in the house as a horrible nightmare, too terrible to be true.

When leaving they ordered all the oxen to be gotten up early next morning.

William Tecumseh Sherman
Letter on His Place in History
January 5, 1865

In a letter to his wife, Sherman discusses his campaign and that he thinks it may be remembered.

SAVANNAH, *January 5,* 1865.

I have written several times to you and to the children. Yesterday I got your letter of December 23, and realize the despair and anguish through which you have passed in the pain and sickness of the little baby I never saw. All spoke of him as so bright and fair that I had hoped he would be spared to us to fill the great void in our hearts left by Willy, but it is otherwise decreed and we must submit. I have seen death in such quantity and in such forms that it no longer startles me, but with you it is different, and 'tis well that like the Spaniards you realize the fact that our little baby has passed from the troubles of life to a better existence. I sent Charley off a few days ago to carry to General Grant and to Washington some important despatches, but told him he must not go farther than Washington as by the time he returns I will be off again on another raid. It is pretty hard on me that I am compelled to make these blows which are necessarily trying to me, but it seems devolved on me and cannot be avoided. If the honors proffered and tendered me from all quarters are of any value they will accrue to you and the children. John writes that I am in everybody's mouth and that even he is known as my brother, and that all the Shermans are now fêted as relatives of me. Surely you and the children will not be overlooked by those who profess to honor me. I do think that in the several grand epochs of this war, my name will have a prominent part, and not least among them will be the determination I took at Atlanta to destroy that place, and march on this city, whilst Thomas, my lieutenant, should dispose of Hood. The idea, the execution and strategy are all good, and will in time be understood. I don't know that you comprehend the magnitude of the thing, but you can see the importance attached to it in England where the critics stand ready to turn against any American general who makes a mistake or fails in its execution. In my case they had time to commit themselves to the conclusion that if I succeeded I would be a great general, but if I failed I would be set down a fool. My success is already assured, so that I will be found to sustain the title. I am told that were I to go north I would be fêted and petted, but as I have no intention of going, you must sustain the honors of the family. I know exactly what amount of merit attaches to my own conduct, and what will survive the clamor of time. The quiet preparation I made before the Atlanta Campaign, the rapid movement on Resaca, the crossing the Chatta-hoochee without loss in the face of a skilful general with a good army, the movement on Jonesboro, whereby Atlanta fell, and the resolution I made to divide my army, with one part to take Savannah and the other to meet Hood in Tennessee, are all clearly mine, and will survive us both in history. I don't know that you can understand the merit of the latter, but it will stamp me in years to come, and will be more appreciated in Europe than in America. I warrant your father will find parallel in the history of the Greeks and Persians, but none on our continent. For his sake I am glad of the success that has attended me, and I know he will feel more pride in my success than you or I do. Oh

WILLIAM WAUD.
Sherman Reviewing His Army on Bay Street, Savannah, January, 1865.
Pencil. 9⅛ x 12¾".
Library of Congress, Washington, D.C.

COLORPLATE 106

JOHN FERGUSON WEIR. *The Gun Foundry.* 1864-1866. Oil on canvas. 64½ × 80″.
Putnam County Historical Society, Cold Springs, New York.

COLORPLATE 107

CONRAD WISE CHAPMAN. *Battery Simkins, Charleston, Feb. 25, 1864.* 1864. Oil on board. 11½ × 15½". Museum of the Confederacy, Richmond. Photo by Katherine Wetzel.

COLORPLATE 108

CONRAD WISE CHAPMAN. *Fort Sumter Interior at Sunrise, Dec. 9, 1864.* 1864. Oil on board. 11½ × 15½″.
Museum of the Confederacy, Richmond. Photo by Larry Sherer, copyright © 1984 Time-Life Books, Inc.

COLORPLATE 109

WILLIAM HEYSHAM OVEREND. *An August Morning with Farragut; The Battle of Mobile Bay, August 5, 1864.* 1883. Oil on canvas. 77½ × 120″. Wadsworth Atheneum, Hartford. Gift of Citizens of Hartford by Subscription. Photo © Wadsworth Atheneum. *The admiral stands in the rigging as his flagship* Hartford *battles the Rebel ironclad* Tennessee.

COLORPLATE 110

ROBERT W. WEIR. *U. S. S. Richmond vs. C. S. S. Tennessee, Mobile Bay.* 1864.
Oil on board. 10 × 16″. The Mariners Museum, Newport News, Virginia.

COLORPLATE 111

XANTHUS RUSSELL SMITH. *Attack on Fort Fisher, North Carolina.* 1893. Oil on canvas.
56 × 123½″. Pennsylvania Academy of the Fine Arts, Philadelphia. Gift of Mrs. Sarah Harrison
(The Joseph Harrison, Jr. Collection).

COLORPLATE 112

FRANK VIZETELLY. *The Interior of the North Eastern Salient of Fort Fisher During the Attack of
the 13th, 14th, and 15th of January.* 1865. Watercolor. 10 × 26″. Harvard College Library, Cambridge.

COLORPLATE 113

GEORGE P. A. HEALY. *The Peacemakers*. 1868. Oil on canvas. 47⅛ × 62⅝″. White House Historical Association, Washington, D.C. Copyright © White House Historical Association; Photo by the National Geographic Association. *At left, Generals Sherman and Grant; at right, Admiral David Porter.*

that Willy were living! how his eyes would brighten and his bosom swell with honest pride if he could hear and understand these things. . . .

You will doubtless read all the details of our march and stay in Savannah in the papers, whose spies infest our camps, spite of all I can do, but I could tell you thousands of little incidents which would more interest you. The women here are, as at Memphis, disposed to usurp my time more from curiosity than business. They had been told of my burning and killing until they expected the veriest monster, but their eyes were opened when Hardee, G. W. Smith and McLaws, the three chief officers of the Rebel army, fled across the Savannah river consigning their families to my special care. There are some very elegant people here, whom I knew in better days and who do not seem ashamed to call on the 'vandal chief.' They regard us just as the Romans did the Goths and the parallel is not unjust. Many of my stalwart men with red beards and huge frames look like giants, and it is wonderful how smoothly all things move, for they all seem to feel implicit faith in me not because I am strong or bold, but because they think I know everything. It seems impossible for us to go anywhere without being where I have been before. My former life from 1840 to 1846 seems providential and every bit of knowledge then acquired is returned, tenfold. Should it so happen that I should approach Charleston on that very ground where I used to hunt with Jim Poyas, and Mr. Quash, and ride by moonlight to save daytime, it would be even more strange than here where I was only a visitor. Col. Kilburn arrived here from Louisville yesterday, and begged me to remember him to you. I continue to receive letters, most flattering, from all my old friends and enclose you two, one from General Hitchcock and one from Professor Mahan. Such men do not flatter and are judges of what they write. . . .

Edward Porter Alexander
On the Last Winter of the War

An artillerist in Lee's army recalls a meeting in February 1865 to negotiate peace, and how it was in the siege lines at Petersburg in the last winter of the war.

By all the rules of state craft, the Confederate government (the executive & the Senate) should have opened negotiations for peace some months before. For at that time we had been in better position to secure concessions than we ever could have reasonably hoped to be again. Since then our position had been growing steadily worse. It would seem, too, that the defeat of the Democrats, & the re-election of Mr. Lincoln in November, might well have been generally recognised as the very funeral of our last chances. But, strange as it now seems to look back upon, our eyes were blinded utterly—at least my own & those of my associates, & we cared not a straw whom the Federals elected, & confidently expected final success to come, some how. And that was the general sentiment in the army. I can only account for it in the generally religious character of our people. They believed in a God who overruled all human affairs, & who in the end brought the right to prevail. They *knew* they were right, & there they were! It was only waiting on God, a little more or less. As one old chaplain, in the army, used to pray, He would surely come down, after a while, & "take a proper view of this situation," & then we would be all right.

Well at last, as it really seemed, by Providential interposition, & not by any initiative of our own a meeting was arranged at Fortress Monroe, early in Feb. 1865, to discuss terms of peace. It was brought about by a[n] Hon. Montgomery Blair, &c. He came to Richmond in January, of his own notion but by Mr. Lincoln's consent, & at last, with some little difficulty, it was arranged that a commission composed of Vice Prest. Stephens, Judge Campbell, & R. M. T. Hunter, should meet President Lincoln & Secretary Seward at Fortress Monroe on Feb. 9th. All the other crises of the war seem to me to be vague & shadowy figures & of uncertain proportions, as compared with the sitting of this conference. For, practically, a proposition was here made to the South, & rejected, which seems absolutely incredible when one reflects that she was then within 60 days of an unconditional surrender! Not from any sudden or unforeseen calamity, either. But from the natural & ordinary operation of forces playing on the side of all men, & only waiting for the winter to pass to produce their inevitable results.

At that date, Feb. 9th, Mr. Lincoln practically offered the South four hundred million dollars as compensation for the slaves set free, & any other reasonable political conditions they might choose to name, if she would return to the Union. But our committee was under instructions. The president & cabinet had absolutely forbidden our delegates to accept any terms, or even to consider any, short of our independence. That was the one thing Mr. Lincoln would not grant. He said to the commission, "Let me write the one word 'Union' at the head of a sheet, & you can fill in the rest of the treaty to suit yourselves." He took Mr. Stephens to one side, & said that it had always seemed to him as only just to the South that the nation should pay for the slaves set free, and that he would recommend to Congress the payment of four hundred millions dollars & believed that it would be granted. . . .

THOMAS C. ROCHE.
A Dead Confederate Soldier, Petersburg, Virginia. April 3, 1865. Photograph. Library of Congress, Washington, D.C.

The future historian may greatly condemn the rejection of such terms by our executive, particularly when the pitiable condition is considered to which we were reduced by unconditional surrender, & by Negro suffrage, & all the iniquities of Reconstruction under the passions engendered by the assassination. But it must never be forgotten that our executive simply carried out the wishes of our army & of the people at that time. We were not "whipped." We were fighting for *Rights*, & we would have scorned the idea of parting with them for money.

Which is all admirable enough, but the trouble was that we were struggling against changes which the advance of the world in railroads & steamboats & telegraphs, in science & knowledge and commerce, &, in short, in civilization, had rendered inevitable.

And as our cause was thus foredoomed to failure, perhaps the most fitting obsequies which could be wished for it, by those who loved it, were those afterward performed at Appomattox. . . .

It was of this period that the story was told of the half-frozen Confederate picket, who sat on a stump & took stock of his nearly bare feet & thin & ragged clothes & empty haversack, & exclaimed, "Well, damn me if ever I love another *Country!*". . . . The Quartermaster Department was on the verge of exhaustion of all supplies of forage & its only chance to get clothing, or such supplies as were needed to keep the worn out railroads even passable, were through blockade running. The Medical Department had always only lived from hand to mouth, through the blockade. And the Ordnance Department, which had already cut up the last turpentine still in the South to make percussion caps from the copper, was now dependent upon the blockade runners for them, as well as for many other essentials. And, about the middle of February, Wilmington was captured & all possible blockade running was ended. Briefly, had not the poem of the deacon's One-horse Shay been written some years before, it might well be supposed to have been suggested by the condition of the Confederacy at this time. Every part had done its duty & lasted its time. And now everything was ready to go to smash all at once!

Walt Whitman
On Rebel Deserters

Whitman sees deserters from the Petersburg lines brought to Washington. Lee wrote at this time of "the alarming number of desertions that are now occurring in this army."

February 23, 1865.

I saw a large procession of young men from the Rebel Army (deserters they are called, but the usual meaning of the word does not apply to them) passing the Avenue today. I stood and watched them as they shuffled along in a slow, tired, worn sort of way; a large proportion of light-haired, blonde, light-gray-eyed young men among them. Their costumes had a dirt-stained uniformity; most had been originally gray; some had articles of our uniform—pants on one, coat or vest on another; I think they were mostly Georgia and North Carolina boys. They excited little or no attention.

As I stood quite close to them, several good-looking enough youths (but O what a tale of misery their appearance told!) nodded or just spoke to me, without doubt divining pity and fatherliness out of my face—for my heart was full enough of it. Several of the couples trudged along with their arms about each other, some probably brothers, as if they were afraid they might somehow get separated.

They nearly all looked what one might call simple, yet intelligent, too. Some had pieces of old carpet, some blankets, and others old bags around their shoulders. Some of them here and there had fine faces; still it was a procession of misery. The two hundred had with them about half-a-dozen armed guards. Along this week I saw some such up by the boat. The government does what it can for them, and sends them north and west.

Charles Royster

FROM THE DESTRUCTIVE WAR
On the Destruction of Columbia

Historian Royster describes the scene when Sherman's army occupied Columbia, the capital of South Carolina, in February 1865.

At dusk, soldiers were wandering throughout the city, under no control. Several buildings in the center of the business district caught fire. The volunteer firemen brought out their remaining engines and tried to bring the hoses to bear on the flames, but soldiers quickly smashed the machinery with axes. The constant straining wind caused the stores to burn fast. With shouts and cheers men moved through the broken and discarded merchandise in the street, the sober as excited as the drunk. Lieutenant Colonel Jeremiah W. Jenkins, the provost marshal who was supposed to police the city, found the task too great. His "youthful, tall lithe and elegant form, in his officers suit and high topped boots" caught the eye of a Columbia woman who sought from him a guard for her house. He walked along the street with her restlessly, rushing into buildings to stamp out small fires. He tried to apologize to her for the disorder, but she denounced the North for making war on women and children after having failed in fair combat. At last Jenkins told her: "The women of the South kept the war alive—and it is only by making them suffer that we can subdue the men."

Not long after sunset, several rockets shot up above the city, leaving bright trails of color. To the soldiers this was a common sight, since rockets were the usual nighttime signals among the separated columns of Sherman's army. But citizens of Columbia read a more frightening meaning into the signal. Some of them had heard warnings about a plan among the soldiers to burn the city. Harriott Horry Ravenel suspected that her slave Martha knew more than she had revealed, because Martha reacted to the rockets by saying: "That's it Miss. Lord hab mussy on us—it's beginning!"

On Main Street a large fire was burning near City Hall. A block north and on the other side of the street, the office of the Southern Express Company was burning. Around the corner, on Taylor Street, A. R. Phillips's store was on fire. In the other direction from City Hall, the buildings on the west side of Main Street in the next block, where the cotton was still burning, also caught fire. Soon fires appeared in many places in the city, especially the upper, northern section, the quarter from which the wind blew. On the east side of town, the Charlotte railroad depot seemed to burst into flame all at once, fire shooting out its doors and windows, quickly spreading to the abandoned furniture and household possessions near the tracks.

THEODORE R. DAVIS.
*In the Carolina Swamp
—The Advance Guard.*
1865. Pen. 6½ x 8″.
Museum of Fine Arts,
Boston. M. and M.
Karolik Collection.
Photo copyright
© 1992 Museum of
Fine Arts, Boston.

New fires were started by some of the soldiers going from house to house, carrying pots of turpentine, balls of cotton, pine sticks aflame, bundles of straw, and lightwood torches. They tossed burning cotton balls in windows and doors, doused furniture with turpentine and lit it. Their shouts and laughter and jokes showed they were having a good time, but the keenest enjoyment belonged to the officers who had escaped from the Confederate prison camp. One of them later bragged that he had fired seventeen houses. Black men led groups of soldiers through the streets to show them hidden valuables, wine cellars, and the homes of certain Columbians. The league of young black men carried out their plan to start fires. The day before Sherman's army arrived, twenty slaves had been flogged at the Market whipping post. This night brought revenge. The father of two of the young men tried to persuade his sons not to take part, but he failed; so he followed them and put out two of the fires they had set. Soldiers knew of specific citizens who deserved punishment and went in search of their homes, asking: "Is this the home of Mr. Rhett?" "Is that the dwelling of Mr. Middleton?" Two aged Charlestonians, Arthur P. Hayne and Alfred Huger, were pulled about and struck. Officers tried to lean from Louisa Cheves McCord the whereabouts of Dr. John Cheves; they blamed him for the land mines that had wounded Federal soldiers outside Savannah and said they would hang him. The devoted secessionist Maxcy Gregg had been killed at the battle of Fredericksburg, but his house was accessible. Soldiers took his gold-headed cane, his gold epaulets and crimson sash, and the trousers he had worn in his last battle. Some former prisoners of war knew which houses they wanted to burn—those of Columbians who had spat on the captured Yankees. A group of soldiers, led by black men and freed prisoners, went to the home of a man who ran a pack of bloodhounds for the capture of escaping slaves and Federal soldiers. They killed the hounds, burned the house, tied the man to a tree, and let the biggest black men flog him.

Men threw burning cotton into the McCord home even after General Howard had made it his headquarters. Howard put out small fires and drily commented that it was remarkable how the cotton was blowing about. Mayor Goodwyn returned home after the fire engines were broken near City Hall and found his house burning. He tried to save some possessions by taking them into the street; but soldiers made fun of him, put pistols to his head and knives to his throat, tore things from his hands and smashed them. People in their homes heard soldiers in the street shout, "Your house is on fire." As the residents rushed out, the soldiers went in to loot. Drunken men ranged through Harriott Ravenel's house on Henderson Street, trying to beat one another to the trunks and closets. They took trinkets, pictures, china, clothing, blankets, and food, then started fires before leaving. The house servants helped put out the fires after the men had gone. Some soldiers seemed to admire the composure of the women in the Ravenel home and stopped long enough to say that they "were sorry for the women and children, but South Carolina must be destroyed." Others were just having a good time: one man left the house wearing a blue silk dress and carrying a lace parasol.

The streets grew more crowded as people fled from burning houses and as more soldiers came in from the surrounding camps. In an arc north and west of the city, thousands of campfires lit the darkened countryside. Sections of the pine woods were burning. The wind pushed those fires: flames jumped among the trees, which threw up streams of sparks within columns of thick smoke. Inside the city, at ten o'clock, all the buildings along Main Street, from the north edge of town to the capitol, were burning. The flames leaned eastward under the steady blast of wind, creeping along Washington Street and other parallel cross streets, toward the churches and the academies. Pulsing globes of fire rose from burning buildings, rushed through the air, and seized more structures. Frantic chickens and pigs, caught by the flames, burned alive. Bursting bales of cotton threw masses of crackling fibers into the air. Burning shingles and fiery debris followed the upward draft of black smoke and hot air hundreds of feet above the city, then fell on roofs, in gardens, and among people in the streets. The branches of shade trees, now bare and black, writhed and snaked under the intense pressure of the heat and the wind. . . .

Sherman had spent the afternoon walking through the city and visiting families he had known as a young lieutenant stationed at Charleston. While walking with Mayor Goodwyn, he had seen the body of a black man, shot by soldiers who took offense at the man's impudence; but Sherman had not arrested the soldiers. In the evening he had remained at the house that served as his headquarters, near the east end of Gervais Street, until eleven o'clock. After supper, he and General Hazen went into the yard and saw the light from the fire. Sherman said: "They have brought it on themselves."

AN END TO WAR

Abraham Lincoln
SECOND INAUGURAL ADDRESS

The president delivers his second inaugural address at the Capitol.

Fellow countrymen: At this second appearing to take the oath of the presidential office there is less occasion for an extended address than there was at the first. Then a statement somewhat in detail of a course to be pursued seemed fitting and proper. Now, at the expiration of four years, during which public declarations have been constantly called forth on every point and phase of the great contest which still absorbs the attention and engrosses the energies of the nation, little that is new could be presented. The progress of our arms, upon which all else chiefly depends, is as well known to the public as to myself, and it is, I trust, reasonably satisfactory and encouraging to all. With high hope for the future, no prediction in regard to it is ventured.

On the occasion corresponding to this four years ago all thoughts were anxiously directed to an impending civil war. All dreaded it, all sought to avert it. While the inaugural address was being delivered from this place, devoted altogether to *saving* the Union without war, insurgent agents were in the city seeking to *destroy* it without war— seeking to dissolve the Union and divide effects by negotiation. Both parties deprecated war, but one of them would *make* war rather than let the nation survive, and the other would *accept* war rather than let it perish, and the war came.

One eighth of the whole population was colored slaves, not distributed generally over the Union, but localized in the southern part of it. These slaves constituted a peculiar and powerful interest. All knew that this interest was somehow the cause of the war. To strengthen, perpetuate, and extend this interest was the object for which the insurgents would rend the Union even by war, while the government claimed no right to do more than to restrict the territorial enlargement of it. Neither party expected for the war the magnitude or the duration which it has already attained. Neither anticipated that the *cause* of the conflict might cease with or even before the conflict itself should cease. Each looked for an easier triumph and a result less fundamental and astounding. Both read the same Bible and pray to the same God, and each invokes His aid against the other. It may seem strange that any men should dare to ask a just God's assistance in wringing their bread from the sweat of other men's faces, but let us judge not, that we be not judged. The prayers of both could not be answered. That of neither has been answered fully. The Almighty has His own purposes. "Woe unto the world because of offenses; for it must needs be that offenses come, but woe to the man by whom the offense cometh." If we shall suppose that American slavery is one of those offenses which, in the providence of God, must needs come, but which, having continued through His ap-

ATTRIBUTED TO ALEXANDER GARDNER. *Lincoln's Second Inauguration.* March 4, 1865. Photograph. Library of Congress, Washington, D.C.

pointed time, He now wills to remove, and that He gives to both North and South this terrible war as the woe due to those by whom the offense came, shall we discern therein any departure from those divine attributes which the believers in a living God always ascribe to Him? Fondly do we hope, fervently do we pray, that this mighty scourge of war may speedily pass away. Yet, if God wills that it continue until at the wealth piled by the bondsman's two hundred and fifty years of unrequited toil shall be sunk, and until every drop of blood drawn with the lash shall be paid by another drawn with the sword, as was said three thousand years ago, so still it must be said, "The judgments of the Lord are true and righteous altogether."

   With malice toward none, with charity for all, with firmness in the right as God gives us to see the right, let us strive on to finish the work we are in, to bind up the nation's wounds, to care for him who shall have borne the battle and for his widow and his orphan, to do all which may achieve and cherish a just and lasting peace among ourselves and with all nations.

John Cheves Haskell

On the Chaos in the Capital of the Confederacy

Colonel Haskell was an artillerist in Lee's army. This excerpt, from his Memoirs, *records the evacuation of Richmond, in April 1865.*

When I got to Richmond, everything was in the wildest confusion. I met my quartermaster just below the town with a lot of much needed horses; one fine pair he had found in

Richmond. April, 1865.
Photograph.
Library of Congress,
Washington, D.C.

336

a drygoods store behind the counter. The low characters of the town had broken into everything, gotten a lot of whiskey, and were looting the place, being aided to a considerable extent by the soldiers, who had broken through all discipline. As I rode by the principal jewelry store, I saw an old woman come crawling backward out of a window. One of the mounted men rode up and whacked her with the flat of his sword. She tumbled out with a yell, and her lapful of plunder from the showcases of Mitchell and Tyler, the leading jewelers of Richmond, poured over the sidewalk. At another store, a party was beating in the door, which burst in only to show the owner armed. He fired on his assailants, one of whom fell, but instantly he was himself shot to death.

A crowd of plunderers filled the Government warehouses down at the bridge. There was a large amount of whiskey in one house, just at the bridge, and the plunderers, filled with it, were throwing out everything they could lay their hands on, utterly regardless of the crowd below. Numbers were crushed by the large bags and boxes and barrels, thrown from the third and fourth stories. No one seemed to pay the slightest heed or attention, but would rush in to plunder as soon as anything was thrown out, though it might have crushed to death someone an arm's length away. This went on as long as I was there, which was for hours as I waited to see the men and guns across.

Ulysses S. Grant

On His Appointment with General Lee at Appomattox

In his Memoirs, *General Grant recounts his meeting with General Lee at Appomattox Court House on April 9, 1865, Palm Sunday.*

I had known General Lee in the old army, and had served with him in the Mexican War; but did not suppose, owing to the difference in our age and rank, that he would remember me; while I would more naturally remember him distinctly, because he was the chief of staff of General Scott in the Mexican War.

When I had left camp that morning I had not expected so soon the result that was then taking place, and consequently was in rough garb. I was without a sword, as I usually was when on horseback on the field, and wore a soldier's blouse for a coat, with the shoulder straps of my rank to indicate to the army who I was. When I went into the house I found General Lee. We greeted each other, and after shaking hands took our seats. I had my staff with me, a good portion of whom were in the room during the whole of the interview.

What General Lee's feelings were I do not know. As he was a man of much dignity, with an impassable face, it was impossible to say whether he felt inwardly glad that the end had finally come, or felt sad over the result, and was too manly to show it. Whatever his feelings, they were entirely concealed from my observation; but my own feelings, which had been quite jubilant on the receipt of his letter, were sad and depressed. I felt like anything rather than rejoicing at the downfall of a foe who had fought so long and valiantly, and had suffered so much for a cause, though that cause was, I believe, one of the worst for which a people ever fought, and one for which there was the least excuse. I do not question, however, the sincerity of the great mass of those who were opposed to us.

ALFRED R. WAUD.
*General Lee Leaving
Appomattox, April 9,
1865.* 1865. Pencil.
9½ x 8⅝". Library
of Congress,
Washington, D.C.

General Lee was dressed in a full uniform which was entirely new, and was wearing a sword of considerable value, very likely the sword which had been presented by the State of Virginia; at all events, it was an entirely different sword from the one that would ordinarily be worn in the field. In my rough traveling suit, the uniform of a private with the straps of a lieutenant-general, I must have contrasted very strangely with a man so handsomely dressed, six feet high and of faultless form. But this was not a matter that I thought of until afterwards.

Elisha Hunt Rhodes
On the End of the Fighting

The men in the ranks learn of the surrender. By then, diarist Rhodes was colonel of the 2nd Rhode Island regiment.

Sunday April 9/65, Near Appomattox Court House, Va.—Glory to God in the highest. Peace on earth, good will to men! Thank God Lee has surrendered and the war will soon end. How can I record the events of this day? This morning we started at an early hour still following the sound of an occasional cannon shot. I found a Rebel Captain from North Carolina by the roadside, and finding him to be a Mason I had him go with my Provost Guard. About 11 A.M. we halted in a field facing the woods and stacked arms. Rumors of intended surrender were heard, but we did not feel sure. I took the Rebel Captain over to Gen. Edward's Headquarters, and we lunched with him. The Captain insisted that Lee would surrender and begged that we would not send him to the rear. Some time in the afternoon we heard loud cheering at the front, and soon Major General Meade commanding the Army of the Potomac rode like mad down the road with hat off shouting: "The war is over, and we are going home!" Such a scene only happens once in centuries. The Batteries began to fire blank cartridges, while the Infantry fired their muskets in the air. The men threw their knapsacks and canteens into the air and howled like mad.

General Wheaton and a party of officers rode to our Regiment and actually gave three cheers for the 2nd R.I. which were returned with a will. I cried and laughed by turns. I never was so happy in my life.

The Rebels are half starved, and our men have divided their rations with them. The 2nd R.I. had three days' rations and after dividing their rations with the Rebels will have to make a day and a half's rations last for three days. But we did it cheerfully. Well I have seen the end of the Rebellion. I was in the first battle fought by the dear old Army of the Potomac, and I was in the last. I thank God for all his blessings to me and that my life has been spared to see this glorious day. Hurrah, Hurrah, Hurrah!

ALFRED R. WAUD. *General George Custer Receives a Flag of Truce at Appomattox Court House, April, 1865.* Pencil. Library of Congress, Washington, D.C.

Joshua Lawrence Chamberlain
On the Surrender of Lee's Army

From The Passing of the Armies, *General Chamberlain describes how he was detailed to take the surrender of the Army of Northern Virginia.*

The dusky swarms forge forward into gray columns of march. On they come, with the old swinging route step and swaying battle-flags. In the van, the proud Confederate ensign—the great field of white with canton of star-strewn cross of blue on a field of red, the regimental battle-flags with the same escutcheon following on, crowded so thick, by thinning out of men, that the whole column seemed crowned with red. At the right of our line our little group mounted beneath our flags, the red Maltese cross on a field of white, erewhile so bravely borne through many a field more crimson than itself, its mystic meaning now ruling all. . . .

Instruction had been given; and when the head of each division column comes opposite our group, our bugle sounds the signal and instantly our whole line from right to left, regiment by regiment in succession, gives the soldier's salutation, from the "order arms" to the old "carry"—the marching salute. Gordon at the head of the column, riding with heavy spirit and downcast face, catches the sound of shifting arms, looks up, and, taking the meaning, wheels superbly, making with himself and his horse one uplifted figure, with profound salutation as he drops the point of his sword to the boot toe; then facing to his own command, gives word for his successive brigades to pass us with the same position of the manual,—honor answering honor. On our part not a sound of trumpet more, nor roll of drum; not a cheer, nor word nor whisper of vain-glorying, nor motion

JOHN R. CHAPIN.
The Surrender of the Army of Northern Virginia, April 12, 1865. 1865. Pencil. 9 x 13½". Library of Congress, Washington, D.C.

of man standing again at the order, but an awed stillness rather, and breath-holding, as if it were the passing of the dead!

As each successive division masks our own, it halts, the men face inward towards us across the road, twelve feet away; then carefully "dress" their line, each captain taking pains for the good appearance of his company, worn and half starved as they were. The field and staff take their positions in the intervals of regiments; generals in rear of their commands. They fix bayonets, stack arms; then, hesitatingly, remove cartridge-boxes and lay them down. Lastly,—reluctantly, with agony of expression,—they tenderly fold their flags, battle-worn and torn, blood-stained, heart-holding colors, and lay them down; some frenziedly rushing from the ranks, kneeling over them, clinging to them, pressing them to their lips with burning tears. And only the Flag of the Union greets the sky!

What visions thronged as we looked into each other's eyes! Here pass the men of Antietam, the Bloody Lane, the Sunken Road, the Cornfield, the Burnside-Bridge; the men whom Stonewall Jackson on the second night at Fredericksburg begged Lee to let him take and crush the two corps of the Army of the Potomac huddled in the streets in darkness and confusion; the men who swept away the Eleventh Corps at Chancellorsville; who left six thousand of their companions around the bases of Culp's and Cemetery Hills at Gettysburg; these survivors of the terrible Wilderness, the Bloody-Angle at Spottsylvania, the slaughter pen of Cold Harbor, the whirlpool of Bethesda Church!

Here comes Cobb's Georgia Legion, which held the stone wall on Marye's Heights at Fredericksburg, close before which we piled our dead for breastworks so that the living might stay and live.

Here too come Gordon's Georgians and Hoke's North Carolinians, who stood before the terrific mine explosion at Petersburg, and advancing retook the smoking crater and the dismal heaps of dead—ours more than theirs—huddled in the ghastly chasm.

Here are the men of McGowan, Hunton, and Scales, who broke the Fifth Corps lines on the White Oak Road, and were so desperately driven back on that forlorn night of March 31st by my thrice-decimated brigade.

Now comes Anderson's Fourth Corps, only Bushrod Johnson's Division left, and this the remnant of those we fought so fiercely on the Quaker Road two weeks ago, with Wise's Legion, too fierce for its own good.

Here passes the proud remnant of Ransom's North Carolinians which we swept through Five Forks ten days ago,—and all the little that was left of this division in the sharp passages at Sailor's Creek five days thereafter.

Now makes its last front A. P. Hill's old Corps, Heth now at the head, since Hill had gone too far forward ever to return: the men who poured destruction into our division at Shepardstown Ford, Antietam, in 1862, when Hill reported the Potomac running blue with our bodies; the men who opened the desperate first day's fight at Gettysburg, where withstanding them so stubbornly our Robinson's Brigades lost 1185 men, and the Iron Brigade alone 1153,—these men of Heth's Division here too losing 2850 men, companions of these now looking into our faces so differently.

What is this but the remnant of Mahone's Division, last seen by us at the North Anna? its thinned ranks of worn, bright-eyed men recalling scenes of costly valor and ever-remembered history.

Now the sad great pageant—Longstreet and his men! What shall we give them for greeting that has not already been spoken in volleys of thunder and written in lines of fire on all the river-banks of Virginia? Shall we go back to Gaines' Mill and Malvern Hill? Or to the Antietam of Maryland, or Gettysburg of Pennsylvania?—deepest graven of all. For here is what remains of Kershaw's Division, which left 40 per cent. of its men at Antietam, and at Gettysburg with Barksdale's and Semmes' Brigades tore through the Peach Orchard, rolling up the right of our gallant Third Corps, sweeping over the proud batteries of Massachusetts—Bigelow and Philips,—where under the smoke we saw the earth brown and blue with prostrate bodies of horses and men, and the tongues of over-turned cannon and caissons pointing grim and stark in the air.

Then in the Wilderness, at Spottsylvania and thereafter, Kershaw's Division again, in deeds of awful glory, held their name and fame, until fate met them at Sailor's Creek, where Kershaw himself, and Ewell, and so many more, gave up their arms and hopes,—all, indeed, but manhood's honor.

With what strange emotion I look into these faces before which in the mad assault on Rives' Salient, June 18, 1864, I was left for dead under their eyes! It is by miracles we have lived to see this day,—any of us standing here.

Now comes the sinewy remnant of fierce Hood's Division, which at Gettysburg we saw pouring through the Devil's Den, and the Plum Run gorge; turning again by the left our stubborn Third Corps, then swarming up the rocky bastions of Round Top, to be met there by equal valor, which changed Lee's whole plan of battle and perhaps the story of Gettysburg.

Ah, is this Pickett's Division?—this little group left of those who on the lurid last day of Gettysburg breasted level cross-fire and thunderbolts of storm, to be strewn back drifting wrecks, where after that awful, futile, pitiful charge we buried them in graves a furlong wide, with name unknown!

Met again in the terrible cyclone-sweep over the breastworks at Five Forks; met now, so thin, so pale, purged of the mortal,—as if knowing pain or joy no more. How could we help falling on our knees, all of us together, and praying God to pity and forgive us all!

Stephen Vincent Benét

FROM "JOHN BROWN'S BODY"

On Mr. Lincoln's Visit to Richmond

Poet Benét describes the president's visit to Richmond two days after the Confederate evacuation.

Richmond is fallen—Lincoln walks in its streets,
Alone, unguarded, stops at George Pickett's house,
Knocks at George Pickett's door. George Pickett has gone
But the strange, gaunt figure talks to George Pickett's wife
A moment—she thinks she is dreaming, seeing him there—
"Just one of George Pickett's old friends, m'am."

                                             He turns away.
She watches him down the street with wondering eyes.
The red light falls upon him from the red sky.
Houses are burning, strange shadows flee through the streets.
A gang of loafers is broaching a liquor-barrel
In a red-lit square. The liquor spills on the cobbles.
They try to scoop it up in their dirty hands.

A long, blue column tramps by, shouting "John Brown's Body."
The loafers scatter like wasps from a half-sucked pear,
Come back when the column is gone.

                                A half-crazy slave
Mounts on a stoop and starts to preach to the sky.
A white-haired woman shoos him away with a broom.
He mumbles and reels to the shadows.
                                A general passes,
His escort armed with drawn sabres. The sabres shine
In the red, low light.
                        Two doors away, down the street,
A woman is sobbing the same long sob all night
Beside a corpse with crossed hands.
                                Lincoln passes on. . . .

Mary Chesnut

On the News of President Lincoln's Assassination

Mrs. Chesnut was in Chester, South Carolina, when she received the news from Washington. Her husband was general of Confederate reserves in that state.

April 22, 1865. This yellow Confederate quire of paper blotted by my journal has been buried three days with the silver sugar dish, teapot, milk jug, and a few spoons and forks that follow my fortunes as I wander. With these valuables was Hood's silver cup, which was partly crushed when he was wounded at Chickamauga.

It has been a wild three days. Aides galloping around with messages. Yankees hanging over us like the sword of Damocles. We have been in queer straits. We sat up at Mrs. Bedon's, dressed, without once going to bed for forty-eight hours. And we were aweary. Mariana in the grange does not know anything about it. No Yankees to spright her or fright her there.

Colonel Cad Jones came with a dispatch, a sealed secret dispatch. It was for General Chesnut. I opened it.

Lincoln—old Abe Lincoln—killed—murdered—Seward wounded!

Why? By whom? It is simply maddening, all this.

I sent off messenger after messenger for General Chesnut. I have not the faintest idea where he is, but I know this foul murder will bring down worse miseries on us.

Mary Darby says: "But they murdered him themselves. No Confederates in Washington."

"But if they see fit to accuse us of instigating it?"

"Who murdered him?"

"Who knows!"

"See if they don't take vengeance on us, now that we are ruined and cannot repel them any longer."

Met Mr. Heyward. He said: "Plebiscitum it is. See, our army are deserting Joe Johnston. That is the people's vote against a continuance of the war. And the death of Lincoln—I call that a warning to tyrants. He will not be the last president put to death in the capital, though he is the first."

"Joe Johnston's army that he has risked his reputation to save from the very first year of the war—*deserting*. Saving his army by retreats, and now they are deserting *him*."

"Yes, Stonewall's tactics were the best—hard knocks, blow after blow in rapid succession, quick marches, surprises, victories quand même. That would have saved us. Watch, wait, retreat, ruined us. Now look out for bands of marauders, black and white, lawless disbanded soldiery from both armies."

An armistice, they say, is agreed on.

Taking stock, as the shopkeepers say. Heavy debts for the support of negroes during the war—and before, as far as we are concerned. No home—our husbands shot or made prisoners. . . .

Walt Whitman
"O CAPTAIN! MY CAPTAIN!"

The poet mourns the leader he had come to admire beyond reckoning.

O Captain! my Captain! our fearful trip is done,
The ship has weather'd every rack, the prize we sought is won;
The port is near, the bells I hear, the people all exulting,
While follow eyes the steady keel, the vessel grim and daring

     But O heart! heart! heart!
       O the bleeding drops of red,
          Where on the deck my Captain lies,
            Fallen cold and dead.

HERMANN FABER. *Death of Abraham Lincoln.* 1865. Pencil on paper. 13⅞ x 9⅞". Armed Forces Institute of Pathology, Washington, D.C. Otis Historical Archives, National Museum of Health and Medicine.

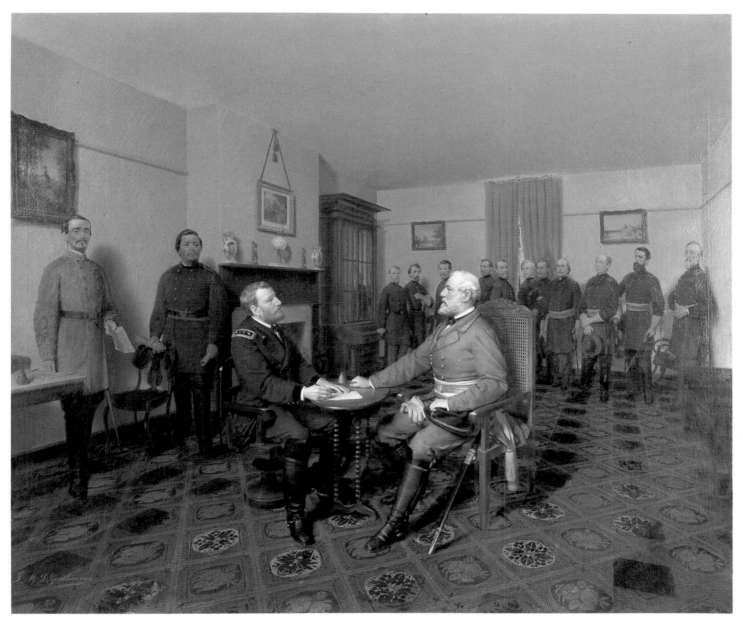

COLORPLATE 114

Louis M. D. Guillaume. *The Surrender of General Lee to General Grant, April 9, 1865.* 1867.
Oil on canvas. 60 × 72″. Appomattox Court House National Historical Park, Appomattox,
Virginia. U. S. Department of the Interior, National Park Service, Washington, D.C.

COLORPLATE 115

Thomas Nast. *Entrance of the 55th Massachusetts (Colored) Regiment into Charleston, S.C., February 21, 1865.* No date. Pencil, neutral wash and oil, heightened with white on board. 14¼ × 21¼″. Museum of Fine Arts, Boston. M. and M. Karolik Collection.

COLORPLATE 116

RICHARD NORRIS BROOKE. *Furling the Flag*. 1871. Oil on canvas. 22 × 30″. West Point Museum,
United States Military Academy, West Point, New York.

COLORPLATE 117

CARL BERSCH. *Lincoln Borne by Loving Hands.* 1865. Oil on canvas. 40 × 60″.
Collection of Ford's Theater, United States Department of the Interior, National Park
Service, Washington, D.C. Photo by Edward Owen.

COLORPLATE 118

FRANK BUCHSER. *The Volunteer's Return.* 1867.
Oil on canvas. 34½ × 30″. Kunstmuseum, Basel.

COLORPLATE 119

THOMAS WATERMAN WOOD. *The Return of the Flags, 1865.* 1869. Oil on canvas.
37 × 30″. West Point Museum, United States Military Academy, West Point, New York.

COLORPLATE 120

EASTMAN JOHNSON. *The Pension Agent*. 1867. Oil on canvas. 25¼ × 37⅜″.
Fine Arts Museums of San Francisco. Mildred Anna Williams Collection.

COLORPLATE 121

WINSLOW HOMER. *The Veteran in a New Field.* 1865. Oil on canvas. 24⅛ × 38⅛″.
Metropolitan Museum of Art, New York. Bequest of Miss Adelaide Milton de Groot.

O Captain! my Captain! rise up and hear the bells;
Rise up—for you the flag is flung—for you the bugle trills,
For you bouquets and ribbon'd wreaths—for you the shores
     a-crowding,
For you they call, the swaying mass, their eager faces turning;
       Here Captain! dear father!
          The arm beneath your head!
            It is some dream that on the deck,
              You've fallen cold and dead.

My Captain does not answer, his lips are pale and still,
My father does not feel my arm, he has no pulse nor will,
The ship is anchor'd safe and sound, its voyage closed and done,
From fearful trip the victor ship comes in with object won:
      Exult O shores, and ring O bells!
        But I with mournful tread,
          Walk the deck my Captain lies,
           Fallen cold and dead.

Richard M. Ketchum

On General Lee's Return to Richmond

The soldier his men called "Marse" Robert returns to Richmond from Appomattox, and is described by historian Ketchum.

———————————

The ordeal in Wilmer McLean's parlor took place on April 9, but Robert E. Lee remained near Appomattox for another three days, until his men stacked their arms and surrendered the worn, faded battle flags which they had followed for four years. Then he set out toward Richmond, pitching his tent each night, sleeping under canvas for the last time. News of his coming preceded him, and along the road women and children waited, some with gifts of food.

On the morning of April 15, 1865, at almost the same time that Abraham Lincoln was dying in Washington, Lee reached the town of Manchester on the outskirts of Richmond. William Hatcher, a Baptist minister, looking out his window at the gray, sodden landscape, saw Lee's party ride by in the heavy downpour. "His steed was bespattered with mud," Hatcher wrote, "and his head hung down as if worn by long traveling. The horseman himself sat his horse like a master; his face was ridged with self-respecting grief; his garments were worn in the service and stained with travel; his hat was slouched and spattered with mud . . ."

The rain was still falling when Lee and five other officers, with Lee's old ambulance and a few wagons carrying their personal effects (one, lacking canvas, was covered with an old quilt) rode into Richmond, and the first people who saw them enter the ruined city wept. As they went along, crowds grew thicker, cheers broke out, and Union troops uncovered when the General passed by. Finally he reached the house on East Franklin Street, dismounted, and made his way toward the gate through a cheering throng, occasionally grasping an outstretched hand. Then he bowed, went into the house, and closed the door on four years of war.

MATHEW BRADY.
Lee in Richmond.
May, 1865.
Photograph.
National Archives,
Washington, D.C.

Worn out, heartbroken, deeply concerned for the future of the South and its people, Lee stayed in the house for days on end, sitting quietly in the back parlor with his family, sleeping the sleep of exhaustion. In those first weeks after Appomattox, Union troops patrolled the streets of the city outside his door; dazed civilians depended for food on handouts from Federal relief agencies. No trains entered the ghostly city; there was no mail. Yet everyone waited for news, mostly to learn the fate of captured troops or of the army still fighting under Joe Johnston. Nearly fifty thousand Negroes had come in from the outlying plantations, but no one seemed to know what to do with them, or they with themselves. After Lincoln's assassination former Confederate soldiers were forbidden to talk to each other in the streets, and between ten and fifteen thousand of them roamed the city, silent, sullen, many of them crippled. At night the desolate city was in darkness, for fire had destroyed the gas mains. There was no light, and there seemed to be no hope.

If Lee had thought to shut out the city and the past he was mistaken, for the South still looked to him for leadership, despite the Union sentinel in front of his house. A stream of callers began to arrive: women seeking husbands and sons, ministers and civic leaders seeking advice, the curious seeking souvenirs or a glimpse of the great man. Confederates still in Libby Prison wrote, asking him to arrange their release, or if that was impossible, just to "ride by the Libby, and let us see you and give you a good cheer. We will all feel better after it." Officers and men came by to bid their old chief farewell before they headed for home. One day two ragged soldiers appeared, saying they were delegates for sixty more whose uniforms were too tattered for them to enter the house. On another occasion, when Lee was trying to answer the flood of correspondence, a tall Confederate soldier with one arm in a sling came to the door and was turned away with an apology by Custis Lee, the General's son. As he turned to go, the soldier said he had been with Hood's Texans and had followed Lee for four years, and now he was going to walk home to Texas; he had hoped to shake his commander's hand. Custis changed his mind and went to get his father, and when Lee came downstairs the soldier took his hand, struggled to say something, and then burst into tears. He covered his face with his arm and walked out of the house.

Thousands who could not see him in the flesh wanted a picture, and one day in April Mathew Brady, the photographer, came to the front door and told a servant he wanted to see the General. When Lee appeared and heard the request he said, "It is utterly impossible, Mr. Brady. How can I sit for a photograph with the eyes of the world upon me as they are today?" But Brady, who had suffered physical and financial hardships and risked danger on a score of battlefields in his determination to document the Civil War, knew this was one picture that had to be taken. It ended the story.

He went to Mrs. Lee and to one of Lee's friends, and they persuaded the General to sit for him. Once more Lee put on the gray uniform, came out into the sunlight below the back porch, and spoke wearily to the photographer: "Very well, Mr. Brady, we are ready." And the photographer with the failing eyesight put his head under the black cloth, focusing the camera until he thought he could see the image sharp. His subject, the commander in chief of the defeated Confederate Army, stood motionless, perfectly controlled except for the pride and defiance written in his eyes.

Walt Whitman
"WHEN LILACS LAST IN THE DOORYARD BLOOM'D"

The president is carried home to Springfield.

When lilacs last in the dooryard bloom'd,
And the great star early droop'd in the western sky in the night,
I mourn'd, and yet shall mourn with ever-returning spring.

Ever-returning spring, trinity sure to me you bring,
Lilac blooming perennial and drooping star in the west,
And thought of him I love.

O powerful western fallen star!
O shades of night—O moody, tearful night!
O great star disappear'd—O the black murk that hides the star!
O cruel hands that hold me powerless—O helpless soul of me!
O harsh surrounding cloud that will not free my soul. . . .

Coffin that passes through lanes and streets,
Through day and night with the great cloud darkening the land,
With the pomp of the inloop'd flags with the cities draped in black,
With the show of the States themselves as of crape-veil'd women standing,
With processions long and winding and the flambeaus of the night,
With the countless torches lit, with the silent sea of faces and the unbared
    heads,
With the waiting depot, the arriving coffin, and the sombre faces,
With dirges through the night, with the thousand voices rising strong and
    solemn,
With all the mournful voices of the dirges pour'd around the coffin,
The dim-lit churches and the shuddering organs—where amid these you
    journey,
With the tolling tolling bells' perpetual clang,
Here, coffin that slowly passes,
I give you my sprig of lilac. . . .

Union Cemetery, City Point.
1864. Photograph. National
Archives, Washington, D.C.

Walt Whitman
"THE THOUGHT OF GRAVES . . ."

Whitman's thoughts came back finally to the land "cluttered with cemeteries" from the war.

There rises in my brain the thought of graves—
to my lips a word for dead soldiers
The Dead we left behind—there they lie, embedded low,
    already fused by Nature
Through broad Virginia's soil, through Tennessee—
The Southern states cluttered with cemeteries
the borders dotted with their graves—the Nation's dead.
Silent they lie—the passionate hot tears have ceased to flow—
time has assuaged the anguish of the living.

Douglas Southall Freeman
"THE LAST PARADE"

The biographer of Lee and historian of the Army of Northern Virginia wrote this tribute on the occasion of the last Confederate reunion in Richmond in 1932.

They thronged the streets of this old town when Bonham brought his volunteers with their Palmetto flag in 1861. They cheered the lads who took up arms when first Virginia called. With doubtful glance they looked upon the men who hailed from New Orleans, the "Tigers" of the bayou state.

When Longstreet led his veterans from Centreville to hold the Yorktown line, all Richmond brought out food and flowers and draped the bayonets. When first the city heard the distant growl of Union guns, each regiment that came to strengthen Lee was welcomed as the savior of the South. The long procession of the carts that brought a groaning load across the Chickahominy from Gaines' Mill was watched with aching hearts.

Another year and solemn strains and mourning drums received the train that had the silent form of him who was the "right arm" of his famous chief. That was the darkest day, save one, that Richmond ever knew, for when the "stonewall" fell, the stoutest bulwark of the South was down. With Jackson dead, where was another such?

When Pickett's soldiers came, a shattered fragment of defiant wrath, to tell how hell itself had opened on that hill at Gettysburg, the townsfolk gazed as if on men who had upturned their graves. The months that followed saw a steady flow into the mills of death. Each night the sleeping street was wakened by the tread of veterans who hurried on to meet the sullen Meade or hastened back to check the wily Sheridan. The clatter of the

horses' hoofs, the rumble of the trains, the drum at dawn, the bugle on the midnight air—all these the leaguered city heard till children's talk was all of arms, and every chat across the garden wall was punctuated by the sound of fratricidal strife.

Ten months of thunder and of ceaseless march and then the end. Brave Custis Lee led out the last defenders of the town, and limping Ewell rode away while flames leaped up and bridges burned and Trojan women waited death. The next parade was set to fastest time, as up the hill and past St. Paul's and in the gates the Federals rode and tore with wildest cheers the still-defiant flag from off the capitol. Dark orgy in the underworld and brutish plunder of the stores, a wider stretch of fire, the mad rejoicing of the slaves, the sly emergence of the spies; and after that the slow return of one gray rider through the wreck of fanes and dreams, a solitary horseman on a weary steed, with only youth and age to pay him homage as he stopped before his door and bowed to all and climbed the steps and went within and put aside his blade to work for peace.

Excited days of preparation then, and pontoons thrown across the James. The army of the victor, Grant, the gossips said, was soon to march through Richmond and to see the ashes of the pinnacles on which its distant gaze had long been fixed. They came. In endless lines, all day they moved, all night, until the city's tearful folk became bewildered in their count and asked, How could the "thin, gray line" have stood so long against that host?

At last the blue-coats left and civil rule returned, in poverty and pain, but with a memory that made the humblest rich. The fallen walls were raised again, the peaceful smoke of busy trade rose where the battle-fumes had hung. For twenty years, the soldiers of the South remained behind the counter or the plow, until the day when Johnston led them out to lay the cornerstone of what the South designed to be a fit memorial to the matchless Lee. A few years more, and when the figure stood upon the pedestal, the word went out that every man who wore the gray should muster in the ranks again and pass before the chieftain on old Traveller. A day that was when love became the meat of life!

Reunions multiplied. A grateful city gladly threw its portals wide each time the aged survivors of Homeric strife returned to view the scenes of youth. A deep emotion rose as Forrest's troopers galloped past and Texans raised the "rebel yell." Today the city has its last review. The armies of the South will march our streets no more. It is the rear guard, engaged with death, that passes now. Who that remembers other days can face that truth and still withhold his tears? The dreams of youth have faded in the twilight of the years. The deeds that shook a continent belong to history. Farewell; sound taps! And then a generation new must face its battles in its turn, forever heartened by that heritage.

Bruce Catton
"A SOUND OF DISTANT DRUMS"

Historian Catton looks back on the Civil War from the perspective of a century and observes its multiple meanings.

The Civil War left America with a legend and a haunting memory. These had to do less with things that remained than with the things that had been lost. What had been won would not be entirely visible for many years to come, and most people were too war-weary to look at it anyway, but what had been lost could not be forgotten. The men who had marched gaily off in new uniforms and who had not come back; the dreams that had brought fire and a great wind down on a land that meant to be happy and easygoing; the buildings the war had wrecked, the countryside it had scarred, the whole network of habits and hopes and attitudes of mind it had ground to fragments—these were remembered with proud devotion by a nation which had paid an unimaginable price for an experience compounded of suffering and loss and ending in stunned bewilderment.

North and South together shared in this, for if the consciousness of defeat afflicted only one of the two sections, both knew that something greatly cherished was gone forever, whether that something was only a remembered smile on the face of a boy who had died or was the great shadow of a way of life that had been destroyed. People clung to the memory of what was gone. Knowing the cruelty and insane destructiveness of war as well as any people who ever lived, they nevertheless kept looking backward, and they put a strange gloss of romance on what they saw, cherishing the haunted overtones it had left.

As the postwar years passed the remembrances became formalized. In cities and in small towns the Decoration Day parade became a ritual; rank after rank of men who unaccountably kept on growing older and less military-looking would tramp down dusty streets, bands playing, flags flying, ranks growing thinner year by year until finally nobody remained to march at all. In the South the same ceremonial was performed, although the date on the calendar was different; and in both sections orators spoke at vast length, reciting deeds of bravery and devotion which somehow, considered from the increasing distance, had the power to knit the country together again. Their stereotyped speeches were oddly made significant by the deeds which they commemorated.

The South had the bitterer memories, and it wrapped them in a heavier trapping of nostalgia. Decaying plantation buildings, with empty verandas slowly falling apart under porticoes upheld by insecure wooden pillars, became shrines simply because they somehow spoke for the dream that had died, the vitality of the dream gaining in strength as the physical embodiment of it drifted off into ruin. There were cemeteries for both sections—quiet, peaceful fields where soldiers who had never cared about military formality lay in the last sleep, precisely ranked in rows of white headstones which bespoke personal tragedies blunted at last by time. There were statues, too, with great men frozen in cold marble, presiding over drowsy battlefields which would never again know violence or bloodshed.

And, finally, there was the simple memory of personal valor—the enduring realization that when the great challenge comes, the most ordinary people can show that they value something more than they value their own lives. When the last of the veterans had gone, and the sorrows and bitternesses which the war created had at last worn away, this memory remained. The men who fought in the Civil War, speaking for all Americans, had said something the country could never forget.

CONRAD WISE CHAPMAN. *Stacked Swords*. 1863. Watercolor on brown paper. 5⅛ x 4⅝″. Valentine Museum, Richmond.

INDEX

Pages in *italics* refer to illustrations.

Copyright © 1992, Hugh Lauter Levin Associates, Inc.
Design by Philip Grushkin
Typeset by U. S. Lithograph, typographers, New York City
Printed in Hong Kong
ISBN 0-88363-970-x

Samuel W. Crawford. *The Genesis of the Civil War*. First published in 1887, Hartford, Conn.

C. Vann Woodward, ed. *Mary Chesnut's Civil War*. © 1981 by C. Vann Woodward, Sally Bland Metts, Barbara G. Carpenter, Sally Bland Johnson, and Katherine W. Herbert. Reproduced by permission of Yale University Press.

Walt Whitman. "Beat! Beat! Drums!" "Ashes of Soldiers." "O Captain! My Captain!" "When Lilacs Last in the Dooryard Bloom'd." "The Thought of Graves." Reprinted from *Walt Whitman's Civil War*. Walter Lowenfels, ed. © 1960 by Walter Lowenfels. Published by Alfred A. Knopf, Inc.

James Russell Lowell. "The Pickens-and-Stealin's Rebellion." From *Political Essays*, vol. V of *The Works of James Russell Lowell*. Published by Houghton, Mifflin & Co., 1899.

Testimony of Mrs. Mary A. Ward. *Report of the Committee of the Senate upon the Relations between Labor and Capital, and Testimony Taken by the Committee*. Published by the U.S. Government Printing Office, 1885.

Warren Lee Goss. "Going to the Front." From *Battles and Leaders of the Civil War*, vol. I. Robert U. Johnson and Clarence C. Buel, eds. New York: The Century Co., 1888.

Ulysses S. Grant. *Personal Memoirs of U. S. Grant*. New York: Charles L. Webster & Co., 1885.

Frederick Douglass. *Douglass' Monthly*, August 1861, March 1862.

Benjamin P. Thomas. *Abraham Lincoln*. © 1952 by Benjamin P. Thomas. Reprinted by permission of Alfred A. Knopf, Inc.

J. B. Jones. *A Rebel War Clerk's Diary At the Confederate States Capital*, vol. I. Howard Swiggett, ed. New York: Old Hickory Bookshop, 1935.

Howard K. Beale, ed. *Diary of Gideon Welles*, vol. I. Published by W. W. Norton & Company, Inc., 1960.

Allan Nevins. *The War for the Union*, vol. II. © 1960 Allan Nevins; copyright renewed 1988. Reprinted by permission of Charles Scribner's Sons, an imprint of Macmillan Publishing Company.

Richard Taylor. *Destruction and Reconstruction: Personal Experiences of the Late War*. New York: D. Appleton & Co., 1879, 1900.

Shelby Foote. *The Civil War: A Narrative*. © 1958 by Shelby Foote. Reprinted by permission of Random House, Inc.

Don E. Fehrenbacher. *Lincoln in Text and Context: Collected Essays*. © 1987 by the Board of Trustees of the Leland Stanford Junior University. Reprinted with the permission of the publisher, Stanford University Press.

Roy P. Basler, ed. *The Collected Works of Abraham Lincoln*, vols. V, VI. © 1953 by Abraham Lincoln Association. Reprinted with permission of Rutgers University Press.

Bruce Catton. *A Stillness at Appomattox*. © 1953 by Bruce Catton. Used by permission of Doubleday, a division of Bantam Doubleday Dell Publishing Group, Inc.

War Letters, 1862–1865, of John Chipman Gray and John Codman Ropes. Cambridge: Houghton, Mifflin & Co., The Riverside Press, 1927.

Thomas Wentworth Higginson. "Regular and Volunteer Officers." *Atlantic Monthly*, September, 1864.

Mark Twain. "The Private History of a Campaign That Failed." *Century Magazine*, December, 1885.

Thomas W. Hyde. *Following the Greek Cross or, Memories of the Sixth Army Corps*. Cambridge: Houghton, Mifflin & Co., The Riverside Press, 1895.

Michael Shaara. *The Killer Angels*. © 1974 by Michael Shaara. Reprinted by permission of David McKay Co., a division of Random House, Inc.

Stephen Crane. *The Red Badge of Courage*. First published in 1895.

Sam R. Watkins. *"Co. Aytch," Maury Grays, First Tennessee Regiment; or, A Side Show of the Big Show*. First published in 1882.

Robert Penn Warren. *Wilderness: A Tale of the Civil War*. © 1961 by Robert Penn Warren. Published by Random House.

Walt Whitman. "A Glimpse of War's Hell-Scenes." "The Wounded from Chancellorsville." "Released Union Prisoners from the South." Letter of Condolence. Reflections on the Battle of Bull Run. Dispatch to the *New York Times*, February 26, 1863. Journal Entry, February 23, 1865. Reprinted from *Walt Whitman's Civil War*. Walter Lowenfels, ed. © 1960 by Walter Lowenfels. Published by Alfred A. Knopf, Inc.

Alexander Hunter. *Johnny Reb and Billy Yank*. New York: Neale Publishing Company, 1905.

John W. De Forest. "Forced Marches." *Galaxy*, 1868.

J. B. Polley. *A Soldier's Letters to Charming Nellie*. New York: Neale Publishing Company, 1908.

Harold A. Small, ed. *The Road to Richmond: The Civil War Memoirs of Major Abner R. Small*. © 1939 The Regents of the University of California. Reprinted by permission of University of California Press.

Carlton McCarthy. *Detailed Minutiae of Soldier Life in the Army of Northern Virginia, 1861–1865*. Richmond: Carlton McCarthy & Co., 1882.

John D. Billings. *Hardtack and Coffee or The Unwritten Story of Army Life*. Boston: G. M. Smith, 1887.

Sidney Lanier. *Centennial Edition of the Works of Sidney Lanier: Letters of 1857–1868*, vol. VII. Baltimore/London: The Johns Hopkins University Press, 1945, pp. 46–49.

C. G. Chamberlayne, ed. *Ham Chamberlayne-Virginian: Letters and Papers of an Artillery Officer*. Richmond: Press of the Dietz Printing Co., 1932.

Norwood Penrose Hallowell. *Selected Letters and Papers of N. P. Hallowell*. Published by The Richard R. Smith Co., Inc., 1963.

Letters written by William Stillwell, James Keenan, Benjamin Abbott, and N. J. Brooks. From *"Dear Mother: Don't Grieve About Me. If I Get Killed, I'll Only be Dead." Letters from Georgia Soldiers in the Civil War*. Mills Lane, ed. Savannah, Georgia: Beehive Press, 1977.

Nathaniel Hawthorne. "Chiefly About War Matters." *Atlantic Monthly*, July, 1862.

Alfred W. Ellet. "Ellet and His Steam-Rams at Memphis." From *Battles and Leaders of the Civil War*, vol. I. Robert U. Johnson and Clarence C. Buel, eds. New York: The Century Co., 1888.

"The Cruise of the *Alabama* and the *Sumter*, from the Private Journals and Other Papers of Commander R. Semmes, C. S. N., and Other Officers." From *Battles and Leaders of the Civil War*, vol. IV. Robert U. Johnson and Clarence C. Buel, eds. New York: The Century Co., 1888.

James Morris Morgan. *Recollections of a Rebel Reefer*. London: Constable & Co., 1918.

John McIntosh Kell. "Cruise and Combats of the *Alabama*." From *Battles and Leaders of the Civil War*, vol. IV. Robert U. Johnson and Clarence C. Buel, eds. New York: The Century Co., 1888.

John C. Kinney. "Farragut at Mobile Bay." From *Battles and Leaders of the Civil War*, vol. IV. Robert U. Johnson and Clarence C. Buel, eds. New York: The Century Co., 1888.

William B. Cushing. "The Destruction of the *Albemarle*." From *Battles and Leaders of the Civil War*, vol. IV. Robert U. Johnson and Clarence C. Buel, eds. New York: The Century Co., 1888.

Sallie Putnam. *Richmond During The War: Four Years of Personal Observation by a Richmond Lady*. New York: G. W. Carleton, 1867.

George Washington Cable. "New Orleans Before the Capture." From *Battles and Leaders of the Civil War*, vol. II. Robert U. Johnson and Clarence C. Buel, eds. New York: The Century Co., 1888.

Herman Melville. "Malvern Hill." Reprinted from *Selected Poems of Herman Melville*. Henning Cohen, ed. Published by Anchor Books, Doubleday, 1964.

William L. Lusk, ed. *War Letters of William Thompson Lusk*. © 1911 by William Chittenden Lusk. Privately Printed, New York.

Oliver Wendell Holmes. "My Hunt After the Captain." *Atlantic Monthly*, December, 1862.

Heros Von Borcke. *Memoirs of the Confederate War for Independence*, vol. I. London, 1866.

Alexander K. McClure. "The Invasion of Pennsylvania." From *The Rebellion Record by Frank Moore. Published by Putnam, 1863.*

George Augustus Sala. *My Diary in America in the Midst of War*, vol. I. London: Tinsley Brothers, 1865.

Robert Hunt Rhodes, ed. *All for the Union: A History of the 2nd Rhode Island Volunteer Infantry in the War of the Great Rebellion As told by the Diary and Letters of Elisha Hunt Rhodes*. Published by Orion Books/Crown, 1991.

Shelby Foote. *The Civil War: A Narrative*, vol. I. © 1958 by Shelby Foote. Reprinted by permission of Random House, Inc.

Henry Ropes. Letter to father, June 3, 1862. 20th Massachusetts Regiment Collection, Boston Public Library.

Rufus R. Dawes. *Service with the Sixth Wisconsin Volunteers*. Reprinted by the Press of Morningside Bookshop, Dayton, Ohio.

William Faulkner. *Intruder in the Dust*. © 1948 by Random House, Inc. Reprinted by permission of Random House, Inc.

Constance Cary Harrison. "Virginia Scenes in '61." From *Battles and Leaders of the Civil War*, vol. I. "Richmond Scenes in '62." From *Battles and Leaders of the Civil War*, vol. II. Robert W. Johnson and Clarence C. Buel, eds. New York: The Century Co., 1888.

John Esten Cooke. *Outlines from the Outpost*. Richard Harwell, ed. Chicago: The Lakeside Press, R. R. Donnelley & Sons Company, 1961.

Thomas H. Johnson, ed. From *The Letters of Emily Dickinson*. © 1958, 1968 by the President and Fellows of Harvard College. Reprinted by permission of The Belknap Press of Harvard University Press, Cambridge.

Ambrose Bierce. From *The Collected Writings of Ambrose Bierce*. Clifton Fadiman, ed. New York: The Citadel Press, 1946. Published by arrangement with Carol Publishing Group.

S. S. Boggs. *Eighteen Months a Prisoner under the Rebel Flag*. Published in 1887.

Julia Ward Howe. *Reminiscences, 1819–1899*. Boston: Houghton, Mifflin & Co., 1899.

Julia Ward Howe. "Battle Hymn of the Republic." *Atlantic Monthly*, February, 1862.

Lydia Minturn Post, ed. Letter from Robert Gould Shaw in *Soldiers' Letters from Camp, Battle-field and Prison*. New York: Bunce & Huntington, 1865.

George W. Cable, ed. "A Woman's Diary of the Siege of Vicksburg. Under Fire from the Gunboats." *Century Magazine*, VIII, 1885.

Allan Nevins and Milton Halsey Thomas, eds. *The Diary of George Templeton Strong*. © 1952 The Macmillan Company, copyright renewed 1980 by Milton Halsey Thomas. Reprinted with the permission of Macmillan Publishing Company.

Gurdon Grovenor in William E. Connelley, ed. *Quantrill and the Border Wars*. Iowa: Torch Press, 1910.

Bruce Catton. *Glory Road: The Bloody Route from Fredericksburg to Gettysburg*. © 1952 by Bruce Catton. Used by permission of Doubleday, a division of Bantam Doubleday Dell Publishing Group, Inc.

Frank Wilkeson. *Recollections of a Private Soldier in the Army of the Potomac*. New York & London: G. P. Putnam's Sons, The Knickerbocker Press, 1887.

Frederic Bancroft, ed. *Speeches, Correspondence and Political Papers of Carl Schurz*, vol. 1. New York: G. P. Putnam's Sons, 1913.

Tyler Dennett, ed. *Lincoln and the Civil War in the Diaries and Letters of John Hay*. © 1939 by Dodd Mead & Company, Inc., New York.

Nathaniel Paige. "The Attack on Fort Wagner," *New York Tribune*. From *The Rebellion Record*, VII. Frank Moore, ed., 1864.

Stephen D. Ramseur. Letter to his wife, October 10, 1864. Southern Historical Collection, Library of the University of North Carolina at Chapel Hill.

William Tecumseh Sherman. *Memoirs of General William T. Sherman*. New York: D. Appleton, 1875.

Herman Melville. "Marching to the Sea." "The Wilderness." Reprinted from *Collected Poems of Herman Melville*. Howard P. Vincent, ed. Chicago: Hendricks House, 1947.

Entry from Mary S. Mallard's Journal. Letter from Charles C. Jones, Jr. From *The Children of Pride: A New, Abridged Edition*; Selected Letters of the Family of the Rev. Dr. Charles Colcock Jones from the Years 1860-1868, with the Addition of Several Previously Unpublished Letters. Robert Manson Myers, ed. © 1972, 1984 by Robert Manson Myers. Reproduced by permission of Yale University Press.

M. A. DeWolfe Howe, ed. *Home Letters of General Sherman*. New York: Charles Scribner's Sons, 1909.

Gary W. Gallagher, ed. *Fighting for the Confederacy: The Personal Recollections of General Edward Porter Alexander*. © 1989 The University of North Carolina Press. Reprinted by permission of the publisher.

Charles Royster. From *The Destructive War*. © 1991 by Charles Royster. Reprinted by permission of Alfred A. Knopf, Inc.

Abraham Lincoln. "Second Inaugural Address." Reprinted from *Messages and Papers of the Presidents*, VI. James D. Richardson, ed. New York, 1904.

Gilbert E. Govan and James W. Livingood, eds. From *The Haskell Memoirs: The Personal Narrative of a Confederate Officer*. © 1960 by Gilbert E. Govan and James W. Livingood. Published by G. P. Putnam's Sons, New York. Reprinted by permission of Gilbert E. Govan and James W. Livingood.

Ulysses S. Grant. *Personal Memoirs of U. S. Grant*. 1885.

Joshua Lawrence Chamberlain. *The Passing of the Armies, An Account of the Final Campaign of the Army of the Potomac*, Based upon Personal Reminiscences of the Fifth Army Corps. New York: G. P. Putnam's Sons, 1915.

Richard M. Ketchum. "Faces From the Past." © Richard M. Ketchum, 1961. American Heritage Press.

Douglas S. Freeman. *The Last Parade*. Richmond: Whittet & Shepperson, 1932.

Bruce Catton. Excerpt from *The American Heritage Picture History of the Civil War*. © 1960 by American Heritage, a division of Forbes, Inc.

PHOTO CREDITS:

ROBERT E. LEE from *The Civil War: Lee Takes Command*. Photograph by Larry Sherer, © 1984 Time-Life Books, Inc.

THE PROCLAMATION OF EMANCIPATION from *The Civil War: Twenty Million Yankees*. Photograph by Larry Sherer, © 1985 Time-Life Books, Inc.

PRESENTATION OF THE CHARGER "COQUETTE" TO COLONEL MOSBY BY THE MEN OF HIS COMMAND, DECEMBER, 1864 from *The Civil War: Spies, Scouts and Raiders*. Photograph by Larry Sherer, © 1985 Time-Life Books, Inc.

A NEWSPAPER IN THE TRENCHES from *The Civil War: Death in the Trenches*. Photograph by Larry Sherer, © 1986 Time-Life Books, Inc.

THE BATTLE OF CHICKAMUAGA, SEPTEMBER 19, 1863 AND GENERAL HOOKER AT LOOKOUT MOUNTAIN, NOVEMBER 24, 1863 from *The Civil War: The Fight for Chattanooga*. Photograph by Larry Sherer, © 1985 Time-Life Books, Inc.

BURIAL OF LATANÉ from *The Civil War: Lee Takes Command*. Photograph by Larry Sherer, © 1984 Time-Life Books, Inc.

PETERSBURG REFUGEE FAMILY from *The Civil War: Rebels Resurgent*. Photograph by Larry Sherer, © 1985 Time-Life Books, Inc.

FORT SUMTER INTERIOR AT SUNRISE, DEC. 9, 1864 from *The Civil War: The Coastal War*. Photograph by Larry Sherer, © 1984 Time-Life Books, Inc.

INCIDENTS OF WAR

SOLDIER LIFE

WAR AT SEA

CIVILIANS AT WAR

SOUTH BESIEGED

4TH. PA. CAVALRY

Oct 1861

29

Str. Nemala, *December* 14, 1864

DEAR JOHN,—I have just passed a whole morning in the company of the greatest military genius of the country in the height of his success. If I were to write a dozen pages I could not tell you a tenth part of what he said, for he talked incessantly and more rapidly than any man I ever saw. A despatch boat goes North immediately on our arrival at Hilton Head with the glorious news of Sherman's success, but I will try to scribble a word or two as we go along in this shaky boat. . . .

First about Fort McAllister, the 'all important capture' of which as General S. terms it, secures an excellent base for such supplies as may be needed. The Fort is very strong mounting twenty-one guns, some of which are field pieces, and many months ago beat off three heavy ironclads, inflicting considerable damage; the assault was made by three columns each of three regiments, and twenty-five minutes by the watch, as General Sherman says, after the first order was given the fort was in our possession. The garrison fought desperately, and several refusing to surrender were killed inside of the Fort. Our loss was about eighty, of whom half were killed and wounded by the explosion of torpedoes buried in the ground which were exploded by our men walking over the works after they were captured. General Sherman set the prisoners to work digging them up and informed the commander of the fort that he had it in consideration to shut him up with a number of his men equal to the number of our men who were killed by torpedoes and blow them up by gunpowder.

General Sherman is the most American looking man I ever saw, tall and lank, not very erect, with hair like thatch, which he rubs up with his hands, a rusty beard trimmed

BRADY STUDIO, WASHINGTON, D.C.
William T. Sherman. 1865. Photograph.
National Archives, Washington, D.C.

WINSLOW HOMER.
*Marching Infantry
Column.* 1862.
Graphite, charcoal,
white gouache.
20¼ x 13¼".
Cooper-Hewitt
National Museum of
Design, Smithsonian
Institution / Art
Resource, New York.
Gift of Charles
Savage Homer, Jr.

and in among the tree trunks, he could see knots and waving lines of skirmishers who were running hither and thither and firing at the landscape. A dark battle line lay upon a sun struck clearing that gleamed orange color. A flag fluttered.

Other regiments floundered up the bank. The brigade was formed in line of battle, and after a pause started slowly through the woods in the rear of the receding skirmishers, who were continually melting into the scene to appear again farther on. They were always busy as bees, deeply absorbed in their little combats.

The youth tried to observe everything. He did not use care to avoid trees and branches, and his forgotten feet were constantly knocking against stones or getting entangled in briers. He was aware that these battalions with their commotions were woven red and startling into the gentle fabric of softened greens and browns. It looked to be a wrong place for a battlefield.

The skirmishers in advance fascinated him. Their shots into thickets and at distant and prominent trees spoke to him of tragedies—hidden, mysterious, solemn.

Once the line encountered the body of a dead soldier. He lay upon his back staring at the sky. He was dressed in an awkward suit of yellowish brown. The youth could see that the soles of his shoes had been worn to the thinness of writing paper, and from a great rent in one the dead foot projected piteously. And it was as if fate had betrayed the soldier. In death it exposed to his enemies that poverty which in life he had perhaps concealed from his friends.

The ranks opened covertly to avoid the corpse. The invulnerable dead man forced a way for himself. The youth looked keenly at the ashen face. The wind raised the tawny beard. It moved as if a hand were stroking it. He vaguely desired to walk around and around the body and stare; the impulse of the living to try to read in dead eyes the answer to the Question.

During the march the ardor which the youth had acquired when out of view of the field rapidly faded to nothing. His curiosity was quite easily satisfied. If an intense scene had caught him with its wild swing as he came to the top of the bank, he might have gone roaring on. This advance upon Nature was too calm. He had opportunity to reflect. He had time in which to wonder about himself and to attempt to probe his sensations.

Absurd ideas took hold upon him. He thought that he did not relish the landscape. It threatened him. A coldness swept over his back, and it is true that his trousers felt to him that they were no fit for his legs at all.

COLORPLATE 29

Conrad Wise Chapman. *Confederate Camp at Corinth.* 1862.
Lithograph. $10\frac{5}{8} \times 15\frac{1}{4}''$. Valentine Museum, Richmond.

Members of 3rd Georgia Infantry, Company D. ca. 1861–1862. Ambrotype: Half Plate. 4¼ x 5½". Museum of the Confederacy, Richmond. Eleanor S. Brockenbrough Library. Copy photography by Katherine Wetzel.

"Then look out, we are going to send you some."

"How are you going to do it?"

"Wait and see."

The Rebs watched the group upon the other side curiously, wondering how even Yankee ingenuity could devise a way for sending a batch of papers across the river two hundred yards wide, and in the meantime each man had his own opinion.

"They will shoot arrows over," said Martin.

"Arrows, the devil!" replied the sergeant; "there never was a bow bent which could cast an arrow across this river."

"Maybe they will wrap them around a cannon ball and shoot them across; we'd better get away from here," hastily answered a tall, slim six-footer, who was rather afraid of big shots.

A roar of laughter followed this suggestion, but the originator was too intent on his own awakened fears to let the slightest movement of the enemy pass unscanned. Eagerly he watched while the others were having all the fun at his expense. Presently he shouted:

"Here they come!" and then in a tone of intense admiration, "I'll be doggoned if these Yanks are not the smartest people in the world."

On the other side were several miniature boats and ships—such as schoolboys delight in—with sails set; the gentle breeze impelled the little crafts across the river, each freighted with a couple of newspapers. Slowly, but surely, they headed for the opposite bank as if some spirit Oberon or Puck sat at the tiller; and in a few minutes had accomplished their voyage and were drawn up to await a favorable wind to waft them back.

Drawing lots, Joe Boteler, who found luck against him, started to town, with a muttered curse, to buy tobacco, leaving his comrades to seek some shady spot, and with pipes in our mouths sink deep in the latest war news from the enemy's standpoint, always interesting reading.

It was a cloudless day,—a day to dream,—and with a lazy *sans souci* manner and half-shut eyes, enjoy to the soul the deep loveliness of the scene which lay around us like some fair creation of the fancy, listening the while to the trills of the blue-bird which

123

Merrimack is going down." And sure enough, upon approaching the river, I saw the huge monster swung loose from her moorings and making her way down the river with the gun boats *Beaufort* and *Raleigh* a little piece in the rear. The morning was unusually fine, in pleasing contrast with the miserable weather that we have been tortured with so long. A good portion of her crew were on top and received the enthusiastic cheers from the excited populace without a single response. Everything betokened serious business, for the heaviest ships of the enemy lay but a few miles below, like sullen bull-dogs ready to seize man or beast by the throat at the slightest provocation. Just imagine a house 150 feet long, sunk three feet below the eaves, pierced about one-half way up for three guns on each side and three portholes at bow and stern through which last two pivot guns worked, and you have an exact picture of the *Merrimack*, now called the *Virginia*.

Although Hampton Roads is a large expanse of water, yet it is not navigable for vessels of such draft as the *Merrimack*, consequently she had to traverse 14 to 15 miles in keeping the channel running down until opposite Sewell's Point and then turning up the James River channel and making for the blockading vessels of Newport News. So quietly did the *Merrimack* go that we could not observe any stir either among the ships or at Newport News batteries, until one of our little gunboats took a short cut and fired at the *Cumberland*. Then some stir was observable on board both the *Cumberland* and *Congress*. Both vessels cleared their decks for action and coolly waited for the nondescript. The *Merrimack* never halted nor fired a gun in reply to the *Cumberland*, which was firing away with desperation. You may be able to partly imagine the great anxiety which prevailed along the shore, now lined with thousands of anxious spectators. Everyone said, "Why don't the *Merrimack* fire? The *Cumberland* will sink her &c. &c." But she kept steadily on making directly for her adversary. When she came within a few yards, she fired her bow gun, which went clear through the other and, yet continuing on her course, drove her iron prow right into the *Cumberland*'s side, crushing all before her. The crew fought as the vessel went down. Their last guns were fired as the men stood knee deep in water. After the collision, the *Merrimack* backed out and started for the *Congress*. This vessel fired rapidly, but seeing the fate of its consort she started to run ashore. This she did. But in the meantime she was so riddled with shot that she became perfectly useless and struck her colors. The *Beaufort* then went up to her to take off the

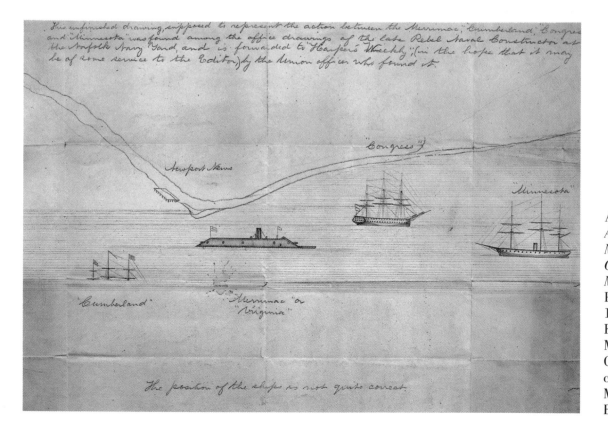

Artist Unknown. *Action between the Merrimac, Cumberland, Congress, and Minnesota.* 1862. Pencil. 11¹³⁄₁₆ x 16¼". Museum of Fine Arts, Boston. M. and M. Karolik Collection. Photo copyright © 1992 Museum of Fine Arts, Boston.